What We Have Heard
from the Beginning

ὑμεῖς ὃ ἠκούσατε ἀπ᾽ ἀρχῆς ἐν ὑμῖν μενέτω
"Let what you have heard from the beginning remain in you."
(1 John 2:24)

This book is dedicated to . . .

G. R. Beasley–Murray
Josef Blank
M.-É. Boismard
F.–M. Braun
Raymond Brown
Rudolf Bultmann
C. H. Dodd
André Feuillet
Percival Gardner–Smith
Barnabas Lindars
Leon Morris
Ignace de la Potterie
Georg Richter
John A. T. Robinson
Eugen Ruckstuhl
Rudolf Schnackenburg
Eduard Schweizer

to . . .

C. K. Barrett
Frans Neirynck

. . . and all those who taught us
what we have known
from the beginning.

Scripture quotations, where not an author's'own translation, are from the
New Revised Standard Version Bible, copyright 1989, Division of Chris-
tian Education of the National Council of the Churches of Christ in the
United States of America. Used by permission. All rights reserved.

Cover Design by Joan Osth

Library of Congress Cataloging-in-Publication Data

What we have heard from the beginning : the past, present, and future of
Johannine studies / [edited by] Tom Thatcher.
     p. cm.
 Includes bibliographical references and index.
 ISBN 978-1-60258-010-7 (pbk. : alk. paper)
 1. Bible. N.T. John--Criticism, interpretation, etc. 2. Bible. N.T. Epis-
tles of John--Criticism, interpretation, etc. I. Thatcher, Tom, 1967-

 BS2601.W43 2007
 226.5'0609--dc22

                              2007028561

Printed in the United States of America on acid–free paper with a minimum of 30% pcw recycled content.

What We Have Heard
from the Beginning

The Past, Present, and Future of Johannine Studies

Tom Thatcher

editor

BAYLOR UNIVERSITY PRESS

CONTENTS

ABBREVIATIONS

AB	Anchor Bible
ABR	*Australian Biblical Review*
Abr.	*De Abrahamo*
ABRL	Anchor Bible Reference Library
AnBib	Analecta biblica
ANL	Annua Nuntia Lovaniensia
ATANT	Abhandlungen zur Theologie des Alten und Neuen Testaments
AThR	*Anglican Theological Review*
BAR	*Biblical Archaeology Review*
BECNT	Baker Exegetical Commentary on the New Testament
BETL	Bibliotheca ephemeridum theologicarum lovaniensium
BIS	Biblical Interpretation Series
BJS	Brown Judaic Studies
BNTC	Black's New Testament Commentaries
BP	The Bible and Postcolonialism Series
BSR	Biblioteca di Scienze Religiose
BZAW	Beihefte zur Zeitschrift für die alttestamentliche Wissenschaft

CBET	Contributions to Biblical Exegesis and Theology
CBQ	*Catholic Biblical Quarterly*
Contempl.	Philo, *De vita contemplativa*
CahRB	Cahiers de la Revue biblique
EstBib	*Estudios bíblicos*
ETL	*Ephemerides theologicae lovanienses*
ExAud	*Ex auditu*
Exsecr	*De exsecrationibus*
ExpTim	*Expository Times*
GBS	Guides to Biblical Scholarship
Gig.	Philo, *De gigantibus*
HBS	Herders Biblische Studien
Her.	Philo, *Quis rerum divinarum heres sit*
HNT	Handbuch zum Neuen Testament
HTKNT	Herders theologischer Kommentar zum Neuen Testament
IBS	*Irish Biblical Studies*
IRT	Issues in Religion and Theology
JBL	*Journal of Biblical Literature*
JETS	*Journal of the Evangelical Theological Society*
JSNT	*Journal for the Study of the New Testament*
JSNTSup	Journal for the Study of the New Testament Supplement Series
JTS	*Journal of Theological Studies*
Leg.	Philo, *Legum allegoriae*
LXX	Septuagint
Mek.	*Mekilta*
MJS	Münsteraner Judaistiche Studien
Mut.	Philo, *De mutatione nominum*
NIGTC	New International Greek Testament Commentary
NovT	*Novum Testamentum*
NovTSup	Supplements to Novum Testamentum
NT	New Testament
NTOA	Novum Testamentum et Orbis Antiquus
NTS	*New Testament Studies*
OT	Old Testament
QD	Quaestiones disputatae
RB	*Revue biblique*
SA	Studia anselmiana
SBL	Society of Biblical Literature
SBLDS	Society of Biblical Literature Dissertation Series

SBLSymS	Society of Biblical Literature Symposium Series
SBT	Studies in Biblical Theology
SHR	Studies in the History of Religions (Supplement to Numen)
SJT	*Scottish Journal of Theology*
SNTSMS	Society for New Testament Studies Monograph Series
SNTSU	Studien zum Neuen Testament und seiner Umwelt
SubBib	Subsidia biblica
TDOT	*Theological Dictionary of the Old Testament.* Edited by G. J. Botterweck and H. Ringgren. Translated by J. T. Willis, G. W. Bromiley, and D. E. Green. 8 vols. Grand Rapids, 1974–
THKNT	Theologischer Handkommentar zum Neuen Testament
TynBul	*Tyndale Bulletin*
TZ	*Theologische Zeitschrift*
VC	*Vor Christus*
VitCont	*Vita Contemplativa*
WMANT	Wissenschaftliche Monographien zum Alten und Neuen Testament
WUNT	Wissenschaftliche Untersuchungen zum Neuen Testament
ZNW	*Zeitschrift für die neutestamentliche Wissenschaft und die Kunde der älteren Kirche*

THE PURPOSE AND PLAN OF THIS BOOK

Tom Thatcher

A few months before this book was finished, my longtime friend and mentor Robert Fortna called to raise a concern. "Your title," he said, "'What We Have Heard from the Beginning'—I'm not really sure what that's all about. Obviously that plays on some references in 1 John, right? But there that means that the reader is supposed to accept John's teachings about Christ, 'what they have heard from the beginning' about the orthodox faith. That's not what this book is really about, is it? I think that will be confusing to people." Further reflection led me to agree that the title might be confusing, so here I offer an explanation that will, I hope, provide a rationale for the existence of this book.

Until about 1993, I had no real interest in the Johannine Literature. I had heard, I am sure, occasional sermons based on verses from the Fourth Gospel and 1–2–3 John, and had probably read through all four books for private edification (at least, I think I had), but I had never studied them in a systematic fashion. I knew about the Gospel of John's awkward relationship with the Synoptics and had heard some things about the Johannine christological formulas, which I tended to view through post–Reformation theological categories as a sort of generic summary of orthodox theology. I had also read Alan Culpepper's *Anatomy of the Fourth Gospel* as a seminary student, but while that book had a dramatic impact on my thinking about the literary nature of the Bible, it did very little to interest me in deeper Johannine things. Essentially, the Johannine Literature was "just there" to me, a division of the canon that seemed fairly repetitive and essentially unremarkable.

Then, I participated in a doctoral seminar on the Johannine Literature led by Gerald Borchert, who was at that time writing his two–volume commentary on the Fourth Gospel for the New American series. I have never confessed this to Dr. Borchert, but I took this particular course only because it happened to be offered at a convenient time and because the workload seemed manageable. I was more interested in method than in any section of the canon and was looking for a dissertation topic that would be readily amenable to interdisciplinary approaches. Yet Prof. Borchert's enthusiasm, and the wise counsel of senior peers on the value of choosing a thesis in line with the current interests of one's advisor, led me to explore avenues outside the boundaries of the required reading list for the course. These preliminary soundings suggested that the Johannine Literature was a ripe target for the approaches that interested me. Scrapping my proposal on "Negative Theology in Paul," I produced a new dissertation outline that would initiate me into the guild of Johannine scholarship. I soon began a regular dialogue with Robert Fortna, whose work was critical to my own study simply because I intended to oppose his thinking at so many points. Together, Professors Borchert and Fortna led me through the maze of theories and the massive bibliography that comprise Johannine Studies.

Now, having lived in the Johannine world for some fifteen years, two things become very clear as I reflect on the development of my modest academic career. First, I now realize that I was born during a golden age of Johannine Studies, and while this can be intimidating at times, it also has allowed me to reap what many others have sown. The monumental monographs and commentaries produced during what John A. T. Robinson called the "New Look" era—roughly the mid–1950s through the 1990s—had already established the issues, methods, and credibility of Johannine Studies long before I came to the table. Viewed in retrospect, the scholarship of the generation before me was remarkable not only for the volume of its output but also, and especially, for the unprecedented sophistication of its investigations into the history behind the Johannine Literature, the unique theological outlook of this remarkable branch of early Christianity, and the literary style and structure of the respective books. Second, I am now increasingly aware of the extent to which the work of this great generation has influenced my own thinking. In general, I characterize myself as a person who is always looking for a new angle on things, as one who tries to say something different—note that the terms "looking" and "tries" are admissions that I often fail to achieve this goal. Yet I find more and more that even my most original ideas tend to reflect things I have read in books that were published twenty or thirty years ago; that my most grandiose methodological moves are tied to a framework of questions laid down by the generation before me; that I am, at every moment, dependent upon the wisdom, insights, and guidance of senior colleagues. Every academic discipline moves forward as new generations of scholars walk on the graves of their ancestors, yet I am beginning to understand how holy that ground is.

These two realizations came forcefully to my attention several years ago while I was talking to a student about something Raymond Brown had written. "Now, who's Raymond Brown?" he asked. After I went back to my office, I looked at the several books by Brown on my shelf and pulled down volume one of his Anchor Bible commentary. Who is Raymond Brown? I had seen Prof. Brown only once, very briefly, at a Society of Biblical Literature meeting just before his death, an encounter that I remember vividly. But my student will never meet him, even if he someday becomes the world's foremost authority on the Johannine Literature and can quote long excerpts from Brown's writings, just as I was never able to meet G. R. Beasley–Murray or Rudolf Schnackenburg. Being a sentimental person and given to the nostalgia typical of Gen–Xers, I feel a twinge of regret when I hold a copy of *Historical Tradition in the Fourth Gospel* and realize that I will never sit down with C. H. Dodd over a cup of coffee to ask him about his work and seek his counsel for my own career. And this realization makes me very thankful for, and very appreciative of, the times when I can sit down occasionally with people like Bob Kysar and John Painter and Gilbert Van Belle, encounters that one day will earn the deep admiration of my own junior colleagues who will never know the wonderful people behind these names.

This book, then, seeks to be a sort of time capsule, a virtual conversation between future students of the Johannine Literature and some of the living legends of a golden era of scholarship—I stress "some of," as the list of contributors to this book is representative, not exhaustive, a sampling of global voices. Each senior contributor was asked to discuss, briefly and in a conversational tone, his or her journey with John. This discussion could include an evaluation of the state of the field, programmatic remarks on questions that merit further attention, a personal history of research, a summary of current work—anything that one might share with an interested student over coffee after class. Taken as a whole, the essays in this volume are intended to provide a deep sounding of the undercurrents that have made the field of Johannine Studies specifically, and New Testament Studies generally, what it is today—to view the issues through the eyes of people who are in a position to see above and beyond current fads and trends. At the same time, this book seeks not only to celebrate the past, but also to forecast the future. For this reason, each major essay is followed by a brief response from a younger scholar who will carry the study of the Fourth Gospel into the next several decades. These respondents were asked to reflect on their senior colleague's comments and to identify questions that remain unanswered. Taken as a whole, the essays and responses in this book survey the past, present, and future of Johannine scholarship (note the subtitle) from the perspectives of individuals who live and work in the ongoing stream of Johannine tradition.

The title of this book, then, is an acknowledgment that "what we have heard from the beginning"—what we have been taught by earlier generations—"remains in us" so long as we keep thinking about the Johannine Literature. It remains in us not only because we have inherited our foundational ideas and methods from these people, but also because we have known them as friends and mentors who have touched our lives in ways that cannot be reduced to a few paragraphs in a history of research. Thus, the past, present, and future of Johannine Studies flow into and out of one another as new hands weave living threads into an ancient tapestry.

Let me close with one final thought, based on my experiences in editing this book and my own engagement with its contents. At the seminary where I teach, the Master of Arts in Biblical Studies (I think that's the official title of the degree) requires a hundred–page thesis for the research component. Many students, particularly those with full-time jobs, active ministries, and/or young families, are intimidated by this project and frequently express disbelief at the possibility of writing such a paper. Their dismay is often compounded by a fear that they cannot think of anything original to say. Just recently, I was enjoying burritos with a nervous student who wanted to discuss possible research topics; the conversation opened with the familiar question, "So do I have to come up with some new idea for this thing? I can't come up with any new ideas, I don't think."

His question took me back to a discussion involving myself and some kids on my block which must have occurred around 1979—I say this because I remember talking about this on the front porch of my friend Dwayne's house, and I visualize myself and everyone involved in the conversation as we would have appeared at about age twelve. In the blue collar neighborhood where I grew up, where many families (including my own) were within a generation of the post–World War II Appalachian migration to the industrial centers of the Midwest, one rarely met a person who had graduated from college. In many families a high school diploma was an outstanding accomplishment, so my friends and I were quite impressed to learn that one of our buddy's relatives—I believe an aunt—was soon to receive a "master's degree." Someone asked what that was, and he proceeded to explain that it was another degree that one could pursue after college. Further, he added—retrospectively, his mother must have explained all of this in some detail to him, as they were heading out of town for the graduation ceremony the next day—after receiving such a degree, one could go on to get a doctorate, the highest level of education available. The word "doctor" referred, in all of our minds, to a person who gives out polio vaccines and permission slips for playing baseball. So I asked this individual how his relative (whose degree was in some field other than medicine) could achieve this status. He clarified that a "doctor" was not just a medical person, but actually anyone who—and I quote—"is able to write a book about something that no one has ever written about before."

This statement filled me with a kind of awe, and it informed my thinking about doctoral degrees for quite some time thereafter—in fact, until very recently. The same sort of awe inspired my student's fear of a master's thesis: his awe arising from the level of work involved; his fear arising from the fact that, after two millennia of scholarship, only the vainest person alive could imagine that she or he might come up with something new to say about the Bible. Over the past decade or so, I have been surprised to learn that this same fear and awe afflicts even those individuals at the very highest levels of biblical scholarship. Perhaps more so, because these erudite scholars, having become more and more aware of what has already been said, acutely realize the difficulty of having anything new to say. Some of those people have contributed essays to this book.

Yet if I may be so bold and, indeed, impertinent, I would suggest that biblical scholarship is not about saying something that no one has ever said before. Biblical scholarship, rather, is about continuing a conversation that has been ongoing since the days of Papias, a conversation that has kept the Bible alive and relevant for two millennia. Those who join that conversation today step into a stream that has run deep and strong through the lives of Ireneaus, Origen, Eusebius, Augustine, Aquinas, Luther, Calvin, Griesbach, Schleiermacher, Wesley, Schweitzer, Bultmann, Dodd, and many, many others. I hope that the book you are now reading may stand as evidence that the conversation will continue for at least one more generation.

CHAPTER 1

SECOND THOUGHTS ON THE FOURTH GOSPEL

John Ashton

When Tom Thatcher approached me with a request for a contribution to
the present volume, he paid me the compliment of calling me "undoubtedly one of the juggernauts of Johannine scholarship." What he meant
of course was that he was greatly impressed by my big book on John,
Understanding the Fourth Gospel, first published in 1991. But his remark
prompted me to ask myself just how much lateral pressure would be needed
to make me veer significantly from the course I had set all those years ago
(more than a quarter of a century) when I decided to embark upon this
work. The pressure has been considerable, compelling me to test afresh
the strength of theories I had argued for in the past but could no longer
take for granted. As I set out to rethink my claims in the light of subsequent scholarship, it occurred to me that it was perhaps time to undertake a complete rewrite of the book in question, and with this in mind, I
asked Oxford University Press to consider publishing a second edition of
Understanding the Fourth Gospel. After some delay, the press agreed and
the reflections that follow are largely drawn from the introduction to this
revised edition, which appeared in May of this year (2007).

On certain points, my thinking about the Johannine Literature has
indeed changed. I no longer believe, for instance, that it can be said with
any confidence that the author of the Fourth Gospel was a convert from

Essenism, and I have therefore transferred the chapter in which this was argued ("Dualism") from the historical part ("Genesis") to the exegetical part ("Revelation") of the new edition of *Understanding the Fourth Gospel*. At other points my thinking has remained the same, but my argument has developed. For example, even before the first edition of *Understanding the Fourth Gospel* had been published—while it was still in press—I had detected a significant gap in my discussion of the reasons for the rupture between the Johannine community and "the Jews." I attempted to fill this gap in a chapter titled "Bridging Ambiguities" in my 1994 book *Studying John*, which now appears in a modified form in chapter 6 of the second edition of *Understanding the Fourth Gospel* under the title "Messenger of God." The other new chapter in the revised edition, "The Search for Wisdom," represents an attempt to fill a second gap by devoting some consideration to the question of the Fourth Gospel's plot. Nevertheless, it would be wrong to pretend that these additions represent any real change of direction in my thinking.

The main purpose of the book published in 1991 was to furnish new and coherent answers to the two big "riddles" dominating the remarkable commentary of Rudolf Bultmann, which had appeared fifty years before. Bultmann's work is largely ignored nowadays, but the two riddles still deserve attention. The first of these, modified so as to ask where the Fourth Gospel stands in the development of Jewish thought, is in fact part of the larger question (probably the most interesting of all those confronting New Testament scholarship) of how to explain Christianity's emergence out of Judaism. My answer to the second riddle, which concerns what Bultmann called the *Grundkonzeption* of the Gospel and focuses upon its curious affinity with Jewish apocalyptic, attracted little interest when *Understanding the Fourth Gospel* was released in 1991, and I am pleased to have had the opportunity of putting it forward again.

In what follows here, however, I want to concentrate on two central issues that are intensely debated even today, where, as I see it, my own approach is most under threat. The first of these is the ongoing argument between the diachronic and the synchronic approaches to interpretation; the second is the broad question of what scholars have called "the Johannine community."

DIACHRONIC AND SYNCHRONIC APPROACHES

In theory, there is no contradiction between the "diachronic" and "synchronic" approaches to the Gospel of John. The former involves tracing the history of the text, the other of studying it in its present form, and there is no obvious reason why the two methods should be regarded as incompatible. But in practice, the partisans of synchronicity, whom I shall call "synchronists," frequently raise objections in principle to the alternative approach. Mark Stibbe, introducing a collection of narrative–critical studies published in 1993, comments on what he calls "the loss of historical consciousness" among current literary critics of John. "First of all, and most obviously, they have rejected historical criticism. Nearly all the books which study the final form of John's Gospel begin with some brief and iconoclastic rejection of former, more historical methods" (Stibbe 1993, 1). Why they should do so is not entirely clear to me, because the starting-point of historical critics is no different from that of literary critics of any persuasion, namely, the text in its final form. Far from opposing the synchronic study of the Gospel, historical critics always begin by taking a close look at the text as a whole. The apparent dislocations and awkward conjunctions that make them want to dig deeper are there already, and their observation of these so-called "aporias" in John's narrative results from a synchronic perception, not from some ingrained inclination to chop and change a smooth and well–integrated piece of writing. Historical critics are not, as one critic has recently put it, "*predisposed* towards aporias in the text" (Segovia 1996, 185; emphasis added) nor are they instinctive deconstructionists. They neither seek out aporias nor invent them; but having found them in the text they prefer to explain them rather than paper them over or pretend they are not there.

Insignificant as they may appear to some, the Fourth Gospel's aporias are in fact of great importance for all its interpreters, because their estimate of the general relevance of these problem spots and their manner of handling them will largely determine their eventual position on the big question of how the text was composed. Alternatively, in some cases it may be that someone's view concerning the composition of the Gospel may affect his or her approach to all or any of the aporias. We have to allow for the possibility that a scholar's reading of the evidence may be distorted by previously formed opinions or unconscious prejudices.

There are, I suggest, five distinct ways of responding to the Fourth Gospel's aporias: (1) ignoring them altogether, (2) explaining them away, (3) treating them seriously and drawing appropriate conclusions, (4) reading them dialectically, (5) interpreting them as intentional elements of the evangelist's literary strategy. The most questionable approach on this list is number 2, because the validity or adequacy of any particular interpretation is always to some extent a matter of opinion. To take but one example, when C. H. Dodd reads Jesus' injunction at 14:31 to "rise, let us be on our way"—the best known of all the Gospel's aporias—as "a movement of the spirit, an interior act of will, but . . . a real departure nonetheless" (1953, 409), most readers will feel that they have just

witnessed an adroit piece of sleight–of–hand. At the risk of being myself
accused of prejudice, therefore, I want to retain this category of responses
on my list. What I mean by "dialectical reading" (number 4 above) is the
attempt to acknowledge perceived disjunctions in the text and yet to go
beyond them by finding new meanings that take into account possible
earlier versions of the text and whatever may have been added since. I
have attempted a reading of this kind in the chapter titled "The Shepherd" in *Studying John* (Ashton 1994, 114–40). There remains a lot of
work to be done along these lines.

In his introduction to *The Gospel of Signs* (1970), published nearly
thirty years after Bultmann's great commentary, Robert Fortna noted
the "tacit moratorium" at that time on the question of possible sources
and earlier editions behind the Fourth Gospel (1 n. 1). The sheer depth
and exhaustiveness of Bultmann's work had, not surprisingly, left most of
his rivals stunned and intimidated. Now, more than sixty years after the
appearance of *Das Evangelium des Johannes* (1941), it is easier to see where
Bultmann went wrong. His revelation–discourse source had never won
much support; his displacement theory was comprehensively demolished
by Ernst Haenchen (1980, 48–57), who concluded, rightly one hopes,
that "the time of displacement theories is past"; Bultmann's proposed
"ecclesiastical redactor," never very robust, was finally laid low, crushed
one might say, by the massive three volume study of Jörg Frey, *Die johanneische Eschatologie* (1997–2000).

Yet while the disappearance of displacement theories and the death
of the notion of an ecclesiastical redactor has cleared the air, the Fourth
Gospel's aporias are still with us, and they still require explanation. Cutting to the chase, I want to suggest that the main aporias can be divided
into three types, which point in three different directions. First, and most
obvious, there is chapter 21, which even C. H. Dodd, despite his commitment to interpreting the text as it has come down to us, dismissed as "a
mere postscript" (1953, 409). Second, there are the aporias that suggest
the existence of a signs source (John 2:23; 4:54; 20:30; etc.). Third, some
of the most important aporias point to the likelihood that there were at
least two separate editions of the Gospel. The most obvious of these are
3:31, 6:1, 10:1 and 14:30–31, all of which are what Fortna calls "contextual" aporias, problems in the flow and presentation of the narrative. Like
many scholars, I have become increasingly doubtful about the usefulness
of "stylistic" criteria for distinguishing between different strands of the
Gospel text, and I am reluctant to turn too quickly to what Fortna calls
"ideological" but might less tendentiously be called "theological" criteria.
It is all too easy, as Frey shows in his discussion of the arguments concerning John 14 in Wellhausen's leaflet, *Erweiterungen und Änderungen,*

to mingle contextual and theological considerations in such a way as to expose oneself to the charge of theological *parti pris* (Frey 1997–2000, 1.53–55, 62). But the most important aporias in the Fourth Gospel's narrative, including 14:30–31, are those that demand the attention not of theologians but of literary critics.

In view of the strong evidence that the Gospel of John went through (at least) two editions, I find it surprising that so few commentators take this possibility into account, for it neatly disposes of the two alternative theories that bedeviled Johannine scholarship for so long: the ecclesiastical redactor and the displacement theory. If one thinks of "the same person" as responsible for virtually the whole text—apart perhaps from (a) a source that he freely adapted to suit his own purposes, (b) a hymn to Wisdom that served him as a prologue (John 1:1–18), (c) the final chapter (John 21), and (d) a few relatively insignificant glosses—then the specter of theological contradiction that many more conservative critics have understandably found so threatening vanishes without trace.

What, then, are we to make of the objections that have been leveled against the use of aporias as helpful clues in interpreting the Gospel of John? These objections are, I think, of two main types. The first is well represented by C. H. Dodd, who conceives it "to be the duty of an interpreter at least to see what can be done with the document as it has come down to us before attempting to improve upon it" (1953, 290). The second type is that of the champions of narrative criticism and the theoreticians of this discipline known as "narratologists." Interested above all in the "story" of the Gospel, they realize that the value of their work depends upon the existence of an unbroken line in the text from start to finish. Here, I will briefly respond to both types of objection to the approach I have suggested.

First, my objection to Dodd, let me be clear, has nothing to do with the target he sets himself—no reasonable person could find anything wrong with seeing "what can be done with the document as it has come down to us." But I do object to his deliberate exclusion of other aims and other methods. Bultmann's purpose, which is to recover as far as possible the original work of John the evangelist in its purity and integrity, is on the face of it just as legitimate and no less laudable an enterprise than that of Dodd. There is a sense indeed in which Bultmann is doing exactly what Dodd requires—seeing what can be done with the document as it has come down to us. Dodd's frank admission "that the work [the Gospel of John] has suffered some dislocation" is disingenuous, in so far as it includes no acknowledgment that the dislocations need to be explained. The unargued assumption that they can have no bearing upon the interpretation of the text is not a strength but a weakness. If, by some freak chance, Bultmann's theory happened to be right and the work of the evangelist has been spoiled by a later ecclesiastical redactor intent on adding elements of sacramentalism and futuristic eschatology absent from the original text, then Bultmann could scarcely be blamed for drawing his readers' attention to these alterations; nor in principle was he wrong to undertake the laborious work of restoring the Gospel to its original state, if indeed it had suffered the kind of disruption that his argument supposes. His fault, if fault there was, is to be sought not in his principles but in his practice.

Dodd himself (except for his exclusion of John 21) stuck rigidly to his principle of focusing on the text as we have it, but only at the price of ignoring certain obvious aporias (e.g. 6:1 and 20:30–31) and explaining others away (9:1 and 14:30–31). More recently, Dodd's lead has been followed by a number of other scholars, such as Fernando Segovia, who believes that by and large "the proposed aporias can be readily explained in other—and, I would add, simpler—ways," and Richard Bauckham, who asserts that "a passage that seems awkward to the source critic, whose judgment often amounts merely to observing that 'he or she would not have written it like that,' can appear quite reasonable to a critic who is attentive to the literary dynamics of the text" (Segovia 1996, 186; Bauckham 2001, 105–6). To these glib assertions that there are better or simpler ways of solving the aporias, all one can say is, "Show me."

A more serious objection to Dodd's approach is put by Jörg Frey, one of the most productive and influential Johannine scholars today. It comes in a small section of the first part of his monumental thesis on Johannine eschatology (1997–2000). Volume I of Frey's study, itself quite a big book, is an impressively comprehensive history of research, but Frey's summary discussion of the Fourth Gospel's aporias, in a section titled *Die Aporie der johanneischen Literarkritik* ("the impasse of Johannine source criticism"), takes up fewer than three pages. Frey wants to argue that source criticism has proved not nearly as useful a tool for the interpretation of the Gospel of John as for study of the Synoptics. Here is the crucial sentence: "When interpreters deliberately renounce any stylistic verification of their theories and follow the old *Tendenzkritik* in relying solely on theological criteria, this can only lead into the vicious circle of individual theological theories" (Frey 1997–2000, 1.431).[1] Robert Fortna, introducing his Signs Gospel hypothesis, distinguishes clearly between ideological, stylistic,

---

[1] Mine is a free translation, but not, I trust, an inaccurate one. Original: "Wo die Auslegung einer philologischen Verifikation ihrer Konstruktion bewußt den Abschied gibt und sich im Gefolge der alten Tendenzkritik allein auf sachliche Kriterien stützen will, führt der Weg nur in den *circulus vitiosus* der eigenen theologischen Konstruktionen."

and contextual criteria. For Frey, however, any argument concerning the Fourth Gospel's aporias that is not based on stylistics (*Philologie*) is bound to be theologically motivated and is therefore worthless—and he is quietly confident that the stylistic criteria are worthless, too.

In the first place, Frey's calm assumption that anyone employing theological criteria is necessarily infected by the demonstrable bias associated with the *Tendenzkritik* of Baur and the Tübingen school is a way of dismissing these without argument. Yet, to take but one example, Fortna's distinction between the low Christology implied in the simple title "Messiah" as employed in the signs source and the high Christology observable in the current context of the Gospel of John is unquestionably correct. Less straightforward theological differences between the Gospel and its sources may be harder to detect and more open to discussion, but are not for that reason to be discarded unexamined. More serious is Frey's apparent assumption that theological (*sachlich*) and stylistic criteria are all we have. For a scholar of Frey's undoubted learning, the failure to acknowledge the existence of Fortna's third category, "contextual" aporias, is more than just an astounding oversight; it is a very serious omission indeed. Shaky as they may seem to some, the contextual aporias are the foundation of all theories of layers of redaction and successive editions of the Fourth Gospel. Fortna rightly favors them because this category is "more objective" than the other two (1970, 18–19), and in fact most of the major aporias are of this kind, readily discernible because of literary or contextual roughnesses and not needing a theologian to spot them. If these are ignored, the other criteria are too weak to stand alone unaided.

The second type of objection to any diachronic approach is the one raised by the so-called narrative critics, who are interested especially and sometimes exclusively in the story or plot of the Gospel of John. They deny a priori that the study of the prehistory of the text has any relevance to the meaning of the Gospel in its present form. The following quotes are notable examples of this approach:

- "dissection and stratification have no place in the study of the gospel and may confuse one's view of the text" (Culpepper 1983, 5)

- "the meaning of the present text is not dependent upon the recovery of the sources. . . . Even if the sources were recovered, focusing attention on them would only serve to distract us from our task of reading the Evangelist's text" (Nicholson 1983, 15–16)

- "questions of multilayered interpolation . . . have no place . . . no more than do questions of 'the author's intentions,' for the assumption of unity endows the entire text with intentionality" (Staley 1988, 29–30)

- "Narrative unity is not something that must be proved from an analysis of the material. Rather, it is something that can be assumed. It is the form of the narrative itself that grants coherence to the material, no matter how disparate the material might be" (Powell 1990, 92)

- "Literary readings presuppose an holistic approach to the text as against a tendency to atomize it into units of earlier material and sources. . . . Stress is placed on the overall coherence of the narrative, and meaning is found in relationship of parts to the whole. Along with this goes an understanding of gaps, lacunae and fissures in the text as purposefully conceived, to be understood and resolved in terms of the rhetorical strategies and ploys of the implied author, or as textual signals inviting the implied reader to actualize the narrative reality or obtain meaning by testing hypotheses and imaginatively filling the gaps. The literary text, on this perspective, becomes 'a dynamic series of gaps'" (Tovey 1997, 21)

What reply can be made to such objections?

Culpepper's bald assertion that "dissection and stratification have no place in the study of the gospel"—strange in a work dealing expressly with the Gospel's "anatomy"—does not withstand scrutiny. But my real complaint against Culpepper (as against Dodd) concerns the exclusiveness of his claim. In other respects, Culpepper's *Anatomy of the Fourth Gospel* makes a real contribution to Johannine scholarship and one can readily understand why it is widely admired. Similarly, it is possible, as Dodd, Culpepper, and many others have shown, to study the meaning of the text fruitfully without delving into its sources, but the search for sources (which also involves an inquiry into the "integrity" of the text) does not have to be a pointless and unprofitable distraction. I am baffled by the blank refusal of people claiming to be literary critics of whatever persuasion to consider any solution to a textual problem except an integral reading of the text as it stands in the manuscript tradition. Simply as an *argumentum ad hominem*, it is worth pointing out that no two manuscripts are the same and no single manuscript is free from error. There are textual variants in almost every verse of the Gospel of John, and modern editions are the result of thousands of tiny decisions on the part of their editors. For example, the latest edition (27th) of the Nestle–Aland Greek text fails to include an important variant for John 7:52, where Bodmer Papyrus II, uniquely, reads ὁ προφήτης ("the prophet") in place of the anarthrous προφήτης ("a prophet") found in all the other manuscripts. Should it be for that reason left out of account?

I have greater problems with assertions such as "the assumption of unity endows the entire text with intentionality" and "it is the form of the narrative itself that grants coherence to the material," largely because I do not understand them. If unity is simply assumed, then the intentionality of the text is assumed along with it. But what if the material, on examination, proves to lack coherence? The suggestion of "a dynamic series of gaps" (Tovey 1997, 21)—a far cry indeed from David Friedrich Strauss's characterization of the Gospel of John as a "seamless garment" (*jener ungenähte Leibrock*)—is clearly an invitation to the implied readers of the Gospel to fill the gaps in for themselves. But how? In accordance with "the perceived strategies and ploys" not, be it noted, of the real author, who guards his independence, but rather of the implied author, always at the beck and call of his inventor, the narrative critic who has designed and constructed him? I cannot take this seriously.

THE JOHANNINE COMMUNITY

No one has followed the course of Johannine Studies over the last three decades more intently than Robert Kysar. So when Kysar concludes, perhaps a trifle wistfully, that in his view "there is now sufficient evidence in these early years [of the twenty–first century] to indicate that the whither of the Johannine community [the future of the theory] is likely to include its demise" (2005b, 76), one has to sit up and take notice. Kysar's reasons for reaching this conclusion are twofold. The first reason "has to do with the evidence for such a hypothetical construction as the Johannine community" (Kysar 2005b, 71). Here we should distinguish the various ways in which individual scholars have explained the origins and progress of the community from the general hypothesis that there was such a community in the first place. Kysar asks, for instance, with regard to the Fourth Gospel's three references to expulsion from the synagogue (John 9:22; 12:42; 16:2), whether these necessarily refer to an event that had already happened. Perhaps not. But the most important reason for believing that the Johannine group was no longer attached to the synagogue at the time the Gospel was written is the uncompromisingly bitter tone of the exchanges between Jesus and "the Jews" in chapters 5, 8, and 10. And as for the existence of the community, how else should we explain the "sheepfold" of chapter 10, or the many-branched "vine" of chapter 15? Questioning whether the sectarian attitude of the Gospel should be explained as a consequence of expulsion from the synagogue, Kysar suggests that there could be other reasons. Indeed. As I explained fifteen years ago, my own theory is that the expulsion was the consequence, not the cause, of the Johannine group's adoption of beliefs incompatible with the strict monotheism of those whom the Gospel calls "the Jews." Finally, Kysar emphasizes that "*simply because a hypothesis illumines the possible meaning of a passage does not necessarily prove that the hypothesis is true*" (2005b, 73, emphasis original). This, as a logical principle, is undeniable. Broadened out to include science as well as literature, it helps to explain why it is still possible to believe in creationism or a flat earth (there are Web sites for both). But most reasonable people will continue to affirm that the earth is round and that the origin of species is best explained by natural selection. When it comes to literature, of course, matters are less straightforward. One cannot, for instance, attribute to those who deny the existence of Q the kind of unreason that seems to afflict the members of the Flat Earth Society. But the continuing disagreement of scholars about questions on which no certainty can be reached does not mean that they should stop searching together for answers to the questions they have raised.

Kysar's second reason for forecasting the rapid demise of the theory of the Johannine community is "the decline of historical criticism" and, more alarmingly, the objections confronting the study of history in general. "The waves of . . . postmodernism have gradually washed away the assumptions on which the study of history was founded during the Enlightenment. . . . If postmodernism prevails it will mean the death of the historical critical method of biblical interpretation and all the historical reconstructions that were the results of the method, including those involving the Johannine community" (Kysar 2005b, 73–74). The greatest challenge, according to Kysar, is "the question of the *locus of meaning*." Perhaps it is true that "a text means differently as it is interpreted by different readers" (Kysar 2005b, 75, emphasis original). Nevertheless, swimming as strongly as I can against the tide of postmodernism, I still believe that it makes sense to look for the meaning that the first readers of a text would have found in it. There is no obvious decline in the study and composition of books on history, and these are still separated from fiction and historical novels in all the bookshops that I know. I trust that the worst of Kysar's fears are ill-founded.

Now I want to consider some more specific objections against the theory of a Johannine community: (1) the notion that the genre of the Gospel of John does not support reading strategies that might reveal the existence of a community behind the text, (2) the notion that the Gospel of John, along with the Synoptics, was written "for all Christians" rather than for a distinct community, and (3) the notion that flaws in J. Louis Martyn's reconstruction of the history of the Johannine community raise doubts about the community's existence.

A Life of Christ?

One enormous obstacle blocking the path to the acceptance of J. Louis Martyn's general theory about the history of the Johannine community is the widespread but largely mistaken belief that the Gospels are lives of Christ—not of course in the same sense as the nineteenth–century "lives" so brilliantly analyzed by Albert Schweitzer, but very much in the same sense as the ancient Greek and Roman biographies (*bioi*) by people such as Plutarch and Suetonius. Richard Bauckham, in fact, declares that "the most damaging criticism of Martyn's two–level reading strategy," the very foundation of Martyn's conclusions about the history of the Johannine community, "is the fact that it has no basis in the literary genre of the Fourth Gospel." Exhibiting an uncharacteristic deference to current scholarship, Bauckham says that "recent discussion of the gospel genre strongly favors the view that first-century readers would have recognized all four canonical Gospels as a special form of Greco–Roman biography" (2001, 104). Bauckham is no doubt right in thinking that this "special form" of biography cannot easily be reconciled with the type of reading that Martyn proposes, and in particular with his reconstruction of the Johannine community.

Crucial here is Bauckham's quite proper insistence that the Gospels cannot be unique. "This word 'unique' is a negative term signifying what is mentally inapprehensible. The absolutely unique is, by definition, indescribable" (Toynbee 1954, 8.255). So far so good. But before searching for a genre into which the Gospels can be slotted and thereby better understood, the first move, surely, is to delineate the Gospels themselves as accurately as possible—to ask, quite simply, what is it that characterizes them as Gospels? We may start by suggesting that the use of the plural form "Gospels" skews this question from the outset, for we should really be asking about the Gospel of Mark. It was Mark, after all, who, whatever model he himself had in mind, introduced the modifications that entitle us to search for a formula to convey the special characteristics of the canonical Gospels that eventually led to their being classed together as "the fourfold gospel." Matthew and Luke had Mark's Gospel before them as they wrote, and the easiest way of explaining the formal similarities between these three and the Fourth Gospel is that John was acquainted with at least one of the others. How, then, is Mark a "biography," and how are Mark and John distinct from other ancient "biographies"?

Martin Hengel begins a lecture called "The Four Gospels and the One Gospel of Jesus Christ" (summarizing a book of the same title) with a zealous defense of the view that the Gospels are biographies. Aware, however, that this is not enough, he adds, referring to Mark, that it is a "kerygmatic biography." "Because 'biography' and 'proclamation' are fused in his [Mark's] work," he continues, "Mark can call his narrative about Jesus '[a] saving message,' that is an account of Jesus' activity which brings about faith and thus salvation" (Hengel 2004, 22). Leaving aside the tendentious translation of εὐαγγήλιον as "saving message," we may question what exactly happens when biography and proclamation are, in Hengel's word, "fused." Fuse oxygen and hydrogen and you get water. It is at least conceivable that the fusion of "biography" and "proclamation" may result in something that cannot properly be called either "biography" or "kerygma." When we speak of a "carrot cake," we mean a cake in which carrots are one of the main ingredients but they are not exactly "fused" with the flour, the eggs, and the oil. Applied to Mark's Gospel, the term "kerygmatic biography" seems to imply that it is a special form of biography, just as the carrot cake is a special form of cake. But is this right? The Gospels unquestionably include certain biographical elements, but it is still permissible to ask whether the novelty that prompted earlier scholars to speak of the uniqueness of the Gospels has any precedent among the *bioi* with which they have been compared.

A fascinating answer to this question is given in an essay by Jonathan Z. Smith, who selects two texts for detailed comparison, Philostratus' *Vita Apollonii* and Iamblichus' *De Vita Pythagorica liber*. He argues that "for those figures [in the relevant ancient writings] for whom an ultimate religious claim is made (e.g., son of god), their biographies will serve as apologies against outsiders' charges that they were merely magicians and against their admirers' sincere misunderstanding that they were merely wonder–workers, divine men or philosophers. From Iamblichus' *De mysteriis Aegyptiorum* and Apuleius' *Apologia* to the Gospel of Mark . . . the characteristic of every such religious biography . . . of Late Antiquity is this double defense against the charge of magic—against the calumny of outsiders and the sincere misunderstanding of admirers. . . . The solution of each group or individual so charged was the same: to insist on an inward meaning of the suspect activities. The allegedly magical action, properly understood, is a sign. There is both a transparent and a hidden meaning, a literal and a deeper understanding required. At the surface level the biography appears to be an explicit story of a magician or a *Wundermensch*; at the depth level it is the enigmatic self-disclosure of a son of god" (1978, 193–94).

Speaking of the work of Philostratus, Smith says that "his biography as biography is unimportant," and of that of Iamblichus, "for mere mortals, a figure like Pythagoras must remain a cipher" (1978, first quote 197, second quote 203). Smith concludes that "what an Apollonius, a Pythagoras, a Jesus reveals in the narratives concerning them, is their own enigmatic nature, their *sui generis* character" and comments provocatively "I would want to claim the title 'gospel' for the *Vitae* attributed to Mark and John as well as those by Philostratus and Iamblichus" (1978, 203–4). Neither Philostratus nor Iamblichus can have influenced Mark, because he preceded them by some two centuries; but then neither can Plutarch or Suetonius, writing around the end of the first century C.E. There are historical features in the work of all three writers, but Mark, Philostratus, and Iamblichus—unlike Plutarch and Suetonius—were more interested in what Hengel calls "proclamation" than in any kind of historical biography. To call them biographers without further scrutiny is to focus on what was for them a secondary aspect of their work. Even Smith's suggested term "religious biographies" has the disadvantage of laying too much stress on the biographical aspect; so for want of a better name, I suggest "proclamatory narratives." This has the double advantage of restricting the range of comparison and of suggesting that the religious aspect of a work (namely, the extreme claims it makes on behalf of its hero) is likely to affect its historical reliability.

When we turn to the problem of the genre of the Fourth Gospel, moreover, there is an additional argument available. This is evident from two major sections of the text, first the acrimonious controversies between Jesus and "the Jews" in chapters 5–10, and second, the farewell discourse and prayer in chapters 14–17. Although projected back into the life of Jesus, these passages clearly display the concerns of a much later period. The violent dissensions of chapters 5, 8, and 10, the way "the Jews" are portrayed in these engagements, the claims made by Jesus about himself, and the consolatory words of the farewell discourse all go to prove that their author, whom we call "the evangelist," was writing for readers whose circumstances were radically different from those of the few followers Jesus had gathered in his own lifetime and who must have read these chapters as a direct reflection of their own experiences (see Frey 2004a, 38 and, more fully, 1997–2000, 2.247–68).

So Bauckham is simply wrong to say that the original readers of the Gospel of John "would not expect it to address the specific circumstances of one particular community" (2001, 104–5). So much seems to me to be evident from the Gospel itself. Bauckham adds that the Fourth Gospel "displays a strong sense of the 'pastness' of the story of Jesus, temporally and geographically located in its own time and space" (2001, 105). But the correct inference from this fact is the need for the very "two-level" reading that he rejects. It is true that this need does not apply to all sections of the Gospel narrative or to all the characters who play a part in it. Composed, as I have already argued, over a long period, the Gospel of John is not a homogeneous text.

A "Gospel for All Christians"?

The Gospels for All Christians—the defiant title of a collection of essays in which Richard Bauckham and others argue that, far from being written for local communities, as most scholars believe, the Gospels were actually intended for distribution throughout the Christian world—begs the question it is intended to answer. For this book presupposes that during the period of the Gospels' composition—between, say, 65 and 90 C.E.—members of local churches thought of themselves as belonging to a much larger organization, already scattered all over the known world. Bauckham indeed asserts that the early Christian movement "had a strong sense of itself as a worldwide movement" (1998b, 33), although he provides no direct evidence in support of this claim. While Paul was alive, as is plain from his authentic letters, the term ἐκκλησία referred to a local church. In the Epistle to the Ephesians, of course, this word refers to some universal church in which all Christians, Jews, and Gentiles alike, were united (see Eph 1:22; 3:21), but it is at least conceivable that Ephesians was written after the Gospels. So the question remains open: Does it make sense to speak of "all Christians" at the time when the canonical Gospels were being composed? Other scholars—particularly Philip Esler (1998), David Sim (2001), and Margaret Mitchell (2005)—have dealt comprehensively with Bauckham's thesis. Here I will confine myself to a 2001 article in which he discusses the special case of the Fourth Gospel (Bauckham 2001).

Bauckham begins by stating that "the most damaging criticism of Martyn's 'two-level' reading strategy is the fact that it has no basis in the literary genre of the Fourth Gospel" (2001, 104), an assertion which, as we have seen, begs the question. The next section of his article headed "A Two-Level Text" accurately sums up the position of his adversaries:

> Closely associated with the two–level reading strategy is the view that FG [the Fourth Gospel] is a multilayered work, in which texts from various stages of the community's history have been preserved alongside one another. This perspective posits a complex history of literary redaction as the key to the Johannine community's social and theological history. The ability to distinguish these various sources and levels of redaction depends primarily on the identification of aporias and theological tensions between different parts of FG. (Bauckham 2001, 105)

Bauckham goes on to assert, without argument, that "literary criticism" has a better way of dealing with these aporias and that "we need to be much more open to the possibility" that the ideological tensions between the different parts of the Gospel "belong to the character and method of FE's [the Fourth Evangelist's] theology" (2001, 105–6, quote 106). Possibly so, but not unless the literary critics are prepared to demonstrate in each instance the superiority of their approach. Such work of theirs that I have read (quite a lot) has left me unimpressed.

The section of Bauckham's article titled "In–Group Language?" is confusing because it is confused. He claims that nowadays the Fourth Gospel is seen as the most accessible of the four to Christians and non–Christians alike, though he provides no evidence for either assertion. That it should be accessible to Christians is easily explained on the basis of centuries of teaching and tradition; but to non–Christians, who have no previous knowledge of Christianity? I doubt it. The explanations the Gospel itself sometimes gives of its riddles (which Bauckham considers a counterargument against the in–group language theory) have nothing to do with the insider/outsider dichotomy of the in–group language, but relate instead to the evangelist's before/after theology: during Jesus' lifetime all is hidden; after the resurrection all becomes clear. Similarly, the riddles employed to lead to a fuller understanding (the Samaritan woman and, arguably, Nicodemus) fulfill, it is true, a different function from the oppositional riddles used in Jesus' confrontations with "the Jews." But this simply means that one has to be precise about the identification of "insiders" and "outsiders." And this, in turn, is different from the two levels of understanding, the first available to the characters in the story, the second to the readers of the Gospel. Bauckham complains that "scholars who read FE's language as the in–group talk of a sectarian community" have "missed the fact that FG seems designed, on the contrary, to introduce readers to its special language and symbolism" (2001, 109). But there is no contradiction here.

The *Birkat-Haminim*

In 1979, J. Louis Martyn published a revised edition of his classic *History and Theology in the Fourth Gospel* (1968). The revision includes a long note (1979b, 54 n. 69) defending his views on the euphemistically titled *Birkat-Haminim*, a "Benediction of the Heretics" (generally thought to have been introduced into the synagogue liturgy in the late–first century C.E. and regarded by Martyn as the key to the Fourth Gospel's allusions to excommunication), against certain objections raised privately by Wayne Meeks and in the published writings of other scholars. Martyn admits "that we are dealing with questions which can be resolved only with some degree of probability," but repeats his personal opinion that the *Birkat–Haminim* "was issued under Gamaliel II and that it is in some way reflected in John 9:22, etc." In another note (1979b, 56 n. 75), Martyn argues against Morton Smith that the Eighteenth Blessing was probably introduced toward the beginning of the period during which Gamaliel II controlled the Jamnian Synod (80–115 C.E.), not toward the end, as Smith proposed. An earlier date would make a connection with the excommunication referred to in John 9:22 more likely. Most of the very considerable scholarly work on this question that has appeared since 1979 is very critical of Martyn's position. Opinions range from Daniel Boyarin's complete dismissal of the Talmudic story concerning a "curse on heretics" ("the aroma of legend hovers over this entire account"; 2002, 220) to the theory of Liliane Vana that the *Birkat–Haminim* was part of the "Eighteen Blessings" even before the destruction of the temple in 70 C.E.—a time when these blessings were not a synagogue prayer at all and when their daily recitation was not compulsory—and that, consequently, it has nothing to do with the exclusion of Jewish Christians from post–70 synagogues (Vana 2003).

If, contra Boyarin, some historical basis is to be accorded to the Talmudic story about the *Birkat–Haminim*, I am persuaded by the argument of Stephen Katz that this "was not directed solely at Jewish Christians when promulgated (or revised) after 70 [C.E.]. Rather, it was aimed against all heretics and detractors of the Jewish community who existed in the last two decades of the first century—including of course but not uniquely Jewish Christianity."[2] Katz continues by reminding us of what he calls "an important hermeneutical consideration—the difference between speaker and hearer." In this case:

> [T]he Jewish leadership directed its malediction against all heretics, while the Jewish Christians, who knew of the animosity against them and of the feeling that they were heretics 'heard' the *Birkat–Haminim* as particularly aimed at them. This was a perfectly natural response. Thus John and other later, second–century Christian sources could well speak of Jews cursing Christians in the synagogue, when in fact the malediction was against *minim* in general. (Katz 1984, 73–74)

---

[2] According to Rabbi Burton L. Visotzky, Katz is too much motivated by apologetic concerns. He himself believes that "the rabbis of Yavneh were a small, politically divided, largely impotent group who only had power over a tiny minority in the late first century, and had little power even in the years beyond" (Visotzky 2005, 95).

To this perceptive comment I would add that, as in a divorce, it is necessary to listen to both sides to get the full story. John's Gospel gives us
one, surely biased, version of the break between the two groups. The
version of "the Jews" would have been very different and may well have
said nothing about excommunication. Pieter van der Horst makes the
point that "the door [of the synagogue] always remained open [to Chris-
tians] even in Jerome's time" (1993–1994, 368). In the case of the Gospel
of John, however, we are dealing with a local dispute that had issued in
an all–too–real and probably rather messy divorce: the Jesus group had
broken away from the synagogue and would never return. In putting so
much stress on the relationship between the *Birkat–Haminim* and the
expulsion of the Jesus group from the synagogue to which texts such as
John 9:22 allude, Martyn lays himself open to the complete rejection of
his theory by, among others, Boyarin. This is unfortunate, because, as I
observed fifteen years ago, Martyn's reading of John 9 is not built upon
his interpretation of the Eighteen Benedictions—"at most it is buttressed
by it" (Ashton 1991, 108 n. 102). Quite apart from the support Martyn
finds for his theory in rabbinical sources, the evidence of the Fourth Gospel itself, read, as it surely must be, in relation not to the time of Jesus
but to that of the Jesus group within the synagogue, points to a decisive
break between "the Jews" and those among them who professed belief in
Jesus. This evidence alone is sufficient to justify research into the history
of this group.

Conclusion

What impressed me most about the United States in the course of my
first extended stay there more than thirty years ago (in truth less than
a couple of months) was the rapidity of change. In the New World, I
reflected, people move more quickly and readily than in the Old. The
remarkable rapidity with which people changed jobs, moved residences,
and revised opinions left me both admiring and bemused. Now, looking
back on the scholarly enterprise that has absorbed my time and energy
more than any other, I have to confess that in all essential respects I have
scarcely budged. As with Fernando Segovia, who cheerfully admits to
what seem to me bewilderingly frequent shifts in his approach to the
study of the Fourth Gospel, I have (indeed I have always had) an interest in "cultural studies" (Segovia 1996, 184). But I would not gloss this
interest as "ideological criticism," nor would I see in this interest any
reason for altering my basic point of view. I was then and remain still an
unrepentant advocate of historical criticism.

So much as I admire, say, Robert Kysar and Dwight Moody Smith for their advised readiness over the years to adapt to changing modes of Johannine scholarship, I will myself stay on the sidelines. Far from applauding the demise of historical criticism (if indeed things are as bad as that), I should like to see much more work done on the history of the ideas of the Gospel of John, in the interest of gaining a fuller understanding of the emergence of Christianity from Judaism; more work, too, on a dialectical approach to the text (what the French and Germans call *relecture*); and, finally, a more positive attitude to the history of the reception of the Gospel over the centuries.

1: RESPONSE

WHY SHOULD HISTORICAL CRITICISM CONTINUE TO HAVE A PLACE IN JOHANNINE STUDIES?

Wendy E. S. North

In part three of *Gulliver's Travels*, the eponymous hero voyages to Glubbdubdrib where he is granted his wish to see the ghosts of Homer and Aristotle together with those of their numerous commentators. Contrary to expectations, he soon discovers that Homer, far from being blind, has exceptional sight, while Aristotle, the celebrated "peripatetic" teacher, is virtually immobile. Gulliver also discovers that these learned "antients" are completely unacquainted with those later ghosts who make up the rest of the company (Swift 1975, x).

Swift's satirical wit was, of course, directed at the received wisdom of his age, which he took as complacency and sought to deflate by completely reversing its norms and assumptions. In many ways, however, Swift's masterpiece remains as fresh today and as vexatious to the world as he predicted it would be on its publication in 1726 (Swift 1975, v). For those of us who inhabit the lesser world of Johannine Studies, the vexation surely lies in raising acutely the whole issue of meaning, and therefore of historicity, in the process of interpreting for today an ancient text such as the Fourth Gospel. Bearing this in mind, and bearing in mind also John Ashton's declared position as "an unrepentant advocate of historical criticism," my response to his admirable and wide–ranging contribution will briefly explore this topic.

To begin with, I am not persuaded by Robert Kysar's claim that the rise of postmodernism could signal the demise of historical–critical methods of biblical interpretation (Kysar 2005b). In the first place, it is unclear to me why the empirical fact that all human endeavor is subjectively flawed should be seen to have burst upon our collective consciousness only just now in the history of ideas. Did we never know this before? After all, the argument itself is scarcely new. Swift, for example, was an incisive proponent of it and wrote *Gulliver's Travels* with the express intention of ridiculing the naïveté of the Enlightenment view of the human being as "animal rationale" (Swift 1975, x). Second, I do not see that it follows from this fact of human frailty that we should abandon the whole historical enterprise. Objectivity may be humanly impossible, but it matters that we try. Not to do so, as Ashton puts it, "would be like saying that if you have a squint there is no point trying to see straight" (1994, 188).

What, then, can historically oriented approaches bring to the task of interpreting John's Gospel in today's climate of hermeneutical alternatives? From a historical standpoint, the Fourth Gospel as we now have it belongs (probably) to the end of the first century C.E. and was written by a real individual who was addressing a real target audience. It follows from this that the text itself, as a vehicle of communication, can be supposed to have "meaning," inasmuch as this will be the burden of what its author wished to convey. The difficulty here arises when we ask what meaning was perceived in the text by its first recipients, which is where reader response theory begins to come into view. However, there are two observations we can make about the Gospel of John which suggest that these original readers' perception of its meaning may not have strayed far from what the author intended. The first, which I have argued elsewhere (North 2003, 466), is the likelihood that John's first readers were a specific group who were already in receipt of his teaching. This circumstance would surely have predisposed them to be open to further instruction. The second observation concerns John's style of communication. With more than 400 asides to the reader distributed throughout his text (Van Belle 1985, 63–104), John was at pains to the point of pedantry to inform his readers how his Gospel was to be understood. This means that his readers would find meaning in his text by attending to what he does say rather than to what he does not say. These considerations surely place a serious question mark against the unrelenting application of the view that readers of John's text would have contributed to its meaning by filling in its "gaps."

One of the effects of historical–critical study is an emphasis on the extent to which John and his text are estranged, both temporally and culturally, from ourselves as commentators—an estrangement that Swift was prepared to exploit with fine malicious glee. This raises problems for those engaged in interpreting John's text for today. The postmodernist solution, as I understand it, is to locate all meaning in the contemporary reader and so dispense with history altogether. Yet it seems to me that to detach John's text from its original context so that it takes on new meaning for the present may be to exchange one set of problems for another. For example, if words mean whatever we want them to mean—what Marie Isaacs calls "the Humpty–Dumpty school of semantics" (1991, 41)—then we have freed John's text from the past only to shackle it to our own presuppositions, for surely in erasing its antiquity we also erase its capacity to be other than ourselves. Moreover, and even more disturbingly, if what the text means to me is as valid a meaning as any other meaning, who is to gainsay me if I decide that John 8:44 means that all Jews have the devil's DNA? Here surely the specificity of historical circumstances offers a much needed restraint.

My overall objective in this contribution is not to argue that the only meaning of John's text resides in the past, nor that we should privilege that meaning above others. It is to argue, however, that "what was from the beginning," as 1 John puts it, is indispensable to our understanding. The evangelist himself would scarcely have disagreed, for what John knew in his bones was that to go forward, schooled by the Spirit to interpret Jesus' meaning for a new day, was also to turn back to the historical reality, the σάρξ ("flesh") that was Jesus' earthly life. It was on this understanding that he wrote his Gospel.

CHAPTER 2

IN SEARCH OF A NEW SYNTHESIS

Johannes Beutler, S.J.

Evaluating the present state of Johannine research, looking backward and forward, is not an easy task. The image of a house under construction comes to mind. While some workers are installing the heating and the oil containers in the basement, others are plumbing the upper floors, inserting the windows, or covering the roof with tiles. Only the architect has in view all the different activities that shall lead to the final form of the house. Who would be such an architect in Johannine research?

Fifteen years ago, I was asked to respond to a Semeia volume titled *The Fourth Gospel from a Literary Perspective*. My contribution was called "Response from a European Perspective" (Beutler 1991). Much of what I wrote on that occasion would still pertain to the present task of summarizing both the state of Johannine research and of my own thinking. In the following discussion, I shall refer to this article from time to time, bringing that discussion up to date and enlarging its vision.

THE PRESENT STATE OF JOHANNINE RESEARCH

As in the article just mentioned, I would still make a distinction between "method and hermeneutics." There has been much reflection on the former and rather little on the latter. Particularly in Europe, there are still studies of Johannine source criticism and Bultmann's literary source theory survives in varied forms. Of Bultmann's sources, the *Semeiaquelle* ("signs source") is still particularly an object of study—sometimes in itself, sometimes as part of a "basic document" (*Grundschrift*) behind the Fourth Gospel. This same source is studied in the United States in the guise of a "Gospel of Signs" or "predecessor" to the Fourth Gospel (Fortna 1988). The other hypothetical literary layer of the Fourth Gospel that is still sometimes maintained is the "ecclesiastical redaction." In contrast to Bultmann's original proposal, this layer is now generally viewed as a sympathetic expansion of the previous layers of the Gospel of John (as "Johannine redaction") and is often believed to include the texts about the Beloved Disciple. Such a model is accepted by a number of Protestant and Catholic scholars (the latter coming mostly from the school of Georg Richter at Regensburg). Other schools of exegesis, however, reject this diachronic approach and favor a synchronic one. Various scholars who write in German concentrate on the existing text of John, sometimes under the influence of Martin Hengel. Proponents of this approach either deny the existence of sources or layers in the text or abstract from them. This distinction is not always made clear. Quite interesting is the case of Hartwig Thyen, who started with a source distinction in the line of his master Rudolf Bultmann but then gradually gave up this position and now argues not only for a synchronic reading of the Fourth Gospel, but even for a coherent text in which sources or layers are no longer discernible (Thyen 2005). In Thyen's current view, such layers would be irrelevant to interpretation.

Thyen arrived at this position partly under the influence of his American doctoral students, who brought from their cultural context the reader response approach that has been popular in North America for almost three decades now. In this approach, the text of the Fourth Gospel is taken as it stands and is interpreted in terms of the way the (real or implied) author tries to convince his (real or implied) reader. A considerable segment of North American scholarship has been dedicated to this approach in the form of rhetorical criticism. The term "rhetorical criticism" is not always used in the same sense: it might just mean the study of the strategy of narration found in a text (in this case being close to "textual pragmatics" as practiced in continental Europe), or it can refer to the study of a text according to the rules of classical or contemporary rhetoric. When emphasis is placed on the rules of classical rhetoric, rhetorical criticism supposes the study of classical philology. In fact, this approach has become prominent not only in Pauline Studies (I think of the school founded by Hans Dieter Betz), but also in a sector of Johannine Studies. This approach seems to have advantages and disadvantages. The advantage comes from the fact that New Testament texts in general and the Fourth Gospel in particular are seen in light of their surrounding culture, the Greco–Roman world. The disadvantage seems to be that the Jewish aspect of such texts remains out of sight. In extreme cases, New Testament exegesis appears as a sub–discipline of classical philology, and the theological aspect of the interpretation of the New Testament may be lost.

Although in the English–speaking world the pragmatic aspect of New Testament and Johannine texts stands at the center of attention, in the countries of the Roman languages (French, Spanish, Italian, and also in the work of Indian scholar G. Mlakuzhyil), semantics have been prominent these last decades. Also in this cultural world, the text of John is normally considered homogeneous and coherent. For some time, structuralism has had an influence on Johannine research. One frequently encounters proposals for the structure of the Fourth Gospel (or parts of it) that are based on key words found in *inclusios* or concentric structures. Such studies sometimes appear artificial. Not every concept used at the beginning and the end of a section of the text is necessarily an "inclusion"; there is also the possibility of "anaphora," the resumption of a concept from one paragraph at the beginning of the next. The acceptance of concentric structures has to be studied and proved in every individual New Testament text, not simply presupposed.

One problem is found in the denial of, and not only abstraction from, literary layers in the Fourth Gospel. Recently, a group of scholars whom I like to call the "Swiss School" (J. Zumstein, A. Dettwiler, K. Haldimann, but also the German K. Scholtissek) has begun to work with the hypothesis of *relecture*, a "rereading" of Johannine texts by successive layers or authors. The best known example is the addition of chapters 15–17 to the original farewell discourses of Jesus in John 13–14. The starting point for such an approach would be the exhortation of Jesus in John 14:31, "Rise, let us go hence." Defenders of the literary coherence of the farewell discourse sometimes give this exhortation a spiritual sense, referring to Cyril of Alexandria's interpretation. But, as I tried to show in an article for the Festschrift G. Ghiberti, Cyril proposes this spiritual sense only as a secondary one after the literal sense. Thus, the exhortation of Jesus retains its original meaning, and John 15–17 can be read as a "rereading" of the original farewell discourse, now emphasizing the impact of Jesus' departure on the disciples. The same orientation toward the disciples of Jesus is found in John 21, a chapter that is viewed as an "epilogue" even by scholars who otherwise defend the homogeneous character of John (like Udo Schnelle). In my opinion (which I share with Barnabas Lindars and René Kieffer), such Johannine "rereadings" or additions may also be found in the prologue (John 1:1–18) and in chapter 6, with its emphasis on the Eucharist, the role of Peter, and the group of the Twelve.

Sociological approaches to the Fourth Gospel have become rare more recently. The reasons are found in the change of paradigm from the historical to the literary approach. Some authors, such as Richard Bauckham and Edward Klink, also doubt in principle the possibility of reconstructing a "Johannine community."

If the historical setting of the origin of the Fourth Gospel gets out of sight, hermeneutical approaches become more difficult. During the past years, hermeneutics of Johannine texts have been proposed only rarely. In the North Atlantic area, feminist approaches are readily available, but contributions from a non–Western background are often less easily accessible. They may be found in dissertations written by students from the Third World and in publications based on international collaborations, such as the new *Global Bible Commentary* edited by Daniel Patte and others (Patte 2004). Biblical reviews from the southern continents are often difficult to locate. One exception may be *Bible Bhashyam* from India, which has gained international acceptance. A selection of articles published in this review has been edited in German by Fr. George M. Soares–Prabhu (1984), who has attempted to address in a creative way the social and religious dimensions of the Gospel of John within the cultural and social world of contemporary India. Recently, a growing consciousness of the need for a New Testament hermeneutics can also be detected in the Western world, as reflected, for example, in recent seminars of the Studiorum Novi Testamenti Societas (SNTS) dedicated to this topic.

TASKS FOR THE FUTURE

Some years ago, I became coeditor of a book, initiated by Karl P. Donfried, on *The Thessalonians Debate* (Beutler and Donfried 2000). This volume documented the debates in a seminar of the SNTS in which scholars from both sides of the North Atlantic exchanged views on the first half of 1 Thessalonians, particularly 2:1–12. In general, North American scholars favored a rhetorical approach while those from Europe preferred an approach based on form criticism, in this case focusing on the format of ancient letters. A final section was dedicated to the question "Is Synthesis Possible,"? which Donfried answered positively in his introductory essay.

An affirmative answer should also be given to similar questions with regard to the multiplicity of methodological approaches to the interpretation of John. In general, there is a growing international consensus that diachronic and synchronic approaches to the New Testament do not exclude, but rather complement, each other. This opinion has been powerfully defended by Wilhelm Egger in his *Methodenlehre zum Neuen Testament* (1999), which has been translated into most international academic languages, including English (but, notably, not French). For Egger, the interpretation of New Testament texts should start with a synchronic analysis, divided into "linguistic–syntactic," "semantic," and "pragmatic" analyses. The last of these coincides with a reader response or rhetorical approach. But in Egger's view, to do full justice to New Testament texts, it is indispensable to apply also the diachronic approach, investigating the sources and traditions used by the author of the text under consideration. In Johannine Studies, such a synthetic view is often viewed as desirable but is in fact rarely achieved. Such a synthetic approach would be expected particularly in commentaries on John, but in general commentaries are characterized by either a more strongly synchronic or a more historical–critical approach. Such variety may be justified, but the need for synthesis should at least be remembered. If the Gospel of John is interpreted exclusively with literary tools taken from Greco–Roman antiquity, the idea of "witness," central to this Gospel, may be lost. In its center stands a historical person, Jesus Christ, who transcends the patterns of the text itself and who is proclaimed a historical figure asking for acceptance by faith. This person is rooted in the history of the Jewish people, and as such, the traditions of Israel are indispensable for a full understanding of the Fourth Gospel. At the same time, from a literary point of view, Hebrew poetry and art of narration must be considered for a correct interpretation of the text of the Fourth Gospel. Jewish–Christian dialogue on such topics seems to be rewarding and would free Johannine scholarship from a too–exclusive link with classical philology.

There has been valuable research on the intertestamental literature in the past few decades, and, in the future, the conclusions of such investigations should be used more directly for the interpretation of the Gospel of John. After the first boom of Qumran studies following the discovery of the Dead Sea Scrolls in 1947, interest in these texts and their connections with the Johannine Literature has faded. The scrolls have meanwhile become increasingly the topic of a sensationalist journalism that has remained fruitless for a solid understanding of the Fourth Gospel. The time may have come for reconsidering these texts for the interpretation of Johannine tradition and theology. Rabbinic studies will complement this approach, even if the extant rabbinic texts—like the gnostic texts—are to be dated later than the Gospel of John. Occasional contributions to this topic (such as that by David Daube, 1984) in the past may serve as a basis for the future. Studies in Hellenistic Judaism are also particularly rewarding. If this form of Judaism is the cradle of New Testament theology in the Diaspora, every contribution will be appreciated. This is evident, for example, in the case of the Johannine Logos theology, which cannot be understood without reference to Philo of Alexandria.

The need for a hermeneutics of the Gospel of John is felt particularly among interpreters from non–Western cultures. This fact is not self–
evident. Indeed, every interpreter may reflect about his or her horizon of
interpretation. The vast majority of participants in the international societies of biblical or New Testament studies still come from the great industrial nations of the North, where the interest falls mainly on the historical
and literary aspects of New Testament texts. A recent seminar of the SNTS
combined "mission" and "hermeneutics," thus giving the impression that
"hermeneutics" is a task for scholars in areas of the world in which the
church is still spreading, such as India or Africa. Of course, this impression
would be quite mistaken: The need for hermeneutical reflection imposes
itself on interpreters from all cultural backgrounds. Only in this way can
we avoid the dichotomy between the wealthy nations of the North and
those struggling for survival in the South. The above–mentioned *Global
Bible Commentary* is a recent example of such consciousness.

LOOKING BACK

The present book seeks to allow Johannine scholars of the "older generation" an opportunity to express their ideas about present Johannine
scholarship, tasks for the future, and their own personal development.
For me personally, this third aspect is the most difficult to deal with.
Again, I would distinguish between "method" and "hermeneutics."
I started my studies in John forty years ago (in 1967) after a licentiate
in Sacred Scripture at the Pontifical Biblical Institute in Rome. I then
moved to the Pontifical Gregorian University, just across the Piazza della
Pilotta, and was accepted for a doctoral dissertation with Fr. Donatien
Mollat, a French Jesuit known, among his many other publications, for
his commentary on the Gospel of John in the *Jerusalem Bible*. Through
him, I became more acquainted with French and French–language exegesis, having also been previously a student of Ignace de la Potterie (in
whose room I now live). Fr. Mollat was, however, very open to scholarship from other schools and languages, in particular to publications from
the Anglo–Saxon world. This met with my own preferences. The subject
of my dissertation (published in 1972 under the title *Martyria: Traditionsgeschichtliche Untersuchungen zum Zeugnisthema bei Johannes*) dealt with a
subject relevant for fundamental theology: the importance of "witness"
for Jesus' claims to be the Messiah and Son of God in John. My interest in
this topic arose from the fact that originally I was expected to teach fundamental theology at the Institute of Philosophy and Theology "Sankt
Georgen" at Frankfurt (Germany). But in the period right after Vatican
II, the kind of apologetics that looked for arguments for Christian belief

on a historical–critical level broke down, and fundamental theology and New Testament exegesis parted ways. I opted for New Testament exegesis and have never regretted doing so.

My approach to the subject was basically determined by the historical–critical paradigm. I looked for traditions that might have influenced Johannine thought in the passages dealing with "witness" in the Fourth Gospel. I noted that this Johannine concept did not show any clear coherence with gnostic thought, although the most important passages reflecting this theme appear in discourses of Jesus (especially John 5 and 8). Rather, the most prominent influences on the Fourth Gospel came from the Old Testament and Jewish texts and traditions. This conclusion determined in a strong way my later orientation in Johannine exegesis. I found close parallels to the Johannine idea of "witness for Jesus" in the context of "witness for Moses" in Jewish Hellenistic texts with an apologetic background (Philo and Josephus), and I also found texts close to the Johannine idea of a "heavenly witness," particularly in Jewish apocalyptic literature and the Qumran documents. In this line of research, I found myself in company with scholars from Britain and the United States, but also from France and the French–speaking world. They have remained my preferred partners of dialogue since the days when I first joined the SNTS (in 1975) and became the cochair of two seminars.

Since these early years, my interests have been oriented toward the Jewish backgrounds of the Fourth Gospel and connections between John and the Hebrew Bible. One early example of this approach was a 1975 article in *New Testament Studies* titled "Psalm 42/43 im Johannesevangelium," which was later expanded into the first half of my book on John 14, *Habt keine Angst: Die erste johanneische Abschiedsrede (Joh 14)* (Beutler 1984). Here I argued that the three main sections of John 14 are built on three different aspects of the Old Testament: Psalms 42–43 (14:1–14), covenant theology (14:15–24), and eschatological promises that focus on peace, joy, and the gift of the Holy Spirit (14:25–29). On the topic of covenant theology, I proposed at a conference and later in an article that the "great commandment" of Deuteronomy 6:4 lies behind John 5:42–44 and 8:41–59 (love of the only God; cf. John 14:15–24 and 21:15–17). Together with colleagues from the SNTS, I discussed the possibility that one may see OT and Jewish ideas and traditions about the Good Shepherd and wicked ones behind John 10:1–18; these conversations eventually led to a book, coedited with Robert Fortna (Beutler and Fortna 1991). These and similar essays are gathered in my collected volume *Studien zu den johanneischen Schriften* (Beutler 1998), and such interests also determined the choice of articles for my 2004 Festschrift *Israel und seine Heilstraditionen im Johannesevangelium* (Labahn et al. 2004).

In 1993 I joined the Pontifical Biblical Commission. From 1996 to 2000, we discussed and prepared a document titled "The Jewish People and Their Holy Scripture in the Christian Bible." I enjoyed the privilege of taking part in this enterprise and later produced the German translation. The document was well received, even by Jewish critics. My work on the Jewish background of John has continued in more recent years. One fruit of this work is a course on "Judaism and the Jews in the Gospel of John," taught at the Pontifical Biblical Institute in 2004–2005 and published in Italian at the Institute's Press in 2006; the English translation (by the same publisher) appeared in the same year. Here in Italy (where I moved in 1998), I have continued to take part in Christian–Jewish dialogue, particularly since 2001 in the ongoing discussions at Camaldoli. Jewish and Christian members of this discussion group celebrated the twenty–fifth anniversary of these meetings with a pilgrimage to the Holy Land in November 2004. For me it was about the fifteenth voyage to Israel, after shorter and longer stays in previous years, sometimes as a leader of study groups.

After finishing my volume on John 14, I accepted the task of writing a commentary on the Johannine Epistles for the "Regensburger Neues Testament" series, but because of various commitments in teaching and administration, it took me fifteen years to complete the manuscript. The book was finally published in 2000. An Italian translation is on the way, and an English one would be welcome. Here again, I did not accept Bultmann's proposal that gnostic dualism lies behind the various "antitheses" in 1 John; in my view, Jewish and OT thought seem closer to this document. In particular, I saw, with Ignace de la Potterie and Edward Malatesta, the influence of OT covenant theology. The main purpose of 1 John seems to be to convince the reader of the conditions for a new covenant relationship with God (walking in the light; living in justice and love). If this perspective is adopted, 1 John and 2 John focus more on anthropology than on Christology and ethics viewed individually.

Of course, I noticed the change of paradigm from historical to literary approaches in the 1970s. The first edition of Eggers' book *Methodenlehre zum Neuen Testament* appeared in 1987, the same year I shifted from typewriter to computer—a good occasion to rewrite my notes for various courses on the Gospels and Acts. For the interpretation of John, I followed Egger's suggestion that interpretation should start with the existing text rather than with hypothetical sources or layers, an approach I have maintained ever since. At the same time, I shared Egger's opinion that synchronic and diachronic approaches should not be seen as alternatives but rather as complementary, with emphasis on the synchronic. In fact, a number of the difficulties in New Testament texts that had once led me to source hypotheses disappeared after more detailed study of the form of the text. This approach allowed a more coherent interpretation of the texts and the discovery of their literary "making" as pieces of art. For the Letters of John, this approach proved particularly rewarding, since no sources seem to have been used by the author (other than the Gospel of John, which is, however, hardly ever referred to directly, with the exception of the prologue). I found in the First Letter of John a scheme that practically every section of the book seems to follow: introduction, three antitheses, and conclusion, with the conclusion often forming an *inclusio* with the introduction and leading into the next unit. Applied to 1 John 3:11–24, this approach allowed me to see vv. 19–20 as the first (negative) part of an antithesis and vv. 21–22 as the positive second part, with substantial consequences for my understanding of the phrase "God is greater than our heart" (rather in the sense of an all–knowing God from whom nothing escapes). I share this interpretation, well–attested up to the time of the Reformation and beyond, with John Court from Canterbury.

In the case of the Gospel of John, the existence and relevance of sources and layers are still matters of dispute. Following the Bultmann paradigm—the evangelist used a σημεῖα source, a gnostic discourses source, and an early passion and resurrection account, and his work was later edited by an ecclesiastical redactor—diachronic models have been and are still proposed (a signs source or a "Gospel of Signs" or *Grundschrift*). At the same time, an increasing number of scholars reject this kind of source criticism, either because these scholars consider such sources and layers indemonstrable or because they believe the sources are irrelevant. I do not quite share this opinion.

Closely related to the source question, valuable work has been done on the relationship between John and the Synoptics. In particular, the Leuven School, led by Frans Neirynck, has made John's use of the Synoptic Gospels more plausible. I have always appreciated the arguments of this school. In some cases, the influence of Synoptic tradition on John may be loose—I think, for example, of the influence of the Synoptic term "kingdom of God," which plays a subordinate role in John but may stand behind some passages of the Fourth Gospel nevertheless. I have repeatedly attempted to read John 14:25–29, 16:4b–33, and 20:19–23 in the light of the tradition of the kingdom of God, defined by St. Paul as "righteousness, peace and joy in the Holy Spirit" (Rom 14:17), most recently in a contribution to Fortna and Thatcher's *Jesus in Johannine Tradition* (2001).

The overall structure of the Gospel of John follows the broad outline shaped by Mark: the appearance of John the Baptist, Jesus' encounter with him, and the call of the first disciples, leading into the healing miracles on the lame and the blind during Jesus' public activity, followed by his last days in Jerusalem and his resurrection. At the same time, however, John's specific sequence of events does not follow faithfully the order of the Synoptics, and the contacts remain rather loose. There are, of course, exceptions—John 6 in particular follows the sequence of Mark (6:6–8:38) closely: the multiplication of the loaves, Jesus' walking on the sea, the request for a sign, a discourse on bread, the division of the listeners, Peter's confession, and the revelation of a "devil" among the disciples. In this chapter, John diverges from his cycle of Jewish feasts of pilgrimage— the Passover mentioned at 6:4 does not fit in, particularly if the feast of John 5:1 is identified with Pentecost—and this time Jesus does not go up to Jerusalem to celebrate the feast with the Jewish community. Instead, John's account seems to reflect a Christian reinterpretation of Passover in terms of the Eucharist. For these and similar reasons, I have adopted the proposal of Barnabas Lindars and René Kieffer and now see in John 6 a later addition, a *relecture*, of the literary context determined by the Jewish cycle of feasts of pilgrimage. In fact, I would propose a re-elaboration of the Fourth Gospel by a redactor (or John himself) under the influence of the Synoptic tradition and early Christian theology and church structures. Such additions would include the prologue (John 1:1–18)—the main subject of which, Christ as the Logos incarnate, is not taken up later on in the Fourth Gospel—chapter 6, chapters 15–17, and chapter 21. The model of the *relecture* of John 6 proposed here differs from Bultmann's hypothesis of an "ecclesiastical redactor" in two respects: I do not see the "redaction" as in conflict with the previous layers of John, but rather as a positive development; and, I do not think that the Eucharist has been inserted into John 6 from v. 51c onward, but rather that the entire dialogue in chapter 6 has been inserted. A strong argument for its coherence is its concentric structure, as I tried to show in a 1991 essay (Beutler 1997, German version 1991).

Looking back, I may say that I have arrived—with other scholars—at a synthesis of the synchronic and the diachronic models of interpretation. The existing text of John should be the starting point for any interpretation. However, diachronic aspects of the text should also merit our interest. The best-known sources of John are the Synoptic Gospels. Among the possible influences on John's presentation, those coming from Judaism and early Christianity merit our particular interest. A gradual growth of the text of the Fourth Gospel should be accepted, particularly in the chapters indicated above.

Let me move, once again, from method to hermeneutics. During the years of my graduate studies, the subject of hermeneutics was hardly taken seriously. In the Catholic institutions in which I studied and later taught, an interpretation of the biblical texts in accordance with the teaching and the tradition of the church was assumed. The Apostolic Constitution "Dei Verbum" of Vatican II and the 1993 document "The Interpretation of the Bible in the Church" by the Pontifical Biblical Commission (in whose vote I took part) gave the reasons and the framework for this perspective. More important for me became the question of how far my interpretation of the Bible in general and of the Johannine writings in particular were conditioned by my own heritage in the Western world. When I joined the SNTS in 1975 and started attending its annual meetings regularly from 1977 onward, I noticed quickly that our dialogues were strongly limited to the Western world, especially Western Europe, North America, and the Commonwealth countries. As a consequence, our discussions remained strongly, if not exclusively, determined by historical and literary questions. Conference speakers hardly ever reflected on their reasons for choosing a particular topic or on the cultural, social, and economic conditions of their interpretations. Such questions would have been (and are to some extent still now) considered *unwissenschaftlich* ("unscientific"). When Wilhelm Egger, my study companion during my years in Rome, suggested in 1987 that hermeneutical reflection should be an aspect of the interpretation of biblical books, he seemed like "a voice crying in the wilderness." It must be said that, since that time, the SNTS has dedicated remarkable efforts to meeting this problem. The papers presented still largely reflect the problem described earlier, but the Society has efficiently tried to enlarge toward the East and the South, and in the meantime new members from these continents have reached committee. This trend—reflected, for example, in the meeting of the annual conference of the SNTS in South Africa in 1999—makes me hopeful for the future.

For me and my exegesis, the encounter with Africa was a decisive turning point. In 1984, I was invited to attend the Second Conference of African Catholic Exegetes, held in Ibadan, Nigeria. There I met a group of fine scholars who reflected on the Acts of the Apostles as a document describing young churches on their way to faith. Since then, I have been in Nigeria four more times, mostly teaching at the Catholic Institute of West Africa in Port Harcourt. Some of my graduate students later came to Frankfurt for post–graduate work, and international students are now the dominant group among my doctoral students here in Rome. I learned from these students and my African colleagues to ask serious questions concerning the text and to see in exegesis no longer *l'art pour l'art*. When I joined the Peace Movement in the early 1980s, I found myself side by side with mostly young people from my own country and abroad, who found in Scripture guidelines for their dedication to peace and justice.

As to the interpretation of John, there was and is the problem that the Fourth Gospel, as the so-called "spiritual Gospel," does not seem to lend itself to social-critical interpretation. It was my work on the Old Testament and the Jewish backgrounds of the Fourth Gospel that helped me overcome this difficulty. The seminar in the SNTS (of which I was cochair) on "The Shepherd Discourse of John 10 and Its Context" (1986–1990) helped us to see Jesus' Shepherd Discourse as a controversy about true leadership. Readers are invited to opt for the good shepherd over the wicked ones (the hirelings, robbers and thieves). When I interpreted this chapter in 2005 at a national meeting of biblical scholars in Bogotá (Colombia), the relevance was noticed immediately. If we view the Johannine texts from this perspective, new horizons are also opened in 1 John. I now read this letter as a document that asks for a decision of faith for Christ Incarnate, in the middle of a community of brothers and sisters but open also for other human beings who need our help. In 1 John 3, Cain is not just a killer of his brother, but the murderer of a human being. Not breaking bread with the brother or the sister who suffers is tantamount to homicide. This is a strong message, and I tried to convey it in my contribution on the Johannine Letters in the *Global Bible Commentary* (Patte 2004). Such conclusions should not be regarded as desired side effects of our exegetical work, but rather as the conditions for its legitimacy.

2: RESPONSE

JOHANNINE EXEGESIS IN TRANSITION
JOHANNES BEUTLER'S SEARCH FOR A NEW SYNTHESIS

Carsten Claussen

When Johannes Beutler began his work in Johannine Studies in 1967, Rudolf Bultmann's commentary was, without doubt, still the most influential interpretation of the Fourth Gospel. Since its first edition in 1941, this commentary has served not only as a landmark study for questions of the religious context and literary strata of the Fourth Gospel, but also as a premiere example of biblical hermeneutics. As these three issues feature prominently in Beutler's contribution, I will use this outline as a background for my own comments on his search for a new synthesis.

For Bultmann, the "religious context" of the Fourth Gospel was fundamentally that of Gnosticism. Thus, Christ was identified as the Gnostic Logos-Redeemer and was interpreted as God walking about the earth in the appearance of a man. This view led scholars such as Ernst Käsemann (1968, 27) and Luise Schottroff (1970, 295) to characterize John's Christology as naive docetism or as Gnosticism adapting the Christian tradition. However, at about the same time, Raymond Brown summarized another approach that had become increasingly popular, especially in North America: "A large number of scholars are coming to agree that the principal background for Johannine thought was the Palestinian Judaism of Jesus' time. This Judaism was far from monolithic, and its very diversity helps to explain different aspects of Johannine thought" (1966–1970,

1.lix; cf. Brown/Moloney 2003, 132). Broadly speaking, one may say that the world of Johannine scholarship was split in those days. While German scholars tended to look for a Gnostic background to the Fourth Gospel, North Americans were interpreting John in light of the Old Testament, Rabbinic Judaism, and the Qumran literature.

Even in his 1972 doctoral dissertation, Beutler indicated his desire to avoid a strict dichotomy of backgrounds for Johannine thought (Jewish versus Gnostic). Here he analyzed the important motif of μαρτυρία ("witness") not only in the Johannine Gospel and two of the Epistles but also in Greek literary and nonliterary texts, the Old Testament and later Jewish writings, Gnostic and other syncretistic texts, and other New Testament documents. Against the prevailing German consensus, Beutler was able to show that this important Johannine motif cannot be traced back to a Gnostic usage. The closest parallels he discovered—Hellenistic Jewish texts, Jewish apocalyptic writings, and the Qumran literature—led him into close collaboration with colleagues from the English- and French-speaking worlds early in his career. Today, an international consensus supports his conviction that the background of the Fourth Gospel is predominantly Jewish with strong connections to the Old Testament.

However, more than Beutler seems to take into account, one should realize that John's background is not only Jewish but *also* Hellenistic. A growing number of scholars (see Frey 2004b, 32; Schnelle 2005, 548) now argue that discussions of the background of John's religious thought should take into account Jewish *and* Hellenistic texts. Recent studies such as George L. Parsenios's work (2005) on the exegetical problems posed by John 14:31 and Craig Keener's commentary (2003) have shown how Hellenistic sources can help our interpretation of the Fourth Gospel even when one acknowledges the Jewish background of John (as these authors do). Thus, Martin Hengel's (1974) influential attempt to overcome the Judaism versus Hellenism dichotomy may finally be bearing fruit for the question of Johannine backgrounds.

Moving to the second point noted earlier, in the late 1960s most Johannine scholars, again following Bultmann's precedent, were still optimistic that a number of sources and literary strata could be uncovered behind the Fourth Gospel. However, by the 1980s only the theory of a presumed "signs source" still found a number of adherents. At least after the release of Alan Culpepper's *Anatomy of the Fourth Gospel* (1983), the signs of the time were clearly pointing toward a synchronic over a diachronic approach to the text. Overall, most Johannine scholars were no longer interested in the composition-history of the Gospel of John, but rather in its final form. Beutler confesses that he—under the influence of Wilhelm Egger's *Methodenlehre* (1987)—was moving toward a synthesis of these approaches, with emphasis on the synchronic. In contrast to scholars who wish to abandon the diachronic perspective altogether, Beutler's argument is an important reminder of the need for balance. For example, when considering the provenance of John 21, even a synchronic approach that tries to treat this chapter as an integral part of the Fourth Gospel cannot ignore the diachronic reality that this text was very likely added later (Culpepper 1983, 96f.). Thus, one cannot simply ignore historical or literary approaches, although today not many scholars would follow Beutler's understanding of the numerous additions that may be identified in the Fourth Gospel.

Finally, coming from a Protestant background, I was somewhat surprised to realize how little Beutler was influenced by the prominent discussions of hermeneutics that were taking place during the time of his graduate studies. After all, Bultmann's most radical, and for some time also most influential, impact was in the area of hermeneutics. Although few scholars today would follow his program of demythologization and existentialist interpretation, Bultmann's occupation with the condition of the exegete is still very relevant and should not be overlooked, especially in light of contemporary contextual interpretations of biblical texts. According to Bultmann, it is simply not possible to engage in exegesis without a preunderstanding (1957b, 409–17). To quote his own words, "Every interpreter brings with him certain conceptions, perhaps idealistic or psychological, as presuppositions of his exegesis, in most cases unconsciously" (Bultmann 1958, 45). These conceptions represent a preunderstanding, based on one's life experience (*Lebensbezug*), that makes it possible to understand a text. In addition, Bultmann also points out that the historical interpretation of a text is part of our preunderstanding, as required by historical–critical research. Although such an existential understanding of history is never definitive but rather open, this does not mean that it is subjective in the sense of being left to the discretion of the individual exegete, which would lead to the loss of any kind of objectivity.

While keeping this in mind, it must first be acknowledged that the encounter with exegetes from different international backgrounds has tremendously enlarged the horizon of the once, but no longer almost exclusively, Western perspective on hermeneutics. Among the finest examples of the globalization of Biblical Studies is the *Global Bible Commentary* (2004), to which Beutler was invited to contribute as one of a very few scholars from a Western background. Among others, postcolonial interpretations, particularly from India and Africa, and Latin–American liberation hermeneutics have become companions in the struggle not only against the evils of globalization but also against a predominantly

Western interpretation of the Bible (cf. Sugirtharajah 2002). By making explicit the specific background from which these exegetes read the Bible, their hermeneutic becomes transparent. However—and this leads us back to Bultmann's hermeneutic—it does not always seem clear whether such "background information" on the context of the exegete reflects upon the person's preunderstanding, or whether such biographical insights are offered to justify subjective prejudgments that are then read into the biblical text. Only when a biblical text is allowed to say what we do not already know will we be able to listen to its meaning anew and not just to our own preconceived ideas. For this reason, not only the life context of the exegete, but first and foremost the historical context of the text must be taken into account for its interpretation.

CHAPTER 3

THE SCRIPTURES AND THE WORDS AND WORKS OF JESUS

Peder Borgen

As I was doing research on the interpretation of manna as "bread from heaven" in John 6, I had also to examine the phrase "He who sent me" and similar terms.[1] Then I realized that the forensic perspective plays an important role in the Gospel of John. I looked further into the background of this idea of "agency"—Jesus as the agent of God—and found that it reflects a distinct Jewish usage within the broader perspective of Hellenism (Borgen 1965, 158–64; 1986, 67–78; 1996b, 101–2, 110). Philo of Alexandria also provided material of interest on heavenly agents. He applies this juridical concept to the personified Logos, who acts as the ambassador of God (*Her.* 205), and to angels, who are envoys between God and people (*Gig.* 16; *Abr.* 115). Philo's ideas illuminate John's understanding that Jesus, as the Son, is the emissary of God the Father. As I looked further into the forensic aspect of John, I learned from Théo Preiss that this judicial concept may also have mystical connotations: the agent can be seen as a person identical with his principal (Preiss 1954, 25). The motif of the union of the agent with the sender is strengthened by John's view that Jesus is the Son of God the Father.

---

[1] I dedicate this essay to C. Kingsley Barrett, a great Johannine scholar and, to me, a treasured colleague and friend.

Among those scholars who have examined the forensic aspect in John, N. A. Dahl and S. Pancaro have made particularly helpful contributions. Dahl recognized that the Johannine concepts of "witness" and "testimony" have judicial connotations. According to him, the forensic perspective was so basic and broad that it determined the Johannine understanding of history: the conflict between God and the world is conceived in forensic terms as a cosmic lawsuit. Christ is the representative of God, and the "Jews" are representatives of the world. The "Jews" base their arguments upon the Law, and Jesus appeals to the witness borne to him by John the Baptist, by his own works, and by the Scriptures. The lawsuit reaches its climax in the proceedings before Pilate, where Jesus, in his very defeat, actually won his case (Dahl 1962). Similarly, Pancaro, in the introduction to his monograph *The Law in the Fourth Gospel*, writes "The confrontation between Jesus and the Jews unfolds itself in John as an impressive juridical trial and, within this dramatic framework, the Law appears as a hermeneutical key to much John has to say concerning the person of Jesus and his 'work'" (1975, 1). Accordingly, in his extensive study, Pancaro deals with (a) the Law as a norm vainly used against Jesus, (b) the way in which the Law testifies against the Jews and in favor of Jesus, and (c) the way in which the transferal of nomistic terms and symbols takes place in the Gospel of John.

Directly and indirectly, at several points I shall touch on this forensic aspect of John's presentation and deal with it further at the close of the essay. In my research, I have given much time to detailed analysis of sections of the Gospel of John, seen within their larger contexts. It is natural that I also use the same approach in this study of forensic motifs in the Fourth Gospel. I begin with chapters 5 and 6.

THEMATIC CONNECTIONS BETWEEN JOHN 5 AND 6

In John's report on the revelatory words and works of Jesus, John the Baptist, Jesus' own works, God the sender, and the Scriptures/Law all serve as "witnesses," as outlined in John 5:30–47. John 5:1–18, the story of Jesus healing a paralytic person on the Sabbath, is followed by a series of judicial exchanges. The story in vv. 1–9 serves as the base text from which words are repeated and paraphrased in the subsequent discussion in vv. 10–18. The accusation against Jesus is twofold: (1) it was not lawful to carry a pallet on the Sabbath, and (2) in his justification of the healing on the Sabbath, Jesus made the blasphemous claim that when he healed the paralytic he was doing the same work as God the Father. He thus made himself equal to God, and the "Jews" sought to kill him (Seland 1995, 59, 236). Here, Jesus draws on traditional exegesis: God cannot be resting on the Sabbath, in spite of the reference to God's rest in Genesis 2:2–3. In the section that follows, John 5:19–30, the relationship between the Son and God the Father is characterized. A conclusion is drawn in v. 30: "I can do nothing on my own. As I hear, I judge; and my judgment is just, because I seek to do not my own will but the will of him who sent me." The remaining section of chapter 5, vv. 31–47, centers on persons, activities, and writings that bear witness to the Son, whom the Father sent—John the Baptist (with reference to John 1), the Son's works, the Father, and the Scriptures all bear witness to him.

Although there is a geographical discrepancy between John 5 and 6—the action in chapter 5 is situated in Jerusalem, while 6:1 indicates that Jesus is in Galilee—a close thematic connection between the chapters can be seen. Several observations will highlight the unity of these chapters.

First, in John 5:36 it is said that Jesus' works bear witness to him that "the Father has sent me." The summary statement about Jesus' healing activity, the report on the feeding of the 5,000, and Jesus' epiphanic appearance to the disciples at 6:1–21 demonstrate this witnessing function of the works: Jesus was more than the Prophet–like–Moses; that is, more than the crowd's misconception of what the miraculous feeding meant. Further, Jesus' appearance to his disciples at the crossing of the sea seems to presuppose the union between God the Father and the Son as outlined in John 5:19–30. The coworking of the Father and the Son is expressed in the epiphanic "I Am" saying at 6:20 (O'Day 1997, 156–57).

Second, in John 5:37, Jesus says, "And the Father who sent me has himself testified on my behalf." Yet the specific "witness" to which this verse refers is not clear. If this testimony by the Father refers to biblical events, such as the revelation at Sinai, then emphasis is placed on a negative reaction to this witness: God's voice has not been heard, nor has his form been seen, and they have not his word abiding in them (vv. 37b–38). Another possibility should not be overlooked, however. In John 6:27–29, there is a verb that belongs to the terminology of "witnessing," σφραγίζω, which means "to seal, to close with a seal, to authenticate, certify, to accredit as an envoy." God has set his seal on the Son of Man, who will give the food that endures to eternal life. Thus, "to set the seal on" can mean to accredit a person, for example as an envoy (Borgen 1993, 272–74, 287–90; Schnackenburg 1965–1971, 2.50; Liddell and Scott 1958, 1742). Thus, the "witness" borne by the Father at 5:37 may be understood in terms of the "seal" to which Jesus refers at 6:27–29.

Third, in John 5:39–40 it is stated in a pointed way that the Scriptures bear witness: "You search the scriptures, because you think that in them you have eternal life; and it is they that testify on my behalf; yet you refuse to come to me that you may have life." Then in 6:31, an explicit quotation from the Scriptures is given: "as it is written, 'He gave them bread from heaven to eat.'" In the subsequent exposition, words from this quotation are repeated through v. 58. In this exegetical commentary it is shown that this text from the Scriptures bears witness to Jesus as the bread from heaven, as explicitly stated in vv. 35 and 48 ("I am the bread of life"), in v. 41 ("I am the bread that came down from heaven"), and similarly in v. 51 ("I am the living bread that came down from heaven"). Thus, chapter 6 seems to discuss the Scriptures that Jesus claims as his witnesses at 5:39–40. If the direct witness by the Father is not referred to by the word "to seal," σφραγίζω, in 6:27, as suggested above, then only the witnessing of Jesus' works (6:1–21) and of the Scriptures (6:30–58) are presented in John 6, and the dialogue in 6:22–29 serves as a bridge between these two units.

Fourth and finally, a connection with John 5 may also be seen in 6:60–71. Following his offensive remarks about eating his flesh and drinking his blood, many disciples left Jesus, and John notes that Judas will betray him. Peter, representing the Twelve, confesses that Jesus has the words (ῥήματα) of eternal life. "The words" may here refer to the positive reaction by the Twelve, over against the doubt expressed in the question of Jesus mentioned in 5:47: "how will you believe in my words (ῥήματα)?" (my translation).

These points show that, as far as ideas and interplay are concerned, there is a close and smooth connection between John 5 and 6, despite the geographical discrepancy. As far as the relationship between chapters 5, 6, and 7 is concerned, it is clear that in 7:1 John picks up the thread from 5:17–18 that the Jewish authorities sought to kill Jesus. Thus 7:1 and 5:17–18 form an *inclusio* around 5:19–6:71.

THE WITNESS OF THE SCRIPTURES

In tracing the relationship between chapters 5, 6, and 7 of the Gospel of John, I have made clear that the works of Jesus—here particularly the stories of the feeding and the crossing of the sea—have weight as a witness, together with the witness of the Scriptures exemplified by Jesus' exposition of bread from heaven. Jesus' comment in 6:26, "you seek me, not because you saw signs, but because you ate your fill of the loaves," shows that the narratives of these events fully bore witness, but the crowd was motivated in their search by a misconception about them.

Within this context, some observations should be made from my analysis of John 6:31–58. Words from the Old Testament quotation, "Bread from heaven he gave them to eat" (6:31; see Exod 16:4; Neh 9:15;

Ps 78:24–25), are repeated all through this section. Several characteristics of Jesus' exposition of this text are particularly notable.

First, the words "bread from heaven he gave them" from the main Old Testament quotation are repeated and interpreted throughout Jesus' exposition in a systematic way. The words ἄρτον ἐκ τοῦ οὐρανοῦ ἔδωκεν from the quotation in v. 31 recur as follows in vv. 32–48:

> v. 32 δέδωκεν ἄρτον ἐκ τοῦ οὐρανοῦ . . . δίδωσιν . . . ἄρτον ἐκ
>   τοῦ οὐρανοῦ
> v. 33 ἄρτος . . . ἐκ τοῦ οὐρανοῦ
> v. 34 δός . . . ἄρτον
> v. 35 ἄρτος
> v. 38 τοῦ οὐρανοῦ
> v. 41 ἄρτος . . . ἐκ τοῦ οὐρανοῦ
> v. 42 ἐκ τοῦ οὐρανοῦ
> v. 48 ἄρτος

In vv. 49–58, the term φαγεῖν, "to eat," (or the synonym, τρώγειν, see John 13:18) is added and takes on a central role.

> v. 49 ἔφαγον
> v. 50 ἄρτος . . . ἐκ τοῦ οὐρανοῦ . . . φάγῃ
> v. 51 ἄρτος . . . ἐκ τοῦ οὐρανοῦ . . . φάγῃ . . . ἄρτου . . . ἄρτος
>   . . . δώσω
> v. 52 δοῦναι . . . φαγεῖν
> v. 53 φάγητε
> v. 54 (τρώγων)
> v. 56 (τρώγων)
> v. 57 (τρώγων)
> v. 58 ἄρτος . . . ἐκ τοῦ οὐρανοῦ . . . ἔφαγον . . . (τρώγων) . . .
>   ἄρτον

Second, the closing statement at John 6:58 refers back to the main statement at the beginning of the section and at the same time sums up points from the entire exposition. Thus, the section begins as the "Jews" remind Jesus that their ancestors ate manna in the wilderness by citing an Old Testament quotation about "bread from heaven" (6:31) and ends as Jesus repeats these themes at 6:58, adding the claim that those who eat the bread he provides will never die.

Third, besides the main quotation from the Old Testament in v. 31, in v. 45 there is a subordinate quotation, Isaiah 54:3, which is built into the exposition. Parallels may be found in Philo's *Leg.* 3:162–168, *Mut.*

253–263, and more stereotyped examples in *Exod R* 25:1, 2, 6 (see Borgen 1965, 28–58).

The subsections in this exposition may be outlined as follows. The Old Testament quotation in John 6:31 is part of the question raised by the crowd in v. 30 ("what sign do you do, that we may see, and believe you?"), and the exposition begins with Jesus' answer in vv. 32–33. A new question is asked in v. 34, and Jesus' answer follows in vv. 35–40. The sequence of exegetical debate between Jesus and the "Jews," covers vv. 41–48. Then, Jesus moves into verses 49–51, in which the word "eat" from the Old Testament text is a central term. A new question is raised by the "Jews" in v. 52, with Jesus' answer given in the remaining part of the exposition, vv. 53–58.[2]

It is important to remember that questions and answers were a typical part of Jewish exegetical activity. Thus, Philo says that when the Therapeutae assemble, the leader "examines some points in the sacred writings, or also solves that which is propounded by another" (*Contempl.* 75). Moreover, the form of questions and answers on exegetical matters is widely used in Philo's writings and also in other ancient Jewish sources (see Borgen 1997, 80–101, cf. 102–39).

It is thus an observable fact that words and phrases from the Old Testament quotation in John 6:31, ἄρτον ἐκ τοῦ οὐρανοῦ ἔδωκεν αὐτοῖς φαγεῖν ("he gave them bread from heaven to eat") are repeated from v. 32 to v. 58. This fact also demonstrates that the Old Testament quotation serves as text, and that these repeated words and phrases from the text are woven together with other words and phrases into an exegetical exposition.[3]

---

[2] Note that Paul Anderson makes a confusing mistake when he writes that "the homiletic pattern identified by Borgen [in John 6:31ff] . . . consists of the following points: (1) The Old Testament quotation. (2) The interpretation. (3) The objection to the interpretation. (4) Point (2), the interpretation, freely repeated and questioned. (5) The answer which can conclude with a reference to point (2), the interpretation" (1997b, 12 n. 21; also P. Anderson 1997a, 53). As can be seen, the points referred to by Anderson are not the same as the points in my characterization of the homiletic exposition, as indicated here. Anderson refers to page 85 of my book *Bread from Heaven*, where I analyze the subsection John 6:41–48. These verses specifically contain what I called "a pattern of exegetical debate."

[3] Some modifications to my outline have been suggested by other scholars, such as those proposed by G. Richter (1969). Richter agrees with me that there is a paraphrasing and systematic exposition of words from the Old Testament text cited in John 6:31ff, and also that the closing statement has many similarities with the opening statement. I maintain that 6:58 is the closing statement, while Richter suggests that 6:51a is the closing verse, because of the agreements between v. 51a and the opening verses in vv. 31–33. In this respect Richter follows those who

Textual Structures

Recent years have seen an increasing interest in structural studies of biblical narratives. Various methods are used. Rather than enter into a general discussion of method, I shall give a few examples of structural similarities and differences that may be seen in the Gospel of John. One example is related to my analysis of the prologue of John, John 1:1–18 (Borgen 1970, 288–95; 1972, 115–30; 1987b, 75–101). My observations suggest that the prologue basically is to be divided in two parts: 1:1–5, which deal with protological and preincarnational "time" (Painter 2003a, 179–201), and 1:6–18, which deal with the appearance of Jesus Christ. Thus, John 1:1–18, seen as a unit, has this structure:

(a) vv. 1–2: Logos (ὁ λόγος) and God (ὁ θεός) before the creation
   (b) v. 3: Logos who created (πάντα διʼ αὐτοῦ ἐγένετο)
      (c) vv. 4–5: Light and darkness (φῶς and σκοτία); darkness has not overcome the light
      (c') vv. 6–9: The coming of light (φῶς) with Jesus' coming, with the Baptist as a witness
   (b') vv. 10–13: The Creator (διʼ αὐτοῦ ἐγένετο) claims his possession by the coming of Jesus
(a') vv. 14–18: The epiphany with the coming of Jesus. The terms ὁ λόγος and God (ὁ θεός) are repeated

R. Alan Culpepper's interest in my studies of the prologue focused on my proposal regarding the structure of the passage. According to him, my outline represented a step forward, but my analysis had some weaknesses, among them that "it is based on only three key terms or phrases while the prologue contains several other equally important terms which when taken into account alter the structure of the text" (Culpepper 1980, 1–31). My response is that Culpepper's comment is inadequate, because it ignores the fact that these "three terms or phrases" come from the authoritative source on the creation, Genesis 1:1-5, which is specifically marked out by the initial words "In the beginning" (John 1:1/Gen 1:1; see Borgen 1987b, 93–96). These words or terms have special weight in the opening section of John's Gospel. Furthermore, Culpepper characterizes

---

see 6:51b–58 as an interpolation about the Eucharist. My answer to Richter is that in all the passages discussed, the closing statement comes at the point where the repetition of words from the Old Testament text ends. In this case, as noted earlier, the repetition of words from the Old Testament quotation in John 6:31 runs beyond v. 51a and ends with v. 58. For further discussion, see Borgen 1983, 32–38.

my understanding of the structure of the prologue of John roughly as chiastic. He then maintains that the two references to John the Baptist (1:6–8, 15) distort my proposed structure, because both lie in the second half of the chiasm (c' and a' in the outline). Here, Culpepper applies his own theoretical model in a mechanical way. One should not overlook the fact that the first half of John's prologue deals with the protological and preincarnational perspective and the second half with aspects related to the incarnation. Logically, John the Baptist can appear only in this second half. Correspondingly, in the *Jerusalem Targum* on Genesis 3:24 the references to "this world" and "the world to come" occur only in the second half of the text, simply because the first half deals with protology and the second half with history and eschatology.

My point here is that structural models are not to be applied in a mechanical way. As much as possible, they should develop from the intrinsic value system and thought forms present in the text itself, with other relevant texts used for comparison. This is the case because, as D. Moody Smith advises, the identification of material on the basis of criteria obtained from outside the Gospel itself seems more easily controllable than one's own personal standards of consistency and coherence (1984, 14–15).

In *Bread from Heaven*, I concentrated my analysis on the Old Testament text quoted in John 6:31b, "as it is written, 'He gave them bread from heaven to eat,'" and the subsequent exegetical exposition. In that book, I dealt with the literary context of the discourse only briefly (Borgen 1965, 41–46). I realized, however, that I needed to look more closely at chapter 6 as a whole and its thematic ties to chapter 5 (Borgen 1993). To emphasize this point, I have already looked at the two chapters together in the beginning of this essay. The contexts of the homilies that I used for comparison from Philo's writings can now be explored further. Observations on one such passage, *Leg.* 3.162–68, will serve as an illustration. Before looking at this text, a point of information about the extant treatises of Philo's *Allegorical Commentary* series on Genesis will prove helpful. This exegetical series consists of a verse by verse commentary that covers the main parts of Genesis 2–41. Thus, in this series there are no running commentaries dedicated exclusively to Exodus—with its section on the manna/bread from heaven in chapter 16—or the other Pentateuchal books. Several sections from these other parts of the Pentateuch are, however, interpreted by Philo in the course of his remarks on Genesis. For this reason, Philo's *Allegorical Commentaries* on Genesis includes sections on texts from Exodus, such as those on the manna (Exod 16), and on other texts from the remaining books of the Pentateuch.

In *Legum Allegoriae*, Book 3, the verses in Genesis 3:8–19 serve as headings for chains of expositions on verses from other parts of the Pentateuch. As one of the parallels to John 6:31–58, I examined Philo's exposition of Exodus 16:4 in *Leg.* 3.162–68. This section is incorporated into an expository chain of units connected to Genesis 3:14c: "dust you shall eat all the days of your life." This chain runs from 3.161–81. The different parts of this broad exposition have as a common theme the idea of "food." In *Bread from Heaven*, I referred to the thematic and transitional words in *Leg.* 3.162a: "That the food of the soul is not earthly but heavenly, the Sacred Word will testify (μαρτυρήσει) abundantly" (1965, 44). This statement introduces a quotation of Exodus 16:4 and serves as a bridge back to the brief exposition on the earthly food of Genesis 3:14c in *Leg.* 3.161. Thus, Philo here moves from earthly food to spiritual/ethereal food.

Scholars such as David Runia and myself have examined some of Philo's "chains" of scriptural quotations and the expositions that follow scriptural quotations in his running commentary. These added links in the chain have been called "secondary quotations." There is no value judgment expressed in this term, because a large variety of relationships exist between the head link and the subsequent links of a chain (Runia 1984, 209–56; 1987, 105–38; cf. 1991; Borgen 1997, 102–39). For example, in the transitional formulation at *Leg.* 3.162a, the verb μαρτυρέω is the key word: "The Sacred Word" will "bear witness" to the heavenly food. Here there is a correspondence to the idea in John 5:39 that "the scriptures" "bear witness" to Jesus, who, according to 6:31–58, is "the bread of life" that came down from heaven.

In summary, the following forensic perspective emerges on John 5:1–7:1. Jesus has committed two crimes: (1) he broke the Sabbath, and (2) he made himself equal to God (5:1–18) violations that place him under the threat of capital punishment. In verses 19–30, Jesus explains the relationship between himself, as Son, to God, as Father, leading him to conclude that "I can do nothing on my own. As I hear, I judge; and my judgment is just, because I seek to do not my own will but the will of him who sent me." Jesus then refers to witnesses who bear witness to him: John the Baptist, the works of Jesus, the Father who sent him, and the Scriptures. The Scriptures bear witness to him (v. 39), and Moses accuses the "Jews"; at the same time, Moses wrote of Jesus (5:44–45). In chapter 6, this "witness" is documented. The witness of the works is experienced by the crowd and by the disciples in 6:1–21. In the subsequent dialogue between Jesus and the crowd (6:22–29), it is made clear that they had misunderstood Jesus' works to refer to food for the stomach. They should rather work for the food that endures to eternal life. Then the crowd asks for a sign and refers to what was "written": "He gave them bread from heaven to eat" (6:30–31). In his exegesis of this text, Jesus identifies the bread from heaven with himself (6:32–58). In this way, the Old Testament text bears witness to Jesus as the bread from heaven. As suggested earlier, 6:22–29 probably focuses on the phrase "for it is on him [the Son of Man] that God the Father has set his seal" (v. 27). By this "sealing," the Father has borne witness to him.

In these two chapters, the different groups react to Jesus' "witnesses" in various ways. The "Jews" first seek to kill him for his crimes (John 5:17–18), then they challenge his exegesis of the scriptural quotation on bread from heaven (6:41–42, 52). The "crowd," who searches for Jesus, misunderstands his feeding of the 5,000 (6:26). When Jesus identifies himself by saying, "I am the bread of life," he criticizes them for their disbelief and says, "you have seen me and yet do not believe" (6:35–36). The disciples are divided in their reactions. Many leave Jesus (6:60–66), while the Twelve, represented by Peter, decide to remain because they have come to know that Jesus is "the Holy One of God" (6:67–69). Finally, Judas, the son of Simon Iscariot, one of the Twelve, has resolved to betray him (6:70–71). After this sequence of crimes, threat of punishment, Jesus' self–presentation, his list of witnesses and the documentation of the witnessing functions, and the various reactions to his claims, John 7:1 returns to the situation of Jesus living under the threat of being killed.

In my view, John Painter's attribution of John 6:1–35, which he calls a "quest story," to the first edition of the Fourth Gospel, and his attribution of 6:41–59 and 6:60–66, which he calls "rejection stories," to a later second edition, breaks down at 6:36–40 (Painter 1993b, 267–86). According to him, the quest is completed by the crowd, and the "Jews" (vv. 41, 52) are the ones who reject (Painter 1993b, 278–81). Against Painter, it must be pointed out that verse 36 specifically says that the crowd rejected Jesus: "But I said to you that you have seen me and yet do not believe." As for the "Jews," they object to Jesus' exegetical identification of himself with the bread from heaven and ask how he could give his flesh to eat. Yet it is not stated that they rejected Jesus. Overall, I agree with Painter that there is a history of traditions behind the Gospel of John, but I question his theory of two editions. The different reactions to Jesus' works and words seen in the Fourth Gospel would also be present—with some variations—in the pre-Gospel period of the tradition. Further, when Painter calls v. 35 ("I am the bread of life") the "text" on which Jesus' exposition is based, he ignores the fact that the term "bread" in this verse is an integral part of the Old Testament quotation in v. 31, which runs through v. 58. Verse 35 also is an integral part of the questions and answers about the scriptural quotation. The central importance of v. 35 is the result of the fact that from here onward the "bread" in the OT citation is explicitly identified with Jesus, as also is the case at 6:41, 48, and 51. In all these "I Am" sayings, words from the OT quotation in v. 31 are repeated.

Many other approaches to the structural analysis of John's narrative are seen in research today (see Beutler 1997). I offer a few scattered comments relevant to this issue. First, when examining the use of misunderstanding and irony in John, one should try to integrate the "theological" aspect into the formal structural categories, for example by combining the analysis of misunderstanding with the theological category of earth and heaven and related ideas. Second, because interpretive and exegetical elements, even on a judicial level, are present in the Gospel of John, one should look into possible learned aspects of this activity. For example, Hebrew philological features are presupposed and used to express interpretive concerns and ideas, such as in John 1:51. Here the Hebrew בֹ in Genesis 28:12 is understood as a reference to a person, meaning "on him," and in John 6:32 and 12:40 variances in the vocalization of the Hebrew text are presupposed (Borgen 1965, 62–66, 172, 179). This is comparable to the combined grammatical and theological point made by Paul in Galatians 3:16: "The promises were spoken to Abraham 'and to' his 'seed.' It does not say 'and to seeds,' as to many, but as to one, 'and to your seed,' which is Christ." Finally, any discussion of structures and rhetoric should pay attention to the forensic character of words and events in the life of Jesus, leading up to his execution as a criminal and his portrayal as God's Son and emissary returning to his Father.

JOHN WITHIN THE EARLY GOSPEL TRADITIONS

In early Christian tradition, the Scriptures had authority and small units of the Hebrew Bible ("verses") were quoted and subject to exegetical exposition. One might ask whether the works and words of Jesus were in the process of being treated in the same or similar way. The answer is "yes." For example, a "Jesus logion" may serve as the basis for various forms of interpretation. The logion, "whoever receives one whom I send, receives me; and whoever receives me receives him who sent me" at John 13:20 may serve as an example.

The traditional saying behind John 13:20 is found in all four canonical Gospels, and thus has a firm place in the gospel tradition. There are two versions. The first mentions a chain of two agents, i.e. the sender (God), the first agent (Jesus) who is sent and who in turn sends the second agent, and the addressee who receives (John 13:20; Matt 10:14; Luke 10:16; Mark 9:37 and Luke 9:48). The other version mentions only a single agent; for example, by seeing God the Father as the sender, the agent (Jesus) as the one who is sent, and the addressee who receives (John 5:23; 8:19; 12:44–45; 14:7, 9; 15:23). Thus, at John 13:20, the Father sends Jesus (= the first agent) and Jesus sends the disciple (= the second agent), whom the addressee receives, while at John 5:23, the Father sends the Son (= the one agent), whom all must honor. There are rabbinic parallels to the formula of single agency, such as those found in *Mek.* on Exodus 14:31: "having faith in the Shepherd of Israel (the agent) is the same as having faith in (the word of) Him who spoke and the world came into being (= the sender)," and "speaking against the Shepherd of Israel (=the agent) is like speaking against Him who spoke (= the sender)." It is of interest that the idea of agency here is applied to the role of Moses in an exegetical interpretation of Exodus 14:31, "the people . . . believed in the Lord and in his servant Moses," and of Numbers 21:5, "the people spoke against God and against Moses."

One form of expository elaboration on this traditional logion is found in John 12:44–50. In this passage, two versions of the logion with single agency serve as Jesus' "text":

He who believes in me (ὁ πιστεύων εἰς ἐμε),
believes not in me, but in him who sent me (εἰς τὸν πέμψαντά με).
And he who sees (ὁ θεωρῶν) me
sees him who sent me (τὸν πέμψαντά με).

In the subsequent exposition, words from this "text" are repeated and woven together with other words and phrases:

(a) Fragments from and related to these two versions of the saying:
　　v. 46 ὁ πιστεύων εἰς ἐμὲ
　　v. 49 ὁ πέμψας με
(b) Fragment from another version that is presupposed (cf. Luke 10:16, "he who . . . rejects me"):
　　v. 48 ὁ ἀθετῶν ἐμὲ καὶ μὴ λαμβάνων . . . μου
(c) Terminology on agency:
　　v. 49 ἐξ ἐμαυτοῦ οὐκ
　　v. 50 καθὼς οὕτως
(d) Legal and eschatological terminology from the gospel tradition and terms used elsewhere in the New Testament and in Judaism:
　　v. 47 ἐγὼ οὐ κρίνω . . . οὐ . . . κρίνω τὸν κόσμον . . . σώσω
　　　　τὸν κόσμον
　　v. 48 τὸν κρίνοντα ὁ λόγος-κρινεῖ ἐν τῇ ἐσχάτῃ ἡμέρᾳ
　　v. 50 ζωὴ αἰώνιος
(e) Other words from the gospel tradition:
　　v. 46 ἐγὼ ἐλήλυθα, ἵνα

v. 47 οὐ ἦλθον ἵνα . . . ἀλλ᾽ ἵνα
v. 47 (?) ἐάν τίς μου ἀκούσῃ τῶν ῥημάτων καὶ μὴ φυλάξῃ
(f) Terminological influence from the Old Testament—the giving of
the Law and the light and darkness in the creation story:
v. 46 φῶς ἐν τῇ σκοτίᾳ
v. 49 ἐντολὴν δέδωκεν

In 1 Corinthians 7:10–16, Paul testifies to such an expository use of
a cited Jesus logion, the traditional saying on divorce: "To the married I
give this command—not I but the Lord—that the wife should not separate from her husband (but if she does separate, let her remain unmarried
or else be reconciled to her husband) and that the husband should not
divorce his wife" (vv. 10–11). In vv. 12–16, Paul adds an exposition in
which he repeats words from the Jesus logion and weaves them together
with interpretive words. Similarly, the Jesus logion on agency cited in
John 12:44–45 is followed in vv. 46–50 by an exposition. Although the
themes differ, both deal with judicial applications. Paul develops rules
for marriage and divorce, while John elaborates on rules of agency to
describe the role of Jesus as the commissioned agent of the Father.

Paul also reveals that a narrative unit in the gospel tradition can be
used as the basis for an exposition. In 1 Corinthians 11:23–25(26) he cites
the institution of the Lord's Supper as a transmitted tradition, then in vv.
27–34 he gives a commentary on this quoted unit of tradition by repeat-
ing words from the story and weaving them together with interpretive
words. Paul's use here of a story from the gospel tradition can give insight
to the rendering and expository application of traditional narratives in
John, such as the story of the healing of the paralytic in John 5:1–9, followed by a subsequent judicial exchange in which words from the story
are repeated and woven together with interpretive applications (5:10–18;
Borgen 1990, 413–17).

John's use of early Christian tradition raises the question of the
Fourth Gospel's relationship to the Synoptics. In my 1959 study "John
and the Synoptics in the Passion Narrative," I concluded that John is
based essentially on an independent tradition. At some points, however,
various elements from the Synoptic Gospels can be seen in the Johannine version of a story. When John appears dependent upon the Synoptic
Gospels only in certain pericopes, it is probable that oral tradition has
brought this material to John. This approach explains the relative freedom with which John has reproduced the synoptic material. Although
there is continuity between this early article and my present view on the
relationship between John and the Synoptics, I have also modified my

perspective and made shifts of emphasis. Today, I formulate my understanding by noting three main possibilities. First, the exposition of an oral or written tradition may have received its form in the presynoptic and pre-Johannine stages; the evangelist has then brought these preformed units of tradition into his Gospel. Second, the evangelist may himself have interpreted and given form to some oral or written traditions that do not come from the present Synoptic Gospels. Third, the exposition may take place after one or more sections of one, two, or all three of the Synoptics were known to the evangelist and were in varied ways utilized by him. This knowledge of and influence from one or more of the other Gospels, or of units from them, may have been brought to John by traveling Christians (Borgen 1992, 1816). Since the publication of the 1959 essay just noted, I have moved more in the direction of points 1 and 2, without excluding the possibility that also point 3 can be at work.

Behind the Gospel of John, there was a process of tradition in which preservation and continuity were present and also in which expository interpretation was at work. A few examples will illustrate this principle and indicate points at which John may be judged independent of the Synoptics.

First, aspects of the use of the traditional saying behind John 13:20 have already been discussed: (a) "He who receives any one whom I send" (b) "receives me," (c) "and he who receives me" (d) "receives him who sent me." The points made in sections (a), (b), (c), and (d) of the saying are found in the parallels in Matthew 10:40 and Luke 10:16 (cf. Mark 9:37 and Luke 9:48). But the words utilized by John differ from those found in the other Gospels. For example, John uses the verbs λαμβάνω ("receive") and πέμπω ("send"), while Matthew 10:40 has δέχομαι and ἀποστέλλω. Moreover, the contexts of the saying differ: John 13:20 appears in the Last Supper after the footwashing (John 13:1–20); Matthew 10:40 places the saying in the missionary discourse (9:36–11:1); Luke 10:16 locates it in the mission of the seventy–two (Luke 10:1–16); at Mark 9:37 and Luke 9:48, it concludes the dispute about greatness (Mark 9:33–37; Luke 9:46–48). For comparison, parallels between Paul's citation of the logion on divorce (1 Cor 7:10–11) and the saying's appearance in the Synoptic Gospels (Mark 10:11) offer helpful insight. The verb in the synoptic version of the saying (ἀπολύειν) differs from Paul's terms for divorce (χωρίζειν and ἀφιέναι), parallel to what is seen from comparison between the Synoptic Gospels and John on the various versions of the Jesus logion on agency. In conclusion, John's use of the logion on agency does not reflect the wording or the literary context of the saying as it appears in the Synoptics. This observation, and the parallel use of another Jesus logion by Paul, supports the view that John draws here on a Jesus logion that was transmitted and interpreted in his community, independent of the Synoptic Gospels (Borgen 1992, 1820–23).

As a second example, both in John 6:51–58 and 1 Corinthians 10:3–4, 16–17, 21, manna traditions are connected with Eucharistic traditions. John 6:51–58 paraphrases parts of the institution of the Lord's Supper, a traditional version of which is presupposed. Similarly, Paul in 1 Corinthians 10:16–17, 21 selects words from the Eucharistic tradition without quoting the story of the institution—here the story of the institution is simply presupposed. The commentary in 1 Corinthians 11:(26)27–37 is also a parallel to John's usage, but here the words of institution have been quoted directly in 11:23–25(26). John and Paul thus use the Eucharistic tradition in the same way, both making expository elaborations of word sets. The sets in John 6:51b–58 are ἄρτος/βρῶσις/σάρξ ("bread/food/ flesh"), αἷμα/πόσις ("blood/drink"), and φάγειν/τρώγειν ("to eat") and πίνειν ("to drink"). The Pauline word sets in 1 Corinthians 10:3–4, 16–17, 21 and 11:27–29 are ἄρτος/βρῶμα/σῶμα ("bread/food/body"), πόμα/ ποτήριον/αἷμα ("drink/blood"), φάγειν/μετέχειν ("to eat") and πίνειν ("to drink"). John and Paul apply the biblical story on the manna and the well to the eating and drinking in the Lord's Supper. In John 6:(31)51b– 58, words from the Eucharistic tradition are made part of the exposition of the Old Testament text on the manna, cited in v. 31. In 1 Corinthians 10:3–4, the Israelites' eating and drinking in the desert typify the Lord's Supper. Against this backdrop, it is probable that John 6:55 ("For my flesh is food [βρῶσις] indeed, and my blood is drink [πόσις] indeed") refers to the manna and the well, just as do the corresponding terms, βρῶμα and πόμα in 1 Corinthians 10:3–4. Finally, in John 6:51b, the phrase ὁ ἄρτος δὲ ὃν ἐγὼ δώσω ἡ σάρξ μού ἐστιν ὑπὲρ τῆς τοῦ κόσμου ζωῆς ("the bread which I will give is my flesh for the life of the world") comes close to rendering a formulation from the presupposed institution story of the Eucharist in the Johannine community. This understanding is supported by the similar wordings in 1 Corinthians 11:24, τοῦτό μού ἐστιν τὸ σῶμα τὸ ὑπὲρ ὑμῶν ("this is my body which [is given] on your behalf") and Luke 22:19, τοῦτό ἐστιν τὸ σῶμά μου τὸ ὑπὲρ ὑμῶν διδόμενον ("this is my body which is given on your behalf"). These similarities show that John is here closer to Paul than to the Synoptics and support the view that John presupposes the practice of a communal, Eucharistic meal. This circumstance gives support to the understanding that John here is independent of the Synoptics. John draws on a tradition, for which Paul gives evidence, and Paul shows that this combination of the manna with the Eucharist already existed in the fifties C.E. Thus, John is here independent of the other written Gospels (Borgen 1990).

To many, it has become an accepted and self–evident principle that, as a liturgical tradition and practice, the story of the institution of the Eucharist was firm and stable in a way different from the rest of the traditional gospel material (Neirynck 1990, 440–41; Labahn and Lang 2004, 455–56). It is interesting to note that those who maintain this view realize that literary methods and analyses are not sufficient in themselves to support this claim; rather, it is necessary to look at the liturgical setting and usage of the Eucharistic story in community life at the pre–Gospel stage. In this way, one may allow for oral tradition and its transmission to be even more decisive than literary analyses and considerations. In my view, it seems difficult to envision that there was only a single gospel tradition in use in any given Christian community before, during, and after the present Gospels were written. Thus, one has to think in terms of various degrees of stability and some varieties in the transmission process. A double process was at work: the need and aim of preserving oral traditions in a recognizable continuity, and the need for interpreting and applying them.

It should be noted that the preserved Eucharistic traditions themselves testify to a variety. As seen earlier, fragments are built into expository contexts. Editorial modifications are made, as at 1 Corinthians 11:26, where Paul formulates a sentence parallel to the words of Jesus in v. 25b so that Jesus seems to be speaking although Paul is clearly referring to Jesus in the third person as "the Lord": "For as often as you eat this bread and drink his cup, you proclaim the Lord's death until he comes." The different versions of the Eucharistic tradition challenge the theory of their unique stability among gospel traditions: the Markan version, the longer and shorter version of Luke, and the version of 1 Corinthians 11:23–25(26) show disagreements and agreements among themselves. Moreover, in Matthew, Mark, and Luke, the Eucharistic stories are parts of the Gospels, placed together with the other traditions about Jesus' words and works (Borgen 1990).

Against this background, one may compare the orally transmitted Pauline Eucharistic material with the versions in Matthew/Mark, Luke, and the Johannine fragments. In this way, one can discover degrees of agreement and degrees of difference that might exist between mutually independent traditions. Thus, a comparison between the version of Paul and the version of Mark can demonstrate the kind of agreements that might exist between two mutually independent versions: there are close verbal agreements in the form of sentences, word pairs and sets, single words, and corresponding variant terms. This approach may also be used in comparing Paul's material with the Lukan versions. Such comparisons will also demonstrate that there are differences that give each version its distinctive character. One difference to be seen is that there are no specific agreements between the context of the passage in Paul and the context in Mark, even though Paul seems to presuppose a passion narrative corresponding to the passion narratives in the Gospels.

In view of considerations such as these, I have drawn the following conclusion with regard to the story of the cleansing of the temple in John 2:13–22 and the Eucharistic fragments in John 6:51–58: in all these cases, the agreements between John and the Synoptics are neither closer, nor more striking, than those between the Pauline passages and Mark. In the case of the story about the healing of the paralytic in John 5:1–18, there are fewer agreements with the Synoptics. As far as these three Johannine passages are concerned, one may conclude that John and the Synoptics are mutually independent.

A note should be added here. Frans Neirynck has suggested that the passage about the healing of the paralytic at the pool of Bethesda in Jerusalem, John 5:1–18, includes elements drawn from Mark 2:1–3:6, the healing of the paralytic in Capernaum and the disciples plucking grain (1990, 445–47). Several comments might be made, but here I will note only that this would mean that John has treated the synoptic material in a radical way, almost in a violent way. In general, research along these lines has not clarified the method that John used in the treatment of these stories from Mark. What is John's understanding of Mark and of tradition, and how and why would his readers find his radical treatment of Mark acceptable and authoritative (Borgen 1990; cf. D. M. Smith 1992, 186 n. 5)?

THE FORENSIC ASPECT

Returning now to the forensic themes raised in John 5 and 6, when the charges brought against Jesus throughout the Gospel of John are put together, they form a crimes report. If the trial and execution are included, a crimes–trial–execution report on Jesus emerges in John's narrative.

The crimes report: Jesus was

- A violator of the Sabbath, of the Law—a "sinner" (5:1–18)
- A blasphemer (5:17–18)
- A false teacher who leads the people astray (7:12, 45–49)
- A blasphemer (8:58)
- A violator of the Sabbath, of the Law—"a sinner" (ch. 9, esp. 9:14–16, 24)
- A blasphemer (10:24–38)
- An enemy of the Jewish nation (11:47–53)

Report on the trial: Jesus was

- Tried as a criminal, an evildoer, and sentenced to capital
  punishment (18:1–19:16a)
- Accused as a false teacher who led the people astray (18:19–
  24)
- Accused as a blasphemer (19:7)

Report on the execution and the burial: Jesus was

- Executed by crucifixion as a criminal and was buried (19:16b–
  41).

According to John, the "Jews'" misunderstanding and misuse of the
Law were behind these charges. In the eyes of the Jews, the Law demands
the condemnation and execution of Jesus: "We have a law and by that law
he ought to die, because he has made himself the Son of God" (John 19:7;
Pancaro 1975, 7–8). According to the contrary view, John's view, the
Scriptures/ Law and other entities bear witness to Jesus, and Moses wrote
of him (1:45; 5:40, 45, etc.). On this basis, John pictures Jesus within a
scriptural framework. A few examples have been given in this essay. I have
shown how the prologue, John 1:1–18, draws on Genesis and deals with
aspects "before," at, and after creation, namely Logos, God, creation, the
light, and then subsequently addresses the corresponding three manifes-
tations in the incarnation. In chapter 5 we read that Jesus, in accordance
with Scriptural exegesis, acted like God when healing on the Sabbath,
and for that reason faced the threat of being killed for blasphemy. As the
Son of God, he makes clear that he is completely dependent upon God,
his Father, and that he acts as the Father's emissary. Jesus refers to the
Baptist, his own works, the Father, and the Scriptures as his witnesses. In
chapter 6, examples are given of these witnessing functions: Jesus' works
are exemplified by the feeding of the 5,000; God, the Father, sealed and
authorized the Son of man; the Old Testament quotation and exposition
of bread from heaven bore witness of him as the bread of life that came
down from heaven. Then in 7:1, the threat of capital punishment referred
to in 5:17–18 emerges again, and the debate about Jesus continues in a
sharpened form. In all these instances, John calls upon witnesses who
might refute the charges that lead to Jesus' execution.

Within the scope of this essay, it is not possible to follow the series of
events and the line of thinking throughout the entire Gospel, but a basis
for further studies has been given. The obvious fact is that the Gospel of
John goes beyond the trial, execution, and burial to tell about Jesus' resurrection appearances. He then commissions his disciples to be his emis-

saries. Forensic/witness themes in these sections of the narrative should also be explored.

PRAGMATIC CONCERNS

What is the pragmatic concern running through the Gospel of John? In *Bread from Heaven*, I saw an antidocetic motif at work in John 6 (1965, 2–3, 172–92). I maintained that an aim of John 6:31–58, as well as of the Gospel in general, was to criticize a docetic tendency that drew a sharp distinction between the spiritual sphere and the external sphere and played down the unique role of Jesus Christ in history. This claim has been challenged by scholars such as John Painter (1997a, 80) and Maarten Menken (1997, 198–99). Menken's comment is to the point: "Borgen, *Bread from Heaven*, pp. 183–92, rightly stresses that the 'Jews' of John 6:41, 52 sharply distinguish between the spiritual bread from heaven and the man Jesus, but his identification of these Jews with the Docetists does not seem to be justified: the Johannine Jews deny Jesus' heavenly provenance, the Docetists deny his humanity that culminates in his death" (1997, 199 n. 61). Further reflection has led me to agree with Menken's understanding. The "Jews" were people who knew Jesus' human family, and they therefore question that he is the Son of God and the bread that came down from heaven (6:42). In a pointed way this tension is present in the trial, verdict, and execution of Jesus: John claims that a criminal, publicly crucified, is the heavenly Son of God, the Father. John 20:31 is to be read against this background: "These [signs] are written so that you may believe that Jesus is the Messiah, the Son of God, and that through believing you may have life in his name." It is by believing in the criminal who suffered capital punishment, and who, nevertheless or just for that reason, is the Son of God, that "you may have life in his name."

Against such a background, I have suggested that structural and rhetorical studies should pay more attention to theological movements between the earthly and the heavenly levels when Johannine stories about misunderstanding and conflict are analyzed. Moreover, attention should be given to the forensic aspect that runs through the Gospel of John and leads to Jesus' trial and execution. This forensic aspect indicates that there is an element of a learned treatment of the Scriptures and tradition.

Finally, the question about John and the Synoptics has been broadened so that gospel material in Paul's first letter to the Corinthians has been included. Observations in support of the view that John is independent of the other Gospels have been listed. The possibility that there may have been some influence on John from (parts of) one or several of the other Gospels has not been excluded completely.

A final remark on the nature of the Gospel of John as a whole should be given. Seeing that the structure of a "crimes and punishment report" is present in John, I have looked into such reports in Philo's *Against Flaccus*, Josephus' *War* (7.437–53, on Catullus), 2 *Macc* 4:7–9:29 (on Antiochus), and Acts 12:1–24 (on Herod Agrippa). It is of interest to note that the Gospel of John, as with *Against Flaccus* and 2 *Macc* 4:7–9:29, begins the crimes and punishment report with the professional activities of the main character as an adult. The activities described ultimately caused the person to suffer capital punishment. Against this background, one might ask whether John (and Mark?), who begins his narrative with the ministry of the adult Jesus, follows the basic structure of a crimes and punishment report but in a recast form, one that gives the activities and death of a criminal a contrasting meaning. In this way, the death of Jesus as a criminal, even suffering execution by means of crucifixion, has been turned "upside down" so as to become a central point of a Gospel (Borgen 2005, 78).

3: RESPONSE

LIVING WORD(S) AND THE BREAD OF LIFE

Michael Labahn

Since the publication of his famous study on John 6, *Bread from Heaven*, Peder Borgen has become a well–known and well–established Johannine scholar. His contributions range from explorations of the religious background of Johannine thought to the quest for the sources of the Johannine tradition. On the former, Borgen, an expert on Philo, is aware of both Jewish and Hellenistic influences on the Gospel of John and has examined the Johannine interpretation of the Old Testament as a lively source for the Gospel's presentation of Jesus. On the latter, his research has brought him into the ongoing debate over John's relationship to the Synoptics (cf. D. M. Smith 2001; Labahn and Lang 2004). His contribution to the present volume beautifully combines his expertise in these different fields of Johannine exegesis. It is very difficult to give a short but well–founded reply to such a rich contribution, but for reasons of space I must limit myself to a few remarks.

To contextualize my comments, I begin with a short overview of my own research on John 5 and 6. In my view, each of these incidents is a distinct literary unit within the Fourth Gospel. The narrator uses traditions present in his community as well as ideas from his theological school to elaborate two conflicts that develop christological, theological, and pragmatic insights (cf. Labahn 1999, 213–304; 2000a; 2000b). John 6 refers back to the preceding healing stories in chapters 4 and 5 but also

establishes distinctive issues. At the same time, I do not deny that the
narrator connects the episodes of his narrative very closely. I am grateful
that Borgen has honored my studies by a friendly and thorough critique
(cf. Borgen 2000) that shows our agreements as well as the differences in
our approaches.

With this brief introduction, I will focus on four main issues in Borgen's article: his understanding of John 5:19–6:71 as a literary unity, his
analysis of the interplay between John and texts from the Hebrew Bible,
his remarks on the relationship between John and the Synoptics, and his
observations on the forensic structure of units of John's narrative.

First, Borgen's innovative approach takes John 5:19–6:71 as a single
literary unit and views 5:17–18 and 7:1 as an *inclusio*. Several observations would challenge this proposal. The literary structures in John 5,
6, and 9 reveal that discussion and monologue often follow a narrated
incident. The geographical distinction between Jerusalem (ch. 5) and the
Sea of Galilee (ch. 6) is accompanied by statements indicating the passing of time ("after this"; 6:1, 4). Also, the new narrative setting in John
6 does not explicitly reflect the plot to kill Jesus (7:1, 25; 8:59; 10:31–39;
11:16, 53) and includes a new group of dissenters, a point that Borgen
himself acknowledges by taking 5:17–18 as a first reaction to Jesus' witness and noting that in chapter 6 there are other reactions. Further, the
God–given works mentioned in 5:36 are more generally connected with
all the deeds of Jesus, including his speeches. Of course, 6:31 may be the
closest (in terms of the flow of the narrative) explicit example of how
Scripture "witnesses" to Jesus in John, but the narrator refers to the witness of Scripture through numerous quotations and allusions throughout
the book. Finally, the confession of Peter in John 6:68 ("You have the
words of eternal life"), linked with the hint about Judas the traitor, is
not to be read as a direct reply to 5:47 ("if you do not believe what he
[Moses] wrote, how will you believe what I say?"). Rather, it is to be read
alongside the testing of Jesus' disciples in John 6:5–8 as an exemplary
reaction to Jesus' appearance. Following Borgen's reading, however, one
may treat Peter's confession as a reply to the question of 5:47, similar to
the reply of the Samaritans in 4:39–42 or even, as 20:30–31 would propose, of the reader.

One might accept that there may be a closer connection between
chapters 5 and 6 than has generally been realized. Borgen's approach also
helps us to read the Fourth Gospel as a horizontal line of thought—for
instance, gradually learning more about the witness motif. John repeats
motifs, taking them up again and again to help the reader join his "universe of thought" (cf. Labahn 2004, 330f.). Nevertheless, I believe Borgen presses the connection between John 5 and 6 too much.

Second, Borgen's research shows that a wide range of conclusions may be drawn by analyzing the intertextual play between John and Old Testament texts. These conclusions include observations on the literary design of the Gospel and its structure: for example, demonstrating that the OT quotation in John 6:31 is an instance of the "witness" of Scripture, which is exposed—as Borgen says, is "repeated and interpreted"—throughout 6:31–58 to support the literary unity of the passage, or referring to Genesis 1:1–5 as an "authoritative source" for John 1:1–18. Borgen convincingly stresses that any analysis of structure—including any intertextual interplay—must be derived from the text itself and its "value system and thought," of course without denying comparison with other relevant texts. According to my view, any intertextual play receives support as well as contradiction from intratextuality in that sense.

Third, regarding John and the Synoptics, we must, I believe, differentiate between at least two questions: (a) did the author of the Fourth Gospel have knowledge of (an)other written Gospel(s), and, (b) was the tradition used by the Fourth Evangelist related to the Synoptic Gospels or their traditions? If the narrator of John's Gospel knew at least one Synoptic Gospel, he obviously did not use it as his overall literary source; vice versa, the Synoptics clearly were not the exclusive source(s) for John (as pointed out by Borgen's contributions). However, there remains the possibility that the author of John knew one of the Synoptic Gospels and used at least some of the synoptic material, a hypothesis that Borgen now seems to accept. Further, Borgen points to continuity and creativity by the Johannine narrator and "various degrees of stability" in transmission. Although we have to reckon with a certain amount of continuity to support the very notion of "transmission," I would like to underscore the creative aspect. It is now generally acknowledged, in contrast to the old *formgeschichtlich* approach, that oral tradition is not a stable entity. However, it is still too easy to refer to written texts as "fixed forms" while treating oral tradition as a fluid form of transmission. Using traditions includes the establishment of new meanings in continuity and in dialogue with one's own public memory; in this way, traditions are kept alive for their intended audiences. Therefore, it is highly hypothetical to label any tradition behind a Johannine passage that seems to parallel a synoptic text as presynoptic, nonsynoptic, or synoptic. Nevertheless, in some cases it seems likely that the tradition used by the Fourth Evangelist—for example, the tradition behind John 6—has its roots in a synoptic text to which it is related through "secondary orality." The Synoptics, in other words, may be the source of the oral traditional material on which John has drawn (cf. Labahn 2000a). In other cases, we may reckon with an independent Johannine tradition, as may be the case with the traditions behind John 5:1–18 and 6:51–58. Each individual text must be addressed with the type of methodological care that characterizes Borgen's style of analysis.

For Borgen, the relationship between John and the Synoptics has to be placed within the larger framework of early Christian Jesus tradition and its transmission, which can also be detected in the letters of Paul. This is a methodologically well–grounded argument. Regarding the different kinds of tradition, however—and the assumption that liturgical traditions are more stable than others does not, of course, rule out the possibility of different traditions within a single community with regard to community rites—and the individual shaping of each, at present we are not able to establish general rules about the nature of the transmission of early Christian Jesus tradition.

Fourth and finally, Borgen underlines the forensic aspect in the overall structure and individual units of the Gospel of John, detecting "a crimes and punishment report." Herewith, he correctly underscores that Jesus' crucifixion became a central point of the narrative, establishing meaning in contrast to the humiliation that is inherently part of this kind of punishment.

By his inspiring studies, Borgen has shown that a close look at the use of sources and traditions by the Fourth Evangelist helps to deepen our understanding of John's Christology and theology. We can learn that the word(s) of traditions—including the Old Testament, synoptic or nonsynoptic sayings and narratives—are living words that were creatively and meaningfully taken up in order to present Jesus as the one who is God's bread of life for all people.

CHAPTER 4

THREE REVOLUTIONS, A FUNERAL, AND GLIMMERS OF A CHALLENGING DAWN

Thomas L. Brodie, O.P.

On Holy Thursday, 1960, I was struck by a preacher's description of Jesus washing his disciples' feet. That night I found the account (John 13:1–20) in an old translation and began to read. The account became a long farewell speech, and it captured me like nothing I had ever read before. More than legends or lyrics, soldiers or sailors, saints or scholars, Greeks or Romans, Wild West or Far East, Jesus' farewell speech gave an extraordinary experience of depth and calm and truth. I decided to learn the beginning of it by heart. Then the entire speech. The wording was somewhat archaic, but it was easier than the wording of the Shakespearean speeches that every high school student in the country had been expected to learn. By autumn, I had memorized the entire Gospel of John.

As time passed, the words began to recede. But not completely. Years later, I read in George Steiner that the custom of learning things by heart has great value—that somehow the text lodges deep within a person, in the heart. And so it seemed. The old words became a kind of treasure, an underlying joy. In an earlier age, that treasure might have remained essentially undisturbed until I went to my grave. But it was not to be. Three succeeding decades—the 1960s, 1970s, and 1980s—all brought benign revolutions to my understanding of the Bible, including the Gospel of John, and having expressed much of what I have learned, especially through five books (Brodie 1993a; 1993b; 2000; 2001; 2004), I now seem to be facing a further change. It is appropriate then to summarize my reflections around these changes.

THE FIRST REVOLUTION

The first revolution in my thinking about John was started by a creature called the historical-critical method, including eventually "social" history. I first encountered this phenomenon in the shape of a throwaway remark. One day an older person said casually that the words in the Gospels were not the exact words of Jesus. My heart sank. Later, the evidence was inescapable. In my formal studies in the 1960s, I was taught in the tradition of Jerusalem's *Ecole Biblique* with its emphasis on history and archaeology—my parents' present on my twenty–first birthday was the *Bible de Jerusalem*—and from Genesis, Jericho, Isaiah, and Jonah to the quest for Jesus' life and words, the historical method showed that the Bible was not the solid building I had imagined. It was necessary, therefore, to give special attention to history and sources. And when in 1968 I was catapulted prematurely into teaching almost all aspects of Biblical Studies, Old and New Testament, in the regional seminary of the West Indies in Trinidad, I did indeed try to do justice to the bold theories of Wellhausen, Noth, and Bultmann, but I also sifted the meticulous historical research of scholars such as de Vaux, Albright, Bright, Benoit, Dodd, and Brown.

Teaching John was a challenge. The Fourth Gospel had earned Saint John the title "The Theologian," but, as Westcott lamented, the historians had driven the theologians from the field. Raymond Brown often recounted how when he was embarking on his Anchor Bible commentary on John, his mentor, William Foxwell Albright, urged him to deal with history rather than theology. Brown had replied that, given how the Gospel begins, he would have to engage theology, which he did. But Brown also engaged history, so that Albright's emphasis tended to dominate the commentary. John's differences from the other Gospels, when combined with the idea of oral tradition, contributed to the notion that John had an independent link to the original events. John's Gospel, after all, was somehow deeply historical. Brown's commentary seemed extraordinarily comprehensive and helpful, and also reassuring. I read it over and over.

THE SECOND REVOLUTION

In September 1972, a second benign revolution struck. To prepare for examinations, I had gone into virtual seclusion in a village in Normandy.

My custom was to study the Old Testament in the morning and the New Testament in the afternoon and evening, and I had spent much of the previous day with Matthew, a Gospel I knew well from teaching it in Trinidad. Now I was focused on Deuteronomy, and I suddenly said to myself, "That is like Matthew, that is so like Matthew"—something about the sense of community, the discourses, the blessings and curses, the mountain setting. I quickly made a half page of notes and told myself not to think about it, because I needed to concentrate on my exams. Yet at lunchtime, I could not resist talking about it. In the following days other similar phenomena emerged. Aspects of the Elijah–Elisha narrative showed startling similarities to Luke–Acts, and the Book of Wisdom's confrontation between Wisdom and the kings of the earth felt somewhat like John's account of the meeting between Jesus and Pilate.

Eventually, when the exams were over and I had moved to Jerusalem for a year's study at the *Ecole Biblique*, I faced a dilemma. Jerusalem seemed an excellent place to study biblical history and archaeology, but I was now concerned that the New Testament appeared to come not only from the land and its people but also from a book—from the Old Testament. I embraced my courses and the excursions on history and archaeology, including unforgettable trips to Hebron, the Negev, Sinai, Galilee, Samaria, and the Holy Sepulcher, but I also bought a copy of the Greek Old Testament—the Septuagint—and, with Matthew in mind, started ploughing through Deuteronomy.

The ploughing was tedious. Connections with Matthew seemed few and flimsy. Then, suddenly, in Deuteronomy 15, the search came to life. The repeated emphasis on remission resonated with Matthew's emphasis on forgiveness (Matt 18). Both use similar Greek terminology. Obviously such similarity proved nothing. But further comparison revealed more links. The Deuteronomic word for "debt," δάνειον, is unknown elsewhere in the Bible—except in Matthew 18. Gradually the pieces of the puzzle began to fall into place. Matthew 18 was based on first–century materials, including Mark, but it had also absorbed Deuteronomy 15. Once I had got inside part of the Deuteronomy–Matthew connection, the rest of it became easier to track, and I kept going over the two texts.

Because of my preoccupation with the emerging OT/NT links, I failed to obtain a diploma from the *Ecole Biblique*, and virtually twenty years passed before my work on Matthew 18 and Deuteronomy was published (Brodie 1992). Yet the *Ecole* provided an invaluable context for initiating the exploration. Langlamet, professor of Old Testament there, said Matthew's dependence upon Deuteronomy made immediate sense to him. He had once thought of the idea, but had never developed it.

Boismard, lecturing on John, simply asked, "Are you learning?" and when
I answered "Yes," he said, "Then stay with it."

Soon the pattern of literary dependence began to emerge. Parts of
that pattern were surprisingly complicated:

- Matthew's use of Deuteronomy was twofold. First, a small kernel
  of the Gospel (a series of enigmatic sayings in Matthew 5 and 11,
  including five beatitudes, five antitheses, and a revelatory cry, "I
  thank you, Father") contain a dense distillation of Deuteronomy.
  Second, the Gospel as a whole contains a further, more expansive
  reworking of the older book. The kernel, the series of sayings, was
  so distinctive, coherent, and complete, both in itself and as a distillation of Deuteronomy, that it looked like a distinct arrangement.
  As a working hypothesis, I gave this arrangement the Papias–related
  name *logia*.
- Luke–Acts likewise contains two modes of using LXX narrative: one
  heavy (in about ten chapters of Luke's Gospel, plus half of Acts [Acts
  1:1–15:35]), the other light. I did not realize then that the variation in the two halves of Acts—heavy usage of the LXX in the first,
  light in the second—was a commonplace among scholars; nor did
  I pay sufficient attention to Evans' detection of the use of Deuteronomy in Luke's travel narrative (Evans 1957, 37–53). However, I
  did become aware that many researchers maintained that Luke–Acts
  once existed in a shorter form, a form that in some analyses contained about half of Acts and was known as Proto–Luke.
- Mark's links to the Old Testament seemed so complex that my investigation halted. But then, in a fallow moment of going nowhere, the
  idea dawned that perhaps Mark knew an epistle. The epistles proved
  to be just one component, but an important one, first for Mark and
  later for the other Gospels. Each Gospel, it emerged, had used both
  the Old Testament and some epistles.
- Each Gospel writer also used the preceding Gospels. To some
  degree, this is accepted—most researchers now hold that Matthew
  and Luke used Mark, and some maintain Luke used Matthew. But
  such views, the results of modern research, began to emerge as only
  one part of a larger pattern of Gospel interdependence.

The tracing of these connections happened very rapidly, through a
trial and error process that I could not articulate but that caused me, for
the first time in my life, not to be able to sleep. I tried to slow things down
and put the pieces together. By the end of the academic year (June 1973)
it was possible to trace the central sequence of literary dependence:

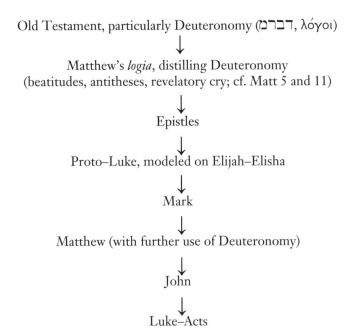

Old Testament, particularly Deuteronomy (דברים, λόγοι)
↓
Matthew's *logia*, distilling Deuteronomy
(beatitudes, antitheses, revelatory cry; cf. Matt 5 and 11)
↓
Epistles
↓
Proto–Luke, modeled on Elijah–Elisha
↓
Mark
↓
Matthew (with further use of Deuteronomy)
↓
John
↓
Luke–Acts

This sequence of dependence was just the backbone of a complex literary and historical process, but it had considerable implications. It gave a fresh framework for approaching the New Testament writings, outlined a solution to the Synoptic Problem, and provided a context for discussing the Gospel of John. The more pressing concern, however, was not the complexity or the implications, but simply whether the basic sequence was correct. I asked for more time and, thanks to the generosity of the Dominican sisters in the village in Normandy, again went into seclusion. There, for two and a half years, I scrutinized the primary texts more closely, elaborating all the time, trying to articulate criteria for establishing literary dependence, and implicitly testing, testing, testing.

The biggest surprise from those years concerned the nature and role of the New Testament epistles. I had not wanted to become entangled with the epistles, but the detail of the Gospel texts was indicating a complex literary process of using extant writings. Many epistles had transformed the great Old Testament narratives, especially the Pentateuch, and—apart from building on one another (itself a huge phenomenon)—they in turn had been transformed into one component of the Gospels and Acts. The process was particularly decisive in 1 Corinthians. Despite its distinctive first–century content, this letter is pervaded by the Old Testament, especially the Pentateuch, including Deuteronomy, and it had contributed decisively to part of Luke–Acts, Proto–Luke.

The overall sequence was confirmed. As with the Elijah–Elisha narrative, but more so, Proto–Luke moved from historiography toward biography (*bios*); Mark, building on Proto–Luke, brought the process further. Unraveling Mark's use of Proto–Luke consumed a huge amount of time. Matthew expanded Mark, especially with discourses. And John, building on Matthew, brought the discourses to a new level. Canonical Luke–Acts retained Proto–Luke in full but expanded it with many sources, including diverse distillations of the other Gospels.

I produced a manuscript and showed it to two publishers in the spring of 1975, but their responses indicated that it was not at all what publishers wanted. Searching for a way forward, I tested the waters in beloved Trinidad and in Ireland, and then, following a long family tradition, sought permission to go to America. Eventually, in September 1976, I got a job teaching Old Testament at the regional seminary in Boynton Beach, Florida. I chose Old Testament to protect the students from my ideas about the New Testament, which had not received any outside approval, and also because I just love the Old Testament. At that time, Old Testament studies were developing quickly, especially regarding history, form criticism, and sources, including the slow–burning idea that Hebrew narrative had reshaped prophetic writings—a partial precedent for the Gospels' use of the epistles. I enjoyed teaching the old narratives and prophets, and at the same time, I started trying to express my NT ideas in articles.

I failed. My proposed articles, despite my increasing conviction of their truth, lacked the appropriate idiom and use of secondary literature. They also lacked other elements.

The Second Revolution Deepens

A new phase in my awareness of the ancient use of sources was sparked by a question from Joseph Fitzmyer. In the summer of 1980, during a visit to Washington, D.C., I showed him some of my work—a piece on Luke's use of Chronicles—and, after considering it, he asked a simple question: "Is the process you are invoking found elsewhere in the ancient world?" I could not answer him.

As never before, I started wading through libraries, and eventually hit on the obvious—the pervasive practice of Greco–Roman literary imitation (*mimēsis*) and its sundry ancient analogues, many of them Jewish. What I had noticed within the Bible was the tip of an iceberg. Here was a whole world of diverse ways of deliberately reshaping far–flung sources. Some of this phenomenon had long influenced Biblical Studies, especially in Old Testament circles, but not much. Biblical studies had developed

·in a world where the very concept of any form of imitation was fading, and aversion to the notion of imitation had affected even classical studies. While our high school curriculum included Virgil and Homer, no one mentioned that one imitated the other. Likewise in biblical studies, no one mentioned that Genesis had absorbed and transformed Homer's *Odyssey*. The centrality of imitation and literary transformation was lost. The discussion of the Synoptic Problem—largely a problem of sources— had made little reference to how the rest of the world used sources. And the discussion of John's possible use of the Synoptics had done likewise. It had tended to pose a dilemma between dependence and independence regarding the Synoptics, without taking account of the many ways in which the two could be combined.

I left the lovely job and people in Florida, received the generous gift of a three–year research fellowship at Yale Divinity School, and having started to publish some articles on Luke's imitative use of the LXX, turned again to John. The question was simple: Was it possible, bearing in mind the standard first–century methods of reworking texts, to establish whether John's Gospel had used known Scripture texts—the OT, the epistles, and above all the Synoptics? Following the lead of Louis Martyn in his search for what was happening in the Fourth Gospel and behind it, it seemed appropriate to give special attention to John 9.

For a year (1982 to 1983), I sat with a page containing two columns of Greek text: John's account of the man born blind (ch. 9), and the synoptic text that seemed closest to it—a Markan sequence involving aspects of sight and insight, from discussing signs to the transfiguration (Mark 8:11–9:8). Some of the other students mocked me gently: "You and that page." The evidence favoring John's dependence upon Mark seemed overwhelming—dozens of links, many of them substantial—but there was no clear pattern, and so the evidence as a whole was not convincing. I realized I was trying to explain how John 9 used sources without knowing John's meaning. I started trying to trace the chapter's meaning, but then found I could not do it without examining other chapters. And so, imperceptibly, at first unwillingly, I was drawn into examining the whole Gospel, into writing a commentary.

Eight years later, I returned to the relationship of John 9 to Mark 8:11–9:8 and within a week or two the pattern was clear. Each text may be said to consist essentially of six scenes or pericopes, but John, instead of using each Markan pericope to color just one scene concerning the man born blind, had subdivided each Markan pericope into three distinct aspects and had systematically "dispersed" these aspects among three scenes in John 9. Ironically, Raymond Brown, in comparing John and the Synoptics, had described the essence of this phenomenon in 1961 but had not pursued its possible literary explanation. He had left it, as did others with such data, to an undefined oral tradition. The systematic dispersal explained the complexity of the data, and suddenly the essential pattern of the evidence became clear. Once the dependence of John 9 on Mark 8:11–9:8 had been secured as a test case, it was possible to give an outline of John's use of Mark, Matthew and Proto–Luke. The outline (Brodie 1993b, 67–134) is not at all as elaborate and articulate as I would have liked, but it is essentially true. The publishing outcome was anticlimactic. Scarcely any reviewer attempted to say whether the test case was valid. Apparently the material was too strange and time consuming.

A THIRD REVOLUTION

Meanwhile, as the writing of the commentary continued through the 1980s, I was undergoing a third benign revolution. Robert Alter's *The Art of Biblical Narrative* (1981) did not shock me as did historical criticism and literary rewriting, but it startled me, and it inaugurated further research—into literary criticism, rhetorical criticism, authors such as Luis Alonso–Schökel, Carol Newsom, Meir Sternberg, Jan Fokkelman, Phyllis Trible, Alan Culpepper, Vernon Robbins, and Gail O'Day. Suddenly a mass of data, formerly assigned to a vague mixture of oral tradition, lost sources, and elusive stages of redaction, began to fall into place as the work of one accomplished writer. Strange syntax made more sense as artistry rather than as poor redaction. C. K. Barrett's view of John as dialogical became clearer in light of Carol Newsom's work on the dialogical nature of biblical narrative. And the importance ancient writers attached to a work's beginning, middle, and end helped explain many elements, including why at these three points Mark is most obviously related to the Elijah–Elisha narrative and John, in turn, is most obviously related to Mark.

I learned much about John 9. Here too was authorial unity, but with at least three levels: the life (*bios*) of Jesus; the experiences of the early church; and, surprisingly, the stages of human living and believing. As in Shakespeare's seven ages, John goes from birth to (evoking) death, but while Shakespeare emphasizes outer detail, John uses details to evoke stages that were largely within, particularly stages of believing.

Eventually it began to become clear that, even if the Gospel of John used dozens of sources, every word from beginning to end had been chiseled into its present shape by a single authoritative writer. The prologue's (John 1:1–18) notorious variations of style, a spiraling change from soaring poetry to mundane prose, made complete sense in light of the prologue's central message—the change from Word into flesh. John's distinctive portrayal of a three–year ministry likewise made sense, when analyzed closely, as a way of portraying major stages of a Spirit–led life—a variation on the stages portrayed in John 9. And the problem of John's "double ending" (20:30–31; 21:24–25) fell into place as part of a three–part conclusion (19:35–37; 20:30–31; 21:24–25), for which Proto–Luke gives a partial precedent (Acts 1:1–15:35; cf. triple "it seemed good," 15:22, 25, 28; note references to writing, cf. Luke 1:1–4). Even John's closing hyperbole (21:25) emerged as a well–crafted variation on the Gospel's opening—a form of *inclusio*. John's startling picture of the extent of the writings that would be needed to describe all Jesus had done/made—so vast that they would not all fit into the entire world—is a culminating, down–to–earth variation on the picture of the Word who had made all things from the beginning (1:1–3). The world–surpassing Word had generated the equivalent of world–surpassing writings—a quantity that leaves one guessing how many books it would take (οἶμαι, "I suppose/think").

THE FUNERAL

The three revolutions brought me some understanding, but one of them also brought me baggage. I had grown up believing the Gospels were the product of four great writers who wrote for all Christians, writers who were divinely inspired, their splendor symbolized by visionary animals, including the soaring eagle for John. But in the 1960s, I learned of theories of composition whereby the central energy underlying the Gospels came from oral tradition. The idea seemed plausible, and even when the New Testament's use of the Old Testament was emerging in my awareness, the idea of oral tradition lingered on. Alter woke me up when he described his experience of reading Robert Culley's presentation of the patterns of oral transmission in Genesis. "As I [Alter] stared at Culley's schematic tables, it gradually dawned on me that he had made a discovery without realizing it. For what his tables of parallels and variations actually reveal are the lineaments of a purposefully deployed literary convention. The variations in the parallel episodes are not at all at *random*, as a scrambling of oral transmission would imply" (Alter 1981, 50). Alter's analysis demonstrated that Culley had misread a literary phenomenon as oral, but it did not explain why Culley, along with other biblical scholars, first came to the idea that biblical narrative depends upon oral tradition. Why impose an oral model on a literary phenomenon? And if oral tradition was questionable in the older scriptures, then even more so in the New Testament, where the time span between events and writing was generally less than a lifetime. To take the closest example, my parents often described clearly and verifiably events that had happened more than sixty or seventy years earlier. Their descriptions, whether oral or written, were direct and did not need a process of handing on, or transmission, as the label "oral tradition" generally implies. They just told it essentially as it was—and as I once imagined the four evangelists doing, either because they were present at the original events or had spoken to someone who had been there. So why the idea of oral tradition?

The answer seemed elusive. Speech is so basic to humans—obviously far more than writing—that the idea of oral communication has an immediate plausibility. This is doubly so regarding the ancient world, in which few people could read and the culture was radically oral. And when I looked into the matter—I ended up reading Walter Ong and once went to St. Louis just to talk to him—I found that even writing, for most of its history, resonated with orality. All ancient writing, until the eighteenth century, reflected orality or oral rhythms; it was aural, geared to the ear, to being heard, unlike modern writing, geared primarily to the eye. Virgil's epic was highly crafted writing and a distillation of earlier literature, but it was saturated with orality; it was geared to oral communication, to being heard, and in fact was being read aloud in Augustus's imperial court even before it was complete. But such orality was still not oral tradition, not oral transmission; it was simply a quality of ancient writing.

Studying nonliterate tribes did not help. For them, oral transmission is largely the only option, and their ability to remember masses of very old material does not solve the essential problem: How do you deduce from a piece of writing that it is based on oral transmission? If the variations in the tribes' accounts corresponded broadly to the variations between the Gospels, then oral transmission could account for Gospel relationships. But tribal variations do not correspond to Gospel variations. And neither do the variations within rabbinical methods of memorization.

Searching further, I found a claim to oral tradition at the heart of Judaism. The Pharisees had justified their practices by appealing to an oral tradition that went back to Moses. This Jewish claim would have provided a context for an analogous Christian claim, but when I examined the evidence for the Jewish claim, particularly by dipping into Jacob Neusner, it became clear that it was not based on historical reality.

Eventually, something obvious began to come into focus—the influence of form criticism. Form critics, especially Gunkel and Bultmann, made a major contribution in recognizing diverse literary forms in the Bible, but their presuppositions about the development of history and peoples led them to interpret those forms as tied to local communities and, above all, as oral, not literary. One of the clearest clues to this logic occurs in the introduction to Gunkel's seminal commentary on Genesis.

Gunkel located the biblical people among the "uncultivierten Völker" ("uncultivated peoples"; 1901, i), and because such people were uncultivated, undeveloped, incapable of composing complex works of art, their method of communication was oral. Therefore, their writings resulted from oral tradition. The idea of oral tradition spread not only to students of Genesis such as Robert Culley, but also to New Testament scholars, especially Schmidt, Dibelius, and Bultmann. The idea then passed to Percival Gardner–Smith, and in 1938 he used it to explain the similarities and differences between John and the Synoptics. The result is well known: John became cut off from the Synoptics, isolated, and his mantle of oral tradition endowed him with the potential for carrying an independent historical tradition.

To this day, few researchers attempt to spell out the logic underlying the claim to oral tradition behind the Gospels. With admirable honesty, James Dunn states that oral tradition is a presumption, and he justifies that presumption by saying it is inescapable (2003, 157). With due respect, it is not. The Fourth Gospel, for instance, can be explained increasingly by John's use of extant sources and his theological and literary purposes. Sometimes, of course, it is easy or convenient to invoke oral tradition. Certainly, it is incomparably easier to call upon irretrievable oral tradition than to try to follow the retrievable but complex processes of literary transformation and genius. And when an undefined Johannine oral tradition is combined with an undefined link to the Synoptics, then all bases seem to be covered. But the result is a world of vagueness in which logic is lost, despite fine erudition.

Two essential phenomena remain. First, the variations among the Gospels, including John, fit well among the variations of ancient literary rewriting, but they do not fit well among the variations of oral transmission. Second, the Gospel of John's orality, strong though it is, fits well into the orality of all ancient writing.

The way back from invoking oral tradition will not be easy. Louis Martyn, speaking at a Society of Biblical Literature meeting in Anaheim, California, once described the notion of the Johannine community, including his own version of it, as a genie that had gone out of control and was proving very difficult to put back into the bottle. Likewise with oral tradition. Once the genie was released, it took on a life of its own. Two generations have become so accustomed to the idea that a radical review seems unthinkable. Yet it is time to bring form criticism to a new level of maturity and to free it of unnecessary complications. We need a gentle funeral.

The Quest for History

Having passed through the three revolutions and the funeral, I came
again to the issue of history. Three aspects seemed essential. First, historical criticism as such is valuable. History is like an extension of life, and
in the quest for understanding, knowledge of the past is generally useful
and often indispensable. To avoid historical criticism is to deny evidence
of reality.

Second, historical criticism needs help, particularly from literary criticism—from analysis of sources and artistry. The literary aspect may not
be first in importance—most biblical scholars are understandably more
focused on history and theology—but *methodologically the literary aspect
comes first*. The situation is like building a house. One wants shelter—a
roof over one's head. But one begins with cold messy foundations. If the
foundation is not built first, the walls and roof will not survive. Several
New Testament projects are now expending vast effort on reconstructing
the history of Jesus and the early church, but they have not undertaken
the preliminary literary studies, and therefore do not understand the
nature of the materials they are handling. With respect, they are making
mansions built on sand.

Third, historical criticism is open to abuse. At times, for instance, it
smothers the text with more information than is helpful—like smother-
ing young David with Saul's armor. At other times, it tries to force the
text to yield information that it cannot. Famous examples include asking
the Bible to decide issues about the solar system, about geological ages
(based on the six days of Genesis 1), and, for Bishop Ussher, about the age
of the world. But a problem is also arising in the efforts to squeeze a life
of the historical Jesus from the Gospels. The quest goes round in circles,
and though the circles carry increasing erudition, normal scientific progress is not happening. Raymond Brown, speaking to the Catholic Biblical Association, once described the task of trying to sift history from the
passion narratives as "infuriatingly difficult." And there is a danger that
history is turning into an idol: faith is sometimes being tied to a human
product, empirical history, in the same way that believing in God was
once confused with external compliance with the Law.

The danger of forcing a text to yield alien information is particularly
acute in the case of the Gospel of John. At times, John seems to offer
hope of a distinctive contribution to the quest for the historical Jesus—he
includes true factual elements of history not found in the Synoptics. For
instance, he declares the existence in Jerusalem of a pool with five porti-
cos. But Virgil, in describing the unhistorical journey of Aeneas to Rome,
makes similar factual declarations about genuine places. Information

about people and places other than Jesus is not information about Jesus. Inch by inch, every feature of the Johannine Jesus is being explained by elements other than history, especially by dependence upon other biblical texts and by the requirements of John's visionary narrative. Such explanations do not exclude a historical aspect, but it means history is no longer needed to explain the data, and so the claim can be neither established nor falsified. Data that can be neither established nor falsified is beyond the discipline of history, and therefore beyond any reconstruction of the historical Jesus. Adding vagueness and probabilities does not solve the essential problem.

CONFIRMING THE THREE REVOLUTIONS — THE NEED FOR TIME

Clarification and consolidation of the developments just outlined will need time. Time is particularly necessary in the delicate process of tracing extant sources. Tracing John's reshaping of Mark and Matthew, for instance, generally requires knowledge of ancient transformative practices, and a rigorous application of the criteria for determining literary dependence. Erudition alone is not sufficient, partly because vast erudition can have pivotal blind spots, and also because erudition can be more at ease with hard science. Tracing transformations often requires sympathy with art.

The presence of blind spots is illustrated by the splendid *Anchor Bible Dictionary*. This valuable resource has no entry for literary imitation, or for the leading literary stars of the ancient world, Homer and Virgil (to be accurate, there is an entry under "Homer": "HOMER [Heb *homer*]. See WEIGHTS AND MEASURES"). Even advocates of ancient rhetoric frequently overlook the role of imitation. But time is helping. Imitation/mimēsis has found a place in the latest editions of the *Oxford Classical Dictionary* and *The Cambridge Guide to Literature in English*.

Time is also needed because of the quantity of material to be processed. In tracing just the historical and literary aspects of New Testament backgrounds, at least five major areas need exploring: (1) first–century life and events, including spiritual experience; (2) first–century literary sources and methods; (3) the epistles' multifaceted intertextuality; (4) the interdependence of the Gospels, including Matthew's *logia* and Proto–Luke; (5) the OT/LXX. The gradual rediscovery of the imitation and transformation of the LXX will do far more for NT studies than the discovery of the Dead Sea Scrolls.

The need for time is illustrated by my own experience. Having realized in 1972 that the Elijah–Elisha narrative was pivotal in shaping the Gospels, I kept working regularly on its role, and eventually developed my study of it into a dissertation and a series of articles, but I could never understand why that particular narrative, rather than some other, was given such a role. Only in the 1990s, when my conditions in southern Africa pushed me to concentrate on Genesis, did the reason emerge: the Elijah–Elisha narrative is a synthesis of virtually the entire Genesis–Kings epic. For someone wishing to build a Christ–centered account in continuity with the Old Testament, the Elijah–Elisha narrative provided an ideal starting point or model. This was illuminating, but it meant I needed almost thirty years to make the transition from sensing the role of the Elijah–Elisha narrative to actually publishing even such a preliminary study as *The Crucial Bridge* (Brodie 2000). And I also needed almost thirty years to publish an adaptation of the manuscript that had been ready in 1975 (Brodie 2004).

Time is necessary also in absorbing and assessing older scholarship. At the Baltimore conference to honor Raymond Brown in 2003, Alan Culpepper concluded that only time would tell whether Brown's legacy represents a pinnacle of synthesis or the last holdout of a bankrupt historicism (Culpepper 2005b, 50). Culpepper may be right, but we hardly need apply that stark dilemma to Brown's work as a whole. Although many historical claims for which Brown fought so hard cannot stand the test of time, much of his larger vision—theological and literary—will surely prove in the long term to have been a central contribution both to the church and to scholarship.

Despite the difficulty and the need for time, the sequence of literary dependence proposed above—OT/LXX, Matthew's *logia*, epistles, Proto–Luke, Mark, Matthew, John, Luke–Acts—is incomparably more verifiable than the elusive sequence of stages or lost documents behind the Fourth Gospel proposed respectively by Brown and Boismard. This does not negate the contribution of such scholars, including their insights into some of the text's literary features. Long before I saw the key role of the Elijah–Elisha narrative, Brown had already detected it and partly described it, and with typical courtesy later sent me an offprint (Brown 1971, 86–104). And Boismard, despite the fragility of his larger theses, indicated many specific connections that I would have missed. Such scholars were generally ahead of their disciplines, but there was not time for their insights to be incorporated into new fields, particularly into literary studies.

GLIMMERS OF A CHALLENGING DAWN

In the meantime, while waiting for insights to be absorbed and revolutions to be consolidated, more change seems to be looming—a difficult dawn that moves beyond questions of history and literary criticism and into the world of philosophy and theology. Philosophy in this case includes the truth–bearing role of imagination and art; theology includes spirituality and mysticism. Philosophy is particularly necessary because forcing the historical issue is part of the larger problem of forcing art, including religion and the Bible, into the post–Enlightenment categories of empirical philosophy and method.

The difficulty seemed overwhelming to me when I was concluding *The Birthing of the New Testament* in 2004. I was unable to say what to do with the results. But writing these reflections has helped, as have recent chance encounters with Mary Warnock's *Imagination and Time* (1994), which indicates that imagination is a guide to truth; Douglas Templeton's *The New Testament as True Fiction* (1999); and David Brown's twin volumes on religion and imagination (1999; 2000). I am uneasy with some of these books, yet part of what they are saying seems crucial. However, I am not sure I have the resources to deal with this new line of inquiry, and certainly not within the deadline for submitting these reflections. For the moment, it seems best just to survey aspects of the problem.

The first task is to clarify what John is—and what he is not. To use the story of the ugly duckling, have we identified the animal correctly? What if it is not a duck at all? Obviously, multilayered John is not to be oversimplified, but is it possible, within this complexity, to gain greater clarity about what John is and is not?

First, on what John is. The Fourth Gospel's defining energies may be seen from two elements: (1) the Beloved Disciple, the Gospel's most distinctive character and professed source, and (2) the cascade of breakthroughs in the major scenes.

The experience of being "beloved" is central to the Bible, especially the prophets and Song of Songs. The beloved's presence is intimated in the unnamed disciple who abode with Jesus (John 1:35–39), but he appears most clearly as a foil to Judas and treacherous darkness (13:21–30), and in the Fourth Gospel's three climactic sections: crucifixion (19:16b–37), resurrection (19:38–20:31), and seashore revelation (ch. 21). His presence deepens the entire narrative, evoking a great underlying drama that is fraught with tension but centered on an outpouring of love—logos that involves love. The tension is not only with Judas but also with "the Judeans," often translated as "the Jews"—and misused horrendously in later centuries—but the essence of the drama is positive; and, inspired partly by Romans 9–11, John's larger vision encompasses harmony with the Judeans/Jews. The Beloved Disciple also repeatedly challenges and inspires Peter and Peter's leadership of the community of the Twelve— however one interprets either the leadership or the community. Thus it is of the essence of the Gospel of John that it is written from the viewpoint of one who bears witness to the outpouring and acceptance of God's love. Ultimately this phenomenon is beyond words, and so makes moderns uneasy, focused as we are on calculable results, but it is at the Gospel's center. It is no accident that, as the Gospel ends, grammar breaks down and the text declares that the books of all Jesus' doings would not fit in the world (21:25).

Furthermore, the Gospel of John is pervaded by a cascade of break-throughs—a succession of scenes in which, as love is revealed (love or life or truth), diverse human beings respond to the revelation or fail to respond. Some instances stand out—for instance, the Samaritan woman (ch. 4) and the man born blind (ch. 9)—but in fact each major scene shows a breakthrough to God's truth. Von Balthasar (1986, 251–55) summarizes the pattern. And as already mentioned, John's overall three–year frame-work reflects yet another dynamic of revelation and response. Thus the Gospel spells out the practical implications of Christ's presence insofar as it sketches the many ways in which God's Christ–mediated Spirit works, especially within the fabric of people's daily lives. Amid huge conflict, the center is peaceful—as seen, for instance, in the repeated references to "abiding" (μένω). The Spirit may seem as unpredictable as the wind, but seeing it as our advocate (παράκλητος) brings it closer, and John gives a map of how diverse people progress toward God, like diverse photos of mountain climbers moving toward the peak of Everest. Thus, the Fourth Gospel is a map of spirituality and of mysticism—taking mysticism as connecting with ultimate reality, including people's needs.

In summary, John is essentially a theologian. He is not primarily abstract, but absorbs the message of Christ and clarifies its full dimen-sions—life, truth, love, and their opposites—and its practical implications in human life.

Now, what John is not. The evidence indicates that John is not trying to report distinct historical facts about Jesus. He refashions well–known texts, particularly other Gospels, without concern to preserve history–like detail. His focus is elsewhere, on a spiritual dynamic—God's outpouring through Jesus into people's daily lives and people's breakthrough into the divine. There is no warrant for claiming that the Fourth Gospel is based on oral transmission. And there is no reliable evidence that John's occa-sional factual information contains factual details about Jesus. John's lack of distinctive historical facts about Jesus compounds the larger difficulty of reconstructing a historical Jesus. Perhaps the quest for the historical Jesus will not get much further than Albert Schweitzer's closing para-graph (1906): those who obey Jesus, be they wise or simple, will learn in their own lives who he is. In Schweitzer's life, the learning involved both mysticism and practical love.

This assessment of John involves both gain and loss: the Fourth Gospel portrays a multifaceted process of divine incarnation into daily life, into its historical and social dimensions, but it does not elaborate verifiable facts concerning Jesus, the one at the center of the Christian doctrine of the incarnation.

So what do we make of John's ambiguity—so history–like, yet so unhistorical regarding Jesus? And is it possible to reflect on the historicity of John without reflecting on the other evangelists?

For the moment, it is difficult to see how to move forward. On the one hand, a revered Christian tradition, expressed in the dogma of the Incarnation, solidly maintains that God became a human (Jesus) unique in history and that, quite simply, Jesus was God. On the other hand, as John's Gospel illustrates, literary and historical criticism provides little or no support for a verifiable historical claim about Jesus. And hovering in the wings is a litany of reflections about the meaning of dogma and the Incarnation. Thomas Aquinas, for instance, described dogma as simply tending (*tendens*) toward reality. And Timothy Radcliffe, when head of the Dominican Order, remembered "as a student the dizzy excitement of discovering that the Council of Chalcedon was not the end of our search to understand the mystery of Christ but another beginning, exploding all the tiny coherent little solutions in which we had tried to box him" (Radcliffe 1999, 60). It seems unfair that my first retake of Jesus' words made my heart sink while Timothy Radcliffe's reassessment of Chalcedon made him dizzy with excitement. Yet from such diverse responses, John maps out opportunities for truth.

We need patient literary critics—ready not only to examine John's relationship to the Synoptics in the light of the full range of literary practices of adaptation but also to incorporate the larger underlying issue of the relationship of all four Gospels to the complex intertextuality of the epistles (Brodie, MacDonald, Porter 2006). We need historians who are even more patient, ready to wait until basic literary issues have been resolved. And above all, we need theologians to clarify: (1) John's uplifting vision, including the struggle with evil and death; (2) the tension between the doctrine of the incarnation and the failure of empirical history to locate Jesus reliably; (3) the tension between the emphasis on history and incarnation as found in the Bible, especially in the Johannine Literature, and the (looser?) relationship to history in extrabiblical religions, especially Islam. Writers such as Mary Warnock and Douglas Templeton may not solve the problem, but they need to be heard; so do

Strauss and Lüdemann, albeit very critically; and so do the cloud of biblical–based traditions—Jewish, Catholic, Orthodox, and Reform.

Meanwhile, it is appropriate to be attentive, as John was, to spiritual
experience, including mysticism, and to the debate concerning mysticism
and incarnation (Murray 1991, 76–87). In the end, mysticism and incarnation are not opposed.

> It is by the . . . Christian dogma of the Incarnation that it [mys-
> tical philosophy] has been able to describe and to explain the
> nature of the inward and personal mystic experience. The Incar-
> nation, which is for traditional Christianity synonymous with the
> historical birth and earthly life of Christ, is, for mystics of a cer-
> tain type, not only this but also a perpetual Cosmic and personal
> process. It is an everlasting bringing forth, in the universe and
> also in the individual ascending soul, of the divine and perfect
> life. (Underhill 1911, 118)

I am painfully aware that these reflections are unfinished. There is great
need now for clarity of method, centeredness of spirit, and courage.

THE LAST DISCOURSE

As for Jesus' last discourse (John 13–17), it is not the spontaneous talk
I once imagined. Its three main sections (13–14; 15–16; 17) include
well–crafted portrayals of three stages of spiritual development, of passage through a mind–surpassing mystery of life and death ("the Passover
mystery"). The cleansing in chapter 13 (the footwashing) is intensified in
the more intrusive cleansing of chapter 15 (the pruning/purifying of the
vine), and progression toward holiness is intensified further in chapter
17. In the Bible's revelation of the Spirit coming into action, the last discourse represents a high point.

Yet its roots are old. Among the discourse's many sources, three may
be mentioned: Leviticus, Deuteronomy, and the Sermon on the Mount.
The *foundation*—the discourse's three stages—reflects something of
Leviticus's three levels of atonement–centered holiness (Lev 1–10; 11–
16; and 17–26, the holiness code). The *form* adapts the conventional form
of farewell discourses, including the closing pronouncements of Moses in
Deuteronomy. And the *central content* includes a distillation of the Sermon on the Mount, simultaneously reflecting and reversing aspects of the
sermon's beginning, middle, and end. In simplified terms, the beginning
stays in place, but the center and the end have been interchanged:

- The sermon and discourse both begin where Moses had ended, emphasizing "Blessed . . ." (Deut 33:29; Matt 5:3–10; John 13:17).[1]
- The sermon's center, the Our Father, contributes to the discourse's end (John 17).
- Part of the sermon's ending—the good/bad fruit tree (Matt 7:15–20)—contributes to the discourse's center (the vine, John 15:1–8).

The details are a matter for further research. What is essential is that John has synthesized the heart of the Torah with the idealism of the programmatic Sermon on the Mount, and he has done so even in the shadow of death. The idealism has not died.

> We shall not cease from exploration,
> and the end of all our exploring,
> will be to return where we started
> and know the place for the first time.
> —T. S. Eliot, *Four Quartets* ("Little Gidding")

---

[1] Within the opening statements (Matt 5:3-12; John 13:12-20)—after Jesus has sat on the mountain (Matthew) and after Jesus has resumed his place (John)—the precise positioning of "Blessed" varies from the very beginning (in Matthew) to the center (in John 13:17). Before the Sermon, Matthew indicates ascent, and John evokes descent (Jesus strips and washes feet—one of John's intermittent evocations of descent or ascent).

4: Response

INSPECTING AN AERIAL PHOTOGRAPH OF JOHN'S ENGAGEMENT WITH SOURCES

Catrin H. Williams

For close to five decades, Dr. Thomas Brodie has undertaken what has clearly been an adventurous, indeed life–changing, journey in the company of John's Gospel. This journey has led him to tackle some of the thorniest issues in Johannine scholarship—including the relationship between John's Gospel and the Synoptic Gospels, its indebtedness to the Jewish Scriptures, its possible historical value—and, ultimately, to ask what makes John "tick." As his overarching aim has been to develop a new theory of the Fourth Gospel's composition, a theory which, by his own admission, takes the form of an overview or "aerial photograph" (Brodie 1993a, 68–69) to be scrutinized by others, one may justifiably ask: What are the implications of Dr. Brodie's research on the Gospel's literary development for our understanding of John's compositional methods? Can John be wholly explained by his theologically creative use of extant (written) sources?

Dr. Brodie belongs to a small, but growing, group of scholars who believe that John's literary independence from the Synoptic Gospels can no longer be maintained. He goes much further than most, however, by proposing a pattern of literary relationships that amounts to John's systematic use—and total transformation—of the whole of Mark, significant portions of Matthew and Luke–Acts, and even the letter to the Ephesians.

His "test" analysis of John 9 in *The Quest for the Origin of John's Gospel* (Brodie 1993a, 48–66) draws, to a significant degree, on his own criteria for determining literary dependence, which include external plausibility, thematic and verbal similarities, and intelligibility of differences (cf. Brodie 2004, 43–49). The next generation of Johannine scholars, if attracted to this maximalist hypothesis, will need to establish even tighter controls and more precise points of contact for a significant number of passages in the Fourth Gospel in order to test whether John has in fact undertaken a complete refashioning of earlier "Christian" material, especially the Synoptics. And if John, as Dr. Brodie claims, had ready access to a wide range of extant sources, could the same be true of his first readers or hearers? With the rise of audience–oriented approaches to New Testament texts, the dialogical function of the Fourth Gospel in relation to its addressees (as well as to its sources) urgently needs to be explored. Did John presume that his audience was adequately equipped to recognize the contours and content of his Synoptic source texts? And if so, how was the audience meant to interpret the evangelist's "complex literary transformation" of that material? Further reflection upon these issues may clarify what is meant by John's "use" of the Synoptic Gospels.

Dr. Brodie forcefully, and rightly, challenges us to revisit the notion that oral transmission offers a partial explanation for the composition of John. Nevertheless, I am less confident that now is the time to begin the funeral of oral tradition. This would surely be a premature move, one that would require the eulogist to examine every relevant Johannine passage and ask whether a theory of oral transmission or a theory of thorough reshaping of written sources more plausibly accounts for the similarities and differences between John and the Synoptics. Dr. Brodie is also right to highlight the important distinction between oral transmission and orality, recalling his illuminating conversation with Walter Ong about the prominence of oral/aural techniques in ancient writings. The impact of Professor Ong's insights is, of course, much in evidence in the work of Michael Labahn, who uses the concept of orality to offer a very different account of John's relationship with the Synoptics. Labahn proposes that the Synoptic Gospels influenced John indirectly, not in terms of literary dependence but rather through a process of "secondary orality." His approach suggests that the Johannine tradition was influenced by the continual oral retelling of the Gospel of Mark (which, as Dr. Brodie would agree, is a function suggested by its oral/aural features), but not by direct copying from that text (Labahn 2000a, 272–76). The extent to which one can describe the product of this process of retelling as "oral tradition" requires further discussion, but the increasing recognition among scholars of the highly oral character of the first–century world and of the communicative effect of the Gospels through their oral performance should have a major impact on future Johannine Studies.

I share Dr. Brodie's conviction that John's Gospel is saturated with scriptural motifs and concepts, and I applaud the fact that several recent studies of John's appropriation of the Jewish Scriptures have ventured outside the relative comfort zone of explicit quotations. There is, however, a great deal more work to be done in this area, particularly as John's allusive modes of reference suggest that much of his engagement with Scripture still remains undescribed. It often proves difficult to isolate the precise source(s) of the Fourth Gospel's scriptural references, to define their mode of contact, and to evaluate their precise function in their new Johannine context. Some progress has, nevertheless, been made since the issue of intertextuality was introduced into studies of "the Old Testament in the New," because intertextual analysis challenges the interpreter to adopt a well–defined method in the study of literary relationships. Because John so often refers to the Scriptures obliquely, one must ask whether every possible point of contact is a conscious allusion intended to be recognized by readers/hearers or simply an echo inadvertently taken up from the source text. Although Dr. Brodie makes only one fleeting reference to the term "intertextuality" in his essay for this volume (but cf. Brodie 2004), his appeal to the Greco–Roman practice of "imitation" (*mimēsis*) suggests that this approach should be subjected to similar scrutiny. Biblical scholars are constantly being challenged to define carefully their use of the term "intertextuality," so here we must ask: what method of "imitation" is envisaged in the case of John? Is the proposed imitative process always conscious and deliberate? Similar questions could, of course, be asked of John's "use" of the Synoptic Gospels.

Whether one appeals to Greco–Roman practices of literary imitation or to Jewish traditions of rewriting, transformation, and synthesis, it is certainly appropriate to undertake a comparative analysis of Johannine and other first–century strategies of engaging with extant sources. Brodie's broad overview of the mimetic or transformative practices employed in Greco–Roman or Jewish texts is helpful, and highlights the need to identify and analyze close parallels between these texts and the way(s) in which John appropriates his Jewish and Christian sources. The bird's–eye view offered by Dr. Brodie has opened up all kinds of interesting possibilities, but observation closer to the ground may prove to be an even more exciting venture.

CHAPTER 5

REFLECTIONS UPON A JOHANNINE PILGRIMAGE

D. A. Carson

I must begin by confessing I feel a bit of a fraud. Looking over the list of Johannine scholars who are contributing to this volume, I am impressed by the quality and focus of their work. Some have devoted their entire scholarly lives to matters Johannine (one thinks, for instance, of D. Moody Smith and R. Alan Culpepper), and others, while maintaining academic interest in broader New Testament discussions, have nevertheless made groundbreaking contributions to the field of Johannine studies (How can I not mention J. Louis Martyn and Fernando Segovia?). By contrast, I have written only two serious books on John, neither of them groundbreaking, plus a popular exposition and fewer than a dozen technical articles on the Johannine corpus. I would like to think that my National International Greek Testament Commentary (NIGTC) work on the Letters of John will be in the press by the time these words appear in print, but since I have great confidence in the applicability of Murphy's Law to publishing plans, this is not an announcement. Meanwhile, my writing interests have been spread out (not to say dissipated) across enough areas to qualify me as a jack of all trades. All of this is to say that the generosity of the organizers of this project in inviting me to join this gathering is greatly appreciated, even if their wisdom may be doubted.

Yet without in any way depreciating the remarkable work of the genuine Johannine specialists, perhaps something can be said for those of us who have plodded along a broad path which, if it does not lead to destruction, nevertheless directs us away from a highly focused vision. For there is at least something in favor of the poet who can write more than sonnets, for the engineer who can manufacture more than thumb tacks, for the pilot who can handle more than a single–engine Cessna. For better and for worse, my broader probing means that I remain fascinated by the parallels between, say, John and Hebrews. Many have remarked on the conceptual parallels between their "prologues," but one can also usefully ponder the parallels and differences between their respective emphases on the mediation of the Son, on their underscoring of perseverance as a necessary ingredient of genuine faith, of their respective toying with the links between believing and obedience, and of their knowledge of matters Jewish. Again, while working on Paul's understanding of "justification" within the context of contemporary debates on the "new perspective," I find it difficult to forget C. K. Barrett's famous observation that certain lines from John 5 are the Johannine equivalent of the Pauline insistence that a person is justified by faith apart from the Law. And what conceptual connections might there be between such a perspective and the logical link between John 1:16 and John 1:17, with the latter providing the explanation of the former—i.e., "the law was given by Moses, grace and truth came through Jesus Christ" provides the explanation of John's insistence that in Christ we have received χάριν ἀντὶ χάριτος ("grace against grace")? What force does αντί have? Yet again, having just updated my commentary on Matthew, I am driven to ask myself a question that derives from Martin Hengel's study of the earliest Gospel manuscripts: What is to be made of the fact that, so far as the evidence goes, the earliest Christians did not think of four "Gospels" but of the one gospel of Jesus Christ according to Matthew, Mark, Luke, and John (Hengel 2000)? And why do so many probe the historical Jesus with scarcely a glance at John? One recalls with a wry smile the clever title of Carl Trueman: "Sherlock Holmes and the Curious Case of the Missing Book" (Trueman 2005).

Such reflections bring me to the first of four headings.

REALISM, REJOICING, AND REGRETS

Although there have been some distinctive advances in the field of Johannine Studies during the last three and a half decades, the notion of an "advance" in fields such as Biblical Studies and other arts disciplines is rather different from an "advance" in the so–called "hard" sciences. I began my tertiary education by studying chemistry, with side interests in mathematics. In such disciplines, if someone "advances" the discipline by publishing an important article or book, that article or book becomes part of the platform for all subsequent researches in the same area. In some sense, of course, that is true in Biblical Studies too. But in the hard sciences, the conclusions of such research have usually been so testable, and tested, that it is not just the article or book that becomes part of the platform, the baseline, for fresh work, but rather the conclusions of the article or book. By contrast, the results of biblical research often generate debates about the conclusions of the work, debates that often play with notions of plurality of meaning and the like. In other words, in the "hard" sciences, scholars are more likely working with "hard" data than is the case with biblical specialists, so that there is a corresponding ease in changing the minds of one's colleagues. Of course, I am not describing the far more complex business of bringing about, or helping to bring about, a Kuhnian scientific revolution. Nor am I denying that even within the "hard" sciences, there are sometimes debates over hypotheses that are put forward to explain physical phenomena: one thinks, for instance, of current debates over whether or not string theory will ever reconcile quantum mechanics and the general theory of relativity so as to generate a unified field theory. Yet that debate is highly likely, with time, to be resolved to the satisfaction of everyone working in the field. In other words, I am merely saying that because published articles in chemistry (or physics or biology, etc.) most commonly deal with "hard" data, the extent and ease with which one changes the minds of one's colleagues is far higher than in biblical and other arts disciplines.

The difference must not be overstated, of course. Occasionally in the field of Johannine Studies articles and books are published that deal with the reasonably hard data of, say, a grammatical construction, and the result is widely and rapidly taken up. One thinks, for instance, of Malatesta's study of μένειν ἐν and εἶναι ἐν—it is hard to imagine any competent student of the Gospel of John or of the Johannine Letters not interacting with this study when he or she comes to the relevant texts (Malatesta 1978). But more commonly our research focuses on possible historical and literary backgrounds to the biblical texts, on ostensible instances of intertextuality, on rhetorical devices, on social science analysis of the groups depicted in, or presupposed by, our biblical texts, and so forth. So many of these constructions and reconstructions turn on a web of complicated judgments. The result is that another scholar of equal competence may read exactly the same evidence and emerge with quite different conclusions.

From this elementary observation spring two others. First, one of the things that surprised me when I was first embarking on a life of biblical scholarship was how seldom the minds of mature scholars are substantially changed by new publications. One easily recalls the exceptions, of course—conservative scholars who have become more liberal, and the reverse; scholars who have gradually added new literary tools to their arsenal; scholars who keep expanding their fields of expertise. In fact, once in a very long while, scholars look back over their lives and chart the changes they see in themselves. Witness, for example, Robert Kysar's book *Voyages with John: Charting the Fourth Gospel* (2005c), which documents his move from historical criticism to the adoption of certain postmodern stances. But even such expansions and adaptations tend to be along a certain trajectory. Those who have read, for instance, the *oeuvre* of Raymond Brown right through can easily chart the development of his thought regarding Johannine communities. But although there are tighter and tighter refinements with time, his line is set pretty early in his career. Something similar could be said of, say, Schnackenburg, Bultmann, Culpepper, and other front–rank Johannine scholars. The same is true across much of the field of biblical studies (witness, for instance, the recent essay by David Hawkins, "The Bible and the Modern World: Taking it Personally" [2005–2006]). Pretty soon, then, the people we become most hopeful of influencing are not our colleagues in the discipline, but rather the new generation of doctoral and postdoctoral students who are coming through and who are looking around for mentors. The combination of relatively "soft" data that can be configured in multiple ways, and the firmness of the trajectories that most Johannine scholars begin to hack out early in their careers, soon drives most of us to this restrained expectation. I hasten to insist, once more, that literary/historical studies, including Biblical Studies in general and Johannine Studies in particular, are not of an entirely different character than the studies of the "hard" sciences: we are dealing with different positions along a single epistemological spectrum. Nevertheless, not least for those of us who received our early tertiary education in the "hard" sciences, we have had to adjust our expectations of what "progress" or "advance" in the field of Johannine Studies means.

My second elementary observation here is described at much greater length in another paper first prepared for the John, Jesus, and History Group in the Society of Biblical Literature, "The Challenge of the Balkanization of Johannine Studies." Unlike some other subsets of the field of Biblical Studies, the subset of Johannine Studies now has many, many, subdivisions, each subdivision boasting its own ranks of scholars who are more or less aware of the work of other subdivisions, but who almost never take them into account as they focus on their own primary fields of interest. I do not want to go over that ground again, including the evidence that supports the balkanization thesis, and my ideas about what may or may not be done about it. Yet here, too, realism about the state of Johannine Studies may prompt us to rejoice over the creative energy displayed in the field, while we regret that there is so little unanimity among Johannine scholars, and so little discussion about why this is so.

Most of us, I suppose, have experienced mild disappointment that proposals we have made have not been taken up by more people, or even seriously evaluated. At the risk of too personal an example, I shall mention one of my own mild regrets. A quarter of a century ago, I published an essay that worked through the many kinds of misunderstandings or failures to understand in John's Gospel (Carson 1982). Many others had treated the theme of misunderstanding before I did, of course, and not a few have done so since. But if my essay contributed anything special, it was the attempt to isolate sixteen of these misunderstandings that explicitly distinguish between what the disciples understood about Jesus "back then"—i.e. before the cross and resurrection—and what they came to understand only after. The first of these appears in John 2:22, regarding what Jesus says about the destruction of the temple and his promise to rebuild it in three days; the last is in 20:9, where the Beloved Disciple acknowledges that even at the empty tomb he had not yet come to understand that the Scriptures themselves predicted that Jesus had to rise from the dead. These sixteen misunderstandings, or failures to understand, are resolved by the passage of time, in almost every instance by the insight gained only after Jesus' resurrection. In other words, they constitute explicit evidence that the evangelist was not only capable of distinguishing between what the disciples understood "back then" and what they came to understand only later, but that he insisted upon it. I do not think that these textual phenomena have been adequately probed for their bearing on the evangelist's ability and efforts to maintain historical distinctions. These phenomena are very difficult to square with any simple "two levels" theory of referentiality: nor have such phenomena been adequately probed for what they say about the evangelist's understanding of how the first disciples came to "read" Scripture in a different way, a Christian way. For on the one hand, the evangelist keeps insisting that the crucial events in Jesus' life and passion and resurrection fulfill Scripture, and on the other hand he acknowledges—indeed, insists—that the disciples themselves did not read Scripture this way until after the events. Thus we come by another route to something analogous to the dominant notion of μυστήριον in the Pauline corpus: the gospel is simultaneously said to be hidden in times past but now disclosed, and prophesied in times past and now fulfilled (see further Carson 2001). I cannot reflect further on such matters here, except to offer my conclusion that John's Gospel treats the mystery theme as tellingly as any New Testament writer, without using the word "mystery"—just as he can rightly be called the evangelist of the covenant people of God, even though he never uses the word "covenant" (see, among many others, Pryor 1992; Chennattu 2006).

Such reflections bring us to the next section.

HISTORY AND HERMENEUTICS

Without wanting to disparage in the slightest the many literary–critical, narrative–critical, biblical–theological, and social–science approaches to the Fourth Gospel around today, one does get the impression that, by and large, the driving forces behind much contemporary Johannine scholarship ignore historical questions. To put it more charitably, when historical questions are raised with respect to John's Gospel, there is widespread assent that some modicum of historical tradition is preserved in this book, but little agreement how much—and in any case, that modicum of historical tradition rarely makes any difference in reconstructions of the historical Jesus. The overwhelming majority of those who engage in such reconstructions focus almost all their attention on the Synoptic Gospels—or, if John is studied at all, he is treated to an extra volume outside the principal discussion.

The reasons for this state of affairs are many and complicated, and they begin with the transparent differences between John's Gospel and the other three canonical Gospels. But among the reasons is the widespread view that John was early praised by the Gnostics and substantially ignored by the orthodox of the second century. As a result, it took quite a long time for orthodox Christians to value this Gospel and to include it in the canon, and they did so primarily under the influence of Irenaeus. This assured result, passed on from scholarly generation to scholarly generation, has now been killed and laid to rest in an important book by Charles E. Hill, *The Johannine Corpus in the Early Church* (2004). What he calls the "OJP" (= the "Orthodox Johannophobia Paradigm") must be abandoned. Whether or not one agrees with all of Hill's detailed arguments, he has certainly established, beyond reasonable cavil, that the situation was precisely the opposite of the OJP. Orthodox Christians, including the author of the long ending of Mark, Aristides, Melito, and Tatian cheerfully used and rapidly accepted John's Gospel, and consequently also the four–Gospel canon. Within one generation of its publication, John's Gospel was accepted as Scripture in Syria, Asia, Rome, and Gaul. With the exception of only one man, John's Gospel was not subjected to a "hands off" policy by the orthodox. By contrast, most of the Gnostics viewed John's Gospel with reserve, not to say outright suspicion. The OJP is dead: R.I.P.

There are two entailments to the death of this notion. First, throughout the second century, if the Fourth Gospel was seen by orthodox believers as part of the fourfold gospel—i.e. as contributing to and supportive of the one gospel of Jesus Christ according to Matthew, Mark, Luke, and John—we probably ought to make more of an effort to attempt similar integration. One begins to wonder whether John was ever quite as sectarian as he is often made out to be. Despite the provocative and stimulating thesis of Richard Bauckham, who argues that all four canonical Gospels were originally written for "all Christians" and not for some Christian community hermetically sealed off from the rest of the Christian world, one must at least acknowledge that the Fourth Gospel is related in some fashion or other to the three Johannine Epistles, and they, transparently, are occasioned by specific problems in specific churches—they are not universal encyclicals, not "general epistles." Still, between the expansive thesis of Bauckham and the narrowness of an assumed sectarianism, there is a lot of room to maneuver—and here, the evidence of Hill must be allowed to play its part. From the time when we can actually measure the reception of the Fourth Gospel, its good news, and thus its Jesus, were seen as of a piece with the one gospel, the one Jesus, of the synoptic tradition.

Second, these realities have a bearing on another discussion that occupies only a fringe of contemporary scholarship, but it is an increasingly vociferous fringe. I suppose it would be more accurate to imagine a spectrum. At one end, a lot of mainstream scholars operate; at the other end of this spectrum, relatively few. Yet the entire spectrum reaches at least a few conclusions that deserve further reflection, and at the minority end of the spectrum, most of us should be throwing down the gauntlet. At the heart of the spectrum that I have in mind is the attempt to make early Christianity astonishingly diverse, with the ostensibly orthodox playing the role of the bad guys as they outmaneuvered and finally managed to crush all opposition and squeeze out those lovely Gnostics (so, in sum, Pagels 2003). Some of this runs back to the influential work of Walter Bauer, *Orthodoxy and Heresy in Earliest Christianity* (1934), whose title, astonishingly, leads the reader to expect an analysis of orthodoxy and heresy in earliest Christianity, even though Bauer focuses his attention on the second century. Many scholars have responded to Bauer, whether in support or in criticism, and this is not the place to review that complicated literature (though see especially Trebilco 2006). From my perspective, a book such as Galatians, among the earliest of the New Testament documents, and a book such as 1 John, among the latest of the New Testament documents, both attest an awareness of a distinction between faithful and unfaithful stances, complete with an anathema, or a label such as "antichrist," for those who are judged too far outside. The real questions, for our purposes, are two:

(1) How far were such distinctions between "orthodoxy" and "heterodoxy" (for want of a better generic word pair) in agreement with each other in the first century, and thus mutually confirming, and how far were they such occasional stances that it would be closer to historical reality to infer that each group was pronouncing what was orthodox and what was heretical, thereby fueling the fires of unbounded sectarianism?
(2) Is there any believable evidence that the kind of movements reflected in second, third, and fourth–century Gnostic sources were alive and well in the first century, contributing to this mix?

It is this second question that interests me at the moment. Perhaps I can address this question by coming at it tangentially. Scholarship is still divided on whether or not there was a single, well–defined document that we call Q. I remain uncertain; perhaps there were several overlapping sayings sources. But as the spectrum I have been discussing narrows down a little toward the Jesus Seminar end, we find some loud claims to the effect that Q was not only a distinguishable and largely retrievable source, but that it should be thought of as the "Q Gospel." This "Q Gospel," linked perhaps with the *Gospel of Thomas*, competes, in the minds of those at this narrower end of the spectrum, with the four canonical Gospels, to help establish the breadth of first–century Christianity. And as the spectrum narrows down yet further and yields to the media's endless infatuation with what is novel, we find a place for the contribution of the *Gospel of Judas* in the re–creation of Christianity's historical roots. And then, of course, we find all this diversity nicely reflected in Dan Brown's *The DaVinci Code*.

I seem to have got a long way from my Johannine pilgrimage. But perhaps not. A handful of observations will delineate the connections that my wandering mind discerns.

First, I return to the fact that the actual evidence makes John part of the fourfold one gospel (i.e., that in the first century, there was simply "the gospel" according to Matthew, Mark, Luke, and John [see especially Hengel 2000; 2005; Piper 2005]). The presentation of this good news began, in all four cases, with the public ministry of John the Baptist announcing one who was coming after him. It surveyed, in all four cases, the ministry of Jesus, including his teaching, miracles, death, and resurrection. His death and resurrection are thus so endemic to this "good news" that the old saw about the canonical Gospels being passion narratives with extended introductions is not entirely without warrant—but in any case, in the first century, there is no evidence that they were considered "four Gospels," canonical or otherwise. Rather, they were four books that bore witness to "the gospel," the one gospel of Jesus Christ. Thus it is more than a little misleading when Johannine scholars, to go no further, begin their attempts at unraveling the nature of the book we call "the Gospel of John" by appealing to second–century distinctions in the meaning of the word "gospel" (e.g., Carter 2006, 4–5).

Second, this is entirely in line with Paul's perception when he wrote to the Corinthians: the gospel he passed on to them as a matter of first importance (I think it is marginally more likely that ἐν πρώτοις establishes the importance of the subject rather than merely the time Paul dispensed it) could be summed up by the assertions "that Christ died for our sins in accordance with the scriptures, and that he was buried, and that he was raised on the third day in acordance with the scriptures, and that he appeared" to various witnesses (1 Cor 15:3–5). In other words, the gospel that Paul preached and that the Corinthians embraced was not only profoundly christological, but it was the Christology of the cross and resurrection. The Paul who declared that he resolved to focus on Christ crucified would not have recognized an ostensible Gospel of sayings detached from the great redemptive events.

Third, whether or not Q ever existed independently as a well–defined document—let us assume for the moment that it did—there is not a single scrap of evidence that it was ever recognized in the first century—or in any century before the twentieth, for that matter—as a "Gospel." How could it be? In the first century, not even the books that came to be thought of as the canonical "Gospels" were thought of as Gospels. One can understand that eventually "Gospel" became a designation for a certain literary form: it is first used to refer to a written gospel–book about the time of Bar–Kokhba (130s C.E.; see the important work of Horbury 2005, 10), and in due course the Fathers could speak of "the gospel of Matthew," and the Gnostics could speak of "the gospel of Peter"; but in the beginning it was not so. To speak of "the Q Gospel" is massively anachronistic and painfully misleading. A document of sayings more or less aligned with what we call Q may well have existed, but in the first century it could not possibly have been called "the gospel of Jesus Christ according to Q" (if we let "Q" stand for a person rather than for "Quelle," [source]).

Fourth, despite the best efforts of some scholars to assign the *Gospel of Thomas* to the first century, many scholars remain unconvinced. There is increasing evidence that it reflects second–century Syrian Christianity. But in any case, a collection of 114 sayings plus a couple of tiny historical snippets is not "the gospel of our Lord Jesus Christ according to Thomas."

Fifth, the same objections apply to the *Gospel of Judas*. Add the confusion furnished by some in the media, who have frequently avowed that the document appears to be "authentic," and the possibility of widespread historical misunderstanding is almost guaranteed. Of course the document appears to be "authentic": it appears to be an authentic third– or fourth–century copy of the *Gospel of Judas* to which Irenaeus referred in *Against All Heresies* about 180 C.E. It is not, however, "authentic" if that word were to suggest any substantive connection with the historical Judas Iscariot. As Simon Gathercole of the University of Aberdeen has memorably put it, the *Gospel of Judas* has the same sort of connection with Judas that a newly discovered CD of Queen Victoria's Journals, in which she gives her thoughts on *The Lord of the Rings*, would have with Queen Victoria; or, in the words of Adam Gopnik in the *New Yorker*, "The finding of the new Gospel [of Judas] . . . no more challenges the basis of the church's faith than the discovery of a document from the nineteenth century written in Ohio and defending King George would be a challenge to the basis of American democracy." The world of the *Gospel of Judas* is the world of late second and early third–century Gnosticism, complete with esoteric teaching that only Judas Iscariot understands, replete with the dualism that Gnosticism typically espouses and that any believer in the resurrection of Jesus had learned to decry (the Jesus of the *Gospel of Judas* wants Judas to betray him and thus "sacrifice the man that clothes me"), devoid of any substantive connection with first–century Palestine or historical references, and promoting a Jesus who sounds like a condescending, smart–mouthed alien rather than the Messiah who weeps over Jerusalem and goes to the cross to give his life a ransom for many.

Yet we find a handful of scholars, at the narrowest end of the spectrum, assuring us that what the *Gospel of Judas* provides is further evidence that nascent Christianity was wonderfully diverse and plastic. Here is Elaine Pagels: "What is clear is that the Gospel of Judas has joined the other spectacular discoveries that are exploding the myth of a monolithic Christianity and showing how diverse and fascinating the early Christian movement really was" (2006). Well, yes, I suppose so, if by "the early Christian movement" one is referring to the middle of the second century and later, and if one takes umbrage at any effort to say another group is wrong, and if one is happy to adopt the most amazing historical anachronisms when the actual historical data get in the way of a well–spun thesis. But if we all take a deep breath and become at least a little suspicious of postmodernism's infatuation with boundless diversity, we may return to sufficient historical rigor to smile at the lack of evidence. It's been fun; now let's get serious.

So we have arrived at the odd place where some scholars will deploy all their considerable skills to make John's Gospel appear as historically worthless as possible, despite the powerful first– and second–century evidence to the contrary, while assigning late second– and third–century Gnostic documents a voice in the creation of first–century history. That these documents were in fact condemned as heretical by second– and third–century Christians gives them an added cachet in the eyes of conspiracy buffs. The more obvious explanation is largely ignored: they were heretical and deserving of condemnation. Nevertheless, the problem with these reconstructions is not, in the first instance, bad theology, but rather bad history, grounded in profoundly flawed hermeneutical practice. One recalls the advice of C. S. Lewis: "Agnosticism is, in a sense, what I am preaching. I do not wish to reduce the skeptical element in your minds. I am only suggesting that it need not be reserved exclusively for the New Testament and the Creeds. Try doubting something else" (1975, 122).

Grammar and Gratitude

Johannine scholarship, as with other branches of biblical scholarship, has felt the impact of adjacent disciplines, and, as a result, has spawned a plethora of cross–disciplinary specialisms: social science approaches to the Fourth Gospel, socio–rhetorical approaches to the books of this corpus, postcolonial readings, and an array of other approaches similarly "against the grain." But one adjacent area in which considerable work has been done, but which has, so far, had relatively little impact on Biblical Studies in general and Johannine scholarship in particular, is the study of Greek, especially as nourished by the burgeoning field of linguistics.

A glance backward will remind us of another time when a seismic shift took place in our understanding of Greek. The Renaissance began the restoration of the study of Greek and Hebrew by Christians in Europe, but of course the *lingua franca* for scholars remained, for a long time, Latin. Partly because of the influence of Latin, during the entire Rationalist period in Europe the Greek verbal system was assumed to be essentially time–based. Straightforward reading of the texts showed that there were countless exceptions, of course, but the controlling paradigm did not quickly change. Eventually, however, the sheer number of exceptions fostered major rethinking, and in the late–eighteenth century and throughout the nineteenth century the category of *Aktionsart* was incorporated into the analysis of the Greek verb as such analysis was undertaken by almost all Western scholars. In the indicative mood, the (morphological) tenses were, by and large, understood to be proper tenses (i.e., the morphemes grammaticalized time distinctions); but outside the indicative mood, the tenses grammaticalized "kind of action." Probably almost everyone who reads these lines was brought up under this analysis of the Greek verbal system, not understanding that three hundred years ago no one was brought up under this analysis of the Greek verbal system.

It was not long before the inadequacies of *Aktionsart* began to become apparent. Already at the end of the nineteenth century, a few probing essays made their way into *Classical Review* and elsewhere. This history is now so well known I need not repeat it here. A French work in the 1940s (Holt 1943) and a Spanish work in the 1970s (Mateos 1977) moved toward aspect theory, but they did not receive the attention they deserved, even though they doubtless helped prepare the way for the groundbreaking works by Porter (1989), Fanning (1990), McKay (1994), and the plethora of essays and books that followed in their train.

Yet it has to be said that far too little of this work has been absorbed by New Testament scholars and incorporated into their commentaries and exegetical essays. We ought to be poised for a major paradigm shift in the study of the Greek verb, but crossover flow from Greek and linguistics to New Testament commentary writing, and, more broadly, to exegetical essays and monographs, is still rather rare. Part of the reason is that some of the groundbreaking work is couched in linguistic jargon that some New Testament scholars find impenetrable. But that is not the only reason. And meanwhile, linguistic developments in other domains pertaining to Greek, apart from the verbal system, have not lagged behind. The study of words has been chronicled most impressively by John Lee (2003): Appeal to translation glosses is becoming less and less respectable. The careful study of relevant words in the papyri pertinent to New Testament exegesis is being capably undertaken by a team in Australia. The recent book by O'Donnell (2005) is now the best survey of the very substantial developments across the entire field of linguistics that pertain to our understanding of the Greek of the New Testament.

One understands the reasons why commentary writers might be reluctant to embark on work that bountifully deploys the vocabulary of these linguistic developments, when so few of our readers are trained in the field. Even if we could get such manuscripts past our editors, we might succeed in nothing more than guaranteeing limited sales. Nevertheless, at some point or other our gratitude for the genuine linguistic advances that have been made in the last fifty years must find expression in our work somewhere. For myself, I am particularly grateful that the editors of the NIGTC series have graciously granted me permission to include a lengthy appendix in my forthcoming commentary on the

Johannine Letters—an appendix that will explain some of the vocabulary and concepts that are used throughout the commentary. Either this will be one more small step toward a wider use of knowledge from this adjacent field within Johannine Studies, or, quite conceivably, it will sink like a stone to oblivion—some would doubtless say, well–deserved oblivion. We shall see.

CONFUSION AND CONFESSIONALISM

Many of us resort to the conservative/liberal polarity for cubbyholing biblical scholars. It can, I suppose, be a useful shorthand. But when I was a graduate student at Cambridge University, I learned in the most powerful way possible—that is, by example—how tricky those categories can be, primarily because they can refer to selective axes. The faculty of the Divinity School of that esteemed university included, on the one hand, John A. T. Robinson, whose views on critical matters to do with John's Gospel were considerably more conservative than mine, but whose understanding of the theological content of John was astonishingly liberal (see, for instance, the eighth chapter of his *The Priority of John*, 1985); and, on the other, John C. O'Neill, who on many critical matters makes members of the Jesus Seminar look like fundamentalists, managing to doubt, for instance, that the apostle Paul wrote more than two–thirds of Galatians (O'Neill 1972), and yet vociferously defending the view that substitutionary atonement is taught in the New Testament documents. One begins to wonder how many separate axes amenable to the liberal/conservative polarity could be identified. For instance, some scholars, temperamentally, drift toward the traditional, though what is judged "traditional" varies enormously; conversely, other scholars are attracted to the innovative, not to say the esoteric. And then, of course, there are more complicated axes: some keep working "behind" the text, some focus on the text itself, and others devote their energy to what is "in front of" the text. Each of these approaches necessarily smuggles in an array of epistemological, theological, and other assumptions.

One of the newer axes—it was essentially unknown when I was starting out—is established by the poles "univocal (= single) meaning" to be diligently pursued (however difficult to attain, and however humbly we articulate what that meaning is) and "open–ended meanings," generated by different methods or by the different stances of the interpreters. In North America, though no longer, by and large, in Europe, this debate is often cast in terms of the impact of postmodernism. However this polarity is assessed, it is important to recognize that there is a spectrum of opinion. For instance, a little in from one end, a scholar might contend that although there is univocal meaning in the text, some part of that meaning very likely remains hidden to people from one culture, yet proves to be transparent to people from another culture who bring another set of questions. Yet this stance remains distinguishable from those who think that each stance is equally insightful or valid or true. After all, a slightly more "conservative" take on this cultural bifurcation would argue that once the people from the first culture have explained their context and questions to the people from the second culture, and vice versa, the two people groups are able to argue back and forth, with reasonable intelligence, as to whether or not any particular interpretation of the text is "really there." If the consensus is positive, this may result in a fresh synthesis of understanding of the text, both people groups benefiting and both finding that the enlarged interpretation is in fact generated by the text itself. Conversely, frank discussion may gradually force belated recognition that at least one of the inherited interpretations cannot in fact be justified by the text itself. Many other points along the spectrum could easily be described.

Yet the poles themselves are so fundamentally mutually antithetical that defenders of these poles can be fairly scathing of one another. It might be useful to give an example drawn from the broader field of philosophy of religion before we remind ourselves of their equivalents in the ranks of Johannine scholarship.

On the one side, we may choose a brief essay by Keith Ward in *Church Times* (2 December 2005) titled "True Protestants Allow Diversity." Ward's argument is that voices within the Anglican communion that seek to establish themselves by appealing to loyalty to "biblical faith" are chasing a chimera. They assume that their interpretation of the Bible is the one and only acceptable interpretation. But the Reformers themselves, Ward argues, rejected a view of the church as a hierarchical organization that had the right to impose doctrinal and moral standards. The Reformers insisted on salvation by faith, i.e. by personal trust in Christ—and "[s]uch faith does not require or entail that all your beliefs are correct." In other words, the Reformation cherished the right of dissent and liberty of conscience: these values "are essential to the very existence of Protestantism." Interpreters of the Bible can and do err but may still have true faith. Ward accepts Kierkegaard's understanding of faith: as a passionate commitment made in objective uncertainty. The early Protestants sought release from the dogmatic strictures of the Roman Catholic Church. In this light, "biblical Protestantism," Ward avers, is "a contradiction in terms," for no human being or group of human beings "has the magisterial authority to issue the 'correct' interpretation of the Bible." Thus, those movements within Anglicanism that seek to return to the Reformation "are in fact committed to undermining the Reformation. They are putting in its place an authoritarian dogmatism of just the sort the Reformers were trying to escape. They are either misunderstanding or betraying the principle of justification by faith alone. Is it not time they began to repent?"

On the other side, we may choose one of the fairly recent essays by Alvin Plantinga (2003). His contribution is full of insight regarding the various trajectories of historical criticism. On the way by, he takes this swipe at postmodern open–endedness:

> Of course, various postmodern hermeneuticists aim to amuse by telling us that in this case, as in all others, the author's intentions have nothing whatever to do with the meaning of a passage, that the reader herself confers upon it whatever meaning the passage has, or perhaps that even entertaining the idea of a text having meaning is to fall into 'hermeneutical innocence'—innocence, oddly enough, which (as they insist) is ineradicably sullied by its inevitable association with oppressive, racist, sexist, homophobic and other offensive modes of thought. This is indeed amusing. Returning to serious business, however, it is obvious (given that the principal author of the Bible is God) that the meaning of a biblical passage will be given by what it is that the Lord intends to teach in that passage, and it is precisely this that biblical commentary tries to discern. (Plantinga 2003, 26)

So Ward's article argues for openness to diverse interpretations, and for principled insistence that any view could be wrong, and for a refusal to promote doctrinal standards that become exclusionary. Plantinga, however, agues that the biblical text enjoys God–given definite meaning that interpreters must in principle pursue and may in fact find. Because these two scholars are targeting quite different opponents, it is possible that both would trim their sails if their opponents changed. On a good day I might optimistically imagine how the two stances could, with a little patience and a lot of discussion, be reconciled. Still, the polarization is remarkable—and it is merely exemplary of much more of the same.

So it is not surprising that the same polarity is found in the world of Johannine scholarship. I have already mentioned the recent book of Robert Kysar (2005c). In his present mood (but will he change his outlook yet again?), Kysar insists that attempts to distinguish tradition, source, and redactions in the Gospel of John, attempts in which he himself was once fully invested, "are now tiresome, exhausted, and largely irrelevant" (2005c, 247). Not only can there be "no purely objective and scientific interpretation of Scripture," but the notion of "the author's intention" is hopeless: we must think, rather, of "the *interpreter's intention for the passage*" (Kysar 2005c, 248, emphasis original). As for John 6 and his own repeated efforts to interpret that passage across the decades, Kysar now concludes that the chapter is "hopelessly ambiguous and no amount of research or study will (or even should) finally resolve that ambiguity" (2005c, 249).

Contrast these assertions with a not atypical passage from C. K. Barrett. Barrett provides a detailed exegesis of John 1:1, then reflects on his own conclusions: "John intends that the whole of his gospel shall be read in the light of this verse. The deeds and words of Jesus are the deeds and words of God; if this be not true the book is blasphemous" (1978, 156). There does not seem to be much room for ambiguity here, yet not for a moment should one dare to think that Barrett is hopelessly naive. I recall with pleasure, and a whiff of terror, the first question he put to me when in 1975 he served as the external examiner of my dissertation at the University of Cambridge. "Mr. Carson," he said, "you have written with clarity on matters Johannine. I think I always understand what you are saying. But tell me, do you think that John would have had the slightest interest in your work?" Of course, the question was wickedly intimidating. The more I thought about it, the more I could peel away layer after layer of subtlety and detect even more ways to respond. I suppose I mumbled enough to get by, since I was awarded the degree, but I am in no place to suspect that Prof. Barrett has not thought long and hard about readings behind the text, of the text, and in front of the text, not to mention the challenges brought by readers located in different cultural settings and different centuries. Yet still he dares to articulate his interpretation of what John means by one of his sentences, and to perceive its personal and even transcendental claim: If what John is saying is not true, he is writing blasphemy. I suspect that Barrett is closer to understanding both John and Irenaeus than either Walter Bauer or Elaine Pagels.

The question, I suppose, is this: Whence this confessionalism? Or, to address the corresponding question to the other side, Whence this dogmatic anticonfessionalism? Even to nibble at the edges of the discussion that these two questions call forth would immediately triple or quadruple the length of these rather personal reflections on my own Johannine pilgrimage. Such answers as there are would drag into the circle of discussion not only all the tools of exegesis and criticism, but epistemological matters, linguistic matters, churchmanship, the broadest exploration of worldview and culture, even moral choices and, in suitably Johannine terms, the gift of God and the work of the Paraclete. But I confess I find myself on the confessional side of this discussion. However much I want to learn charitable caution and suitable humility not only from my colleagues but from the impact of some strands of postmodern thought, I doubt that "humility" is the right term to describe the boundless creativity that uses the Johannine corpus as a springboard for nothing more than the projection of contemporary ideas. Although his whimsical language belongs neither to John nor to the guild of Johannine specialists, G. K. Chesterton's oft–quoted passage on humility springs to mind.

> What we suffer from today is humility in the wrong place. Modesty has moved from the organ of ambition. Modesty has settled upon the organ of conviction; where it was never meant to be. A man was meant to be doubtful about himself, but undoubting about the truth; this has been exactly reversed. . . . The new skeptic is so humble that he doubts if he can even learn. . . . There is a real humility typical of our time; but it so happens that it's practically a more poisonous humility than the wildest protestations of the ascetic. . . . The old humility made a man doubtful about his efforts, which might make him work harder. But the new humility makes a man doubtful about his aims, which makes him stop working altogether. . . . We are on the road to producing a race of man too mentally modest to believe in the multiplication table. (Chesterton 1957, 31–32)

I hope that when I die I will be remembered as a Johannine scholar who wanted above all to be a Christian pilgrim and a churchman. Is it the virtue of humility being displayed when John's confidence is entirely lost? Should not at least some Johannine interpreters echo John's testimony, "I write these things to you who believe in the name of the Son of God, that you may know that you have eternal life" (1 John 5:13)? This, I suggest, is not a weaker position or a merely traditional position. Every approach brings with it the capacity to ask questions and hear answers that might not be allowed by some other approach. I freely admit that I might not ask all the questions raised by, say, a colleague who is primarily driven by postcolonial concerns. But equally, I submit that he or she is unlikely to ask some of the questions that I am likely to bring to the text.

For instance, the fact that the Johannine corpus does not mandate love for one's enemies but has a great deal to say about love for the others in the Johannine community is often taken as one of the bits of irrefutable evidence that this community is sectarian. Entire doctoral dissertations have been constructed out of this initial observation and inference. But I suspect the chain of reasoning is flawed. I mention three factors. First, Matthew's Gospel, which does preserve the command to love one's ene-

mies, characterizes opponents in language every bit as blistering as anything found in the Fourth Gospel and the Johannine Epistles (Matt 23).
In short, is the presence or absence of a command to love one's enemies
proof (or even strong evidence) of anything about the sectarian nature or
otherwise of the community? Second, within John's Gospel, God's love
for the "world" (John 3:16) is of a piece with the "grace and truth" par
excellence that have come to us in the gospel (John 1:14–18): God's love
is to be praised not because the world is so big, but because the world is so
bad. In other words, in his own idiom John emphasizes God's love for his
enemies without using the word "enemies," and sweeps Christ's followers
up into the same love–prompted mission (e.g., John 15:27). Granted that
John's array of ethical injunctions is (as everyone acknowledges) considerably narrower than that found in Matthew, nevertheless it has its own
peculiar depth and must not be domesticated by mere appeal to the latest sociological theories as to what constitutes sectarianism. Third, and
above all, love among the believers is in certain respects to be an imitation
of, a correspondence to, the love between the Father and the Son (John
17), a reflection of God's love (1 John 4). Are we being quite faithful to
John's thought when we infer that the love between the Father and the
Son on which the believers' mutual love is patterned is intrinsically sectarian? Surely, something is wrong with the categories.

    In short, the confessional approach I bring to the interpretation of
the Johannine corpus, whatever its limitations, sanctions a certain independence from strong currents within the guild of New Testament scholars, and I do not find that to be a disadvantage. In fact, a confessional
approach may even claim that it is more likely to listen sympathetically to
the text than some others. Isn't that a good thing?

5: Response

PROGRESS AND REGRESS IN RECENT JOHANNINE SCHOLARSHIP
REFLECTIONS UPON THE ROAD AHEAD

Andreas J. Köstenberger

It is an entirely undeserved privilege to be allowed to add a few reflections of my own to those of my esteemed mentor, D. A. Carson. Most of what I know about matters Johannine I have learned from him, so I can hardly hope to add anything substantive to his highly perceptive observations. My brief comments will revolve around the following two questions raised in Carson's essay: (1) Why do so many probe the historical Jesus with scarcely a glance at John?, and (2) What constitutes "progress" in biblical scholarship, in general, and in Johannine Studies, in particular?

The answer to the first question is, of course, that John is very different from the Synoptics, so that many feel they have to choose between the two. Most opt for the Synoptics and hold that John is interested in theology, not history. This conventional wisdom, however, has recently been challenged by a remarkable phalanx of scholars (M. Thompson 1996; Hengel 1999; Blomberg 2002; Köstenberger 2002). The establishment of the John, Jesus, and History Group in the Society of Biblical Literature is also indicative of the dissatisfaction felt by many regarding this simplistic way of construing the relationship between the Synoptics and John. The reassessment, if not rehabilitation, of the historical reliability of John's Gospel—call it the "second look"—is one of the most heartening recent developments in Johannine scholarship.

The other fascinating question raised by Don Carson's essay is that of "progress" in biblical scholarship. As recently as 1990, D. Moody Smith could state without fear of contradiction that J. Louis Martyn's version of the "Johannine community hypothesis" constituted one of the assured paradigms in Johannine study on which others could confidently build their own theories (1990, 293 n. 30). A decade and a half later, this consensus has significantly eroded. In fact, some former proponents of the hypothesis have publicly renounced it (e.g., Kysar 2005b; cf. Kösten-berger 2004, 1–3), while others have severely criticized it as inadequately taking into account the testimony of the early church (Hengel 1993) and as being at odds with first–century Christianity (Bauckham 1998), not to mention the difficulty the Johannine mission theme presents for radically sectarian readings of John's Gospel (Köstenberger 1998).

What only a short while ago seemed to be a common foundation of Johannine scholarship has thus given way to a state of things in which "the center does not hold." The Johannine Literature Section of the Society of Biblical Literature has turned increasingly to an exploration of diverse readings in the spirit of postmodernism. Don Carson speaks of the "bal-kanization" of Johannine Studies and notes the absence of widely accepted paradigms. In fact, it appears that, efforts at integration notwithstanding, the discipline is in considerable ferment if not disintegration (cf. Guth-rie 1999). This state of affairs, in my view, is tied to the just–mentioned notion of "progress" in biblical scholarship. Too often, traditional views in Johannine scholarship have been overturned not on the basis of new, bet-ter evidence, but rather on the basis of different philosophical presupposi-tions that have led scholars to abandon long–held views in favor of those more in keeping with their larger perspectives on Scripture (Köstenberger 2001). At the end of his article, Don Carson suggests that there may be certain benefits to what he calls "confessional" Johannine scholarship (as well as perils to "dogmatic anticonfessionalism"). I think he has put his finger on a key question, namely whether rejecting various doctrinal com-mitments as out of bounds for biblical scholarship has really advanced the discipline and led to discernible progress.

In fact, I would go even further than Carson. If much of recent Johannine scholarship turns out to be a blind alley, if not a step in the wrong direction, I submit that we should not politely compliment such scholars for their valuable contribution to the field; we should, rather, refuse to call this "progress." "Progress" in Johannine scholarship should not be conceived in evolutionary terms, as if "more recent" necessarily means "more accurate." Rather, the burden of proof should be placed on newer theories to show how they are superior to conventional ways of conceiving of the nature of John's Gospel. Can it be that at least in certain ways precritical exegesis may be superior to recent scholarship (Steinmetz 1980)? Can doctrine and historical research coexist? Is it possible that what is viewed by some as progress may in fact be regress? In this postmodern world, paradigms are increasingly rare. Most likely, the future will witness increasing atomization and polarization between "confessional" and "critical" scholarship. Ideally, the text of John's Gospel and the available evidence could serve as common points of reference and as a proving ground for the hypotheses of scholars from a variety of viewpoints and faith commitments. Time will tell whether this is a realistic possibility. I must confess I am not too optimistic in this regard.

I close with a brief *desideratum* for further research. In short, I believe it would be a mistake to divorce the study of John's Gospel from historical questions. The literary turn of biblical scholarship, including Johannine Studies, has yielded some interesting readings and genuine advances in understanding the Fourth Gospel's narrative. Yet these insights must be grounded in a proper understanding of the place of John's Gospel in the first–century world and Christianity, including such considerations as the matrix of the Gentile mission, the emergence of Gnosticism, and the destruction of the temple (Westcott 1971, xxxvii–xxxviii; cf. Köstenberger 2005, 207 n. 4). If the "Johannine community hypothesis" in its various permutations were found wanting, the solution, I submit, is not a turn toward postmodernism but a search for more plausible alternative paradigms and historical settings for John's Gospel. I am thinking here, among other things, of the Johannine temple theme (an internal datum) in relation to the destruction of the temple (an external datum) as part of the milieu in which John's Gospel took shape (Köstenberger 2005 and literature cited). Perhaps it is in avenues such as these that there lies a certain measure of hope and promise for future Johannine research.

CHAPTER 6

PURSUING THE ELUSIVE

R. Alan Culpepper

This morning, I ran several miles of the Longleaf Trace, a beautiful asphalt path through the woods of southern Mississippi outside Hattiesburg. The path is straight and flat, mileage is noted every half mile, rest stations at regular intervals offer restrooms and water, and various species of trees are labeled along the way. In contrast, the path of my experience in studying the Gospel of John has been marked by sharp turns, surprising new vistas, and constant uncertainty about what I was seeing. In short, studying John has been an expedition into still uncertain territory rather than a jog over a measured course.

The trek started in my first semester of M.Div. studies (1967), when I took an elective course on the Gospel of John with Dr. William E. Hull and read the first volume of Raymond Brown's Anchor Bible commentary. The cocktail of an engaging professor delivering beautifully prepared lectures; a masterful commentary surveying Johannine scholarship and astutely engaging John's setting, literary artistry, and theology; and the intriguing challenges of this "spiritual" (Clement of Alexandria), "maverick" (Robert Kysar) Gospel proved to be irresistibly seductive. I began a lifelong love affair with the Fourth Gospel, which involved taking graduate seminars from Hull, James Price, and Moody Smith, and writing my dissertation on John.

The Johannine School

Early on, I decided that I might never write a full-scale commentary on the Gospel of John—after Bultmann, Barrett, Brown, and Schnackenburg, another commentary hardly seemed to be needed, though many fine commentaries on John have been published over the last thirty years. I would work instead on various topics in Johannine studies. As a graduate student at Duke under Moody Smith, W. D. Davies, and James H. Charlesworth, and taking a minor in classics, the natural place to start for me was with John's background.

I was intrigued with the historical setting of the Fourth Gospel, particularly recent work by J. Louis Martyn (1968) and Wayne Meeks (1972), as well as the scattered allusions to "the Johannine school" in the literature on John, the Epistles, and Revelation. I discovered that this term had a long history in the debates over the authorship of the Gospel and that it had served as a mediating position between defenders of apostolic authorship and critics who maintained that the Gospel was written at a later date (and not by the Apostle John). Years later, I discovered that the term "Johannine school" can be traced to David Friedrich Strauss, who said that the Fourth Evangelist was "a venerator of [the Apostle] John, issuing perhaps from one of his schools" (1972, 330). The Gospel, Strauss maintained, was written not by John but by someone in his circle. The theory of a Johannine school also served to explain the similarities and differences among the five New Testament writings attributed to the Apostle John. The similarities in language, style, and thought among the Gospel, Letters, and Apocalypse can be explained by their common ties to the Johannine school, although the similarities between the Apocalypse and the other writings are not as strong as the similarities shared by the Gospel and Letters. The differences can be accounted for on the basis of the different authors and editors from within this school who contributed to the composition of the various documents.

It was a useful and plausible theory, but can the internal probabilities be supported by the external evidence of comparative studies of other "schools" in antiquity? My supervisory committee gave me more than enough rope to hang myself, and I launched into a study of the Pythagorean school, the Academy (Plato), the Lyceum (Aristotle), the Garden (Epicurus), the Stoa (Zeno), Qumran (the Teacher of Righteousness), the school of Hillel, the school of Philo, and the "school" of Jesus, trying to understand the role and common characteristics of these diverse, ancient school traditions. I defined nine common features of these ancient schools:

(1) they were groups of disciples that usually emphasized φιλία ("broth-erhood") and κοινωνία ("community/commonality");

(2) they gathered around and traced their origins to a founder whom they regarded as an exemplary, wise, or good man;

(3) they valued the teachings of their founder and the traditions about him;

(4) members of the schools were disciples or students of the founder;

(5) teaching, learning, studying, and writing were common activities;

(6) most schools observed communal meals, often in memory of their founders;

(7) they had rules or practices regarding admission, retention of membership, and advancement within the membership;

(8) they often maintained some degree of distance or withdrawal from the rest of society; and

(9) they developed organizational means of ensuring their perpetuity. (Culpepper 1975, 258–59)

Not all of these characteristics are exclusive to schools, but these schools shared a commitment to carry forward the work, teaching, or traditions of their founders. Within the Johannine tradition, it seemed possible to distinguish between the influence of the founder (referred to by the community as "the Beloved Disciple"); the early history of the community that separated from the synagogue; and the later history of the community, when its debate turned inward, concerned with keeping its traditions, ethics, and organization intact (as evident in the three letters written by the Elder).

In retrospect, my dissertation would have been stronger had it been organized around unifying themes rather than specific schools: the roles of the founders, boundary issues, the rhetoric of interschool and intraschool debates, initiation rituals, meals and community life, and the production of written materials and their uses. But at the time, I had to bite off one piece at a time and did not know enough to take this more synthetic approach. The dissertation would also have been stronger had I investigated the legacy and record of the Johannine school in the second–century in more depth—a topic to which I returned later. Nevertheless, the theory of a Johannine school still seems to me to be the best explanation for the origin of the Johannine writings. It was indeed, as Brown (1979) said, the "community of the Beloved Disciple," but at the core of this community there was a group of associates who preserved and extended this individual's teachings, guided a network of related churches, taught, preached, debated, and committed their tradition to writing—the Johannine school.

ANATOMY OF THE FOURTH GOSPEL

Course preparation, teaching, parenting, committee work, and speaking in churches left little time for writing between 1975 and 1980. "The Pivot of John's Prologue" (Culpepper 1980)—which argued for a chiastic structure in John 1:1–18 that turned on the phrase "he gave them authority to become the children of God" (John 1:12b), an important authorization and self–identification for the Johannine community—was a transitional piece, dabbling in literary structure but still ultimately concerned with the Johannine community. Two forces shaped my plans for a sabbatical project for 1980–1981. Raymond Brown's *The Community of the Beloved Disciple* (1979) constructed the history of the Johannine community in such detail that it blocked, at least for the moment, any further work along this line. One could only respond to Brown and suggest alternate interpretations—for example, challenging Brown's understanding of the role of the Samaritans, the emergence of a Prophet–like–Moses Christology within the community, the departure from the synagogue as a key to the community's Christology, and his argument for placing the Johannine tradition in the mainstream of early Christianity. A second factor opened a new line of inquiry. The Parables Group, the Mark Group, and the new Literary Aspects of the Gospels and Acts Group in the Society of Biblical Literature were beginning to engage the work of secular literary criticism bringing a new arsenal of concepts and perspectives to bear on the interpretation of the Gospels. Johannine scholarship had lagged behind synoptic research in the development of source, form, and redaction criticism, so it seemed to be an opportunity to "catch the wave" of a new approach to Gospel studies and examine the Gospel of John as a coherent literary composition before returning to questions of its sources, composition history, and community setting.

Frank Kermode, of King's College, Cambridge, guided my research and read an early draft of what became *Anatomy of the Fourth Gospel* (1983). My objective was to explore the narrative texture of the Gospel of John, the functions of each of its literary elements, and their effects on the reader. Wayne Booth (1961), Seymour Chatman (1978), Gérard Genette (1980), and to a lesser extent Wolfgang Iser (1974) were my primary guides to literary theory. Successive chapters explored the role of the narrator; various aspects of the narrator's point of view; the sequencing of exposition; the relationship between telling and showing; the crafting of authority and verisimilitude; the Gospel's handling of narrative time (duration, order, and repetition); the basic elements of John's plot (the conflict between the responses of belief and unbelief and its episodic character); the evocation of John's characters and their function as representations of various responses to Jesus; John's use of implicit commentary through misunderstandings, irony, and symbolism; and the construction of John's implied reader.

Anatomy of the Fourth Gospel continues to receive praise and criticism.[1] Some reflections a quarter of a century later are in order. First, the work was exploratory and experimental. There were no guides to follow. It was an intellectual exercise in suspending historical issues long enough to raise questions about the literary design of the Gospel of John. My aim was never to replace historical criticism, only to open a new line of study, which David Rhoads and I and other members of the Literary Aspects of the Gospels Group began calling "narrative criticism" to distinguish it from older forms of "literary criticism." As the preface indicates, *Anatomy* explores how the author(s) of the Fourth Gospel constructed various elements of the narrative, whether or not they recognized those elements as such. The modern critic can be aided in understanding the "anatomy" of the Fourth Gospel by analyzing elements that are inherent in every narrative text (as well as those peculiar to John) without assuming that the author(s) were aware of these patterns. It would be anachronistic to retroject modern narrative theory onto an ancient author; it is not anachronistic to use modern concepts in the analysis of the elements of an ancient narrative.

In *The Print's First Kiss*, Jeff Staley builds on *Anatomy of the Fourth Gospel* but also criticizes it at points, especially for not maintaining a clear distinction between the narrator and the implied author (1988, esp. 11–15). Others have charged that *Anatomy* betrays an underlying historical interest when it argues that the way in which the Fourth Gospel

---

[1] Stephen Moore was critical of *Anatomy of the Fourth Gospel* for my focus on the narrative unity of the text: "in its preoccupation with narrative coherence . . . current literary criticism of the Gospels shows itself to be trapped in a hall of mirrors" (1994, 80). Carson was concerned about the implications of narrative criticism for the truth claims of the Gospel and therefore questioned "the unqualified transfer of categories developed in the poetics of the *novel* to Gospel literature" (1991, 63). Stibbe, on the other hand, was excessively positive: "Recent research on the Fourth Gospel has, in a sense, been footnotes to Culpepper" (1993, 10). Surprisingly, Bartlett missed the importance of close literary analysis for preaching: "Culpepper and Staley imagine an implied reader who looks a good deal like an undergraduate literature major, sitting before the text, pen and paper in hand, taking notes on the intricate interweaving of the symbolic structures and the ironic recapitulations in *Madame Bovary*. It is an interesting and often illuminating exercise, but it is not clear just how it relates to the question of how the text might evoke faith, either in the first century or the twenty–first" (2006, 58). For a more complete response to these and similar criticisms, see Culpepper 2003, 73–93.

constructs the implied reader can be used to shed light on its intended or first readers. In retrospect, I should have argued this point more carefully. The implied reader is a literary construct that may or may not resemble the intended or actual first readers of a text. Modern fiction can construct an implied reader that forces the actual reader to play a role or adopt an assumed persona, but that is not the case with the Gospel of John. It is a fair assumption that the actual author(s) wrote for intended, actual readers, and that the implied reader fits the profile of the intended reader closely. The narrative asides may also provide evidence of the adaptation of the Gospel for a wider circle of readers. The narrative critic need not make inferences about the actual first readers, but for those interested in the historical setting of the Fourth Gospel narrative criticism may offer additional data that can supplement or corroborate historical research.

In the flush of excitement over the development of narrative criticism of the Gospels and questioning the "assured results" of historical criticism, some narrative critics have viewed any engagement with historical investigation as a return to the assumption that only that which is grounded in history is valid or that only historical studies really matter. While striving to make a place for narrative criticism and its concern with the literary design and dynamics of the Gospels (esp. in Culpepper 1984), I have never thought that the Gospels can be understood apart from study of the historical and social contexts in which they were written. Such historical study can no longer be viewed as the sole concern of Gospel studies, but it is indispensable. Historical criticism and narrative criticism raise different questions. In pursuit of answers to the questions each raises, the interpreter will use different methods, but the two need not be mutually exclusive and indeed may be complementary. The modern critic can infer from the implied author's assumptions about what the actual reader would know or not know, or about how the reader would respond to various characters, ironies, or symbols, insights that can be correlated with the proposals advanced by interpreters concerned with understanding the history of the Johannine community. In the quest to understand the Gospel of John, there is no place for methodological exclusivism.

The field of Gospel studies was moving rapidly in the 1980s (see Moore 1989; Segovia 1996). Even before the theory, methods, and potential of narrative criticism could be explored fully, new perspectives from reader response criticism, ideological criticism, poststructuralism, and postcolonial criticism were being advanced. The sheer proliferation of perspectives was both energizing and debilitating. I have attempted to make some sense of the field and its assumptions regarding the nature of the text and the role of the reader with a grid or logical square (see figure 6.1).

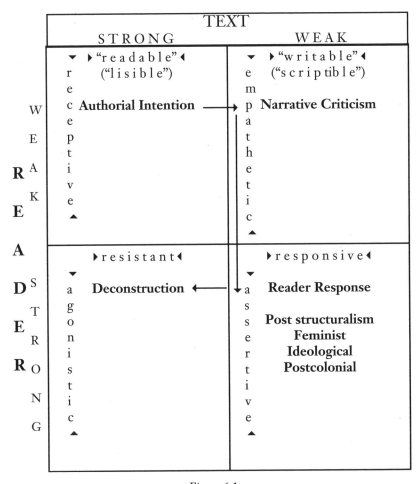

Figure 6.1

By arranging literary theories in a logical square along the axes of "text and reader," "strong and weak," one can begin to understand more clearly the relationships among contemporary theories. We may adapt Roland Barthes' analysis of texts as "lisible" or "scriptible"—"readable" or "writable" (1974, 4). In the logical square, as one moves clockwise beginning in the top left quadrant, the text moves from being open and clear to requiring constructive response from the reader, to once again being dominant but now resisting interpretation. Correspondingly, the reader may be receptive, empathetic, assertive, or agonistic.

Beginning in the top left quadrant of the grid, if the text is strong (and lucid) and the reader is weak, the text transmits the author's intended meaning, and the reader receives or discerns the meaning the text was intended to convey. The text is "readable" and "author–itative." This position has been defended by E. D. Hirsch (1967 and 1976). One typically assumes that this is the case with discursive texts such as articles, lectures, or letters, but in narrative texts the writer's voice is more remote and mediated by the role of the narrator. Narrative texts therefore require the reader to construct meaning from the narrative features of the text.

Moving across the square, we find the place of narrative criticism, which I would contend views both the text and the reader as weak. The text is "writable" in the sense that its complexity, openness, and ambiguities require the reader to construct the sense and subtleties of the narrative from the way the reader employs the various features of a narrative. Narrative criticism therefore requires an empathetic reader, one who can follow the lead of the narrative voice and discern the functions of the other narrative entities (setting, character, plot, imagery, irony, etc.). The fact that narrative criticism views both the text and the reader as "weak" does not mean that the method itself is weak or deficient. It means, rather, that for narrative criticism the interpretive process is less confrontational than in methods in which text and reader are strong, and less one–sided than in approaches in which either the text or the reader dominates.

Moving to the lower right quadrant, the difference between narrative criticism and reader response criticism is one of degree: the role of the reader moves from empathetic to assertive, while the text is still understood to be responsive, if at times more opaque or resistant. The reader therefore takes a more dominant role in the interpretive process. In this quadrant, we may also place poststructuralist, feminist, ideological, and postcolonial readings, though with these methods the reader becomes even more assertive (Russell 1985; Weems 1988; J. Anderson 1991; Moore 1993; Staley 1995; Kitzberger 1998; Segovia 2000). The reader must struggle to construct meaning from a hostile or offensive text. Because the text strives to impose an untenable ideology, reading requires that the reader aggressively block the text, subvert its ideology, and expose the ideology of conventional readings.

The final quadrant—strong text and strong reader—includes contemporary methods that view interpretation as the confrontation between a resistant text and an agonistic reader. In this quadrant, I have placed deconstruction. Deconstructive criticism highlights the gaps and openness of literary texts that are filled by the reader in various ways as the reader strives to impose coherence on a text that defies coherent interpretation. Reading is therefore understood as a struggle with a text that never succumbs to the efforts of the reader but keeps its enigmas intact (e.g., Moore 1994).

Although the critical options for approaching the text of the Fourth Gospel have proliferated during the past two decades, the work of narrative criticism has continued, both in the United States and elsewhere: England (Stibbe 1992; 1993), Germany (Zimmermann 2004), Switzerland (Zumstein 2004), and South Africa (Tolmie 1995; van der Watt 2000). *Anatomy of the Fourth Gospel* has also recently been translated into Korean and Japanese.

JOHN THE SON OF ZEBEDEE: THE LIFE OF A LEGEND

In the mid–1980s, Moody Smith invited me to take on a project that would lead me in a new direction—writing a volume on John the son of Zebedee for the "Personalities of the New Testament" series. Nine years of intermittent but taxing work followed as I collected all the references to the apostle I could find and tried to trace the development of the legends about John in the church fathers, the apocryphal Acts of John, medieval traditions, church calendars, and modern scholarship.

The development of traditions about John in the second century is particularly important—and difficult. The historical record is very thin in the first half of the second century. Then, as one begins to find references to the Gospel of John, one also begins to see defenses of its apostolic authority. The earliest commentaries on John come from the Gnostics Ptolemy and Heracleon. Irenaeus asserts the apostolic authorship of the Gospel, citing a chain of testimony that runs from those who heard the Elder John in Asia, through Papias and Polycarp, and ultimately to his own day, as he places himself in this tradition with the claim that he, as a child, heard "the blessed Polycarp" speak of John the apostle. From that point on, the Gospel of John's place in the canon was assured. Charles E. Hill has recently published a full review of the second–century evidence regarding the Johannine corpus, in which he demonstrates that the allusions to John show that it had a more established place in the church than scholars have recognized (Hill 2004; cf. Culpepper 2005c). He argues further that the Gnostic writers merely exploited what they found congenial in John, that Irenaeus did not have to defend John's orthodoxy, and that there is continuous evidence of the Johannine corpus of writings from the early part of the second century. Hill works carefully, like a spider weaving a web. He accepts the testimony of the ancient authors, placing the burden of proof on those who question their veracity. He argues that ancient writers quoted from memory and often deliberately altered or adapted texts. Therefore, he accepts most of the debated "allusions" and "parallels" as evidence that the writers knew the text of the Fourth Gospel. Hill's work is a *tour de force* that will revise our estimate of the reception of the Gospel of John in the second century, but as with most *tours de force* it overstates the case and will no doubt be qualified by future work. The role of the Fourth Gospel and the roles of the Apostle John, the Elder of the Johannine Epistles, the seer of the Apocalypse, and the John the Elder referred to by Papias will continue to engage scholars and offer fruitful areas for further research.

OLD QUESTIONS AND NEW DIRECTIONS

In 1995, I became the founding dean of the McAfee School of Theology, and the time available for research and writing was limited by the work involved in starting a new program. In addition, my work on the Gospel of John has been further restricted by the writing of a commentary on Luke (Culpepper 1995), a biography of my father's life (Culpepper 2002a), and a commentary on Mark (Culpepper 2007). Nevertheless, new ideas and insights have continued to find expression in scattered articles and lectures.

The Gospel and Letters of John, a textbook for courses on the Gospel and Epistles written at the invitation of Charles Cousar, is a combination of teaching material I have used in courses on John, abbreviated sections of my commentary *1 John, 2 John, 3 John* (Culpepper 1985), and a new chapter titled "The Gospel of John as a Document of Faith." The goal of the volume was to introduce students to the historical, literary, and theological issues posed by these writings and to offer a brief running commentary. Its primary contribution to Johannine scholarship is a brief section that argues that John's episodic plot includes a series of scenes in which various characters respond to Jesus and either recognize or fail to recognize who he is. John therefore contains a series of recognition scenes (*anagnorisis*) similar to those found in ancient dramas that support the conflict of belief and unbelief as responses to Jesus (Culpepper 1998, 72–86).

Invitations to participate in conferences and to write essays for *Festschriften* offered opportunities to extend longstanding interests and explore new ideas. Almost fifteen years after the publication of my first essay on anti–Judaism in the Fourth Gospel, I was invited to participate in a conference on this subject in Leuven, where I read "Anti–Judaism in the Fourth Gospel as a Problem for Christian Interpreters" (Culpepper 2001). In this essay, I argue that the Gospel of John was written after the separation of the Christian community from the Jewish community, in part in an effort to define and assert the Christian community's identity in its new setting. Building on Wayne Meeks's observation that the Gospel of John is most anti–Jewish precisely where it is most Jewish, I

catalogued the list of Jewish elements claimed by the Christian community—particularly that Jesus and his followers are the fulfillment of the
Scriptures and the Jewish festivals and that believers are the true heirs of
the promises made to Abraham, Moses, and the prophets. The Johannine Christians were the true Israel, the "children of God." The Fourth
Gospel is anti–Jewish in the sense that it envisions no continuing role for
Judaism, but its anti–Judaism is theological, not ethnic, racial, or social.

Work on a collection of essays in honor of Robert Kysar allowed
me to continue to reflect upon the ways in which the fledgling Christian community that produced the Gospel of John dealt with social and
theological inclusivism and exclusivism. This interest is evident in the
concluding paragraphs of my 2002 essay "Inclusivism and Exclusivism":

> At least in its historical context, that of a struggling commu-
> nity separated from the synagogue and establishing its own
> self–identity, John advocates a sharp social exclusivism based
> on one's response to the revelation that has come through
> Jesus. On the other hand, as we have seen, all other bases for
> social exclusivism are swept aside. John narrates scenes of Jesus
> accepting persons from every segment of society and then call-
> ing for the unity of the Church, offering for it the images of the
> vine, the flock, and the untorn net.
>
> The tension between John's theological exclusivism and
> inclusivism is even more subtle. John affirms free will in that
> every person is challenged to respond in faith to the light of the
> Logos, while maintaining that faith is never a matter of one's
> own doing. John affirms determinism in that God calls, draws,
> and chooses, but insists that God's election is universal, and
> every person is responsible for his or her response to God's call-
> ing. Jesus is the only way to the Father, but the Logos incarnate
> in Jesus has been and is the light of God's truth from the begin-
> ning and for all people. One does not fully understand the Logos
> until one grasps that the Logos was in Jesus, and one cannot
> understand Jesus fully until one sees that the Logos he embodied
> is the Logos that is eternally calling people to God. (Culpepper
> 2002b, 105–6)

Looking back, the reference to the "images of the vine, the flock, and
the untorn net" foreshadowed my current interest in the "designs for the
church" that are embedded in the Fourth Gospel.

The invitation to present one of the main papers at the 2004 meeting
of the Society of New Testament Studies meeting in Barcelona prompted

me to revisit a paper I had presented at the 1997 SNTS in South Africa. In "Designs for the Church in the Gospel Accounts of Jesus' Death," I trace the ways in which all four Gospel accounts of Jesus' death intimate features that defined the respective early Christian communities behind each text (Culpepper 2005a). This paper focuses on the didactic function of the interpretation of Jesus' death in each of the Gospels as conveyed through the narrative's implicit commentary. I suggest that the evangelists tied the developing self–understandings of their emerging Christian communities to the death of Jesus. Mark interprets the church as a new "temple not made with hands." Matthew relates the death of Jesus to the signs of the end–time and the hope of resurrection. Luke provides ethical instruction for the church, interpreting Jesus' martyrdom as a noble death. John develops a rich portrait by which the church could define itself through the themes, images, and allusions of the Johannine passion narrative.

> With John we find the development of a relatively full design for the church through the gospel's account of Jesus' death: a new family of faith, one without division, claiming Jesus as their king, embracing all people, imbibing living water provided through his thirst, and—as the new Temple—receiving his Spirit, as he promised.
>
> Because the gospels were written during the period when the early Christian communities were separating from the synagogues and establishing their own identity, it is not surprising that these early communities looked to the core events of the gospel story to validate their self–understanding. Through implicit commentary, therefore, the evangelists connected the church with Jesus' death, progressively suggesting that his death served in various respects as a model for the emerging church. The early church, I believe, reflected not only on the significance of the resurrection for its mission; it traced its foundation to the cross. (Culpepper 2005a, 392)

For a conference on Johannine imagery in Eisenach in the summer of 2005, I was able to extend this notion to the account of the great catch of fish in John 21:1–14. These verses develop the tradition of the great catch (cf. Luke 5:1–10) in a distinctively Johannine fashion. I became more firmly convinced that John 21 is an integral part of the Gospel. John 21 is thoroughly ecclesiological, but not more so than John 1–20. The ecclesiological overtones of the great catch of fish are established primarily by the connotations of fishing in ancient rhetoric, the connection of "drawing" the net with John 12:32, and the emphasis on unity in the description of the net as "untorn" (21:11), an emphasis that had particular significance in the Johannine context. The number 153 (21:11) seems to have symbolic significance related to the church, even if we cannot decipher it with confidence. The fish on the fire evokes various associations, including Jesus and the Eucharist, and for John the meal of bread and fish probably celebrated the ministry and resurrection of Jesus.

REFLECTIONS

In retrospect, one can see that an interest in the relationship between text and community is apparent in most of my work on the Gospel of John. I hope it is more nuanced in my later research, drawing upon both historical criticism and narrative criticism.[2] The difficulties in reading the Fourth Gospel as a reflection of its own community setting are much clearer to me now than they were thirty years ago. On the other hand, it still seems to me to be axiomatic that John was written in and for a particular community, or, more likely, a set of communities, though its proclamation of the gospel for this community was relevant for the church at large. This broader relevance is the bridge for much of the Fourth Gospel's relevance to contemporary readers and churches. John communicates directly and indirectly, and the fascination of his Gospel resides in the way it uses imagery and irony for implicit commentary that, whether kerygmatic or didactic in function, is always elusive. The interpreter may focus alternatively on historical, literary, or theological issues, but all of these must be considered in the interpretation of this Gospel.

The path has not been straight or clearly marked in advance. Understanding the Gospel of John, its message for its first readers, and how that message is conveyed in the Gospel's narrative therefore remains endlessly fascinating and rewarding.

---

[2] As de Boer notes, "Culpepper's own recent work shows that the historical and literary approaches need not be mutually exclusive" (1996, 50).

6: RESPONSE

TO WHAT END, METHODOLOGY?

Stan Harstine

The career of R. Alan Culpepper is a synopsis of the movements in Gospels scholarship during the past forty years. Indeed, Culpepper has been an integral force in exploring, educating, and encouraging the changes that have occurred. It was my pleasure to study and work with him during his years at Baylor University. His example as a scholar, teacher, and mentor challenged and shaped many of my views regarding the Johannine corpus.

As indicated in his essay, Culpepper's career is a portrait of the changes in methodology since 1967. From historical reconstructions of the Johannine community to the myriad literary theories applied to the New Testament narratives, Culpepper has been knee–deep in the moving flood that has deluged Johannine scholarship. His earliest monograph, *The Johannine School*, applied an essentially historical–critical methodology, based on the question "What can we know?" to the problem of the Johannine community (Culpepper 1975). As rhetorical issues became more prominent in the late 1970s, Culpepper applied chiasm to the prologue of John (Culpepper 1980). *Anatomy of the Fourth Gospel* was an early exploration into the feasibility of applying a relevant methodology from secular literary studies to this classical text (Culpepper 1983). Since that time, Culpepper has stressed the importance of rigorously establishing our methodological choices. In his mind and practice, there is no room for haphazard scholarship.

Culpepper's emphasis on methodology promotes reflection upon the question, "To what end, *methodology?*" In the introduction to *Anatomy*, he provides some reflection of his own. "My hope is that the present effort will be judged on the basis of its capacity to expose new considerations, explain features of the Gospel, and stimulate greater appreciation for its literary design" (Culpepper 1983, 11). One answer to our question, then, is simply this: methodology applied to the biblical text should illuminate and explain the text. Scholarship must reassess any methodology that fails in this regard, no matter its status or entrenchment.

It is understandable when graduate students mimic their senior professor's approach and when recent Ph.D.s either strive for tenure or hang tenaciously to their temporary appointments, but it is vital for scholars to evaluate the effectiveness of their methodological models and to refine their approaches to research. Those scholars who initiate a radical shift in the methodological paradigm are rare, but those who radically appropriate and effectively apply current methodologies may be equally rare. Adopting a methodology purely for its popularity, its ease of publication, or its shock value are insufficient reasons for investing academic energy. A second answer to our question, then, is this: Scholars must critically evaluate their own methodology for its effectiveness and appropriateness.

Having given some reflection to method, it is important to investigate the other part of our question: "To what *end*, methodology?" Though it is acceptable and customary to speak of the ancient author and audience of the Fourth Gospel (authorial, implicit, or otherwise), scholarship is seemingly tainted when conscious regard is given for a specific modern audience. Just as discussion of the Johannine community includes studies on exclusivism and inclusivism (Culpepper 2002b), Johannine scholarship would profit from active discussion in this area. When Alan Culpepper relocated his office from the Tidwell Bible Building in Waco, Texas, to Atlanta, Georgia, to guide a new seminary at Mercer University, he acted on his personal preference regarding the audience he would pursue with his scholarship. Perhaps the most common audience of Johannine scholars, indeed the likely audience for the current volume, is other Johannine scholars. The "guild," however limited it may be, holds the distinction of being the primary audience for many scholastic efforts. Articles are written, papers presented, and books published for the purpose of gaining a hearing from those within the Society of Biblical Literature. A specific methodology is often required for a paper or article to be accepted by a group or journal; methodological code words are therefore strategically located within the abstract to draw preferential treatment. If there is a major problem with the guild as primary audience, it is its finite quality, indeed its exclusiveness.

For some unstated reason, biblical scholarship increasingly avoids what is clearly the larger, and more obvious, audience of the canonical literature: the community of faith. The religious community as an audience for "pure" scholarship seems to be an outmoded or restrictive model, yet it may be suggested that this audience is frequently in the back of a biblical scholar's mind. Whether to console or challenge, to comfort or disturb, the scholar consciously or unconsciously pursues methodologies with the audience of Christendom partially in view. If Johannine scholars are to demonstrate inclusivism, then this audience must receive ample consideration.

Although a specific audience may be forced upon a scholar by an editor or publishing contract, it remains necessary to confront the role of the audience for Johannine scholarship, indeed for scholarship as a whole. The question, "To what *end*, methodology?" does not call for a single end. Proposed audiences will remain restricted or open, exclusive or inclusive. However, raising the question highlights the problem—a lack of open, scholarly discussion regarding this very substantive issue for scholarship. Professional views frequently assign value judgments to the work of any scholar who chooses to address an audience different from the one predominately addressed by the guild. Is the value of scholarship based merely upon the methodology selected or the audience chosen? I would propose not. Can this discussion be more finely nuanced in the future? I strongly encourage the debate. Perhaps what Culpepper notes regarding the pursuit of the son of Zebedee might also be true regarding Johannine scholarship:

> If a resolution to the historical difficulties surrounding the apostle is not forthcoming, *one can only hope that the future will be as fruitful as the past*, that the legend will continue to inspire both piety and imagination, art, and scholarship. Who can measure the power of the legend or its influence on persons, cultures, and communities of faith? (Culpepper 2000, 328; emphasis added)

CHAPTER 7

THE GOSPEL AND THE EPISTLES OF JOHN READ AGAINST THE BACKGROUND OF THE HISTORY OF THE JOHANNINE COMMUNITIES

Marinus de Jonge

Invited to indicate what I judge to be the critical issues for Johannine Studies, the best I can do is to retrace my own steps in Johannine research and to indicate what proved to be important at various stages.[1] The first section of my essay will give a short review of my book *Jesus: Stranger from Heaven and Son of God*, consisting of a number of essays written between 1970 and 1975 (M. de Jonge 1977a). This volume appeared in the year that also saw the publication of *L'Évangile de Jean. Sources, rédaction, théologie*, reflecting the proceedings of the Colloquium Biblicum Lovaniense 1975, in which many prominent Johannine scholars participated and of which I had the honor of being president (M. de Jonge 1977b). Because a comparison between the two books helps to illustrate how my views interacted with the scholarship of that time, a characterization of what happened at the Leuven conference precedes the review of my own book below.

Although Johannine subjects figured regularly in my academic teaching until my retirement at the end of 1990, and though I wrote a few articles as I went along, it was not until 1996 that I published a short commentary on John in Dutch, in which I summarized my insights as they had

---

[1] I wish to thank my colleagues Martin C. de Boer (for helpful discussions about a number of central issues) and Gilbert Van Belle (for good advice).

developed over the years (M. de Jonge 1996). I also wrote a number of further essays in the period 1990–2000 (M. de Jonge 1990; 1992a; 1992b; 1993; 1995; 2000). These later publications will form the background of the second section of this article, in which I will attempt to assess some more recent trends in Johannine scholarship. How much has happened in the past thirty years in research on the Fourth Gospel and the Johannine Epistles becomes particularly evident when one compares the volume on the 1975 Leuven conference with *John and the Synoptics*, which contains the papers of the colloquium at Leuven in 1990 under the leadership of Adelbert Denaux (Denaux 1992), and with the lectures at the recent 2005 Leuven colloquium on "The Death of Jesus in the Fourth Gospel," with Gilbert Van Belle as president (Van Belle 2005). However, in particular the comparison between the colloquia of 1975 and 2005, which were completely different in scope and approach, has brought home the fact that, for me at least, one problem has remained central over the years: the relationship between a literary and a historical approach to the Johannine writings. Commenting on a number of issues that were and are important to me, I shall concentrate on this question.

LOOKING BACK TO 1975

In my introduction to the volume from the Leuven conference in 1975 I wrote:

> There is widespread agreement on the fact that the Fourth Gospel shows a unity of vocabulary, style and theology; Johannine exegesis will have to give a prominent place to redaction–criticism. But there is variety in this unity, there are sudden transitions in language and content, and (seeming) inconsistencies. The problem is how to explain them. Here the question of sources comes up, and the problem of various stages in the redaction of the Gospel. Both questions were hotly debated at the conference, and different answers are given in the papers in this volume. (M. de Jonge 1977b, 13)

I added that I expected that the readers of the volume would find the rich variety of approaches and the great diversity of results in Johannine Studies at the same time stimulating and perplexing. Let me single out just a few of these approaches for our present purpose.

At the 1975 conference, Rudolf Schnackenburg, who had just completed the third volume of his commentary on the Fourth Gospel, gave a survey of Johannine research in the period 1955–1975 (Schnackenburg 1977). Of the many points reviewed by him, I note his assessment of the various linguistic–semiotic approaches then coming into fashion, which were represented at the conference by Pierre Geoltrain, who gave a paper titled "Analyse structurale du chapitre 9 de l'Évangile de Jean" (unfortunately not included in the conference volume). Schnackenburg remarks:

> Von dieser Methode können wir lernen, zunächst die literarische Ebene für sich zu betrachten (synchronisch); die Frage der Entstehung des Werkes (diachronische Blickweise) darf nicht zu schnell eingebracht werden, um fragwürdige Modelle für den literarischen Werdeprozess zu vermeiden. (1977, 42)[2]

This judgment remains valid also with regard to other forms of new literary criticism current today.

Second, in his lecture "Johannine Language and Style: The Question of Their Unity," Eugen Ruckstuhl defended the main thesis of his *Die literarische Einheit des Johannesevangeliums* (Ruckstuhl 1977; 1988). He argued that we cannot speak about a vocabulary or a specific theological tendency typical for the "Gospel of Signs," the pre–Johannine source reconstructed by Robert Fortna (Fortna 1970). Fortna was present, and a lively discussion followed.

Third, in a solid contribution on "John and the Synoptics," Frans Neirynck defended the thesis that in a number of cases we are able to prove that the Fourth Evangelist did not use traditions lying behind the Synoptic Gospels, but was instead dependent upon these Gospels themselves (Neirynck 1977; Sabbe 1977). Neirynck consistently preferred meticulous literary comparison with existing documents to theories about the use of more or less hypothetical pre–Johannine sources. Also in the following years, the New Testament section of the Faculty of Theology at Leuven remained focused on this approach to the Fourth Gospel. The relationship between John and the Synoptics would later form the central topic of the colloquium of 1990 (Neirynck 1992; Sabbe 1992).

Finally, I mention the paper read at the 1975 colloquium by J. Louis Martyn, the author of *History and Theology in the Fourth Gospel* (Martyn 1968), who continued his search for clues in the Gospel of John to the circumstances in which the book was written. The full title

---

[2] My translation: "This method reminds us to analyze first of all the literary text before us (synchronically); we should not tackle the problem of the origin of the work too early (the diachronic point of view), in order to avoid using dubious models to explain its genesis."

of his contribution indicates that he wanted to present "Glimpses into
the History of the Johannine Community from Its Origin through the
Period of Its Life in Which the Fourth Gospel Was Composed" (Martyn 1979a). Martyn distinguished three redactional stages in the Fourth
Gospel corresponding to three periods in the history of the Johannine
community. His lecture, fascinating and suggestive, provoked much
discussion at the conference. In an added note, Martyn, commenting on
Ruckstuhl's critique of Fortna's hypothesis, conceded that it constituted
a renewed challenge regarding the use of stylistic observations, but
added, "the major criterion for strata differentiation, however, [namely]
the criterion of the aporiae, remains intact" (1977, 149 n. 3).

JESUS: STRANGER FROM HEAVEN AND SON OF GOD

My own contributions to Johannine research at the time of the 1975 colloquium had originated on different occasions over a number of years.
Also in edited form, as chapters in the volume *Jesus: Stranger from Heaven
and Son of God*, they remained separate successive attempts to shed light
on the theme expressed in the book's subtitle, *Jesus Christ and the Christians in Johannine Perspective*. Yet, as I wrote in the preface, behind all
these studies lies the assumption that the Fourth Gospel in its final form
is a meaningful whole, highly complicated in structure, with many paradoxes and many tensions in thought and syntax, but asking to be taken
seriously as a (more or less finished) literary product in which consistent lines can be detected. Literary sources may have been used, and a
long literary process with different stages of redaction may lie behind the
present Gospel, but it remains difficult, if not impossible, to distinguish
between sources and redaction or to detect different redactional layers.
Supposedly redactional and supposedly traditional elements have to be
treated as integral parts of a new literary entity that has to be studied on
its own. Consequently, one should pay attention to the composition and
structure of the Fourth Gospel as a whole (M. de Jonge 1977a, vii–viii,
cf. 197–200).

This (at least primarily) literary approach proved useful and led to a
number of discoveries. The essays in *Stranger from Heaven* show that it
makes sense to read the Gospel of John in its present form as a concerted
effort to explain to its readers what it means to believe in Jesus, the Messiah and Son of God, sent as a unique envoy by the Father, and to have
eternal life through him (cf. John 20:30–31). On the other hand, it cannot
be denied that this approach has led to a neglect of other aspects of the
Gospel of John. The possibility of sources or (rather) earlier redactional
layers was left open and not really explored as a possible solution for the

presence of tensions in the narratives or discourses in the present Gospel. Attention was paid to the historical background presupposed in the Gospel as a whole, but earlier stages in the history of the Johannine communities, possibly reflected in the text, received little notice. Some of the major points I made in these essays, however, seem to me still valid and of importance for present–day study of John.

First, there is the main thesis of the opening chapter (M. de Jonge 1977a, 1–27), expressed in its title, "The Fourth Gospel: The Book of the Disciples." The disciples, as eyewitnesses to Jesus' acts and as hearers of his words, are sent out by Jesus after his resurrection: "As the Father has sent me, so I send you" (John 20:21). Through their message, future generations are able to believe in Jesus, the Son of the Father—see 17:20–21, "I ask not only on behalf of these, but also on behalf of those who will believe in me through their word, that they may all be one." To support them in their mission, the disciples receive the Holy Spirit (20:21; cf. 7:39 and the Paraclete sayings in chs. 14–16). The disciples may have displayed a lack of insight on several occasions and may have been in need of correction during Jesus' earthly mission, but after his return to the Father they received full understanding (2:22; 12:16; 13:7; 20:7). The Gospel of John, as the record of a number of signs performed by Jesus in the disciples' presence, enables its readers to believe in Jesus as Messiah and Son of God and to have life in his name (20:30–31). Future generations of believers must remain united with Jesus' disciples as eyewitnesses through the Spirit who provides true understanding. The Fourth Gospel is thus an essential component of the Spirit's testimony.

Chapter 5, "Signs and Works in the Fourth Gospel" (M. de Jonge 1977a, 117–40) tries to interpret the passages dealing with Jesus' σημεῖα ("signs") not on the level of a hypothetical "signs source" or "Signs Gospel," but, in connection with statements about Jesus' ἔργα ("works"), on the level of the Gospel as it lies before us. For the person(s) responsible for the Gospel in its present form, the σημεῖα are demonstrations of Jesus' special power and authority; they can, however, only be properly understood and interpreted by people who are initiated into the secret of the relationship between Son and Father—such as the disciples (imperfectly during his lifetime and fully after his glorification). The relationship between the Son and the Father is the secret of Jesus' ἔργα—the word preferred by Jesus himself when he speaks about his actions. Jesus' works are God's works performed by and through Jesus. Together, the ἔργα ("works") form the one ἔργον ("work") that Jesus was called to perform in unity with the Father who sent him (John 4:34; 17:4). The word ἔργα, referring not only to acts otherwise called σημεῖα but to all that the Son does in obedience to the will of the Father and empowered by him, leads us to the center of John's theocentric Christology. Together "works" and "words" point to the unity between Father and Son; but if people, outsiders or disciples, find it difficult to believe in Jesus' message about his union with God, it is the works that provide the final convincing evidence (10:32–38; 14:8–11).

Chapter 4, "Jewish Expectations about the 'Messiah' according to the Fourth Gospel" (M. de Jonge 1977a, 77–116), deals with passages in which Jews express Jewish beliefs concerning the Messiah (in particular those in John 7; see also 12:34). A few things stand out clearly. The statements concerned are entirely subordinate to a clearer exposition of Johannine Christology, and add little or nothing to our knowledge of Jewish expectations concerning the Messiah known from other sources. In the stories and discussions found in the Fourth Gospel, representative people (disciples, ordinary Jews ["the crowd"], Jewish leaders, Samaritans [ch. 4]) express representative beliefs and raise representative objections. But these persons are "literary" persons; they are like actors in a play, whose utterances help move along the course of events and, even more, the development of thought. In Jesus' debates with outsiders and discussions with sympathizers in chapters 2–12, in his conversations with his disciples in chapters 13–17, and in the opening chapter and final chapters 18–21, everything leads to, and centers around, the secret of Jesus' unique union with the Father. All that is told serves to strengthen and deepen the faith and the insight of the communities for which the Gospel of John is intended. This fact makes it difficult to determine a particular situation in and for which the Fourth Gospel was written. John gives theological reflection on the real issues in the debate between Christians and Jews and does not aim at providing arguments in a concrete struggle. One may add that there is also implicit or even explicit (7:40–44) criticism of Christological beliefs current in other, non–Johannine, Christian groups. Often we are told about persons who, at least initially, react favorably to Jesus' teaching. They are all Jews, but it is often difficult to decide whether one should call them Jewish sympathizers or Jewish Christians. For John, it is only important to understand that their faith is imperfect and insufficient; the reader should realize that they do not belong to the group of true believers.[3]

I conclude this survey with some points made in the final chapter of *Stranger from Heaven*, "Variety and Development in Johannine Christology" (M. de Jonge 1977a, 193–222). Looking back on the preceding chapters, I emphasize that my approach

[3] On this topic see also chapter 2 of *Stranger from Heaven*, "Nicodemus and Jesus: Some Observations on Misunderstanding and Understanding in the Fourth Gospel" (M. de Jonge 1977a, 29–47), and chapter 3, "Jesus as Prophet and King in the Fourth Gospel" (1977a, 49–76).

tends to play down the differences and inconsistencies in a certain writing, for the very reason that it views them as differences and inconsistencies within the framework of this writing. It also tends to be unhistorical, not because it denies the *Sitz im Leben* and the 'communication–in–situation' aspect of the literary document, but because it realizes that some writings, particularly a Gospel, may be used only with great circumspection as historical sources. (1977a, 199)

I continue with the question, "Does this mean that, given the limitations of the chosen method, we are not in a position to discuss any developments in Johannine Christology at all?" The answer is that we are able to compare the christological statements in *related* documents, in our case those in the Gospel of John, with those in the Johannine Epistles (particularly in 1 John). If we find significant differences we may ask to what extent those differences point to developments in the Christology of the Johannine communities; the next question is then whether these developments are in any way reflected in the Fourth Gospel itself.

In the Epistles (1–2–3 John), the combination "Jesus Christ" (found twice in the Gospel) occurs no fewer than eight times. Separately, Χριστός ("Christ") is used as a title, closely related to, and practically interchangeable with, ὁ υἱὸς τοῦ θεοῦ ("the Son of God"). The author(s) emphasize(s) that the Son of God who came to earth was fully human (see ἐν σαρκὶ ἐληλυθότα, "who has come in flesh," in 1 John 4:2; cf. 2 John 7) and died a human death (see ὁ ἐλθὼν δι᾽ ὕδατος καὶ αἵματος, "who came through water and blood," in 1 John 5:6–8; cf. 1:7). This emphasis is clearly directed against secessionists who have left the communities addressed by the Epistles and disagree on this issue (1 John 2:18–25; 4:1–6). In the Gospel of John, two strategically situated passages clearly state that the Son who appeared on earth was a person of flesh and blood: the prologue (John 1:1–18), which includes the central statement "the Word became flesh" (1:14–18) and at the end of the book, the story about Thomas at 20:24–29, which follows the passage about Jesus' appearance to the disciples without Thomas (20:19–22); and immediately precedes the so–called "first ending" in 20:30–31. The reader need not be in doubt: the resurrected Christ died a human death on the cross (20:20, 25, 27). It is difficult to imagine that 1:14–18 and 20:19–29 played a prominent role in the Jesus traditions known to the Johannine secessionists attacked in the Epistles; on the other hand, there is no sign that these passages were only added to the present Gospel later, with a polemical purpose.

Two additional passages require our attention. First, John 20:19–29 refers back to the specifically Johannine pericope 19:31–37, with v. 34

telling us that "blood and water" (cf. 1 John 5:6–8) came out of Jesus' side when a soldier pierced it with a spear. In an aside in v. 35, we are told that "he who saw this has testified so that you also may believe." This remark, which can be connected with 21:24 and (perhaps) also with other references to the Beloved Disciple, clearly stresses the importance of the information in the preceding verse—but the reason for this is not made explicit. Second, there is the much discussed pericope, 6:51–58, in which Jesus tells "the Jews" that he, "the living bread that comes down from heaven," will give his "flesh" "for the life of the world." "Those who eat my flesh and drink my blood will abide in me, and I in them." These words are "hard," not only for "the Jews" but also for many of Jesus' disciples who leave and follow him no longer (6:60–66)—in contrast to the Twelve (except for Judas) who confess Jesus as the Holy One of God who has words of eternal life (6:67–71). Here, we find a clear reference to a rift within the community of followers of Jesus, and the issue is the true interpretation of his death. The many who have left are clearly wrong; those who side with the Twelve have chosen the right course. These verses at the end of John 6 may reflect the situation addressed in 1 and 2 John. Yet it seems that what is a major issue (in a situation of acute dissent, in the Epistles) is a minor one in the Gospel. Of course, one can go a step farther and hypothesize that originally the discourse on the heavenly bread in John 6 did not contain 51b–58 and that 19:34b–35 or also John 21 (perhaps plus the other passages that mention the Beloved Disciple) were added later, but to prove this beyond doubt is another matter.

On this cautious note, I end this sketch of the issues that were important in Johannine research around 1975 and of the positions taken up by the present author. It is now time to look at later developments.

AFTER 1990

In 1992, Martinus C. de Boer wrote a perceptive article titled "Narrative Criticism, Historical Criticism, and the Gospel of John" in which he discusses the relation between a literary and a historical approach to the Fourth Gospel (De Boer 1992). He later returned to this matter in his *Johannine Perspectives on the Death of Jesus* (1996, 43–52). As an example of narrative–critical readings, De Boer takes R. Alan Culpepper's *Anatomy of the Fourth Gospel: A Study in Literary Design* (1983), but, he says, "the basic concerns and aims of this narrative–critical approach were signaled, somewhat ironically perhaps, by a historical critic, M. de Jonge" (1992, 35). He describes how I proceed with the assumption that the Fourth Gospel is a meaningful whole and how I insist that our study should focus on the finished form of the document. De Boer emphasizes that a strong case can be made that the Gospel of John is not entirely conceptually coherent nor narratively cohesive, even if it is stylistically uniform; also, he notes, Culpepper and I both admit that the Gospel is the product of a long and complex history of composition. We may perhaps not be able to give word–for–word reconstructions of sources or earlier redactional layers/prior editions of the Fourth Gospel, and we have to be cautious in our efforts to connect those with certain events and circumstances in the history of the Johannine community. But we have not finished our task as interpreters before we have tried to establish a correlation between the composition of the Gospel and the history of the group for which it was written. Narrative criticism is intrinsically and rigorously ahistorical; it concentrates on the story, and it explores the ways in which an implied author determines an implied reader's response. Yet, De Boer says, "within the methodological constraints of narrative criticism itself, in fact, the possibility has to be left open that in the Gospel's literary world the implied author presupposes knowledge both of a communal history and a composition history on the part of the implied reader" (1992, 47).[4] He concludes: "There is no reason, it seems, why narrative criticism cannot be another useful tool in the repertoire of the historical critic" (1992, 48).

In his book *Johannine Perspectives on the Death of Jesus* (1996), De Boer distinguishes, on the basis of the literary and theological "aporias" that can be detected in the present text of the Gospel of John, at least four distinct, major editions, each composed within the Johannine school. In his search for a suitable motivation for the production of each new edition and for a distinctive coherent and distinct theological point of view at each stage, he analyzes four different perspectives on Jesus' death, which he correlates with three crises that threatened the faith and identity of Johannine Christians. De Boer proceeds carefully, but does not hesitate to give a clear–cut picture of the four stages in Johannine history. His picture of Johannine communal history is most indebted to the works of his teachers J. Louis Martyn and Raymond Brown (for instance, Brown 1979) but differs from their reconstructions on several points (see De Boer 1996, 53–71, particularly the "Bibliographical Note" on pp. 67–70 and the chart on p. 71). With regard to the Fourth Gospel's history of composition, De Boer stresses (a) that the person responsible for each edition was the composer of a complete Gospel; (b) that it is often not possible to assign a verse or a paragraph to a particular stratum; (c) that

---

[4] In this context, De Boer (rightly) criticizes my statement that the Fourth Gospel "functioned as a whole among people that did not take its prehistory into account" (M. de Jonge 1977a, 198).

each layer of the Gospel deserves as much attention as any other; and (d) "that the theology of each layer has not been lost or rejected, but taken up into the subsequent editions and 'recontextualized,' thereby becoming part of a 'new literary identity' (De Jonge)" (1996, 72–82, quotation 79).

In the flood of publications on the Fourth Gospel, De Boer's book has not, perhaps, received the attention it deserves; in any case, the methodological considerations behind it deserve a more detailed debate. For me, it provided an incentive for a reconsideration of a number of issues (and for starting a discussion with Martin de Boer that continues to the present day). In my article "Christology, Controversy, and Community in the Gospel of John" (M. de Jonge 2000), I pointed out that De Boer's remarks on John's composition–history, particularly point d) above, raise the question of whether his presentation of the development of Johannine Christology, beginning with a reconstructed stage one and working down to the Gospel in its present form, can give an adequate description of the complex Christology at the final stage. Should we not rather work our way backward, starting with the Gospel as it lies before us and using the information that may be gleaned from the Johannine Epistles? If we choose this approach, I argued, it becomes a lot more difficult to make the step from John's "narrative world" to the situation(s) for which the Fourth Gospel was written. The Fourth Gospel's Christology was shaped during a long period of refining certain issues, no doubt in discussions among "insiders" and also in debates with "outsiders," Jews and (Jewish) Christians. The stories and discourses recorded in the Gospel may reflect that period and contain recollections of past events, but in their present form they serve to clarify and to strengthen the Christological beliefs of the Johannine school, which realizes that its Christology is the outcome of a long process of learning and unlearning in the school of the Spirit.[5]

In the end, my article of 2000 amounts to a restatement of my position in 1977. My primary concern remained an analysis of the Christology of the Gospel of John in its final form. I tried to explain its "high" Christology—centering around belief in Jesus, the Son sent by the Father

---

[5] On pp. 213–15 of the same article, I briefly discuss the thesis put forward in De Ruyter 1998 (a doctoral dissertation defended at Leiden); see also H. J. de Jonge 2001. I quote from De Ruyter's English summary: "From John's perspective the rejection of the unity of Jesus and God places his Christian opponents on equal footing with the adversaries of Jesus who rejected Jesus during his public ministry. The only polemic in which the writer of the gospel is engaged is that against the Christians of inadequate faith" (1998, 201). This approach does not explain why John's depiction of Jesus' debates and discussions is so complex and why so many different figures appear on the scene. The result is a two–dimensional rather than a three–dimensional picture of Johannine Christology.

as his final envoy—as the outcome of a complex process, and I noticed the struggle in Johannine circles to combine this belief with the notion that Jesus was a real human being who died on the cross. On many issues, De Boer offered fine exegetical observations, but I could not follow him in his detailed reconstruction of the composition history of the text and in his picture of the communal history resulting from it. Nevertheless, De Boer's insistence that New Testament scholars should not restrict themselves to pure literary analysis but rather should combine it with historical criticism, remains pertinent.

An important step forward in connection with the problem before us has been made by Jean Zumstein in his stimulating book *Kreative Erinnerung. Relecture und Auslegung im Johannesevangelium* (Zumstein 2004), a collection of essays in which he introduces the French term *relecture* to Johannine research and connects it with (among other things) "recontextualization," a term also used by Martin de Boer.[6] The term *relecture* is used in diachronic analysis to denote a creative process of continuation in which an initial text leads to the composition of a second text that acquires its full significance only in relation to the first. In the case of the Fourth Gospel one may note, for instance, earlier redactions that are succeeded by later ones that in turn incorporate the earlier text, reflect upon it, and actualize it to meet the challenges of a new historical context.

In the first essay in the collection, dealing with the history of Johannine Christianity, Zumstein rightly works his way backward, beginning with the reception of the Gospel of John in the second century and dealing next with the conflict over the interpretation of the Gospel reflected in the Johannine Epistles. The preceding stages in the history of the community are closely connected with the reconstructed stages of the composition of the Gospel. The final redaction of the text is represented (mainly) by chapter 21; the production of the main edition of the Gospel preceded this final version; before this was a period characterized by successive "*relectures*" that cannot be ordered chronologically. Zumstein is critical toward the historical reconstructions of J. Louis Martyn, Raymond Brown, and (earlier) Oscar Cullmann and stresses that the Fourth Gospel is not a history book or a *roman à clef*. Later on, speaking about the main edition, Zumstein points out that its aim was to strengthen and to deepen the faith of the Johannine circle of believers (20:30–31). The stories and discourses in the first part of the Gospel show reactions to Jesus

---

[6] For an introduction to Zumstein's approach, see especially the first two essays in *Kreative Erinnerung*, "Zur Geschichte des johanneischen Christentums" (2004, 1–14) and "Der Prozess der Relecture in der johanneischen Literatur" (2004, 15–30).

on the part of various types of persons (faith variously expressed, sympathy, rejection); the second part, concentrating on Jesus' revelation to the inner circle of disciples, is concerned with the faith of Jesus' disciples after Easter. According to Zumstein, the main edition presupposes a group of Christians who have been expelled from synagogues dominated by Pharisees and who are now attempting to come to terms with the implications of their new situation. Zumstein does not give a detailed analysis of this situation, but rather concentrates on the history of the composition of the Gospel in which a variety of *relectures* played a prominent part, successive "rereadings" that spell out the implications of received traditions for new circumstances—trying to reinterpret them, not to negate or to criticize them. These successive *relectures* were, after all, handed down until and including the final redaction. This presupposes the activity of a "school" that was responsible for the traditional process in the Johannine churches. Zumstein states "Das Joh ist nicht der geniale Entwurf einer einzigartigen Persönlichkeit, sondern das Zeugnis eines organisierten Kreises" ("the Gospel of John is not the brilliant design of a unique personality, but rather the testimony of an organized community" [2004, 13]). This school was also active in the situation in which the Johannine Epistles were written, when a conflict arose about the interpretation of a number of Johannine tenets of faith laid down in the Gospel.[7]

With regard to the final redaction reflected in John 21, Zumstein's main argument depends on what he perceives to be a shift in emphasis (2004, 8–9, 23–24, 27). In the main section of the Gospel of John (1–20), Christology is the central theme, whereas the final chapter is ecclesiologically oriented. Here we find a clear case of "recontextualization" connected with a historical change—Zumstein puts this redaction at the time of a migration of the Johannine Christians from Syria to Asia Minor. Next, it is important to note that 20:30–31 is left in place; the redactor has thus shown respect to the earlier edition, to which he added the last chapter of the present Gospel. A similar phenomenon may be found in 14:31. The words "Rise, let us be on our way" at the end of the first farewell discourse (13:31–14:31) were not omitted when later, as Zumstein also argues in several other essays, a second farewell discourse (chs. 15–16, followed by ch. 17) was added. This second farewell discourse is also ecclesiologically oriented, whereas the first (chs. 13–14) centers on Christology.[8] Other elements ascribed by Zumstein to the final redaction

[7] Here Zumstein does not mention the possibility that the Fourth Gospel, as we know it, received its final form after the crisis mentioned in 1 and 2 John. See my remarks earlier on John 19:31–37 and 6:60–71.

[8] Sometimes, this second discourse is subdivided into three parts: 13:31–14:31; 15:18–16:4a; 16:4b–33. Elsewhere, this third part (16:4b–33) is referred to

include glosses on traditional eschatology and the sacraments, and the end of chapter 3 (vv. 31–36). Here, I think, we may have *relectures*, but it is uncertain whether they belong to this final stage in tradition or to the period *before* the main edition of the Fourth Gospel was produced, in which Zumstein rightly refuses to distinguish chronologically between different layers of redaction.

Zumstein's approach is helpful in a number of ways. I appreciate his concentration on the literary processes that helped to shape the present text of the Gospel of John, and the fact that he starts with the Gospel in its final form, working backward toward the increasingly uncertain first stages. I welcome his restraint in connecting composition history with the history of the community; the nature of the evidence does not allow us to go into details. Further, Zumstein's *relecture* model leads to a balanced picture of the tradition process, with attention to the element of reinterpretation and explication (in interaction with changed circumstances) as well as for the aspect of continuation. I also note that his use of the relecture model is directly connected with the notion of collective authorship in a Johannine "school."

Yet with regard to the final point noted above, an important question remains: How may we be sure that repetitions and variations in the Gospel of John are the result of the work of several authors/redactors in succession? May these not be a characteristic of the style of one author or of a particular "school" at one point in time? Two lines of argumentation, I think, may lead to a hypothesis of successive redactions and more than one author. First, there are the arguments advanced by Zumstein with regard to chapter 21 and chapters 15–16. The fact that a substantial portion of the text shows a difference in emphasis with the main text is in itself important, but not decisive; combined with evidence of noninterference with the end of the preceding text, however, these differences may point to editorial activity of a later hand. Here we find at least one type of "aporia" (to use a term popular among earlier scholars; see, for example, De Boer 1996, 72–75) that is relevant for a theory positing more than one stage in the composition–history of the Fourth Gospel. Second, as I stressed earlier, we may compare the Fourth Gospel with the Johannine Epistles, in particular with 1 John, a letter that shows many points of agreement with the Gospel as well as significant differences—a situation that Zumstein views as a typical case of *relecture* (2004, 18–21). With due caution, we may perhaps go further than he and use the differences

---

as "the third farewell discourse" and described as a *relecture* of the first (15:1–17). Zumstein mentions in this connection the work of his pupil Andreas Dettwiler (Dettwiler 1995).

between the specific christological features in 1 John and the main christological emphasis in the Fourth Gospel to distinguish relectures within
the Gospel itself. [9]

At this point, it is useful to mention Klaus Scholtissek's suggestion
that *relecture* should be distinguished from *réécriture* (Scholtissek 2000b;
cf. 2000a, 105–6; 2004b, 458–60). Scholtissek limits the use of *relecture*
to diachronic analysis and uses *réécriture* to describe an analogous process in the synchronic relationship of passages within the Gospel of John,
where one basic theme is taken up, varied, and expressed differently by
the same author. Time and again, the reader of the Fourth Gospel is confronted with a complex argumentation, using repetition, amplification,
and variation of sentences or parts of sentences and of significant words.
Such an argumentation does not necessarily presuppose a situation calling for "recontextualization"; it may simply be inspired by the author's
wish to clarify a point or to go more deeply into the matter in hand.
Scholtissek regards *relecture* and *réécriture* as two complementary aspects
of a continuous process of reflection within the Johannine communities:
a constant "anamnesis/remembering" which is, according to John 14–17,
guided by the Spirit. Scholtissek does not, however, explicitly indicate
how one is able to distinguish between *relecture* and *réécriture*. Elsewhere,
he emphasizes that tensions and incoherences in a text must first be dealt
with synchronically: we begin with the final form of the text and will
always have to come back to the final form at the end of the interpretation process (Scholtissek 2000a, 98–101). Nevertheless, we should resort
to diachronic analysis where necessary and ought to take the historical
circumstances (the *Sitz im Leben*) reflected in the text into account. Thus,
we shall never be able to dispense with historical criticism.

In his surveys of research, Scholtissek notes several times the pre-
dominance of the synchronic approach (together with narrative criticism)
in modern studies on the Gospel of John (for instance, Scholtissek 2002,
117–18, 144–46). He mentions especially Thomas Popp's study *Grammatik des Geistes. Literarische Kunst und theologische Konzeption in Johannes
3 und 6* (2001; see Scholtissek 2002, 129–31; 2004a, 77–81; cf. Van Belle
2003a).[10] Popp analyzes John 2:23–3:36 and 6:1–71 and argues that the
repetitions, variations, and amplifications present in these sections are

---

[9] A complicating factor is that repetitions with variations similar to those
found in the Fourth Gospel can also be found in the various sections of 1 John
and between different sections in that letter.

[10] Van Belle calls Popp's work pioneering and innovative with respect to the
study of both Johannine style and Johannine Christology and states that it will
be a leading resource for the Leuven research project "The Literary Unity of the

the result of *réécriture* rather than of *relecture*. In fact, in Popp's view the Fourth Gospel is the result of the intense theological activity of an evangelist who joins together the various traditions circulating in Johannine circles into a homogeneous whole. This Gospel has to be taken seriously as a work of literary art, and we have to approach it as the work of a great spiritual leader rather than as the outcome of a number of editorial activities of anonymous persons. Popp shares this view on the Gospel of John not only with his *Doktorvater* Udo Schnelle, but also with other scholars—Scholtissek mentions especially Martin Hengel and Jörg Frey (2002, 125–28)—yet with regard to John 21, many are prepared to admit later editorial activity.

Not so Hartwig Thyen, who begins the introduction to his recent 800–page commentary with the statement, "In what follows we interpret the Gospel that has been handed down to us in the canon, from John 1:1 to 21:25, as a coherent and highly poetic literary and authorial text" (Thyen 2005, 1). This declaration is all the more remarkable in view of the fact that Thyen, who started his work on John under Bultmann, had earlier contributed many studies promoting a source and redaction–critical approach to the Fourth Gospel. At the Leuven Colloquium of 1975, for instance, Thyen conducted a seminar that led to a lengthy essay on the developments in Johannine theology and the history of the community, "Entwicklungen innerhalb der Johanneischen Theologie und Kirche im Spiegel von Joh. 21 und der Lieblingsjüngertexte des Evangeliums" (Thyen 1977).

THE COLLOQUIUM BIBLICUM LOVANIENSE 2005

Thyen's change in approach may, to some extent, be regarded as representative of the change in direction that can be discovered in Johannine research at large over the past thirty years. At the Leuven Colloquium of 2005, the subject "The Death of Jesus in the Fourth Gospel" was approached from various angles. By and large, the speakers at the conference assumed the unity of the Gospel of John and the basic coherence of its theology. The president, Gilbert Van Belle—whose opening address was titled "The Death of Jesus and the Literary Unity of the Fourth Gospel"— remarks in his report that during the panel discussion toward the end of the colloquium "it was correctly pointed out that some speakers were inclined to neglect the literary and historical critical background to the Fourth Gospel. This is an evident trend among many authors: they

---

Fourth Gospel: A Study of the Language and Style of the Fourth Evangelist with Special Attention to Repetitions and Variations."

read the Gospel synchronically, on the basis of the text as we have it, and are inclined to ignore its complex genesis and evolution" (Van Belle 2005, 578). Van Belle emphasizes that he himself remains convinced of the need to continue the tradition of historical–critical research, in which his own early thinking was formed, in confrontation with new methods.

As was to be expected, Martin C. de Boer's *Johannine Perspectives on the Death of Jesus* was a subject of discussion at the colloquium. De Boer himself conducted the Dutch speaking seminar and discussed the subject "Johannine History and Johannine Theology: The Death of Jesus as the Exaltation and the Glorification of the Son of Man." After a careful analysis of the relevant passages (cf. De Boer 1996, 157–217), he concluded that John uses the language of exaltation to describe Jesus' death by crucifixion. Likewise, the theme of "glorification" has not just Jesus' resurrection–ascension in mind but also his death/crucifixion. Johannine believers are being asked to see Jesus' death as his passage to the Father and the means whereby he reaches the presence of God. To what end, for whom, and in what circumstances has this identification of Jesus' crucifixion as his exaltation and glorification been made? Distinguishing between conflict followed by expulsion on the one hand and persecution with execution on the other, De Boer opts for the situation presupposed in John 15:20 (cf. 5:16–18) and 16:2b, belonging to the literary unit 15:18–16:4a. The experience of martyrdom led to a reinterpretation of Jesus' death, whereby his crucifixion was evidently understood to be in some way paradigmatic of the experience of the Johannine community.

In the English speaking seminar dealing with the subject "Does John Have a Coherent and Unified View of the Death of Jesus? A Discussion of the Tradition, History, and Theology of John," conducted by John Painter, De Boer's approach was compared with other theories that interpret the Fourth Gospel as a coherent composition. Painter prefers to use the term "editions" loosely and opts instead for the designation "watersheds." In his introductory paper for the seminar he writes, "It seems that the tradition, and the language in which it is expressed, were shaped in a succession of critical situations, which act like dams that will not let the tradition pass through until it has been reshaped to meet the particular crisis." Painter takes the view that one central figure, the evangelist, was responsible for earlier and later developments and for the genesis of the Fourth Gospel in oral communication over a long period of time, both inside and outside of Judea. Yet the "aporias" (Painter mentions particularly the Farewell Discourses and ch. 21) imply some written forms of the tradition within the process. In the end, Painter distinguishes four "watersheds" in the Fourth Gospel's composition–history.

The first is to be connected with the response to the experience of abandonment by Jesus (John 14:18). The second was produced by the expulsion of Johannine believers from the synagogue (9:22, 34; 12:42; 16:2). The third watershed seems to be the time that the Johannine group found itself surrounded by a hostile world, without the buffer of the broader Jewish community. The final redaction of the Gospel, evidenced by chapter 21 (and especially 21:24), took place at the crisis caused by the death of the Beloved Disciple. Painter himself was not primarily interested in the differences between the various stages in the composition of the Gospel; most of his seminar was devoted to the thesis "that the gospel is to be read in the light of the prologue, which is placed at the beginning, even if at a late stage in the composition."

The Present Situation

The present trend to give priority to synchronic analysis and (among other things) to take narrative criticism seriously, is to be applauded. But if we focus on the study of the final form of the text of the Fourth Gospel and proceed with the assumption that it is a meaningful whole, we should not overlook, as M. C. de Boer has emphasized, that the Gospel is not entirely conceptually coherent nor completely narratively cohesive, notwithstanding its uniformity in vocabulary and style. And if we emphasize that one of the typical elements of Johannine style is repetition with variation and amplification, we should not necessarily conclude to *réécriture* by one author rather than to *relecture* by different, succeeding authors. *Réécriture* and *relecture* represent two different aspects of the same process, and even when there is only one author involved, this person may want to vary in order to respond to a different community situation. I still think that the hypothesis of a Johannine "school" has much to recommend it. In any case, I remain hesitant with regard to the tendency to assign (again) a decisive role to a theologically gifted person of great authority, supposedly active during a long period of the Johannine community's history and responsible for the Gospel in its final form. Even if such a person existed, he did not operate in a vacuum but had to respond to changes in the situation of the believers.

We shall always have to start with the Gospel of John as it lies before us. We have to realize that the great variety of traditional and redactional elements that may be detected in the text today served to guide and strengthen the Johannine community in its allegiance to God and to Jesus Christ as the unique Son of God. As it stands, the Fourth Gospel is the outcome of a long period of internal discussion, and it also reflects debates with others; but, as far as I can see, acute conflicts with outsiders are a thing of the past. Bearing this in mind we should, however, *at the present juncture* concentrate on the question of the extent to which the composition–history of the Fourth Gospel can still be reconstructed and how it can be used as a window on the history of the Johannine community. Old style literary criticism may have been one–sided, but now the pendulum has swung too far in the opposite direction. We will not be able to distinguish in detail between a great number of editions of the Gospel, but if we could succeed in locating more "watersheds" (as defined by Painter), this would be an advance. I also think that especially the *relecture* model can be applied more intensively; comparison, in particular, between 1 John and the Fourth Gospel may still yield new results. It would pay off, I suspect, if one would review the many detailed analyses in M. C. de Boer's monograph, keeping consistently the *relecture* model in mind.

Exegetes can never limit themselves to synchronic analysis. I remain convinced that only literary analysis combined with historical criticism will lead to a full picture of the state of affairs.

7: RESPONSE

THE COMBINATION OF A LITERARY AND A HISTORICAL APPROACH TO THE GOSPEL OF JOHN

Peter G. Kirchschlaeger

Marinus de Jonge ends his interesting contribution to this volume with the affirmation that "exegetes can never limit themselves to synchronic analysis. I remain convinced that only literary analysis combined with historical criticism will lead to a full picture of the state of affairs." Before arguing for the combination of a literary and a historical approach to the Gospel of John, he discusses the progress of academic discussion during roughly the last thirty years, following his own steps within Johannine research and indicating different periods of thought. I agree with De Jonge that only in the combination of a literary and a historical approach to the Gospel of John may we find answers to the many questions this Gospel is raising. I would go even further than De Jonge by saying that only with a carefully executed combination of methods can we avoid the risk of too premature and superficial answers to important but very complex questions. What do I mean by that? Let me formulate the issue in a question that will focus my short response to De Jonge's essay: Where are the limits of both approaches and where are the undiscovered potentials of both approaches?

I understand the Gospel of John as a narrative that relies, as every fiction does, upon its socio-historical context without being a historical report. First of all, then, the important impulses from narrative criticism have to be considered: the text as a narrative has its narrative structure. This structure is built from different narrative elements and components: the plot (system of relations and system of actions—what and why), the different characters and their characterizations (who), the point of view (why), focalization (who sees) and the setting (when and where). But, second, because the text is related to its socio-historical context, an interest in the historical situation of the time of the formation of the text is legitimate. As Hans–Josef Klauck pointed out in his introduction to the inaugural session of the Corpus Hellenisticum Novi Testamenti Seminar at the 2005 Society of Biblical Literature meeting, the contextualization of the biblical texts is part of all traditional historical–critical exegesis and not merely an idiosyncratic element of the *religionsgeschichtliche Schule*. Both approaches, narrative and historical, must be pursued in isolation from one another but, at the end of the day, ultimately combined dialectically.

The literary approach has given us new insights about the meaning of the Gospel of John. One difficult challenge, however, is the need for the cautious implementation of some very attractive theoretical models. Let me demonstrate what I mean by returning to an example noted by De Jonge. The question raised by Klaus Scholtissek regarding whether we are dealing with *réécriture* or with *relecture* in the Gospel of John is very important and of significance for Johannine research (see Scholtissek 1999–2004; 2000b; 2004b). The problem, however, as De Jonge notes, is that Scholtissek "does not explicitly indicate how one is able distinguish between '*relecture*' and '*réécriture*'" while he "regards '*relecture*' and '*réécriture*' as two complementary aspects of a continuous process of reflection within the Johannine communities."

An undiscovered potential I see in the persistent search for a figurative meaning is to take more seriously the genre of the Gospel of John: a "Gospel" does not aim to report historical facts, but rather the message of Jesus Christ. At the same time, its historiographical character stands for the importance and significance of history for the Gospel of John. Because I see highlighting the historical approach as my more urgent task, and considering the brevity of this response, I will end my reflections on the literary approach and elaborate further only on the limits and undiscovered potentials of the historical approach.

The historical approach to the Gospel of John has to consider that every text can create a new historical situation. Therefore, the relation between the text and its historical context has to be—based on the interaction theory—a dialectical one. In the case of the Gospel of John, the text of the Gospel itself is the most important source of information about its socio-historical context. Although we can find relevant indications about its context, we have to consider the genre of the Gospel. We cannot directly apply historical indications to our construction of the sociohistorical context behind the text because, first of all, a Gospel does not aim to give a historical report but rather to reveal a "good message." Of course, we have to ask questions about the historical context of the text, but we must be very careful before answering them in any way. I will try to indicate what I mean with some examples.

First, the alleged expulsion from the synagogue and the assumed persecution of Christians are based on several references in the text of the Gospel of John. The Gospel uses the word ἀποσυνάγωγος ("put out of the synagogue") three times; this is often understood, in combination with the *Birkat–Haminim*, as an indication of the historical expulsion of the Johannine community from the synagogue. Yet more and more Johannine scholars doubt the link to the *Birkat–Haminim* because of the character of the *Birkat–Haminim* and the historical character of Judaism at that time. The latter issue is also the reason why, in any case, it would be more adequate to speak of one synagogue among many, rather than of a universal decree. Furthermore, the Gospel of John shows us that the synagogue is not to be understood as antithetical to Jesus. Finally, the alleged expulsion from the synagogue is not a legend of foundation for the Johannine community (as it seems to be understood by some scholars), as is evident from the fact that there is in the narrative of the Gospel still a very strong link between the Jewish Jesus and his fellow Jews. The conflict between Jesus and the "Jews" is a conflict within Judaism. Therefore, the term ἀποσυνάγωγος must be understood more precisely as an illustration of the denial of Jesus and his followers, not as a direct indication of a historical fact—by its very genre, the Gospel of John does not necessarily want to give us historical facts. There can be seen a reality of separation that is reflected within the Gospel of John and that has influenced the text, although we do not know how this separation was provoked and the dimension that it took.

The need for a clear definition and differentiation between separation, disrespect, discrimination, and systematic persecution becomes obvious. The growing skepticism within the scholarly community concerning the missing evidence for a persecution of Christians in the first century points in the same direction. Did not the narrated persecutions function to underline a component of the Christian message, namely, that the greatest suffering would not harm Christian commitment and would be irrelevant to believing Christians after the death and resurrection of Jesus Christ? The necessity of a careful distinction between immediate historical indications and narrative elements is evident. The use of the term "Jews" in the Gospel of John and its meaning has taught us a very significant lesson in this regard.

Second, any reference to a Johannine "school" or "community" cannot rely on very solid evidence. Of course, we can argue that these are extremely helpful models to explain certain points. But when we use these models, we run the risk that they not only help us to illustrate some aspects of the situation, but also frame our point of view as well. The text of the Gospel of John invites us, as Zumstein has shown (2004, 1–14), to think of several authors. If we speak only of "authors," we lose, of course, the important element that these authors are in a certain way related to one another, although the text shows us this only implicitly. The same point can be made regarding the addressees and the links between authors and addressees, e.g., by considering 1 John and 2 John (see 1 John 2:19; Klauck 1989, 59–68). Because a better model is missing, I still would argue for the use of the terms "school" and "community." But it would be a somewhat more prudent answer to these relevant questions to admit the limits of the evidence and to provide a precise definition of what we can and what we cannot prove.

Another undiscovered potential of the historical approach is a broader consideration of the ancient literary context of the Gospel of John (e.g., Dion of Prusa, Plutarch, Philo, Epictetus, Seneca, etc.) to get an idea about its sociohistorical setting. One must always respect the genre of the sources without falling into "parallel–mania," but a more consequent search for the figurative meaning of the text that takes seriously its literary genre would be appropriate, noting, again, that a Gospel does not aim to report historical facts but to announce the message of Jesus Christ.

Where are the limits of both approaches? Where are the undiscovered potentials of both approaches? Of course, I cannot answer these questions in an essay of this length. Here, I simply have tried to underline the point made by Marinus de Jonge and even go a little further. While writing this response, the image of the pendulum mentioned by de Jonge remained in front of my eyes. Maybe it could help us to make a clear distinction between knowledge and imagination while leaving the framework of ideological schools behind us.

CHAPTER 8

THE GOSPEL OF JOHN AND THE
SIGNS GOSPEL

Robert T. Fortna

In the early 1970s—when I was still a raw young scholar and not long after my doctoral dissertation had been published as *The Gospel of Signs*— I went for the first time to an overseas annual meeting of the Society of New Testament Studies (SNTS). I was introduced to two senior Europeans (I would guess recovering Bultmannians), each of whom said upon hearing my name, more or less, "Ah, so you are Fortna; you are quite wrong." My children enjoyed that story. At the time, I concluded it was at least good to know that my book had not been ignored. Since then, to be sure, there have been many more detractors.[1] But not a few supporters (for example, Cope 1987), and from some of them I have learned to

---

[1] Folker Siegert, whose recent work *Der Ertsenwurf des Johannes* (2004) builds heavily on my reconstruction, observes that especially in Germany it brought me "scorn and derision." This was partly, I believe, because I claimed to recover the original Greek text of the source. Siegert believes that the signs source, or what he calls the "pre–Johannine non–synoptic tradition," was not written but oral and used from memory by John the Elder (of 2 and 3 John)—the author, as he holds, of the still Christian–Jewish "first version" of the Johannine Gospel. If so, I would contend that the text of that oral tradition was so fixed that when reused by the first Johannine writer, it created many of the aporias in the Fourth Gospel. Siegert is about to publish a commentary on his reconstruction.

adapt my reconstruction (I prefer of course to think of it as a recovery) of the "Signs Gospel," the source from which, I believe, the Fourth Evangelist derived stories about Jesus' miracles and death. Further, I would claim that my early work, and the subsequent work of others, has revealed the extent to which the Signs Gospel hypothesis is more than a study in source criticism. Any answer to the question of possible documentary sources for the Fourth Gospel reflects also on one's beliefs about: (1) the circumstances in which the text of the Fourth Gospel was produced, (2) its literary unity, (3) its relationship to the Synoptics, and (4) the question of historicity. My subsequent work has led me into all these questions. It is now twenty years since the sequel to the 1970 book—and my principal redaction-critical work on John—*The Fourth Gospel and Its Predecessor* (1988) appeared. Despite the fact that in the meantime my attention has turned away from Johannine Studies, how has my mind changed on the existence of the source and these four issues?

I remain fairly sure that a source *once existed*, a relatively brief written (or if still oral, firmly worded) text containing virtually all the narratives in John that happen to be like the Synoptics. In *The Gospel of Signs*, I was rash enough to include a complete, reconstructed Greek text of the source, and I would no longer hold that that reconstruction is legitimate in its detail. Among other revisions, D. Moody Smith (1984, 90–93) convincingly proposed that John 12:37–40 derives from the Signs Gospel, an explanation for the plot against Jesus and a transition into the passion story. But that a document not unlike my somewhat revised version of a signs source in *The Fourth Gospel and Its Predecessor* underlies our Gospel of John does not seem to me any less tenable.

I began my exploration with Bultmann's proposed *Sēmeiaquelle* ("signs source"), attempting to refine his criteria and leaving aside matter not essential to the sign stories themselves. What remains is a barebones account of some of Jesus' notable miracles: water, a lot of it, turned into wine (John 2:1–11); a young man's healing from a distance (4:46–54); an astonishing catch of fish (21:2–11); a shepherd's lunch turned into a meal for thousands (6:1–12); a dead man raised (11:1–45); a man, blind from birth, enabled to see (9:1–7); and a man lame for thirty–eight years healed (5:1–9). In the source, these episodes were called "signs" and were evidently numbered (vestiges remain in 2:11a, 4:54a, and 21:14a) and arranged in a geographically logical sequence. They offered a terse, vivid account of Jesus' ministry first in Galilee and then in Jerusalem—a spellbinding list, in which Jesus acts not out of sympathy for those in need—and scarcely an account of a ministry in any strict sense. Rather it is a collection of stories that demonstrate *who* Jesus was, no less (and no more) than the Messiah of Jewish expectation (20:31a).

THE GOSPEL OF JOHN AND THE SIGNS GOSPEL

As I continued examining the Fourth Gospel's narrative, I also found myself following, in briefest form, Bultmann's outline for a "passion source"—stories about Jesus' death (and its sequel) pulled together and recounted by the same editor as the signs. These two, probably originally distinct sources recounting Jesus' signs and apologizing for his passion and death, had been brought together and made to follow one another so neatly that Jesus' resurrection at the end became the crowning sign of his identity (as indicated by what is now found at John 2:19). In view of this christological emphasis, the Fourth Evangelist's source could scarcely be called anything but a very simple and straightforward *Gospel*, a Gospel of Signs, the story of Jesus' life and death calculated to promote its author's theological vision. The purpose of such a Signs Gospel was solely to show Jews within the synagogue that Jesus had demonstrated his messianic status and that his death was in fulfillment of Scripture. On the basis of these signs, so it argued, Jews ought to join the Christian movement growing within first–century Judaism. This, I believe, rather than any sort of conversion, is the best way to describe what a Signs Gospel intended. It clearly did not promote the incarnational Christology that characterizes the current text of John, found within the first–person discourses, and it was not concerned with a Gentile mission. I therefore date the source somewhere in the 40s or 50s C.E.

Now to the subsequent questions that have arisen. First of all, I will address the circumstances in which the Fourth Gospel was produced. Despite recent attempts to lay it to rest, I cleave to J. Louis Martyn's identification of the crisis confronting the Johannine community in the late first century as both valid and vital (Martyn 2003). Martyn's approach is vital because it almost alone accounts for the creation of our Gospel of John. It seems to me as likely as ever that official post–70 C.E. Judaism disowned the Christian–Jewish movement within the synagogue, a movement that reflected the type of faith in Jesus as the Jewish Messiah advocated by the Signs Gospel. This crisis—the excommunication of the Johannine Christians because of their belief in Jesus (ἀποσυνάγωγος) appearing three times and only in John—led to a revising of the Signs Gospel and, further, to the creation or consolidation of the Johannine discourse material that so differs from the third–person prose narrative. With the official decision late in the century that such believers could no longer think of themselves as Jews, the relatively brief, and by that time perhaps long–standing, Signs Gospel was no longer of much validity and certainly was of little use. It had either to be discarded or, as I believe, revived and greatly expanded—quoted almost verbatim, corrected by brief inserted comments, and expanded and interpreted by the addition of the distinctly Johannine discourses. The uneven, aporia–laden narrative of the Fourth Gospel suggests such a compositional process.

Second, on the question of the literary unity of John: the pronounced contrast between brief narrative and the long discourses of Jesus, the latter unlike anything in the other canonical Gospels (including their various collections of Jesus' sayings), seems to me to be an obvious indication of at least a two–stage development in the text.[2] The canonical book reads in an almost Talmudic fashion—relatively brief stories greatly interspersed with poetic discourses that in some way or other comment on and widely differ from the prose accounts. How would one author have alternately written both?

The signs pericopes have been barely edited internally, but almost entirely rearranged in their order (reflecting the Johannine Jesus' movements to and from Jerusalem), with a few very brief sayings of Jesus inserted (for example, 2:4; 4:48). These changes have produced the numerous aporias, the difficulties within the text (cf. 2:1; 4:54; 6:1) that are virtually absent from the Synoptics. An earlier document (or fixed oral tradition) has been so carefully preserved, with scarcely any rewriting, that we are clearly reading the work of two authors. And, I hold, the Signs Gospel, the earlier, can more or less readily be lifted out of our Gospel of John.

As to literary style, there is simply no way to demonstrate any stylistic unity. One can only disprove the stylistic disunity between hypothetical reconstructions of two or more literary stages. Ruckstuhl and Dschulnigg have attempted the latter (1991), but the former, which they also claim, cannot be done (see below). Of course, many have argued against the existence of such a source on the grounds that it cannot be reconstructed from the current text of the Fourth Gospel. This is the case, my detractors often claim, because the text of John evidences a high level of stylistic unity. But that alleged unity is a chimera. The Gospel of John is, of course, one literary document; the author/redactor intended to create a coherent narrative, and it almost reads as such. But the study of a document's style as a whole can only prove the existence of its sources when they demonstrate a style notably different from that of the document that hypothetically used them. The major twentieth–century studies of John's style could, at best, attempt to falsify particular source theories. Ruckstuhl and Dschulnigg (1991) sought to show that my proposed Signs Gospel does not evidence a style different from that of the Fourth Gospel

[2] Siegert's hypothesis (2004) of a relatively early, rudimentary yet Johannine Gospel, later developed into our Gospel of John, needs further study. If valid, it suggests a three-stage development.

as a whole. But they used a stylometrically naïve method. More recently, a highly sophisticated stylometric and statistical modeling argues to the contrary, namely that my Signs Gospel does show a distinct style, by a statistically significant margin (Felton and Thatcher 2001). In any case, I believe it is nearly obvious that the reconstructed Signs Gospel does have a distinct style.

As an aside, I want to defend redaction criticism, which has acquired a rather poor press of late, somewhat deservedly. It was the need to provide for the redaction criticism of John that led me in the first place to attempt a reconstruction of sources. A principal achievement of a Signs Gospel theory, as I attempted to demonstrate in a series of articles in the 1970s and in *The Fourth Gospel and Its Predecessor*, is that it makes redaction criticism of John possible. I quite agree that the Gospel of John, or any Gospel, ought to be read as it now stands, not divided for the reader into earlier and later elements. And, further, the text ought not be read with blinders, ignoring the prevailing sociological and political situations (so far as they can be known) of both the author and the intended audience. Thus, I focused on the crisis that evidently required the source, if it was not to be abandoned entirely, to be greatly adapted so as to speak to the Johannine Evangelist's new circumstances. And when I compare the redaction with the source, I seek to show how those very circumstances evoked many of the additions and corrections made by the Johannine author/redactor. Again, yes, of course the modern reader needs to deal with the text lying before her or him. But an auxiliary look over the Fourth Evangelist's shoulder, as the source was presumably adapted, aids considerably in understanding the given text as a response to what author and community had experienced.

On the subject of the Johannine sayings material, I have cast doubt on the likelihood that the composition–history of the discourses can be recovered. My reconstruction of the Signs Gospel includes almost no sayings. In these stories, Jesus merely gives terse directives or asks simple questions relating to his ensuing action—"Fill the jars with water" (2:7) or "Where have you laid him?" (11:34). Even if historically factual, these utterances tell us virtually nothing about the historical Jesus, and it is impossible to say whether they are more than window dressing necessary for the stories. But what about the lengthy Johannine discourses? In *The Gospel of Signs*, I simply left open the question whether the Johannine Evangelist had used traditional sayings material not included in the Signs Gospel. I had not set out to find a purely narrative source, but the more such a source emerged the less I could believe that the discourses stemmed from the same origin. Over time, as evident in *The Fourth Gospel and Its Predecessor*, I came to recognize a rather fundamental distinction between story and saying in John, with the stories coming from the signs source and the discourses essentially added as theological commentary on the signs and on the controversy with the synagogue. I now see rather clearly that the late–first century crisis I have mentioned may have given rise to the discourses, in at least their final form, out of a more inchoate Johannine tradition; the crisis certainly demanded their addition to the Signs Gospel. And it is even possible that the contentious debate the crisis produced between the evangelist's community and the synagogue accounts for the creative invention of some of the discourse material altogether. In John 5:17–47, for example, the evangelist says that the Jews wanted to kill Jesus because of his self–proclaimed unity with the Father, and he defends his claims on the testimony of a number of "witnesses," including Moses; this appears to reflect the debate with the synagogue as the initiating element. Whether the crisis gave rise to the discourses altogether or in some cases only occasioned their codification, it argues for a later date for John than has sometimes been proposed but not so late a date as others have suggested. The best estimate for the date of the earliest version of a fairly complete version of John's Gospel would be some time after 85 C.E. (or whatever date can be given to the revision of the Twelfth Benediction that required Christian Jews to leave their synagogue and cease thinking of themselves as Jewish).

Third, on the question of John's relationship to the Synoptics: quite obviously, if there was dependence of John upon any of the Synoptics, then no narrative source of the sort I propose would have reason to exist. So what follows is hardly dispassionate. I believe that the Fourth Evangelist did not make use of the Synoptics for three reasons that can be succinctly stated. First, so far as I know, there is in John no evidence of patently redactional matter from the Synoptics, the claims of Frans Neirynck and the Leuven School notwithstanding (Neirynck 1977). If the present Gospel does include material that was clearly created by the Lukan author, for example, the evangelist must have borrowed that from Luke; but I find no material like that in John. This being the case, one cannot hold that information in John was derived from the Synoptics themselves; rather, the Gospel of John depends upon the same general stock of tradition that *underlies* the Synoptics. Second, it requires a very complicated game to explain just how the Fourth Evangelist would have used the Synoptics. There is no way to trace it except by the most ingenious reconstruction. Occam's razor suggests we not try. Third, if the author of John knew and used the Synoptics, this fact would tell us virtually nothing redaction–critically about its meaning. This, of course, is not an argument against dependence as much as it is a reason to look at a redaction–critical analysis of John to see to what extent it proves useful and self–validating.

There does appear to be at least some connection between John and the Synoptics. John's narratives are not unique in the New Testament the way the discourses are. The narratives are, to be sure, like the Synoptics and in some instances have synoptic parallels, but they are different from their synoptic parallels, sometimes appearing in a more primitive form. Further, the miracle stories in John are more direct, if sometimes even more heightened, than their synoptic counterparts, and the use they are put to is also simpler and, in fact, quite unlike the Synoptics. This situation is readily explained by the Signs Gospel hypothesis. Such a source was dependent upon the same oral tradition that would underlie Mark, Matthew, and Luke. Yet it uses this common tradition differently from the Synoptics in a singular respect, attributing to Jesus' working of miracles the claim that they are fundamental evidence ("signs") of his messiahship. In the Synoptics, of course, Jesus rejects any request for a sign to account for his activity (Mark 8:11–12; Luke 11:29). Further, in the source the signs stem from Jesus, not "from heaven" as Mark's Pharisees demand, and it is the resurrection that satisfies the expectation for signs (2:18–19). Using the kind of oral tradition lying behind the Synoptics, all that was needed was to select a number of Jesus' miracles, arrange them in a logical geographical order, and treat them as demonstrations of his messiahship. The overlap between John and the Synoptics is, once more, best explained by holding that, in a way that reflected its special interests, the Signs Gospel drew from much the same tradition as the Synoptics and that the Fourth Evangelist then absorbed this material into the much fuller Gospel.

Fourth and finally, the tortured question of the Fourth Gospel's value as a source for the historical Jesus. As I have said in the past, there may be details in what I assign to the Signs Gospel that reflect memory from the time of Jesus. This possibility raises several questions about the Johannine claims that the information in the finished Gospel reflects the "witness" of the Beloved Disciple, a close associate of Jesus (John 13:23; 19:25–35; 20:1–10; 21:7, 20–24). I have never been able to fathom with any confidence the provenance of this figure. Yes, possibly there was such a person, whose special relation to Jesus was possibly created within the Johannine tradition. The lack of any such character in the synoptic tradition obviously argues against his full–blown existence from Jesus' time. But it is just as possible, I believe, that the Beloved Disciple is mythic and was created to fill a purpose, very likely no longer discernible, at the time of the completion of the Fourth Gospel (see Thatcher 2001). He first appears in the narrative only at 13:23 (the unnamed disciple of the Baptist in John 1:35–40, like the disciple "known to the high priest" in 18:16, can scarcely be the Beloved Disciple). This argues for his creation, or at least the maturation of his tradition, at the time of the Johannine community's crisis with the synagogue and in connection with the finished form of the story of Jesus' last days. For me then, the question of John's historicity is essentially a question of the historicity of the Signs Gospel, from which virtually all the narrative material derived.

Some stories in the source, as I mentioned, have a simpler form than their synoptic parallels. Does this mean that it can take us back closer to the deeds of the historical Jesus? Probably not to any useful degree. I say this first because I believe that Jesus himself, contrary to the source's presentation, had no Christology. He neither claimed for himself any special status nor viewed himself as Messiah, still less as the Johannine Son of God. This being the case, I cannot accept that Jesus did deeds that he intended to be taken as "signs" of Christology about himself. Second, when this Christological reading is subtracted from the Signs Gospel's stories, one gains very little that can be attributed to Jesus beyond what the Synoptics already offer. The source's presentation evidences a consistent tendency to heighten the miraculous element of Jesus' deeds. At John 2:6, no less than 120 gallons of water are about to be turned to wine; at 4:51–53, the boy is healed at the very moment that Jesus pronounces him alive; at 5:5, the man at Bethesda has been lame for thirty–eight years, and the man in John 9 has been blind from birth; Lazarus was dead in the tomb a full four days before Jesus raised him (11:39); and the miraculous catch of fish is so great that Peter's net was in danger of tearing (21:11). One can easily imagine how the oral tradition came to understand the miracle stories in this enhanced way and especially, how the Signs Gospel would add to them to justify its claims about Jesus' messiahship.

A somewhat different set of problems relates to the Signs Gospel's passion story, which like the pre–Markan (but not the Markan) passion is fundamentally apologetic. The account was no doubt built up from traditional materials and written to counter claims that no one could be Messiah whose life had ended in crucifixion by Rome. Similarly, the source's passion was produced to demonstrate, from the Jewish Scriptures, that the Christ had been destined to die just as Jesus did, according to a series of prophecies. (In Matthew, the same claim is more explicit: what Jesus experienced happened *in order* to fulfill Scripture.) As in the pre–synoptic passion tradition, the Signs Gospel's account was most likely based as much on these OT proof texts as on any historical memory of the events. But, as I have suggested, the source's passion account has to be earlier than the version we have in Mark. The Markan author has reinterpreted the story so that the death of Jesus is no longer something that needs to be explained away, but rather the very central focus of that Gospel's message. The Signs Gospel in no way reflects this reinterpretation. Its passion story is so driven by apologetic impulses that its overall accuracy is difficult to determine.

But I do think we can find traces of authentic memory in the Signs Gospel's passion account. On Jesus' action in the temple (John 2:13–20)—which would have appeared in the Signs Gospel as a prelude to the passion, rather than as now in the present Gospel among the signs, following the Cana story—we are told that there were oxen and sheep in the temple, that Jesus used a whip, and that he "poured out" the coins. None of these details appear in the Synoptics. The differences, alongside the many parallels, between the Signs Gospel's version and the Synoptics perhaps make it unlikely that the story was entirely fabricated on the basis of Old Testament texts. More likely, the two versions of the story represent independent attempts to relate the same historical event, and which of the details are historical is probably difficult to determine.

Several features of the anointing at Bethany (John 12:1–8) are possibly factual. I would think that Jesus' premonition that the anointing is a foreshadowing of his burial could be historical, without implying any special self–understanding on his part. Jesus' scriptural quote to Judas, "The poor you always have with you," may be a remembered detail; even his addition, "But you do not always have me." And the opening note that these events took place "six days before Passover" appears gratuitous and, therefore, just possibly factual.

On Jesus' final meal, I believe it is not easy to identify a source behind the present account in John 13. At the same time, John's story, unlike the Synoptics, has no hint of the later Lord's Supper and also shows no evidence of being a Passover meal. The footwashing that replaces the synoptic bread and cup is consistent with the lack of self–aggrandizement found in much of the Jesus tradition, and so perhaps may include authentic memories.

On Jesus' arrest (John 18:1–12), the image of Peter's attack on Malchus, the high–priest's slave, is either a skillful elaboration of the tradition or a gratuitous memory. And it seems highly unlikely to me that stories showing such a prominent leader of the early church having denied Jesus could be fictitious (18:15–27). Jesus' crucifixion, if not the Johannine elaboration of the trial before Pilate, is surely factual, and the memory of the locale (Golgotha), along with Mark and Matthew, appears likely (19:17–19).

Beyond such instances as these, it is now impossible to say whether we are mostly dealing, in Crossan's words, with "history remembered" or "prophecy historicized" (1995, 2–4).

What, finally and parenthetically, of the slight possibility that the Johannine discourses, not in any way deriving from the Signs Gospel, may also take us back toward the historical Jesus? It seems obvious that Jesus' proclamation of the kingdom of God would have been at best over-shadowed and all but contradicted, if he taught that he had a very high christological status, the central premise of the Fourth Gospel's lengthy portrayal of his teaching. What is striking about the Synoptics, which are of course decidedly christological, is that this central focus of his public work (the kingdom of God) could still remain intact. In John, it is missing altogether. If Jesus spoke as he does in John, then the voice of the Jewish rabbi, the itinerant teller of subversive parables that we hear in the Synoptics, is simply false.

So we seem to have a certain amount of original, if mainly incidental, information about Jesus' deeds in the Signs Gospel, some of which may reflect authentic memory. John's discourses have been developed, either from previously disconnected traditions or wholesale, as a theological response to the crisis of excommunication. They tell us virtually nothing about the historical Jesus. Emphatic as I am on this last point, and largely convinced on the others, I look forward to the responses and dialogue that may ensue.

8: RESPONSE

THE FOURTH GOSPEL IN
FIRST–CENTURY MEDIA CULTURE

Tom Thatcher

Robert Fortna's lucid essay, a solid summary and update of his work on
the background of the Johannine Literature, leaves me (as his work has
always left me) with the following question: How might recent research
on the media culture of early Christianity impact our understanding of
the traditions behind the Fourth Gospel and its value as a source for the
historical Jesus?

Fortna's work on the Johannine Literature in the 1960s, 1970s, and
1980s both epitomized his generation of scholarship and forecast the current revival of interest in the setting and historical value of the Fourth
Gospel. His career as a Johannine and Jesus scholar has been driven by
two essential questions. First, what sources lie behind John's witness?
Where did this information come from and, as a corollary concern, why
does the Gospel of John so seldom enjoy multiple attestation? Second,
how should we understand the relationship between the Gospel of John
and the career of the historical Jesus? On numerous occasions, John insists
that his "witness" is based upon the best testimony available, in support of
the more significant assertion that what he records is "true." But "true" in
what sense? And how might we go about answering these questions when
the conventional methods and criteria of Jesus research seem inadequate
to the Fourth Gospel's peculiar problems?

Viewed in hindsight, Fortna's answers to these key questions clearly reflect the spirit of the age in which his Signs Gospel hypothesis was born. His ingenious proposal was appealing on three fronts: first, because it seemed to explain the Fourth Gospel's notorious literary and theological "aporias"; second, because it secured a seat for Johannine scholars at the banquet table of redaction criticism; and third, because it promised to shed new light on the twisted path from John back to Jesus. If the Fourth Evangelist did, in fact, borrow much of his material from an earlier source, one could easily explain why the Gospel of John sometimes makes Christ subordinate to the Father while elsewhere elevating him to complete equality; why the narrator cannot seem to remember whether or not Jesus actually baptized people (cp. John 3:22 with 4:2); why Jesus criticizes the royal official for asking for a sign when, in fact, he has not asked for one (4:48). These and other problems could now be readily resolved in terms of John's editorial work—his failure (Fortna would say, "refusal") to hide the theology and style of the Signs Gospel under his own compositions. In fact, John's beliefs could now be more fully understood in diachronic perspective by comparing his expansions and assertions (primarily the discourse material) with the claims of this earlier document. Finally, even if the Signs Gospel ultimately could not answer the question of John's historicity, it certainly could take us closer to Jesus, reaching back past Mark to the dimmer period of Paul and Q and offering a glimpse of the genesis of narrative Gospels.

Aside from its explanatory power, Fortna's thesis remains interesting simply because (as Fortna himself has often noted) it cannot be disproved. There is, in other words, no inherent reason why the Fourth Gospel could not be based on earlier written documents, and many notable scholars have suggested particularly that John's "signs" stories are likely based upon earlier accounts. Support for this conclusion may be easily garnered by analogy with the two–source theory, which suggests that at least some early Christian authors (Matthew and Luke) utilized available documents (Mark and Q) in writing stories about Jesus. Indeed, Luke seems to refer directly to books similar to the Signs Gospel when he reminds Theophilus that "many have undertaken to set down an orderly account of the events that have been fulfilled among us" (Luke 1:1). One can therefore easily imagine that a Johannine Christian produced the first edition of the Fourth Gospel by expanding and revising an earlier account of Jesus' activity. Indeed, the novelty of Fortna's approach lies not so much in his claim that John used documentary sources, but rather in his belief, typical of recent Johannine scholarship in North America and Britain, that these sources were independent of the Synoptics.

In my view, however, the ease with which modern scholars can imagine John quoting, adapting, and expanding an earlier Signs Gospel raises the most substantial red flag against Fortna's proposal. The notion that John read, reflected upon, quoted from, and added to earlier documents—a Signs Gospel, a discourse source, the Synoptics—carries explanatory power for us simply because this is exactly how we use written texts today. But John's first–century media culture was not like our own. In that world, the vast majority of people could not read and even fewer could write; oral speech and collective memory were the technologies through which authors organized and presented their thoughts; written texts were "published" through recitation to gathered groups; and even the most sacred books were paraphrased ad hoc in service of exhortation. Simply put, the Fourth Evangelist lived in an oral world, a world in which "texts" were generally understood in acoustic terms and in which "composition" was a function of speech. But while this fact has been widely recognized by biblical scholars—Werner Kelber's *The Oral and the Written Gospel* is now twenty–five years old—it has not yet had an impact on studies of the Johannine Literature in a significant way. A more adequate understanding of John's media culture would substantially influence our understanding of the Fourth Gospel's sources and historical value at several points. Three such implications will be briefly noted in dialogue with Fortna's groundbreaking work.

First, in discussing the Fourth Evangelist's appropriation of the Signs Gospel, Fortna suggests that John quoted his source "almost verbatim." This is a somewhat softer version of his earlier claim that John has reproduced the Signs Gospel word for word, sometimes adding or taking away material but never substantially revising the text (Fortna 1988, 1–10). Although this model allows for a more detailed reconstruction of John's source, in my view it does not accurately reflect the way that people used documents in John's cultural context, not even sacred ones. A quick look at Philo's writings or Josephus' *Antiquities* will reveal the extent to which even very literate Jews felt quite comfortable "revising" their sacred texts to serve rhetorical interests, and one could scarcely argue that Matthew and Luke handled Mark and Q in the way that Fortna describes. While it remains unclear exactly what it might mean to "quote" or "cite" a text in the first century, it clearly did not mean what it means to modern literate students of the Bible. This fact should serve as the backdrop to all future considerations of John's documentary sources and the Fourth Gospel's relationship to the Synoptics.

Second, the emerging new perspective on early Christian media culture calls for a substantial reconsideration of the very notion of "aporias"—the backbone of all recent source proposals and developmental theories—in the text of the Fourth Gospel. One can scarcely deny that John's style and presentation are frequently puzzling, but it is also quite clear that the label "aporia" has often been applied to any aspect of the text that a particular interpreter, or school of interpreters, cannot readily understand. Here again, John's narrative must be evaluated in terms of its own media dynamics. It comes as little surprise if modern scholars—who are among the most literate individuals in the history of the human race, deeply ingrained in the logic of print and film—do not appreciate the literary aesthetics of a text that was, at least in its earliest formative stages, composed and published orally. Similarly, modern readers, who are accustomed to "doing theology" with diagrams and flow charts, are likely to find tensions in John's oral theological thinking. But while a sharp distinction between verses that reflect a "low (= Jewish) Christology" and those that promote a "high (= Greco–Roman) Christology," or between verses that promote a "realized eschatology" and those that promote a "future eschatology," may be meaningful to us, would John see the problem? How would John even understand the notion of "verses"? I would suggest that all use of the term "aporia" should be suspended until we can answer these questions in a more sophisticated, and historically viable, fashion.

Third, a thorough consideration of oral sensibilities and collective memory would, in my view, have a substantial impact upon the very notion of "the historical value of the Fourth Gospel." At the very least, a more sophisticated approach to first–century media culture would highlight the extent to which the canons of historical Jesus research reflect a literate mentality that would puzzle early Christians such as John, Mark, and Paul. Even the most foundational assumptions of Jesus scholarship—that older texts are more likely to be historical, that multiple attestation supports historicity, and that people can remember bits of data that are dissimilar from their current beliefs—quickly evaporate in the heat of any recognition that all early Christian texts were foundationally oral and equiprimordial and that the Jesus tradition behind all written Gospels was a function of social memory. This being the case, future approaches to John's historical value must proceed along fundamentally different lines from all past efforts, lines that have yet to be drawn.

So would a more careful consideration of the media history of Christian Origins prove that a Signs Gospel did not exist? No. In the end, the most we could say is that John might have used written sources in compiling his book and that he certainly would not have used such sources the way we would use them today. Such considerations might also undermine Fortna's suspicion toward some of John's historical claims and his confidence in others, but they could not definitively resolve the historical problems he highlights. They would simply ask entirely new questions.

CHAPTER 9

WHAT'S THE MEANING OF THIS?
REFLECTIONS UPON A LIFE AND CAREER

Robert Kysar

Probably we have all asked the question, "What's the meaning of this?," especially those of us who have spent years teaching and reading student papers we were grading. And who, in the process of interpreting Scripture, hasn't asked, "What's the meaning of this text?"

For a number of reasons, I have chosen this question as the title of these reflections upon my life and career. I have asked such a question of my whole career, and I suggest that this simple question about meaning lies at the heart of my scholarly, as well as personal, endeavors, although it has become increasingly complicated for me to answer. Moreover, one could track my publications and papers and find that they have all, in some way, reflected a view of "meaning." Therefore, the theme of these reflections upon my career is simply, "How have I sought to determine what meaning is and what texts mean?"

REFLECTIONS UPON A CAREER

From the vantage point of some seventy years, I now see how important the question of "meaning" became for me very early on. The search for a meaning for life itself was the reason I became involved in the church and decided to undertake a career in the clergy. Not only was the question,

"What's the meaning of this?" an essential ingredient in my maturation, it was also influential in my college career. With very little premeditation, I decided to major in English literature. In my classes, I met a professor whose life's work was devoted to asking the question of the meaning of the great English classics. From Prof. Ralph Berringer, I had my first lesson in hermeneutics (although that word was never used) and realized that the whole of human life is a hermeneutical search for meaning. Consequently, my focus became the search for meaning.

Looking back upon my career, several other things become clear. First, I have lived and worked in what has been (and still is) an exciting and tumultuous period in New Testament studies. When I ventured into serious biblical scholarship for the first time, form and redaction criticism were sweeping the field. In Johannine Studies in particular, the historical–critical method was leading us into the issues of sources, redaction, stages of composition, and the history of the community we came to call "Johannine." The towering figure was, of course, Rudolf Bultmann, whose work solicited what at the time seemed to be endless debate over major issues in New Testament interpretation.

This has also been an exciting half–century because the community of scholars has expanded in bursts of change. Thankfully, women and persons of different ethnic groups have entered the discussion and have made inestimable contributions to the investigation of biblical texts. Roman Catholic scholars have aligned themselves with a research community that had been dominated by Protestants, and Jewish colleagues likewise took their places around the table. Gradually, our discipline has become more and more pluralistic and global in scope. What an exciting time to undertake scholarship!

Still another event (this one more personal) stands out in the early years of my career. I don't remember the precise date, but sometime in the early 1970s, Raymond Brown, Wayne Meeks, J. Louis Martyn, George MacRae, and others formed a seminar in the Society of Biblical Literature devoted to the Fourth Gospel. Somehow, I—a young, immature, fresh Ph.D. in New Testament—was graciously invited to join the group. At the time, Brown was just finishing his monumental Anchor Bible commentary, Martyn was working on his reconstruction of the history of the Johannine community, and Robert Fortna was developing the implications of his theory of the "Signs Gospel." Wayne Meeks had published his definitive study *Moses Traditions and the Johannine Christology*, and in the context of this seminar prepared his groundbreaking essay, "The Man from Heaven in Johannine Sectarianism." D. Moody Smith had distinguished himself by explaining Bultmann's confusing and elaborate theories of sources, redaction, and rearrangement of the Fourth Gospel, and

Alan Culpepper had tantalized us with the idea of a "Johannine School." With weak knees and feverish anxiety, this potato–picking, small–town Idahoan (with his slightly dyslexic and attention–deficient mind) took a seat among these esteemed figures.

I doubt that I said a word during the first few years of the meetings. However, it was not long before I sensed that something enormously significant was taking place in Johannine Studies, and I worked my tail off trying to keep up with the discussion. When I went to Yale for my sabbatical leave in 1973, Wayne Meeks gently guided me toward the idea of trying to draw together all that was happening in the seminar and beyond. It was as though a door had opened and research, proposals, and studies on John came pouring out in an intellectual tidal wave. I tried to grasp what was at stake in this research, giving birth to *The Fourth Evangelist and His Gospel: An Examination of Contemporary Scholarship*. From one perspective, this endeavor was my effort to interpret what scholars were writing about the Gospel of John. In several ways, then, with my first published book, I began vaguely to recognize the role that the question "What's the meaning of this?" would play in my life. Along the way, I wrote and published an article that argues that theology itself is a systemization of the quest for meaning.

The Journey to New Understanding

My career may best be summarized in a sketch of my quest to understand meaning. I now see in hindsight that there were three major stages in my journey.

The Beginning: Historical Criticism

In the beginning, historical–critical methods of interpretation determined the answer to the question of meaning for me. I was led to believe that the sense of a text was found in the original intention of the author, who wrote out of a specific historical situation and occasion. My study of English literature in college was built on these same assumptions. John Donne's poems were properly interpreted only in the context of seventeenth–century English history. Consequently, those who majored in English literature were required to complete a course in the history of England. If you wanted to find meaning, you peeked around or through the text to what was behind it. I slowly learned how important this perspective on meaning was and would continue to be.

Like nearly everyone in the mid–twentieth century, I assumed a certain view of history and of how one studied the past—in this case, the original setting of a text. History, we believed, was a scientific endeavor. The historians gathered the "facts" (that is, the supposedly unquestionable events and characters in a given period of time) and from that body of data they sought to define relationships among events, persons, and settings. Biblical interpreters were required to become historians, or at least to avail themselves of respected experts on relevant eras. With a reconstruction of the historical conditions and characters in a certain time and place, the interpreter could discern the possible meanings (if not always the exact, indisputable meanings) of texts. Furthermore, the historical–critical method worked on the assumption that the biblical texts were the result of the intentional efforts of an author to express and communicate material significant in her or his day. The whole enterprise of writing history and of seeking an author's intention was founded upon a confidence that human inquirers could be "objective" in their work. Historiography shared with all the sciences (social as well as physical) the burden of suspending our own predilections, views, commitments, and emotions so that we could observe, record, and analyze the data at our disposal. The discipline was part of the optimism that swept Western culture in the centuries following the Enlightenment. It resulted in a time of blissful freedom from dogma and tradition, which set in motion a tidal wave of change. Biblical interpreters were to become scientists, however difficult that might be.

I was never terribly comfortable with such a model for determining meaning. During my graduate studies, I became significantly committed to existential philosophy and theology. Along with the so–called "new hermeneutic," these perspectives would not allow me to relax entirely and continue business as usual. Frankly, I did not really want to be a historian, but I believed that I had no choice if I wanted to discover meaning in biblical texts. However, in my dissertation I sought to investigate the ways in which presuppositions (particularly of a theological kind) influenced Dodd's and Bultmann's interpretations of the prologue of the Fourth Gospel (John 1:1–18). The dissertation had serious flaws, including its repetitious and plodding structure. Nonetheless, the process helped me come to a clearer assessment of the historical–critical method. To me, this method seemed naive in its assumptions about discovering history and understanding the meaning of a Gospel by means of history. So early on, I suppose, I was interested in the ways in which meaning is born in interpreters in the light of their own presuppositions and social locations.

Another formative experience early in my career undermined the exclusive role of history in Biblical Studies: reading Bultmann's provocative 1957 article, "Is Exegesis Without Presuppositions Possible?" In this essay, Bultmann writes, "To understand history is possible only for one who does not stand over against it as a neutral, nonparticipating spectator, but himself [or herself] stands in history and shares responsibility for it." This reading posture presupposes a "life–relationship" between the interpreter and the text (1960, 294). Alongside Karl Barth's revolutionary interpretive approach, I believe Bultmann accelerated a movement that contributed to the qualification, if not the collapse, of the historical–critical method—even though Bultmann himself sometimes employed the historical–critical method with a vengeance. The eventual result was what has been called the "realist fiction" of "objective meaning" and the fallacy of the subject–object model of interpretation (Palmer 1969, 223). As early as 1973, Walter Wink published the radical statement that the historical–critical method was "bankrupt" (1973, 1). I was hardly aware of how consequential that declaration would become, but without exception the senior scholars surrounding me at Yale that year casually dismissed Wink's assessment.

We gradually came to understand how objectifying a text was simply a way of trying to take control of it. If we could master a text, we could then turn it into an object to be studied, as one might study an insect under a microscope.

Along the Way: Literary Criticism

As I was assessing the value of historical–critical approaches, along came the new literary criticism with another answer to the question, "What's the meaning of this?" I thought I was just beginning to understand redaction criticism (at least, as it could be practiced on the Fourth Gospel) when this new movement intensified my discontent with the interpretive method I had learned in seminary. My good friends Alan Culpepper and Fernando Segovia upset the fragile applecart of the historical–critical method with their applications of the new literary criticism to the Gospel of John. In this model, the discovery of a text's meaning is not accomplished by investigating the distant past, but rather by attending to the present reading of the text in its literary context. I confess that I at first tried to play it safe by learning and practicing something of this new approach without entirely abandoning all the work I had put into the historical–critical enterprise. However, I could no longer believe that meaning hid behind the text in the darkness of the past. It lived or came to life in the reading of the text itself, without any necessary reference to the past. Of course, the new literary criticism was not a simple and single discipline but an umbrella under which numerous ways of reading gathered—reader response, narrative, rhetorical, and eventually autobiographical approaches, among others. Jeff Staley suggested how I might answer the question of meaning in ways peculiar to me and my background and thereby opened the possibilities of what might become an autobiographical criticism (Staley 1988, 1995).

The new literary criticism required that I give the text itself and the interpreter a larger role in discerning meaning than I had previously allowed. Now, there was no "author's intention" to take responsibility for the meaning of a text. I, the reader, must accept responsibility, even if I somehow nuanced the importance of the text itself. However, it was not as simple as it might at first have seemed. We were also talking about structuralism and the way in which texts themselves tell us their meaning. Meaning is encoded in a text, and our job as interpreters was to decipher the code. Narrative and reader response criticisms assume that we can find the plot, or a so-called "implied author," within the text and thereby find what a passage means. Hence, the difference between diachronic and synchronic approaches became blurred, and the relative roles of the text and the reader were highlighted.

My migration into reader–response criticism was cautious and admittedly clumsy. I continued to try to use historical–critical methods to supplement my literary readings. At one point, I characterized myself as an "essentialist." However, I began to find much more satisfaction in asking how the text worked on a reader than in inquiring after the historical context of its composition. An intense submersion in a passage allowed me to develop some new skills of sensitivity and immediacy. Such an interpretive method, however, resulted in a very personal meaning for the text. The most I could say was that "this reader" (myself) experienced, found, or glimpsed a "meaning" in the text.

Gradually, the discipline moved more and more away from formalism toward a reevaluation of the role of readers. Guided by the writings of Edgar V. McKnight, I was finally forced to acknowledge that readers, not texts, *mean*! If the reader and not the text is the source of meaning, then clearly we had to face some new questions. It was very difficult to surrender all pretense of looking for the "true meaning of a text." To give up on the idea that we could no longer assume that written texts even hint at their meaning proved to be a revolutionary admission. What in the world were scholars going to do if we had to surrender the search for the *true* meaning of the text? All of our efforts were designed to argue that ours was the "truer meaning" than that proposed by others. Were we out of work? Fernando Segovia and Mary Ann Tolbert taught us that we all read from a "place" and, when that place is different, meaning will be different. If there is no single meaning to a text, how do we talk together, or even read together? Is meaning entirely relative? Does meaning arise only for a particular community at a particular time?

The Destination: Postmodernity

Only after my retirement did I gradually admit that we were living in a new era. With more time to read, think, and write, I learned to admit that the assumptions of the modern age that arose in the Enlightenment were (or would soon become) a thing of the past. This was now a postmodern age! I caught a number of my colleagues in Johannine Studies totally off guard by enrolling in the school of postmodernism. I have angered some by the change in my views and puzzled many more. I can imagine that some may suspect an early deterioration of my mental capacities. Old age had taken its toll—and I must confess that sometimes I have no idea what I am doing. There are times when I marvel myself that I would shift my perspective so radically and surrender the role I had earned in Johannine Studies. What a crazy thing to do! "It's just like you, Kysar, to screw things up in your final decades of scholarship!" However, in the twilight of my career, with arthritic knees and increasing forgetfulness, I am feeling my way toward a new perspective. I am still not sure where this is going to lead me, but I am pretty sure about a few things.

First, I am pretty sure about the *problematic* character of meaning. I have gradually crept toward the belief that readers create meaning, sometimes even in spite of the text. However, the whole meaning of meaning has become problematic. That is, what sense does it make to say "this is the meaning" of a text? How is meaning recognized, attributed, and constructed? What is meaning? What happens in the mind when we say that a text "means" something? Even now, the deeper issue of what the word "meaning" designates continues to haunt me. Of course, the nature of meaning has been debated for years—even centuries. To oversimplify the issue, the question became whether language has a permanent relationship with a nonsemantic reality—that is, with an objective and universal reality—or whether language is purely a social phenomenon. Some have argued that language cannot be just a creation of society. On the contrary, I now believe that human rationality as a whole is entirely a social–cultural product. If this is so, then it is logical to hold that language and communication are part of that same social product. In spite of the fact that we have assumed for centuries that language refers to some objective reality, I must now insist that words do not have inherent reference. Meaning is not objective, but social. Furthermore, I have been compelled to believe that meaning is constructed almost exclusively on the basis of our own experience. This is to say that (1) the human mind constructs meaning—is the source of meaning—and (2) that this construction arises on the basis of what we already think we know. What we think we already know, however, is doubtless the result of a complex of influences.

In *Preaching to Postmoderns*, Joe Webb and I suggest that there are two basic and complementary ways of determining the source of meaning (Kysar and Webb 2006, 196–208). The first entails the Heideggerian concept of *vorhanden* (the unfamiliar) and *zuhanden* (the familiar). In *Being and Time*, Martin Heidegger argues that humans understand experiences in terms of what we already think we know, what we have already experienced, so that it is "at hand" (1992, 192, 242, for example). To oversimplify a typically obscure Heideggerian concept, we understand what is unknown and newly encountered by relating it to past experience. So, we discern the meaning of a biblical passage based on what we have come to know about other passages and the whole of what we believe is in some sense "true." To quote A. K. M. Adam, "all interpretation is allegorical interpretation" (1995b, 175). The radically important implication of this understanding of meaning is that it requires human imagination. We imagine the relationship between the new and the known. Bernard Brandon Scott's declaration makes sense to me: "Meaning is an act of relation or association that takes place in our imagination" (1985, 17). In my case, the role of imagination in discerning meaning arose from efforts to understand how sermons can assist listeners to see new and different lives for themselves. The preacher has an opportunity to guide the listeners' imaginations toward an alternative to their self–understanding. Preaching entails presenting the unfamiliar in ways that allow listeners to see connections with what is familiar in their lives.

However, Joseph Webb understands meaning in terms of symbolic interaction. Our systems of thought, Webb says (following Kenneth Burke) are socially constructed and entirely dependent upon our experience within a culture. We humans construct meaning in terms of the symbol system we have inherited from others (Webb 1998, 22–25). Symbolic interaction requires that we construct meanings that are consistent with the system we have inherited. Such a view of the construction of meaning is, of course, consistent with what we have recently learned about the social location of the reader.

The existentialist and symbolic interaction theories propose that readers construct meaning out of what they are given in their social location and their previous experience. Language does not refer to an objective body of realities and, in the final analysis, is not referential. If this is true, we will need to acknowledge the fictitious notion of the so–called "true meaning" and end our efforts to demean other interpretations in order to establish our own. Regrettably, much of our time and energy is expended in the effort to put down other views so that ours can step over them to become what we think is "the truth." All of us share the same quandary. We understand meaning in terms of our own constructions in our own social setting. However disturbing this conclusion may be, it is the only one I have been able to embrace with any integrity.

The meaning of meaning suffered this transformation, in part, as a result of the demise of what postmodernists call "metanarratives." The emphasis on the social construction of meaning arose in large part because we are no longer so confident of some grand scheme of rationality as the basis on which something "means." Meaning arises, we once thought, from the relationship between a particular text or experience and an underlying absolute reality. Thus, meaning arises when we can make a rational connection between the experience (in our work or the words of a text) and the vast imagined objective and rational substructure of reality. The suspicion toward and assault upon the grand metaphysical theories of the modernist thinkers has had a far–reaching impact. The opposition to these metanarratives constitutes part of what has been called the "antifoundationalism" and "antitotalization" of postmodern thought. A. K. M. Adam defines "'metanarratives' (or 'grand narratives')" as "stories we tell about the nature and destiny of humanity" and calls them "intellectual expedients that plaster over cracks in the projects of modernity" (1995b, 16–17).

The modernists' search for foundations was essentially the assertion that "final truths" are beyond question. Reason, it was claimed, is integral to the whole of the cosmos and reality. Connected with reason is the modern propensity toward explanations of the universe. Modernism made what has been called the "epistemological turn" (e.g., Penner 2005, 22), in which reason was used in an effort to enthrone a number of beliefs as infallible. The ultimate goal was to claim the existence of a "body of certainty." Postmodernists rightly deny that humans can discover or discern any such absolutely unquestionable truth. On the contrary, we live in the midst of uncertainty and a plurality of beliefs and perspectives. Although we may be hesitant to admit it, we are only able to create communities that temporarily and tenuously live as though this or that is true, never pretending that such belief is rooted in the universe and grounded in the essence of life. The grand universal constructs we created in the name of reason have or will give way eventually to "local stories," the concepts of meaning for specific groups (Kysar 2005c, 247–50).

Such antifoundationalism is nothing new to Western philosophy. In their day, Kierkegaard and Nietzsche attacked Hegel and the whole metaphysical enterprise in general. Both sought to make rationality problematic particularly because they saw in it the mistaken idea that humans could *control* the world through reason. (Cloning seems to be a supreme example of the goal of rational reality.) The anti–metaphysics posture of

Martin Heidegger, as well as Camus, Sartre, and others anticipated the postmodern perspective.

The construction of metanarratives (or ontology in general) is motivated by some basic assumptions about reason and truth in an effort to overcome the inherent uncertainty and uneasiness (i.e., the *angst*) with which humans are destined in life. All this rests on the foundational assumption that human reason is rooted in the very essence of existence. That is to say, we want to believe that the whole of reality is ultimately rational, in spite of the inescapable irrationality evident throughout the world and history. In my own case, the demolition of the grand metaphysical schemes arose from my own personal inescapable uncertainty and doubt. Out of my own experience in seventy plus years, I must conclude that there is no such thing as absolute certainty to be had. The best we can do, I believe, is find companionship and like–mindedness in small communities.

The third postmodernist thesis that has become important to me is this: historical studies are their investigators' fictionalized constructs. This has been difficult for me to accept, given the role of history in our discipline in the past and the far–reaching consequences of rejecting historical methodology. My suspicion toward histories, however, was stimulated in the 1970s when a colleague in political science at the liberal arts college where we both taught observed that, for the most part, scholars in the social sciences no longer make any pretense of writing "scientifically objective" history. Some postmodernists propose that history, as it has been conceived in modernism, is no longer possible. Unlike our predecessors, we can no longer believe there is a "past" that has some sort of ontological reality and can be known by means of research tools (Adam 1995b). Moreover, for me and others, postmodernism has deconstructed modernist history along with other metanarratives (Phillips 1990, 28, 33). Because history is both an epistemological and ontological enterprise at odds with postmodernism, it cannot claim to discover and preserve the past as it actually was. A history is the result, always, of other histories, all of which are fictional narratives saturated with their authors' ideological stances, and hence is only a "sign that refers to itself" (Burnett 2000, 106–12, quote 106). Furthermore, some conclude that one way to understand postmodern history is to say that the historian's task is "that of writing realistic fiction which mediates narrative truth" that we properly evaluate in "aesthetic terms" (Burnett 1990, 64).

Because the past is essentially unknowable, some hold that the construction of metanarratives is impossible, unnecessary, and finally deceptive (Adam 1995b, 16–23). Instead of these large, sweeping, universal stories, "little narratives" may serve as a means of discourse among those concerned with texts related to the past; but these small stories have absolutely no ontological reference. They are expressions of each individual's stories, and they enrich the symbolic world in which we live. The biblical narratives themselves are such "little stories," which in turn invite interpreters to construct their own little stories about themselves (Hens–Piazza 2000a, 164–66). Consequently, as a means of knowing the past as some objective reality, neither the biblical documents themselves nor our efforts to understand them can be successful. The intertextual historical task (which some call the "new historicism") never pretends to discover the past but only to investigate fragments of other texts in ways that merge the past and the present. Hence, the study of the development of the Fourth Gospel, for instance, is as much a study of the investigators' own ideologies as it is a search for what that text tells us about the past. For some, then, postmodernity brings to an end what we have known as the objective and scientific re–creation of the past. The postmodernist assessment of the historical enterprise, however, recognizes the value of "little stories" and of the relationship of texts that come from the past. Examples might include the Genesis creation stories as well as Darwin's work.

Somewhere in the years since my retirement, I began to realize the utter ridiculousness of many of our historical reconstructions in New Testament studies. It was relatively safe for me to decide that the entire Q hypothesis is a skyscraper built upon the end of a toothpick. However, it was a different matter when I questioned the popular theory that the Fourth Gospel was written soon after the Johannine Christians were expelled from their synagogue. Much the same was true of my paper on the Johannine community at a recent conference that honored the memory of Father Raymond Brown. For me to challenge the concept of a Johannine community was close to intellectual suicide, especially after I had propagated such a theory for years. I apologize to any who feel betrayed by my "postmodern turn," but I could do no other. I am convinced that our historical reconstructions are too fragile to hold the weight of our interpretations. We may be able to unearth literary references to name persons and events. However, when we venture to link events, to propose insights into persons and their actions, and in general to construct the "meaning of the past," we are doomed to claim as true only what profits us.

The reasons for this disability are too complex to pursue in this paper. Needless to say, historical reconstructions are inevitably driven (almost always unconsciously) by motives other than the increase of human knowledge—that is, they are ideological. The emergence of the theory of the expulsion of the Johannine Christians from their synagogue cannot be separated from the post–Holocaust struggle to explain and "soften" the Fourth Gospel's devastating presentation of the "Jews." I, too, sought desperately for some way to deal with the anti–Semitism of the New Testament as a whole and in particular the Fourth Gospel. When one openly labels the Johannine portrayal of the Jews "anti–Semitic," the results are disturbing, to say the least. However, our historical reconstructions and their maintenance are also often unconsciously motivated by still other efforts, such as a concern to create a private scholarly world of the knowledgeable over the ignorant. Historical constructions are, I am saying, invariably influenced by our own needs for power, promotion, and prestige. I do not want to exclude history from one of the basic concerns of human life, but I do want us to warn one another of the dangers lurking in the shadows of this process.

I became increasingly cynical as a result of this realization that interpretation is always tainted by our own vested powers, prejudices, and presuppositions, including personal, social, economic, political, and cultural. Of course, this follows logically from the understandings of meaning itself discussed earlier. In its earliest stages, the predecessors of postmodernity viewed all social practices and institutions as desperate attempts to control people. We should not be surprised, then, that all interpretation becomes ideological investigation. I now realize that my naive venture into Dodd's and Bultmann's presuppositions, as displayed in their discussions of the prologue to John, clearly illustrates the ideological nature of interpretation (even as my study of their ideologies betrayed my own). Without knowing in the 1960s what I was doing, I realized how radically different Bultmann's view of John 1:1–18 would have been had he been a Roman Catholic and not a Lutheran.

Finally, in my quest to understand how meaning occurs, I have also learned how flimsy language is. Call it the instability of language. Call it the "surplus of meaning" in any linguistic expression. Call it endless ambiguity. Whatever you name this recognition about language, it leads in one direction: language cannot mean without equivocation. So, there goes the whole pretense of our ability to conclude what texts mean. Or, does it? That seems to me the most significant question in biblical interpretation. Stephen Moore has boldly and persistently dared us to take seriously how unstable language is, and especially the language of ancient texts (Moore 1989). Deconstruction, of course, does not set out to annihilate a text or to reduce it to rubbish. Rather, it seeks to show us what could be taken to be the almost unlimited richness of a text. It invites us to play with possible meanings and to construct various implications. We do not violate the nature of language when we say it means so–and–so. However, we do violate it when we claim that it *only* means so–and–so. Furthermore, it seems to me that the instability of language forces us to take ourselves less seriously than we might like.

Glimpses of the Future

All these postmodern convictions have drastic implications for the whole process of reading Scripture. Of course, if we look into the future of Johannine Studies, we see very different scenes, depending upon our present convictions. If we should embrace postmodernity (or something comparable), what understandings of reading would emerge? In all honesty, I must confess that I have no idea, but some scenes might look something like what follows.

First, I do not believe that postmodernity will result in a radical individualism. If my current view of interpretation is true, what will follow, I believe, is a far more radical dependence upon reading communities. Gone are the days of interpretation done in the solitude of our offices. The new day calls forth a clearer understanding of our mutual interdependence. I am not speaking of denominations or even religions but of groups drawn together for various reasons that make biblical interpretation significant in some way. These reading communities will provide contexts for the discussion of interpretation and the expression of various readings. Such communities may embrace a kind of "local story" out of which they read. An example of such reading communities might be those small, local study groups that read and discuss Scripture in search of understanding and direction to overcome oppression (e.g., "the ecclesial base communities" [*comunidades eclesias de base*] in South America).

The sort of interpretation I believe might emerge in a postmodern context would in no way profess to result in the only "right" reading. To the contrary, variety in interpretations would provide the reading communities their topics of discussion. Gone will be the day when we dare to say that our interpretation is "truer" or more correct than others. There will be no absolutely "true" or "correct" reading. Imagine what that would mean. We could not debate fine points or declare the errors some have made. However, this does not mean we will become cavalier about our readings. It will mean only that we will make no claims for having discovered what the biblical author had intended.

This sort of plurality of readers and readings means, of course, that we will honor a great variety of interpretive methods. One could argue that we already are on our way to an appreciation of pluralism of methods. Just scan the topics of groups and papers in the program for an annual meeting of the Society of Biblical Literature. Multiplicity is upon us, and a postmodern perspective rejoices in that fact. However, just as we will not be able to claim that our readings are superior to others, neither will we be interested in embracing some methods and putting down others. Imagine what discussion will be like in such an atmosphere. None of the harsh remarks that we sometimes find in our journals or footnotes. Specialization will by no means become outmoded; however, no single specialization will be able to "lord it over" others.

Will the Bible even matter in such a culture as I imagine will come to be? Yes, I believe that there will still be interest in probing this collection, just as we will want to explore the Qur'an and other literary classics along with contemporary literature. However, religious communities that claim exclusive ownership of the truth will be marginalized, and this includes, I believe, the current gigantic wave of conservative literalism in all the world's religions. With the demise of the metanarratives and the ontological realm, religions will take a different form, which is a subject for future papers.

Pressing the question of meaning has brought me to a strange conclusion for my career, but one that should not surprise me. Interpretation requires that interpreters know themselves. Every interpretation is really autobiographical, as Jeff Staley and others are teaching me. The existential posture of the interpreter is then nothing more than what it is for every human being: the desperate and agonizing task of being authentic, genuine, honest, and having the courage to be all these things, while standing stark naked in the face of our mortality. At my age, this means interpretation requires the kind of self–discovery and disclosure that the reality of death imposes on us all. Of course, reading texts and asking what they mean teaches us a great deal more about ourselves than about the texts, much less the authors of those texts.

My perspective, however, would be self–contradictory if I were to claim that these propositions alone are true and that all who reject them are wrong. I can no longer be certain of the error of other methods and would not claim the qualifications to critique other approaches. The direction of the future, I hope, will be toward a global, pluralistic multitude of views, each of which is embraced by some identifiable group. The attitude toward other such groups will, I trust, not be tolerance but mutual respect and appreciation.

Because of the nature of its language and narratives, the Gospel of John may figure prominently in this new understanding and practice of interpretation. Its endless ambiguity, irony, and drama might allow it a premier role in the emergence of a postmodern interpretation. However, such a view is doubtless an expression only of my own bias.

I need to say one more thing in conclusion. Throughout the whole of my quest to understanding meaning, I have been and remain indebted beyond measure to my colleagues in Biblical Studies, philosophy, and theology. I am especially gratefully to those with whom I have worked and from whom I have learned through these years within the shelter of the Society of Biblical Literature and other groups. What would I have done without you? Just as I got my start in that seminar chaired by Ray Brown, so through the years have I thrived on our mutual commitments to Johannine Studies. Thank you all so very much.

IS HISTORY HISTORY?

David Rensberger

In American popular culture, "history" is a pejorative term. If someone is done for, finished, no longer relevant, they are "history." Worst of all is for something to be considered "ancient history," not only irrelevant but not even worth mentioning.

For some postmodern theorists, the notion of history itself seems to be "history." Ancient texts can be read "without any necessary reference to the past." Their authors' putative intentions no longer obtrude into our quest for meaning, which we now recognize requires only our own subjective experience. "Historical studies are their investigators' fictionalized constructs," as Bob Kysar puts it, and nothing more.

Frankly, I don't buy it.

Since we are in the postmodern autobiographical mode, let me acknowledge a few things about myself. I've always loved history and historical study. I love trying to connect with other realities, with people who are different from myself and yet somehow still knowable. I've welcomed the arrival of literary criticism, but have taken a fairly intuitive (rather than theoretical) approach to it. Perhaps that is why I am less willing to rule out the historical in favor of the literary: I'm not really interested in getting the hermeneutics right, just in interacting faithfully with the text. A quarter century of teaching in an Afrocentric environment has added to my love of history the realization that the desire to cut ourselves off from contact with the past is a uniquely Euro–American phenomenon. In African and Asian cultures, interest in and even respect for ancestors remains strong.

There is also this: I tend to see both sides of every argument, which works out to mean that I always disagree with everyone. I'm not really a reactionary modernist; I only sound that way when I'm reading postmodernists.

Perhaps it is this instinct for the other side, for the density and complexity of what is real, that leaves me annoyed with some aspects of the postmodern program as it seems to be developing. Having rediscovered an important factor in human culture and the interpretation of texts, some of us seem to think it is the *only* significant factor. The results can be weirdly totalizing and intolerant. It really is astounding to see people asserting that "there is no such thing as absolute certainty" with such absolute certainty. The whole enterprise seems to suffer from a severe and unacknowledged entanglement in the classic "all generalizations are false" paradox.

Now, what postmodernists and their predecessors and congeners propose as true certainly is true. "Meaning is not objective, but social." Every interpreter and every interpretation is involved in self–interest and rooted in personal experience, including social and ideological location. Therefore, there is no "one right interpretation" or "one right meaning" of a text, and no one can be entirely certain of an author's intentions or of any other phenomenon of the past. All of that is true, but it is not all of the truth. Reality, I believe, is too complex for any such simple, one–sided explanation to capture it rightly. Twenty–five years of immersion in Johannine paradox has convinced me that the Fourth Gospel conceives of the truth about Jesus as something too deep, thick, and rich to be expressed in a single statement such as "Jesus is God" or "Jesus was a prophet." This immersion has also encouraged me in my own unwillingness to accept accounts of reality that are less than complex and many–sided.

One problem I have with postmodern rejection of historical criticism is that it confuses what is possible with what ought to be attempted. The past cannot be objectively or exactly recovered; but to claim that ancient texts can be read "without any necessary reference to the past" is sheer self–deception. "What's a cubit?" as Bill Cosby once asked. People who read texts that mention cubits and synagogues and purification and shepherds cannot help making a great deal of reference to the past, however imperfectly understood, and ought to acknowledge it.

I must add that I have always found it both funny and exasperating to hear the accessibility or even the existence of authorial intent solemnly

denied by people who author streams of books and essays with quite clear
and definite intentions.

Authors do have intentions, I believe, and meaning arises when the
intentions of readers interact with them. The past cannot be fully or
objectively known, but we can enter into dialogue with it, fully recognizing the experiences and biases we bring to this dialogue. There seems
to me something oddly purist, even puritanical, about saying we cannot
perfectly know the past and therefore we should drop the subject. All our
interpretations come from particular perspectives and are ideologically
tainted—which is why we need more such interpretations interacting and
dialoguing with one another in the hope of enhancing everyone's understanding, not only of everyone else now, but also of the past.

To say we cannot objectively know the past is no different from saying we cannot objectively know our contemporaries. Yet inevitably we do
want to know what makes our spouses and partners, our colleagues, our
neighbors tick. We listen to them. We filter it through our own experiences. We listen and filter some more. Somehow in this impure and
imperfect process, our genuine knowledge does increase (as does our
fictitious knowledge). We do actually come to know something about
one another, something that is not just the product of our own experiences and imaginations. It is harder to do this with the past, because the
ancient authors cannot tell us, "No, that's not what I mean." But with
patience, self–knowledge, openness, and multiple participants, I believe
such knowledge is possible.

Indeed, I believe we have a kind of moral duty to know and acknowledge our predecessors and to study them assiduously. Particularly in the
case of those who have suffered oppression, if we do not do this—because
we regard them *only* as constructs—we victimize them again, and permanently. To abandon historical study would be to hand ourselves over to
the Holocaust–deniers and their ilk. For the Holocaust is no more certainly recoverable than any other past event. Isn't it also a construct like
other constructs, a "fiction" like other "fictions"? To describe all history
as fictionalized as though this were the only truth about it can lead us to
no other place than that.

This brings us to the subject of the Johannine community and their
expulsion from the synagogue. This theory was indeed constructed in a
post–Holocaust environment that had to come to grips with anti–Judaism
in the New Testament (which apparently is real and not a construct for
Kysar). It has a motive and an ideological bent, maybe more than one—
and so what? I, for one, have no desire to "soften" the unbearable harsh-
ness of the Johannine hostility to "the Jews." Explaining this hostility as
a reaction (not the only or best possible reaction) to something else that

happened is not the same as explaining it away. If I wanted to say "only what profits" me, I would say that Christianity parted amicably with Judaism in the late first century and that both sides behaved nobly and justly. But the discomfiting truth is that some Christians behaved horribly, and some non–Christian Jews probably acted badly as well. I don't know if that's a grand narrative or a little story, but I think it's a human story, and I don't think it becomes *merely* a "fiction" simply because its tellers are not pure of ideological interest.

My plea, then, is simply that we always consider the other side of the other side. "We do not violate the nature of language when we say it means so–and–so. However, we do violate it when we claim that it *only* means so–and–so." There I agree with Bob Kysar, and for precisely that reason I disagree with much of the rest of what he says. If people are to be *changed* by a sermon or a text, they require what can only be called a moral or ethical quality of openness to that which is outside themselves and their interests. That same openness to what is "other" is the thing that makes scholarly dialogue and historical study possible. If we renounce the quest for any reference point outside ourselves (even an imperfect, constructed one), insisting that we only tell ourselves what we already know and want to hear, then nothing new—no learning and no change—is imaginable at all.

CHAPTER 10

THE JOHANNINE COMMUNITY AMONG JEWISH AND OTHER EARLY CHRISTIAN COMMUNITIES

J. Louis Martyn

Because responding to Tom Thatcher's gracious invitation to participate in this volume necessarily involves a bit of reminiscence, we find ourselves briefly at Yale University in the 1950s. To a large extent, the period was marked in Protestant American Biblical Studies by a concentration on issues handed across the Atlantic, so to speak, from Germany and Switzerland. We knew that there was genuine learning in England and Scotland, but the interpretive work that exercised our minds came our way largely from the continent. So when the time arrived for proposing a dissertation topic (1954), I thought in European terms without noticing it. I turned first to Johannine matters, partly because Rudolf Bultmann's commentary on John seemed to me both enormously impressive—it is still worth reading!—and seriously inadequate. I found it impossible to avoid ambivalence while paying close attention to the writings of this scholar, a true giant and also imperfect.

TIMELESS AND PLACELESS READING OF THE FOURTH GOSPEL IN THE POST–ENLIGHTENMENT WESTERN UNIVERSITY

As I reflected on Bultmann's work, I saw, on the one hand, that there was an uncanny congeniality (*Verwantschaft*) between the first–century Johannine Evangelist and this twentieth–century interpreter. At juncture after juncture, one came to a deeper understanding of a passage after pondering and wrestling with Bultmann's comments on it. On the other hand, there were what impressed me as direct and unqualified reflections of the philosophy of Martin Heidegger. Noting earlier a linguistic habit of Bultmann—equally evident in his books and articles on Jesus, Paul, and John—I had concocted a humorous story for the amusement of my fellow doctoral students. Bultmann's publisher, I said, had ordered a special typesetting machine for the production of his works: the depression of a single key brought up the word *Möglichkeit* ("possibility"); the depression of another produced the term *Entscheidung* ("decision"). But were possibility and decision actually central categories in the teaching of Jesus, in the theological systems of Paul and John, and in the thinking of many other early Christian authors as well? Or were those categories borrowed from Heidegger and imposed on the ancient texts? I noted, for example, in John 6:44 that the evangelist puts the verb ἑλκύω ("to draw") in Jesus' mouth in a way that seems emphatically to deny the human capacity of autonomous decision: "No one can come to me unless drawn by the Father who sent me" (cf. 12:32). There was no doubt that the Gospel of John evidences patterns of dualistic thought; but did Bultmann's expression "decision dualism" really stem from that document itself? Those seemed to me weighty questions.

Wide reading in the critical literature soon caused me to be further puzzled. To be sure, Clement of Alexandria had dubbed John the "spiritual Gospel" in the late–second century. Why, however, did post–Enlightenment biblical interpreters so seldom apply old–fashioned historical analysis to the Fourth Gospel, thereby leaving this ancient text to timeless, placeless interpretation in the hands of scholars whose antecedent loyalties lay with Plato and Philo, and now with twentieth–century, existentialist, thoroughly individualistic philosophers? We all knew, to be sure, that Leopold von Ranke was naive in saying that the historian's task was to reconstruct a given ancient picture as it actually was: *wie es eigentlich gewesen war.* We read with great interest Wilhelm Dilthey, thereby outgrowing von Ranke by learning that even the historical exegete is to understand ancient texts "empathetically." But had Dilthey's insights legitimately eclipsed the need for hard–headed historiography? Had I known at that time the writings of Leo Beck, I would have found an ally in my concern that we should learn some things from Dilthey while maintaining our von Rankean interest in everyday history. Beck wrote his dissertation under the direction of Dilthey, thereby savoring what Hugo von Hofmannsthal characterized as Dilthey's ability to convince his students of their own involvement in the exegetical task by stimulating around himself an atmosphere of "impassioned conversation, impassioned listening." In Beck's case, however, empathetic understanding of ancient texts was not purchased at the cost of historical accuracy, as one learns in reading his thoroughly candid response to Adolf von Harnack's *What Is Christianity?* Noting the astonishing extent of Harnack's ignorance of Jewish matters, such as the high value placed on poetic homily by the rabbis, Beck wastes no time with artificial politeness: "Whoever reaches judgments like those of Mr. Harnack knows nothing of a vast area of Jewish life *as it actually existed* in the time of Jesus and the early church; or he compels himself to know nothing of it" (Martyn 1997, 47–69, quote 51; emphasis added).

Giving special attention to Jewish sources as I prepared for general examinations, I noted that, like Harnack, Bultmann had a truly skimpy knowledge of Judaism, while being remarkably learned in non–Jewish materials of the Hellenistic era. Formulating a dissertation topic, I now began to ask whether this imbalance was taking a toll on his interpretation of the Fourth Gospel. Had he leapt over the old–fashioned requirements placed on the *wissenschaftlich* historian, in order—however unconsciously—to make use of the Fourth Gospel in his devotion to the timeless and thoroughly individualistic existentialism of Heidegger? Had the time (the post–Enlightenment period) and the place (the Western university) paradoxically facilitated a timeless, placeless reading of an ancient document (John) as though it had fallen from heaven into the lap of Bultmann (cf. the work of a fellow old–Marburger, Hans Georg Gadamer)? In the case of the Gospel of John, I thought both questions were to be answered in the affirmative, mainly because that document had not been consistently and rigorously subjected to historical analysis by reading it in relation to Second Temple Judaism.

An Attempt to Read the Fourth Gospel in Its Own Setting

In my dissertation, then, two matters claimed major attention: the evangelist's repeated references to οἱ ᾽Ιουδαῖοι ("the Jews"? "the Judeans"?) and the attention he gives to the matter of scriptural interpretation (midrash; Barrett 1947; Moloney 2005a). I attempted to provide a sober and fundamental exegetical analysis of both, leading to the conclusion that, for John, the term "the Jews" is more than a disembodied symbol for the unbelieving world, but instead often refers to real flesh–and–blood Jewish authorities in John's city. And a third focus accompanied those two: because it seemed to me imperative to wrest the Gospel out of the hands of timeless, placeless, philosophical interpreters, I ventured away from the ivy–covered study that is the normal habitat of those of us who labor as lonely, "individual" interpreters. From the beginning of my own work, both in my 1957 dissertation and in *History and Theology in the Fourth Gospel* (essentially written in 1964, published in 1968), I referred to "the Johannine community," the "corporate" setting in which the evangelist penned his Gospel and the one in which that Gospel was first interpreted. When I transformed the dissertation, using it as a third of *History and Theology*, the Johannine community assumed even greater importance.

> Our first task . . . is to say something specific about the actual circumstances in which John wrote his Gospel. How are we to picture daily life in John's church? Have elements of its peculiar daily experiences left their stamp on the Gospel penned by one of its members? May one sense even in its exalted cadences the voice of a Christian theologian who writes in response to contemporary events and issues which concern, or should concern, all members of the Christian community in which he lives? [A positive answer necessitates our making] every effort to take up temporary residence in the *Johannine community*. We must see with the eyes and hear with the ears of that community. We must sense at least some of the crises which helped to shape the lives of its members. And we must listen carefully to the kind of conversations in which all of its members found themselves engaged. Only in the midst of this endeavor will we be able to hear the Fourth Evangelist speak in his own terms, rather than in words we moderns merely want to hear from his mouth. And initially it is only in his own terms that he can speak to our own time. (Martyn 1968, xviii; 2003, 29; emphasis added)

New to *History and Theology*, vis-à-vis the dissertation, were (a) the suggestion that the peculiar Johannine locutions ἀποσυνάγωγος γένηται ("be put out of the synagogue," John 9:22; 12:42) and ἀποσυναγώγους ποιήσουσιν ὑμᾶς ("you will be made outcasts from the synagogue," 16:2) were probably related to the Twelfth Benediction (the *Birkat–Haminim*), and, (b) a more developed emphasis on the thoroughly theological nature of the Fourth Gospel as a "two-level drama," one that to some extent told the story of the Johannine community while narrating the story of Jesus of Nazareth *because* in the work of the Paraclete the risen Lord continues to determine the life of his new community.

The reviews of and references to *History and Theology* over the decades since its initial publication require no rehearsal here beyond my saying that the extensive enthusiasm was genuinely surprising to me. To become in some degree a part of the establishment by publishing a work written somewhat in opposition to the (earlier) establishment can throw one a bit off balance; but that was a matter of merely personal concern. I must admit that I have sometimes been reminded, as recently as last year, of a friend's *bon mot:* "The highest compliment to a person's labors is not imitation, but rather mild larceny." I was sobered by the works of Reuven Kimelman (1981) and Steven Katz (1984; also van der Horst 1994; Boyarin 2004). Scholars having a far greater rabbinic expertise than my own expressed skepticism about directly connecting the ἀποσυνάγωγος references in John's Gospel to the Twelfth Benediction. Wayne Meeks identified that part of my work as a red herring (it did indeed prove to be a pink one), and Moody Smith called it a tactical error in the sense that a few Johannine interpreters were taking the work of Kimelman and Katz as proof against the larger thesis that the Fourth Gospel is a two–level drama shaped in part by the experience of a group of Christian Jews who had suffered—against their wills—the trauma of being severed from their undisturbed membership in their synagogue.

The history of the *Birkat–Haminim* is, to be sure, a somewhat uncertain matter inviting debate—I say only "somewhat uncertain" partly because of the work of William Horbury (1982). The word ἀποσυνάγωγος, on the other hand, is there in the text, and it was not coined in an individual's private fit of paranoia: the occurrences of this term are communal references to a communal experience. Further, we have similar data in the Pseudo–Clementine literature (Martyn 1979a, ch. 2; Klauck 2005). And as odious as we find the Nazi–like thesis that Christian persecution of Jews is "'justified' by the theory that Jews did the first persecuting [Paul, for example]," I still contend that "modern relations between Jews and Christians are not helped by an anti–historical interpretation of biblical texts" (Martyn 1979a, 56). I remain thoroughly convinced on two matters. First, working chronologically backward and forward from the ἀποσυνά–γωγος references, it is possible to sketch the history of the Johannine community "from its origin through the period of its life in which the Fourth Gospel was composed." Second, so sketched, that history "forms to no small extent a chapter in the history of *Jewish Christianity*" (Martyn 1979a, 121, emphasis added; D. M. Smith 1999; Attridge 2006).[1]

---

[1] Regarding the Johannine community and Jewish Christianity, see now the weighty study of M. Theobald (2006). If there was a Signs Gospel—as Fortna successfully argued—it too belongs to the history of Jewish Christianity.

READING THE FOURTH GOSPEL IN TWO SETTINGS

Given the work of Kimelman and Katz on the *Birkat*—work I found instructive in some regards, to be sure—there was now the danger, I thought, that parts of the discourse between Jewish and Christian scholars might take a tumble into pure apologetics, all participants being then the poorer.[2] There are significant differences between indulging in apologetics and being truly sensitive to the Other, notably when the Other is a sibling. Especially when focused on the matter of Christians persecuting Jews and Jews persecuting Christians—Christian Jews—juvenility is as unhelpful as are ad hominem and inaccurate reports of personal conversations, both being forms of childishness that, easily falling into anachronistic readings, dishonor the Other. What liberates us from the *Tendenzen* of our exegetical conversation partner is not our own *Tendenzen*, but rather the text. In short, the relationship between John's community and its parent synagogue(s) was certainly somewhat complex. It was, however, fundamentally different from the relationship between the mighty post–Constantinian church and the synagogue of its era. Dispassionate historical analysis clearly tells us that, at the time of the Fourth Gospel's origin, the later pattern was to some degree reversed. At its origin, the Johannine community was a small conventicle faced with a truly more powerful parent in the local Jewish establishment (e.g., John 19:38; 20:19; cf. Matt 10:17).

Even so, the question remains: Are there passages in the Gospel produced in this separated and threatened community that cause us justly to identify that document itself as "anti–Judaic"? It is an important question. It is also one that cannot be answered in precisely the same way by every person in every time and in every place. I myself cannot pose it without recalling the time in the 1960s when Abraham Joshua Heschel took a leave of absence from the faculty of Jewish Theological Seminary to cross the street and join for a year our faculty at Union Seminary (the board of directors temporarily changed the Trinitarian elements in the professorial induction ceremony). In addition to his classroom teaching, Heschel organized a small discussion group, drawing three members from each of the two faculties. The book we were to produce, each writing a chapter (mine on Romans 9–11), never came to fruition—for it was to begin with a manifesto signed by all, and there were always sentences to which one member or another could not agree. In our discussions, however, there

---

[2] I was amused when, upon the appearance of the pertinent works of Kimelman and Katz, some Christian scholars assumed that, whereas Christian interpreters have *Tendenzen*, Jewish interpreters, being totally objective, have none.

was much valuable fruit, not least in our various stories. Heschel, markedly reserved about scholarship for its own sake, was a master at eliciting frank and candid narratives from us about earlier periods in our lives. We sometimes had as much *haggadah* as *halacha*.

Here I was provided with my first sustained exposure to the possibility that in the New Testament itself there are *sustained* strains of rhetoric and thought that can be correctly identified with the expression "anti–Judaic." At Yale, I had paid some attention to the odious use of the Fourth Gospel by the *Deutsche Christen*, the Nazi–sponsored, anti–Semitic German Christian Church (a possible dissertation subject, I thought), but I had not before asked myself whether in important regards some of the church's foundational documents were *themselves*, and in a sustained manner, anti–Judaic. Formulated that way, the question had occurred to me neither in writing my dissertation nor in my later attempt to produce an exegetically *wissenschaftlich* monograph. Now, however, partly because of some of Heschel's stories, that question arose. He spoke, quite simply and without personal heroics, of his early youth in Warsaw, mentioning, for example, his mother's dispatching him to fetch the day's bread. He had to travel a roundabout route to the baker, he said, to avoid walking by the huge cathedral. Why? Because simply finding himself in its shadow produced uncontrollable trembling. Why? Because, literally overshadowed by that giant monolith, he inevitably recalled stories about one or another of his rabbinic forebears who had been summoned there for a disputation, the outcome of which would fundamentally affect for some time the life of the Jewish community. It was for me a highly affective and truly effective introduction to the degree to which the power of the Christian church hovered menacingly over the life of the largely powerless Jewish community in Warsaw and elsewhere. And, trying to see through the eyes of the frightened little boy, I had to ask myself whether the monolithic nature of that power—so well represented by the literal monolith of the cathedral's structure—was truly separable from its various parts. Was the glorious church music implicated, the scriptural oratorios of Handel and Felix Mendelssohn? Did the Christian Scriptures themselves play a role in the persecutory shadow of the cathedral? Heschel suggested no such thing, but this question occurred to me when I visualized the little boy in short pants trembling in the shadow of a towering edifice that should have been for all human beings a secure place of refuge.

And that question takes us back to the Gospel of John and the matter of anti–Judaism. Would it be salutary to focus the anti–Judaic question on the setting in which the Fourth Gospel had its origin, before carrying it farther?

From its birth, the Johannine community was conscious of its existence as a conventicle with its own fund of images and its own language, as Wayne Meeks insisted (Meeks 2002). It was not, however, a monolith. We can be confident that one of its subgroups consisted of ἀποσυνά-γωγοι with deeply loved kinfolk who remained in the synagogue. What would members of this subgroup have heard as the Fourth Gospel was read aloud in the community? They would presumably have warmed their hands over John 4:22, in which Jesus says to the Samaritan woman, "You worship what you do not know; we worship what we know, for salvation is from the Jews." But how would they have heard 8:31–59, and especially 8:44, "You [Jews] are of your father the devil"?[3] I suppose they would have regretted that verse. They would surely have heard the words of life in the Christology of the entire passage, while feeling, perhaps, that it goes too far with the specific application of its uncompromising dualism to their flesh–and–blood kinfolk. It was, of course, the Johannine community's peculiar history applied to the absolute nature of its dualism and its equally absolute Christology that produced such passages. And because the result is not greatly different from the absolute dualism of Qumran, we inevitably ask ourselves why that passage should present us with an intensified form of the regret experienced by those members of the Johannine community who had beloved kinfolk in the local synagogue. The answer lies, one hardly needs to say, with the subsequent history of the church and the Jewish people (Alexander 2001). There was no Qumran cathedral in Warsaw.

But, precisely in thinking of that history, we are reminded of the fact that the church we know has never lived—and cannot live—solely on the basis of John 8:44. As Brevard Childs has taught us, some form of canonical criticism has to bind the modern Christian interpreter to all of the church's foundational documents, and that means that John 8—indeed the whole of John's Gospel—is always read and preached together with, for example, Romans 9–11 (Harrisville and Sundberg 2002, 304–28). For when we imaginatively find ourselves in the company of Johannine community members whose beloved kinfolk remain firmly in the synagogue, we can remind ourselves that some members of Paul's churches—and especially members of the church in Rome—were similarly situated (perhaps even Paul himself). Here, then, we cannot resist the impulse to read to ourselves—and imaginatively to these special forbears of ours—the whole of our canon, interpreting John on the basis of Paul and Paul on the basis of John, thereby honoring both.

---

[3] The odious potential of this verse reached a crescendo when Hitler's mentor Dietrich Eckart quoted it in his *Der Bolschewismus von Moses bis Lenin: Zwiegespräch zwischen Adolf Hitler und mir* (1924, 18).

10: Response

READING HISTORY IN THE FOURTH GOSPEL

Adele Reinhartz

It is an honor to respond to J. Louis Martyn's reflections upon his own intellectual formation and upon an issue that has preoccupied both of us for many years—the Johannine community. Of course, as Martyn well knows, this is by no means my first response to his work; much of my thinking and writing on the Fourth Gospel has been inspired by his research, in particular his *History and Theology in the Fourth Gospel*. In this I am not alone. Indeed, for those of us who became interested in the Gospel of John in the 1970s and 1980s, Martyn's work served a role that was very similar to the role he ascribes to Bultmann's commentary in stimulating his own work on the Gospel of John. That my own position differs from his by no means diminishes my deep appreciation of and indebtedness to his work.

In his comments, Martyn quotes a paragraph from *History and Theology* that I memorized long ago and will never forget. In this passage, he enjoins us to hear the Fourth Evangelist speak in his own terms rather than ours, and to "see with the eyes and hear with the ears" of the Johannine community (Martyn 2003, 29). For a young graduate student entranced by the highly volatile era that laid the foundations of what we now refer to as "Judaism" and "Christianity," these words were the Pied Piper's melody, leading me on to an engagement with the Gospel of John and its earliest audiences. Martyn's work held out the hope that if I could only listen carefully enough and set aside my own *Tendenzen*, background, and baggage, I would indeed hear the Fourth Evangelist speak in his own words, in his own terms; I would become an honorary member of the Johannine community and see and hear this Gospel as they did.[1]

Furthermore, Martyn's imaginative retelling of John 9 (in which Jesus heals a man born blind) as a two–level drama brought the Johannine community to life for me in a compelling and elegant way. His theory that Johannine Christians were expelled from the synagogue for believing Jesus to be the Messiah provided a coherent and relatively simple answer for much that had puzzled me about the Gospel of John. Martyn's histor-ical–critical approach to the Gospel as a document produced by and for a particular community embroiled in conflict with its local Jewish com-munity helped to explain, but not to excuse, some of John's negative com-ments about Jews and Judaism and to assign to the Gospel a prominent role in the processes that eventually led to the so–called "parting of the ways." Finally, his approach provided a vehicle for an ongoing engage-ment with Jewish–Christian relations, by inviting us to listen with empa-thy to the distress of Johannine Christians bound by family and affection to those who remained within the synagogue—that is, to those who did not follow their faith and join in their fate.

I do not recall exactly when I began to question the expulsion theory (cf. Reinhartz 1998a; 1998b; 2001). In looking back, however, it is clear that one important factor was my increasing sense that historical criti-cism of the New Testament had to be supplemented—or, more precisely, informed by—attention to its literary and rhetorical nature. In this ven-ture, I was educated and emboldened by Alan Culpepper, whose book *Anatomy of the Fourth Gospel* (1983) showed how useful literary criticism and theory could be for our understanding of the Gospel of John. My conviction that the Gospel of John must be viewed first and foremost as a literary work did not cause me to abandon the quest for its historical context. But it continues to shape my approach to the text as a commu-nication between an (implied) author and an (implied) audience and to suggest that meaning does not reside within the text or in its historical context but rather in the interaction between text and reader.

From this perspective, then, I have addressed a number of questions to Martyn's compelling theory. First, should we not keep in mind that the "Johannine community," plausible as it is, is nevertheless a construct, a creation of our scholarly approach rather than an incontrovertible histor-

---

[1] My use of the masculine for the Fourth Evangelist reflects my own sense of the narrator and implied author of this Gospel as male.

ical datum? Second, is the Gospel of John a two–level drama through and through or only in the ἀποσυνάγωγος passages? In theory, the method should be applicable to the entire Gospel, but my own experiments with a more comprehensive application have led to an incoherent, even contradictory, set of results, with limited usefulness for historical reconstruction.[2] Finally, if we see the Gospel as a communication between implied author and implied audience, what is the message communicated therein? This, in effect, returns us to the major challenge that Martyn himself posed. If we place ourselves in the position of the implied audience of the Gospel, and if we listen with the ears of an implied group or community, what messages might we hear?

According to Martyn's construction, we would hear a story of our own experiences in contact and conflict with the Jewish community among whom we live, transposed back into the time of Jesus. In the process, we would also hear a validation of our own difficult path, in the face of past and present exclusion, persecution, and perhaps also separation from many whom we love. But there are other possibilities. We might hear, not our own specific experience, but rather an acknowledgment of and explanation for our current situation of separation or estrangement from the synagogue. In other words, we might hear the Fourth Gospel's answer to the question of how a group that believes a Jewish man to be the Christ and Son of God came to see itself as an entity separate from Judaism, a group that requires explanations for Jewish practices (e.g., John 2:6) and refers to the sacred texts of Judaism as "your" Torah (not "ours"; 8:17; 10:34; 18:31). Second, we might hear in the Fourth Gospel a story not of our *historical* experience but of our *emotional* experience. Although our current separation from the synagogue may have resulted from forcible expulsion or from more subtle modes of exclusion, it may also have come about through our own sense that the "synagogue," which as an entity did not embrace Jesus as messiah, was no longer the appropriate community and liturgical context for our own developing identity that takes faith in Jesus as its center point. Strong feelings of exclusion do not arise only or necessarily from overt acts of exclusion or persecution. Third, we might hear a warning: Do not even think about leaving this community and turning, or returning, to Judaism! If you do, you will experience exclusion, persecution, maybe even death! Furthermore, why would anyone cast aside a faith that assures eternal life to align oneself with a people who have the devil as their father? (cf. John 8:44)

---

[2] For an attempt to read the role of women out of the Fourth Gospel, see Reinhartz 2003.

These possibilities are of course not mutually exclusive, nor are they incompatible with the expulsion theory itself. Rather, they suggest the need to remain open to other interpretations that alone or in combination may also reflect something of the experience, whether historical, social or emotional, of the earliest audiences of this text. Yet even the act of exploring other readings of the Fourth Gospel, and of broadening the theoretical basis to include literary considerations, could not have taken place without Martyn's important work. He has enticed us to look beyond the text to discern, if dimly, and to empathize with, if imperfectly, its earliest readers as they told and retold Jesus' story in their struggle for identity in response to and in conflict with their own historical, cultural, social, and religious circumstances. Seeing with their eyes and hearing with their ears may be acts of historical imagination more than historical reconstruction, but our encounters with the Gospel of John are the richer for trying.

CHAPTER 11

INTO NARRATIVE AND BEYOND

Francis J. Moloney, S.D.B.

In 1972, I was completing a master's thesis on the use of Daniel 7 and/or Suffering Servant language in Mark 10:45: "For the Son of Man came not to be served but to serve, and to give his life a ransom for many." I asked all the expected questions of that period. Was there sufficient linguistic and thematic contact between the OT and the Markan texts to claim that the former influenced the latter? Was it likely that here we have *ipsissima verba* of Jesus? Was it possible that Jesus understood himself in terms of the Danielic Son of Man and the Isaianic Suffering Servant? For the information of the reader, this much researched and deservedly never–published study decided that the ransom saying was a composition formed in the early church. It reflected Jesus' own use of the expression, "the Son of the Man," and the early Christian community's presentation of him as the Suffering Servant.

THE OXFORD EXPERIENCE

Destined to go on to doctoral studies, I was in touch with the then–lecturer in New Testament at the University of Oxford, Dr. Morna D. Hooker, later the Lady Margaret Professor of Divinity at the University of Cambridge. We had agreed that she would direct my work at Oxford,

described as "Son of Man and/or Suffering Servant as Christological Categories in the New Testament." I eventually submitted a dissertation to
the University's Board of Theology with the title "The Johannine Son of
Man" (Moloney 1978). I had already been solidly trained at the Pontifical
Biblical Institute in the biblical languages and in the dominant historical–
critical methods. I recall those days with affection. The biblical text came
to life for me as I began to use my newly acquired skills to rediscover the
situations in the life of Jesus and the life of the church that gave it birth.
Taught and guided by gifted Jesuit scholars from Germany, Belgium,
England, the United States, France, and Italy, I was a ready learner. As a
recently ordained Roman Catholic priest, a member of a religious congregation dedicated to poor and abandoned young people (Salesians of
Don Bosco), I sensed that I was privileged to be given the opportunity to
become familiar with the Word of God that was also the words of men
and women (see Levie 1961).

My time in Oxford helped me to develop these skills, but my close
association with Dr. Hooker was a major factor that I have only come
to recognize in recent years. Trained in traditional form and redaction
criticism, two approaches to the New Testament that depend very heavily upon each other, I worked assiduously to detect "strata" of different
traditions and to suggest what may have led to their being juxtaposed to
generate the canonical form of the Gospel of John. Preeminent at this
time was the seminal first edition of J. Louis Martyn's classic *History and
Theology in the Fourth Gospel* (1968), which was so influential on all subsequent Johannine scholarship and especially on the work of major figures in American Johannine Studies, including Raymond Brown, Dwight
Moody Smith, and Robert Kysar. But Dr. Hooker had little time for these
methods. Well ahead of her time, she insisted that the only text that carried the "finished" theological perspective of an author was the "finished"
text. She respected work done to establish how the text may have come
to have its present shape, but her guidance led me toward the production
of a dissertation that presented a Johannine understanding of the traditional title "the Son of the Man." She was not alone, of course, in working
with the Johannine text in this fashion. Side by side with her influence
was the work of Wilhelm Thüsing (1970) and the slightly later study of
Severino Pancaro (1975). Only now, looking back, can I appreciate that
the eloquent and intense studies of the Gospel of John from Thüsing and
Pancaro, which devoted little or no attention to the history of the Johannine tradition, along with Dr. Hooker's insistence on the hermeneutical
importance of the final text for any "theological" reading, were formative
experiences that mark my approach to the Fourth Gospel to this day.

THE "IN-BETWEEN TIME"

It was some years before I returned to serious critical scholarship. Several occasions became available as I taught in Roman Universities (the Gregorian University, the Biblical Institute, the Salesian Pontifical University), but my major commitment was to seminary education. I used the skills acquired during my years of intellectual formation to teach the Gospels and the letters of Paul to seminarians and in the increasing number of courses and lecture series dedicated to the biblical education of an older generation of clergy and a newer generation of questioning lay people. At first glance, this may appear to have been a rather stagnant period in the development of my scholarly understanding of the Fourth Gospel. Nothing I wrote during that period reflected any change in the method I used to approach the Gospel (Moloney 1977; Moloney 1986). I thought I was simply doing what I had learned to do, as I taught New Testament studies in various settings. But more was going on.

Especially creative in this post–Vatican II period in the Catholic Church was a renewed interest in the Bible. Many people were flocking to the once very clerical seminaries to follow traditional courses, and even more attended extra–curricular classes offered in schools, church halls, and other public venues. These were heady days in the Catholic Church and, again looking back, I can sense that I unconsciously imbibed another element that became formative for my present approach to the Fourth Gospel. The young seminarians, and especially the many laypeople who attended evening lectures at the end of a day's work, made me aware of what we now call "the readers in front of the text." The passion that the systematic unfolding of the Gospel of John aroused in them was often surprising. In those days, I taught and answered questions that focused very much upon the "world behind the text" (form and redactional questions) and the "world in the text" (initially redactional questions). But something was going on in those contexts that was outside my control, and it certainly was not the result of my scholarly methodology. In a later stage of my career, I began to recognize the significant role that the world in front of the text plays in the interpretive process.

THE TURN TOWARD NARRATIVE

The turning point in my journey, as with many others of my vintage, was Alan Culpepper's trailblazing book *Anatomy of the Fourth Gospel: A Study in Literary Design* (1983). Prodded by this courageous study, traditional historical critics were asked to contemplate the suggestion that, although there was no doubt an author "of the text" (the never–ending debate over the identity of the Beloved Disciple), this person is long since gone, and we have no way of ever being certain who he was or what he was trying to do with his story. But a more important "author" emerges "from the text" (via the voice of the narrator) in John 1:1–18, 19:35, and 20:30–31. This so–called "implied author" can be heard, and we can trace his literary and theological strategies as he tells a story to a reader who is also to be found "in the text." Within the narrative itself, the contemporary critic—following the principles of literary criticism—is asked to trace the dialogue going on between an implied author and an implied reader. The former shapes the latter by systematically leading the reader in the text to a final acceptance of a point of view at the end of the story. He does this by his use of time, plot, characters, and other narrative strategies, such as explicit and implicit commentary (Moloney 1997, 219–33).

After the timeless poetry of the prologue (John 1:1–18), a period of at least two years passes in the events reported in 1:19–12:50. Jesus' story is set within the time span of three celebrations of Passover (2:13, 23; 6:4; 11:55, 12:1). Across these years, major characters emerge: John the Baptist (1:19–35; 3:22–30), the disciples, the mother of Jesus (2:1–5), "the Jews," Nicodemus (3:1–21), the Samaritan woman (4:7–30), Samaritan villagers (4:39–42), a royal official (4:46–54), the crowd, the man born blind (9:1–41), Martha and Mary (11:1–44). The interplay between Jesus and these characters often leads to misunderstanding, enabling the level of the discourse to deepen as Jesus takes his interlocutors into discussions and confrontations that they find puzzling and generally too difficult to accept. However, the final celebration of the Passover, announced in 12:1, is the setting for 13:1–20:31 (and on to 21:25 [13:1; 19:31]). The allocation of a single temporal context, the celebration of the Passover, for the final eight chapters of the Gospel (nine if chapter 21 is counted), after at least a two–year span as the backdrop for the first twelve chapters, says something about the relative importance of 13:1–20:31. The speed of the plot slows dramatically, and the characters become more focused: Jesus interacts only with his disciples, "the Jews," and the Romans. This slowing down is imposed upon the implied reader by the implied author, and the real reader follows the process. The success or failure of a story depends upon the quality of the relationship that is generated between the implied author and the implied reader. On the basis of the example just provided, is this dramatic slowing down of the plot and the closer focus upon Jesus, his disciples, "the Jews," and the Romans effective?

In a good story, dialogue between the implied author and the implied reader is so effective that any real reader is drawn into the story and shares the experience of the implied reader. We do not know who wrote the original story, and we do not know who might pick it up to read or to have it read. What we do know is that John's story has stood the test of time, and has continued to fascinate flesh–and–blood readers from many times and cultures. It has been read and reread over the centuries because of its claim upon real readers, and not only because it found its way into the Christian canon in the second century. Close attention to what was happening "within the text" offered a new possibility to the interpreter. Maybe we could now better understand why this story has made such a significant impact upon readers "in front of the text."

These categories and language, all narrative–critical jargon, are familiar to most interpreters now, even though many historical critics had good reason to be suspicious and have not embraced it. Nevertheless, by the late 1980s, the so–called "narrative–critical approach" had introduced a fresh way of thinking about the Gospel of John. Many "narrative" studies of various aspects of the Fourth Gospel appeared: the use of irony; the plot; the characters as a group, singly, or in categories (e.g., women in the Gospel of John); the use of anonymous characters; the "speed" of the narrative and its use of time; the explicit and implicit commentary found within the narrative—to mention but a few.

Narrative Is Not Enough

However exciting the emerging focus upon the world within the text and its impact upon the world receiving the text, narrative readings have problems. Some of those problems were external to the interpretive process itself. For example, students no longer saw the need to study Hebrew, Greek, and the other languages and cultures of antiquity. It was sufficient to immerse oneself in narrative theory and to trace the exploitation of this theory within the Johannine Gospel. Further, it became clear that narrative criticism contained within itself the potential for a new fundamentalism. Narrative theory suggests that an interpreter should trace the emerging implied reader to capture the point of view that the real and the implied author wish to communicate to a real reader. In a successful communication, the real reader identifies him or herself with the implied reader and "enter[s] the fictional contract" (Chatman 1978, 191). However, many readings of the Fourth Gospel from this period, my own included, ran the danger of a communication that ran in the other direction. The interpreter traced an implied reader that reflected the ideological and often ecclesial situation "of the interpreter." The communication that some narrative critics found in the dialogue between the implied author and the implied reader expressed a point of view that resonated with the "interpreter's" point of view. The real reader finds herself or himself in the implied reader. In other words, as Albert Schweitzer said of the first quest for the historical Jesus, and as has also been said of the redaction critics (Hooker 1975, 28–44), the brilliant use of narrative techniques to discover the so–called implied reader in the Fourth Gospel's narrative all too often discovered the ecclesial, theological, and even social perspectives of the interpreter.

My initial enthusiasm for a narrative–critical approach to the Fourth Gospel, most clearly expressed in the first volume of my narrative reading of John, *Belief in the Word: Reading John 1–4* (Moloney 1993), had to be modified in later "readings." It was not enough to follow the principles of narrative–critical theory. This theory had its birth within the academic analysis of the English novel, a relatively recent literary phenomenon. There is much that we can learn from that approach, but the texts that responded so well to it were modern and contemporary fiction, not ancient texts written in Hebrew and Greek. The biblical narratives emerged from social, religious, and historical settings that were very different from the modern and contemporary world and claimed to be something other than "fiction." Another gulf that lay between modern narrative fiction and the biblical texts was the issue of canonicity. The study of English literature had, of course, produced something that could be regarded as a "canon"—a group of books regarded by the scholarly guild as "classics." The accepted literary canon is under severe criticism these days, but that need not detain us here. The biblical texts, on the other hand, developed in the ancient Jewish and Christian communities as normative texts. They have been handed down as such for almost three thousand years (in the case of the Hebrew Bible) and for almost two thousand years (in the case of the Christian Bible). For this reason, the debate over the origin and the criteria of the biblical canon cannot be placed in the same arena as that surrounding the accepted literary canon (Moloney 2006, 7–20). To state the point bluntly, in my opinion one cannot place D. H. Lawrence's *Lady Chatterly's Lover* side by side with the Gospel of John and the same could be said, but for different reasons, of the *Gospel of Thomas*.

Contemporary narrative approaches to these ancient and canonical texts had to situate themselves more critically within the scholarly disciplines developed during the historical–critical period, especially form criticism and redaction criticism. What gave birth to the Johannine story? What cultural influences can one find within it? Is it Jewish or Greek? Is it Christian or Gnostic? How are we to explain the aporias present in the text as we have it? Do they reflect the juxtaposing of traditions from various stages in the development of the narrative? If such is the case, who and what are responsible for the various stages that one might trace

within the narrative as we now have it? Old questions that have never
been definitively resolved must still be asked. We must take a position on
the figure of the Beloved Disciple. Does the use of this character reflect
a literary technique or the role of a historical figure at the beginning of
the Johannine story? In other words, it is dishonest scholarship to interpret an ancient and (for some) a normative text without asking historical
questions. An honest interpretation of the Gospel of John must reflect a
literary and religious world "from the past" that can be found "within the
text." Thus, even a narrative approach to the Gospel of John must continue to ask all the difficult questions about "the world behind the text."
As Adela Yarbro Collins has eloquently argued, we should

> give more weight to the original historical context of the text.
> This context cannot and should not totally determine all sub-
> sequent meaning of the text. But if . . . all meaning is context
> bound, the original context and meaning have a certain norma-
> tive character. I suggest that Biblical theologians are not only
> mediators between genres. They are also mediators between his-
> torical periods. (1988, 150)

TODAY: THE STRUCTURE AND MESSAGE
OF THE FOURTH GOSPEL

The story of my journey as a scholarly reader of the Gospel of John,
and the various theoretical stances that have influenced it since the early
1970s, reflect a parallel journey on the part of many of my contemporaries. We have, of course, each taken our own direction. I think of the
continued serious historical scholarship of Udo Schnelle (1992; 1998).
Similar quality historical scholarship, not without knowledge and interest in more contemporary literary perspectives, comes from the work of
John Painter (1993a). Dwight Moody Smith continues to pursue a strong
interest in the history and character of the Johannine community and the
theology that emerged from it (1995; 2005, 52–62). Fernando Segovia
has moved vigorously away from an earlier career marked by a sophisticated use of historical criticism to readings that are strongly determined
by the historical and cultural situation of contemporary readers (1991).
Robert Kysar has also moved more determinedly away from mainstream
Johannine interpretation into what might be called a "postmodern" or less
stable form of interpretation that contends that there is no such thing as
"the meaning" of a text. For the contemporary Kysar, we must resist any

attempt to develop "an interpretation," and humbly accept that "nothing is certain" (2005a, 161–72; 2005b, 65–81).

Recently called away from scholarly activity for service to the church and my religious congregation, I am now in a position where I can indicate the fruits of thirty–four years' attention to the Gospel of John. What follows is an outline of my present understanding of the Fourth Gospel. It will be interesting to test the following in several years' time, when my social and ecclesial setting will have been long separated from an academic and university context. My reading of the Gospel, both as a whole and in more detailed analysis of particular Johannine texts, is the result of an osmotic process. Over the years, traditional historical criticism, narrative criticism, and some of the less stable methods that focus more and more on the readership of the text have blended to form my interpretive procedures. I still stand by certain positions that have been with me from my earliest days. For example, under the influence of the work of M.-J. Lagrange, E. C. Hoskyns, Rudolf Bultmann, C. H. Dodd, C. K. Barrett, and Raymond Brown, I would still claim that the Fourth Gospel is made up of a prologue (John 1:1–18), a long section dedicated to Jesus' public ministry (a Book of Signs; 1:19–12:50), an intense section dedicated to the last discourse, the passion and resurrection (a Book of Glory; 13:1–20:29), and a conclusion (20:30–31). Unlike many contemporary narrative critics, I do not regard chapter 21 as part of the original narrative, but I see it as an integral part of the overall presentation of the Johannine theological, and especially ecclesiological, message. For the purposes of this reflection, I will present my overall understanding of the Johannine narrative from 1:1–20:31, sending my readers elsewhere for my reading of John 21 and its historical and literary relationship to the preceding chapters (Moloney 1998a, 547–68).

A history of commitment to historical criticism and to the literary and theological unity of the Fourth Gospel, despite clear evidence of a complex prehistory, leads me to read and interpret the Gospel of John as follows.

The prologue (John 1:1–18), despite its intensity, plays a literary and theological role that was widespread in antiquity (D. E. Smith 1991, 1–9). In the classical Greek tragedies, the chorus appears on stage first and informs the audience that great foibles have been committed by human beings and that a portrayal of these foibles will shortly be acted out before them. Already provided with the *fact* of the particular aspect of human frailty and its consequences that form the plot of the play, the action begins. Already aware of *what* is to take place, the audience follows the dramatic portrayal of *how* the tragic events of an Oedipus or an Orestes or an Antigone unfold. Knowledge that something will happen does not distract from the power of the portrayal of *how* it happens. The audience is drawn into the drama. They know *what* is about to happen, and they follow carefully as they see *how* it happens. This same technique is found in the Synoptic Gospels. Mark (1:1–13), Matthew (1:1–4:16), and Luke (1:1–4:13) have long prologues that inform the reader *who* Jesus is and *what* he is bringing to Israel and to all nations. However, the rest of the story must be read so that the reader might come to understand *how* this has taken place. The use of this technique in the Gospel of John, however, is particularly effective because of the "misunderstanding" that develops across the narrative, as Jesus' self–revelation is not understood by the characters in the story. They have not read the prologue. But the reader has and is being called to decision in each narrative. Is the presentation of Jesus provided by 1:1–18 true? The author's focus upon the reader is made clear at the end of the story (20:30–31). The closing statement is directed explicitly to the reader. You have now read a prologue, telling you *who* and *what* Jesus is. This story of *how* he is such has been written so that you may go on believing and have life in his name (20:30–31).

Four "days" mark the time span of John 1:19–51 (vv. 29, 35, 43), and the first Cana miracle takes place "on the third day" (2:1). The setting of four days of preparation culminating with the revelation of the δόξα ("glory") "on the third day" matches exactly the celebration of the Jewish Feast of Pentecost, as it is regulated in the *Melkilta de Rabbi Ishmael*, an early Jewish midrashic commentary on Exodus. Starting with the threefold repetition of "on the third day" found in Exodus 19:11, 15, 16, first–century Jewish liturgical practice extended the days of preparation (Exod 19:10–11, 14–15) to four days of more remote preparation. On the last of the four days of remote preparation, the first of the "three days" begins. It is against this background of the revelation of the glory of God in the gift of the Law at Sinai that these first days of the ministry of Jesus are told in the Fourth Gospel. There is a gradual revelation of Jesus in the witness of the Baptist (vv. 19–28 [first day], vv. 29–34 [second day]) and the movement for the first disciples who recognize Jesus as an expected messianic figure (vv. 35–42 [third day], vv. 43–51 [fourth day]). On the fourth day, Jesus makes himself known in a promise to the disciples, whose confession of Jesus, in categories that are part of their own expectations ("Rabbi," "Messiah," "the one of whom Moses and the Law and the prophets wrote," "of Nazareth," "of Joseph"), is corrected. They will see the opening of the heavens and the communication of the heavenly in the Son of Man (1:50–51, correcting Nathanael's confession in v. 49, but directed to all the disciples).

If the confessions of faith by the disciples in John 1:35–49 are insufficient, what is expected? John 2:1–4:54 provides a response to the question raised for the reader by 1:19–51. In an admirable example of early Christian catechesis, the author has assembled eight narratives. They are framed by the two Cana miracles (2:1–12; 4:46–54) in which the mother of Jesus and the royal official respond unquestioningly to the word of Jesus (2:1–5; 4:50). The criteria for authentic Johannine faith is articulated in the frame: unconditional acceptance of the Word of God, as expressed in the revelation that takes place in and through Jesus. Between the two framing events one finds six further stories, three set in Israel and three set in Samaria. There is a steady progression from rejection ("the Jews" in 2:13–25) to conditioned acceptance (3:1–21, Nicodemus) to an unconditional reception of the word of Jesus (3:22–36) in Israel. The same sequence of responses to Jesus follows in Samaria (4:1–42). Jesus' revelation is rejected (4:1–15, Samaritan woman), conditionally accepted (4:16–38, Samaritan woman), and then unconditionally accepted (4:39–42, Samaritan villagers). The reader has now been instructed, by means of a collection of narratives that deal with numerous responses to the word of Jesus, on the possibility of no faith, partial faith, and correct faith in Israel (2:13–3:36) and in Samaria (4:1–42), set between models of true faith: the mother of Jesus (2:1–12) and the royal official (4:46–54).

Additional problems emerge for the reader. If access to God is available through unconditional commitment in faith to the revelation of God found in the word of Jesus, then what of Israel's traditional access to God through the annual "memories" of God's saving acts in the Feasts of Israel? The author turns to this issue immediately: "After this there was a feast of the Jews" (John 5:1a). Israel's so–called "pilgrim feasts" were Pentecost, Passover, and Tabernacles. The celebration of Pentecost, transcended by the revelation of the δόξα/glory at Cana (2:11), has already appeared in the narrative. In the chapters that follow, the author deals with the fundamental Jewish celebration, the Sabbath (5:1–47; see 5:9b); two Pilgrim Feasts, Passover (6:1–71; see 6:4) and Tabernacles (7:1–10:21; see 7:2); and the celebration of Dedication (10:22–42; see 10:22). The theology and rituals of the Jewish feasts are not discarded. They provide the background for the presentation of Jesus as the giver of life and judge (Sabbath), the true bread from heaven (Passover), the living water, the life of the world, the sent one of the one true god, the shepherd Messiah (Tabernacles), and the one sent and consecrated by God (Dedication). The celebration of the Jewish feasts is a sign and a shadow of the fullness of God's gifts that took place in Jesus Christ (1:16–17). The use of the recently established feast of Dedication, celebrating the reconsecration of the temple in the time of Judas Maccabeus (164 B.C.E), enables the author to point to Jesus as the *place* where God can be found in the world. It closes this series of pastoral and theological reflections upon the

Jewish feasts with a significant Christological claim that lends credence to Jesus' claims across chapters 5–10: "I and the Father are one" (10:30); "The Father is in me and I am in the Father" (v. 38).

The memory of the traditional life of Jesus now imposes itself on the narrative. In chapters 11–12, Jesus turns toward his death and resurrection. Jesus moves to Jerusalem upon hearing that Lazarus had died (John 11:15). He tells his disciples that the miracle to come will play a role in his mission and in the life of the disciples. On the one hand, "this illness does not lead to death; rather it is for God's glory so that the Son of God may be glorified through it" (11:4). On the other, he tells his disciples that he is glad of his absence at the moment of Lazarus' death, "so that you may believe" (v. 15). At no stage in the story does anyone come to faith. Thomas suggests that they all become martyrs with Jesus (v. 16), but that is not what Jesus asked of them. He wants them to believe that he is the one sent by the Father. Martha and, to a lesser extent, Mary are drawn into the weeping and disappointment that the death of their brother has generated, but which Jesus could have prevented. They do express faith (vv. 21, 27, 32), but they are not able to go beyond their own hopes and expectations. This is even the case for the famous words of Martha, "I believe that you are the Messiah, the Son of God, the one coming into the world" (v. 27). If she has come to final and perfect faith with these words, why does she object to Jesus' command to take away the stone from Lazarus' tomb, only to be reprimanded for her little faith (vv. 39–40)? Jesus' weeping and deep disturbance (John 11:33, 38) are not primarily over the loss of his friend, although he is misunderstood in that way (vv. 36–37). As he stands at the tomb, he again announces the reason for all that has happened and is about to happen in a prayer to his Father. "Father, I thank you for having heard me. I know that you always hear me, but I have said this for the sake of the crowd standing here, so that they may believe that you sent me" (vv. 41–42). The miracle is not an end in itself. It is a further summons to the people in the story and the readers of the story to reach beyond their own expectations, to accept Jesus as the unique sent one of God, making known the glory of God, and thus coming to his own glorification (v. 4).

Jesus' body is anointed for burial (John 12:1–8). He enters Jerusalem amid threats that both he and Lazarus must be slain because the whole world is going after him (vv. 9–19). Indeed, Greeks seek Jesus, and he is able to announce that the hour has come for the Son of Man to be glorified (v. 23). In a brief discourse, he insists that the time has come for the revelation of the glory of God and his own glorification. This will take place when the prince of this world is cast out and Jesus, lifted up from the earth, will draw everyone to himself (vv. 31–32). In the Fourth Gospel, the crucifixion of Jesus is a moment of glory (12:33) and the place where all will be gathered, but "the Jews" reject the promises and Jesus leaves them (vv. 34–36). Jesus' next public appearance will be during his passion.

The narrative slows down dramatically. Gathered with his own, Jesus washes their feet, gives them the morsel, instructs them, and prays with them and for them. The first part of the Book of Glory (John 13:1–17:26) shows all the signs of a careful working and reworking of traditions that have come to the author. Earlier traditions about the footwashing, discourses, and a final prayer are gathered, and themes basic to the Gospel stated and restated: Jesus as the revelation of the love of God and the call for disciples to love one another (13:1–38; 17:1–26); the departure of Jesus and its consequences (14:1–31; 16:4–33); the need for believers to abide in Jesus and to love one another on the basis of Jesus' previous choosing of them in the face of hatred and rejection (15:1–16:3). The apparent repetition of many themes is evidence of the author's teaching technique. His stating and restating enables him to make the same point several times but to take it to greater depth with each repetition.

> *A. John 13:1–38*—Jesus makes God known in the perfect love that he shows for his fragile disciples. In and through his loving, Jesus is glorified and God is glorified in him. The disciples are to be recognized as the sent ones of Jesus by the unity created by the love they have for one another.
>
>> *B. John 14:1–31*—Jesus instructs his failing disciples on his departure and on the conditions and challenges they will face. Guided by the Paraclete in his physical absence, love, faith, joy, and peace should be theirs, swept up into the love that unites the Father and Jesus, the sent one.
>>
>>> *C. John 15:1–11*—The oneness and joy created by abiding in Jesus, the true vine, and being swept up into his abiding oneness with the Father.
>>>
>>>> *D. John 15:12–17*—The disciples of Jesus are to love as he has loved, as a consequence of all that he has done for them.
>>>
>>> *C'. John 15:18–16:3*—The hatred, rejection, expulsion, and slaying of the disciples that will result from the actions of "the Jews," the false vine that has rejected Jesus and the Father.
>>
>> *B'. John 16:4–33*—Jesus instructs his failing disciples on his departure and on the conditions and challenges they will face. Guided by the Paraclete in his physical absence, joy and confidence should be theirs, loved by the Father who sent Jesus.

A'. John 17:1–26—Jesus makes God known in the perfect love that he shows for his fragile disciples. In and through his loving, Jesus is glorified and God is glorified in him. The disciples are to be recognized as the sent ones of Jesus by the unity created by the love they have for one another.

This structured presentation of the message of John 13:1–17:28 indicates the cyclic nature of the Johannine argument (13:1–38 = 17:1–26; 14:1–31 = 16:4–33; 15:1–11 = 15:18–16:3 [in a contrasting fashion]; see Brown/ Moloney 2003, 291–97). At its center is the crucial teaching on the new commandment of love (15:12–17). The stage is set for the story of Jesus' glorification, "the hour" when he is "lifted up" to draw everyone to himself, making known the love of God.

Up to this point, the word "kingdom" has been used only twice in the Fourth Gospel, and both times in a traditional passage referring to "the kingdom of God" (John 3:3, 5). In the passion account, the term appears three times in one important verse (18:36). Thus far in the Gospel, the title "king" has been found four times (1:49; 6:15; 12:13, 15). On each occasion, people who would like to make Jesus a king address him in a way that reflects false messianic hopes. Throughout the passion narrative the term "king" appears ten times. Jesus is crowned and dressed as a king, and he acts out his role as king, "lifted up" from the earth. Thus, although John tells the story of an arrest, a Jewish and a Roman trial, a crucifixion, a death, and a burial, his presentation of these events ironically proclaims that Jesus is a king. A carefully written and articulated use of the passion tradition enables the author of the Fourth Gospel to bring his story of Jesus to an end with an account of his death that is, at one and the same time, his being lifted up on a cross and his exaltation as king (3:14; 8:28; 12:32). Summarily stated, the passion narrative unfolds as follows.

A. *John 18:1–11*—Jesus in a garden, with his enemies
   B. *John 18:12–27*—The Jewish Hearing: The community as the bearer of the Word
      C. *John 18:28–19:16*—The Trial before Pilate: Jesus as King
   B'. *John 19:17–37*—The Crucifixion of Jesus: The community founded and nourished
A'. *John 19:38–42*—Jesus in a garden, with his friends

Jesus allows himself to be taken in the darkness by enemies, who must bring lanterns and torches (John 18:1–11). The passion narrative begins in a garden and it closes in a garden, where Jesus is buried in a new tomb, anointed as a king (19:38–42). Before and after the Roman trial, the storyteller addresses the Christian community. As Peter denies him, Jesus tells his interlocutors that he has spoken openly to the world. It is now time to ask those who have heard him. They know what he said (18:20–21). Followers and disciples may fail, but they have been entrusted with the word of Jesus (18:12–27). Lifted up on the cross and proclaimed as king, he gathers his seamless garment in the figures of his Mother and the Beloved Disciple. He pours down his Spirit upon them and bathes them in the water and blood that flow from his side (19:17–37). At the center of the narrative, Pilate ironically proclaims Jesus "King of the Jews" and crowns and clothes him as a king (18:28–19:16). Overall, the passion of Jesus in the Fourth Gospel is more about what Jesus does for the believer than what happened to Jesus.

So much that is positive takes place in the passion narrative. What need is there for a resurrection story? Not only was it a part of received tradition, but the Johannine author has told it in his own way to address his readers (John 20:1–29). As the story comes to an end, he focuses more intensely on his readers: those who have not seen, yet believe. Three features of this resurrection account appear only in the Gospel of John: the experience of Peter and the Beloved Disciple in their journey to the empty tomb (vv. 2–10); the appearance to Mary Magdalene (vv. 11–18); and the episode of "doubting Thomas" (vv. 24–29). The Gospel of John opened with an indication of the possibility of a journey from no faith to complete faith in the experiences recounted in the journey from Cana to Cana (2:1–4:54). It ends with further indications of such a journey, yet at the end of the Gospel, there is a difference. Original members of the Christian community, Peter and the Beloved Disciple, Mary Magdalene, and Thomas, all begin in a situation of unbelief (John 20:2–3 [the disciples], 13–15 [Mary], 24 [Thomas]). However, they are led by the risen Lord, through their various experiences of little and partial faith (vv. 9–10 [the disciples], 16–17 [Mary], 25 [Thomas]), into a final total commitment in faith (vv. 19–22 [disciples], 18 [Mary], 28 [Thomas]). Further, it must be noticed that the Beloved Disciple "saw and believed" (v. 8) without "seeing" Jesus. The initial responses of Mary Magdalene and Thomas are very physical. Mary wishes to cling to Jesus (v. 17), and Thomas will only believe when he can physically penetrate Jesus' wounds (v. 25). In the end, they overcome these limitations and come to faith. But the risen Jesus reminds Thomas that he believed because he saw Jesus (v. 29a). Jesus' final words are, "Blessed are those who have not seen and yet have come to believe" (v. 29b). As the Beloved Disciple believed without seeing, all who follow the way of the Beloved Disciple are specially blessed.

The Gospel of John, at the end of the first Christian century, points back to the foundational experience of the church. The encounter with the risen Jesus has led the very first believers from the poverty of their unfaith to true belief. In his final words, the risen Christ blesses in a special way those who did not have the experience of seeing Jesus himself, but still believe (v. 29). They will all be "beloved disciples." The story of people struggling to come to a deeper faith in Jesus must not be limited to the characters in the story. The author wishes to touch readers of the story. Jesus' final words are addressed to all who read and listen to the Gospel.

The Fourth Gospel closes with words from the narrator: "Now Jesus did many other signs in the presence of the disciples, which are not written in this book. But these are written so that you may come to believe that Jesus is the Messiah, the Son of God, and that through believing you may have life in his name" (John 20:30–31). We have been led to a point of decision. "God so loved the world that he gave his only Son, that everyone who believes in him may not perish but may have eternal life" (3:16). No middle course is feasible; there are only two possibilities—to perish or to have eternal life. This Gospel sees humankind as inexorably caught between two cosmic forces. On the one side there is darkness (blindness, evil, this world, the prince of this world) and on the other is light (life, sight, the Spirit). To choose darkness means death, but the possibility of light and life has now been revealed in Jesus Christ. We judge ourselves by our own decision for or against the God revealed in and through Jesus Christ. He has revealed God so that men and women of all times—living in the presence and under the guidance of the Paraclete, sent by the glorified Jesus (14:16, 26; 15:26; 16:7, 13–15)—might gaze upon him and be saved (3:13–14; 8:28; 12:32; 19:37). Do you believe this?

CONCLUSION

I have come to the above reading of the Gospel of John after many years of study, reflection, teaching, and writing. I am aware that there are many difficult turns and apparent nonsequiturs within the narrative. However, it appears to me that the above reading respects the text itself and is also able to accept that the Fourth Gospel had a long prehistory. The tensions in the text reflect that prehistory, and they guide us in our attempts to understand why the final text was handed down to later generations in this shape. I am also aware that many would disagree with my assessment of the Johannine plot and that my own social location as a Roman Catholic scholar living in a well-developed Western society influences my reading strategies—perhaps more than I recognize.

I wonder if, in the future, Johannine Studies will continue to focus on the text itself and to pay attention to the world that produced the text. My reading is based upon a world behind the text that is at least Greco–Roman, Jewish, pre–Gnostic, early Christian, and early Johannine. The ability of the author to marry all these cultural and religious traditions into a coherent and compelling narrative is a sign of genius. The early reception of this Gospel was in doubt because of that genius. It was so different from everything else in early Christian tradition and played too easily into the hands of the Gnostics. It continues to be a fascinating and troublesome Christian text for the same reason.

To what extent will the world in front of the text determine future Johannine interpretation? I have no doubt that my world (in front of the text) has been influential on my reading of the Fourth Gospel. I have no difficulty with interpretive stances that are increasingly influenced by culture, postcolonialism, feminism, womanism, and the many other "–isms" that arouse passion. I do have difficulty with a future that loses touch with the world behind the text, the world of the text, and the two thousand years of tradition that have given us the Fourth Gospel as a major book within the Christian Scriptures. As Peter Rabinowitz has warned:

> [O]nce you take seriously the notion that readers 'construct' (even partially) the texts that they read, then the canon (any canon) is not (or not only) the product of the inherent qualities in the text; it is also (at least partly) the product of particular choices by the arbiters of taste who create it—choices always grounded in ideological and cultural values, always enmeshed in class, race and gender. (1989, 94)

From where I stand, the Fourth Gospel and the tradition that has delivered this text to the third millennium deserves better than that (Moloney 2005b, 19–39).

THE BEYOND BECKONS

Mary Coloe

Frank Moloney's paper succinctly chronicles the history of Catholic biblical scholarship in the last century. Following Pius XII's encyclical in 1943, Catholic biblical scholars were free to engage in the historical–critical methods pioneered by Protestant scholars from the nineteenth century. In many ways, the 1940s and 1950s were an exciting "wake up" in the Catholic biblical community, and priests from around the world descended upon Rome and Jerusalem to acquire new skills of interpretation. At the same time that the Catholic world was beginning to reap the benefits of this historical–critical research, women and men in the Protestant tradition were already appreciating its limitations and moving into narrative criticism. In Johannine Studies, Moloney was one of the first Catholic scholars to take the plunge into these new narrative waters in his three–volume narrative commentary on John. These works were later crystallized in his Sacra Pagina commentary on John, displaying the convergence of both historical and narrative–critical methods.

As one of Moloney's graduate and doctoral students, I received my biblical training in both historical and narrative methodologies. When contemplating the vast repertoire of Johannine scholarship of the twentieth century, new entrants into this field may well ask, "What's left to do?" Brown and Martyn have opened up the "world behind the text" with their historical–critical methods. Culpepper and Moloney have shed light on the "world within the text" through narrative criticism. Segovia and Kysar are making forays into the "world in front of the text." Where do we go from here? What is "the beyond" that Moloney's title intimates?

Without naming them explicitly, I believe Moloney's paper does indicate some critical issues for future Johannine research. I will describe these issues under the heading "hermeneutics," a word I did not hear in my undergraduate studies. What are we doing when we seek to find the meaning of the text and where do we think this meaning lies?

Moloney's essay describes well the development of a variety of methodologies that the modern scholar can draw upon in engaging the biblical text, but these methods and skills need to be placed at the service of a self–conscious understanding of *what* we do when we interpret a text and the type of text that we are interpreting. Knowing what we aim to achieve should determine the methods chosen and should result in a more selective and sharpened use of these methodological tools. The methods are the tools at the service of the enquiry; they should not be what drives and directs the enquiry. What difference does it make that we interpret a text considered sacred within the community, particularly when the interpreter is part of that believing community? What criteria can we use to evaluate the validity of an interpretation? Should consideration of ethics guide the interpretive task or is this to be left to practitioners in their pastoral ministries? These questions could be called the hermeneutics of the "world in front of the text." The work of feminist and postcolonial critics especially draws these hermeneutical concerns to our attention.

As well as these hermeneutical considerations, I think we need to consider also the hermeneutics of "the world behind the text." To my mind, European scholars have been leading the way in this area. Franz Mussner and Christina Hoegen–Rohls have explored the post–Easter perspective that gives this Gospel its unique style. Jesus, in John's Gospel, is the risen and glorified divine Word who is now a living presence within the community mediated through the Spirit. The ongoing experience of Jesus within the community provides the normative hermeneutic for understanding the Jesus of history, and this hermeneutic shapes the Gospel's narrative. Here, I see a need for considering the theological implications of Gadamer's "fusion of horizons." My own work has developed from this interest in the spirituality and theology of the community that gave birth to the text.

Finally, there is the need to attend to the hermeneutics of "the world within the text." Once again, I find the work of European scholars such as Jean Zumstein and Andreas Dettwiler most insightful. These two scholars have pointed to literary relationships within the text, which they describe as *réécriture* and *relecture*. These terms describe a process that is more than a literary technique or repetition or intratextuality. According to them, the text itself shows signs of a self–conscious reinterpretive process, perhaps to meet new historical circumstances or perhaps to offer further clarification. The works of Andreas Obermann and Klaus Scholtissek show a similar interest in the hermeneutical principals operating in the process of writing the Fourth Gospel. A recent article by Moloney on the issue of the Fourth Gospel as Scripture indicates that he too is moving "beyond" biblical criticisms into biblical hermeneutics (Moloney 2005a).

Alongside these hermeneutical concerns, "the Beyond" will continue to need sound historical, archaeological, sociological, and religious knowledge of the world of the first century. Part of this "world" is a more nuanced and sensitive reading of the relationship between emerging rabbinic Judaism and emerging Christianity. Moloney's work on the Jewish festivals in John, and my own studies, clearly situate the Gospel of John within a strong Jewish heritage that is highly valued and, at the same time, seen as insufficient in the light of Christian faith in Jesus. How do Christian interpreters today speak of this Jewish–Christian relationship, honoring the continuation of God's covenant with Israel while professing Christian faith in a new and unique revelation of God in Jesus? How do Christians interpret the harshly anti–Jewish statements in John, conscious of the anti–Semitism such statements have engendered? Our reading and interpretation of the Fourth Gospel needs a new, sharply critical theology, a new language, and what I have heard called a "hermeneutic of repentance."

In summary, scholars today will need to be equipped with the tools that previous scholarship has manufactured and refined. However, scholars today will also need a richer philosophical and theological awareness of the art of interpretation. Scholars such as Sandra Schneiders, Craig Koester, Dorothy Lee, and Ruben Zimmermann—all of whom emphasize the symbolism in the Fourth Gospel—have made a beginning in asking how metaphor and symbol function to convey meaning and in exploring the theological significance of symbolism in the Fourth Gospel. Christians who believe that this Gospel is a sacred text will need to develop this initial work on symbolism and meaning to consider the Gospel itself as symbol, to test its theological claim to be a text offering "life" to its reader (John 20:30–31).

The "Beyond" beckons as a fertile field of rich possibilities.

CHAPTER 12

THE PROLOGUE AND CHAPTER 17
OF THE GOSPEL OF JOHN

John F. O'Grady

I started studying the Gospel of John more than forty years ago. Since that time, certain chapters or sections have become part of my never–ending quest to understand the mentality of the author, or the inspirer, of this Gospel, as well as the community from which it came. I have particularly struggled to grasp the relationship between the farewell discourses, especially chapter 17, and the rest of the Gospel. I have also wondered about the origin of the prologue (John 1:1–18) and the relationship between these opening verses of the narrative and all that follows. Sometime in the future, exegetes will have to pay more attention to the seventeenth chapter, in particular verse 19: "For their [the disciples'] sakes I sanctify myself so that they also may be sanctified in truth." In my opinion, this chapter, along with the prologue, can offer insights into the mentality both of the author of the Gospel of John and of the community from which this text arose.

INTO THE WHIRLWIND

Over the centuries, those who have read or studied the Gospel of John have recognized the poetic quality of this last written Gospel. The prologue is easily recognized as poetry, and I contend that the same can be said of chapter 17. Readers usually accept that the meaning of this Gospel goes far beyond a simple analysis of the words employed. While every Gospel is both spiritual and theological, the Fourth Gospel, to many, offers more to the person of faith than the other three. John's symbolism, irony, plays on words, and allusions to the Old Testament, Hellenism, Gnosticism, and a host of other possible influences can leave the reader caught in a whirlwind that returns us again and again to the place of origin and that allows us to see again for the first time (Kysar 1975, 2). C. K. Barrett refers to this circular motion of both the prologue and the larger narrative when he says, "The gospel [of John] was intended to be read many times. . . . after the first reading the process is a circular one. The next time I read the prologue I shall read it in the light of the whole book and when I go on to read the rest of the book, I shall read it in the light of the knowledge of the prologue" (1972, 29). Something similar may be said of chapter 17. Such rereading seems to be not only an aspect of an approach to good literature, but also an approach to understanding life. Surely this has been part of my experience of this Gospel. In the words of T. S. Eliot,

> We shall not cease from exploration
> And the end of all our exploring
> Will be to arrive where we started
> And know the place for the first time
> Through the unknown remembered gate.
>
> (*Four Quartets*, "Little Gidding")

As a Roman Catholic growing up in the 1950s, I was most familiar with John's prologue as the "last Gospel"—in every Mass, the priest read the first thirteen verses of the Gospel of John between communion and the final blessing. These verses exemplify many characteristics of the entire Gospel. In some ways, the seventeenth chapter of John also exemplifies many of the characteristics of the entire book. Symbolism abounds in both the prologue and the seventeenth chapter. In the prologue, we find word and flesh; light and darkness; irony; the world was made through him but the world knew him not; he came to his own and his own received him not; "In the beginning God created the heavens and the earth"; "In the beginning was the Word"; and references to the λόγος ("word"); allusions to Greek philosophy and Hermetic literature; an understanding of the *memra*, Wisdom traditions. The whirlwind continues in the seventeenth chapter, where the author begins with relationship to God as Father; speaks of "glory"; makes reference to power over all flesh; eternal life; discipleship; words; truth; the world; acceptance and rejection; and, finally, union with God through Jesus. Just as the Word that became flesh remains in the bosom of the Father whom Jesus has made known (prologue), now the union with God the Father includes Jesus' disciples (ch. 17).

The image of the whirlwind seems applicable. In reading this entire Gospel, the reader goes around and around, returning to familiar themes again and again and developing an ever–deeper understanding. In the prologue, the whirlwind moves the reader from heaven ("In the beginning was the Word . . . all things came into being through him") to earth ("And the Word became flesh and lived among us"), and finally back to heaven ("No one has ever seen God. It is God, the only son, who is close to the father's heart, who has made him known"). Similarly, chapter 17 begins with a reference to the Father and glorification and ends with a revelation to the disciples of God as righteous Father.

Parallels between the Prologue and the Rest of the Gospel

As did many students of the Gospel of John, I at first viewed the prologue as an independent poem—perhaps originally having as its subject Wisdom, which was changed to λόγος ("word") because of the feminine gender of the Greek word σοφία ("wisdom"), or focusing originally on John the Baptist and later adapted to Jesus. I also struggled in deciding whether this independent poem should be treated as a true "prologue" to the Fourth Gospel or rather as an epilogue adapted to the narrative after the Gospel was written. These are only two of the many questions that scholars still ask about the opening verses of the Gospel of John. Where did the prologue come from? Did it exist apart from the Gospel within the Johannine community or perhaps outside this community? Did the author of the prologue compose the remainder of the Gospel? Did it originate in a Christian, Jewish, or Gnostic group, or a combination of groups and individuals? What is the origin of the word λόγος? Did it come from Jewish speculation on wisdom, Greek philosophy, the *memra* of the Targums, Gnosticism, or some other source? The more I saw that ideas in the prologue are repeated throughout the Gospel, the more I concluded that somehow the prologue came from the same community as the Gospel. I also came to see that the source behind the word λόγος is a combination of Jewish speculation on Wisdom and currents of thought at the time, and the prologue acts as an overture written at approximately the same time as other parts of the Gospel.

Table 12.1

Theme	Prologue	Gospel
Preexistence of the Logos or Son	1:1–2	17:5
Logos/Jesus and God	1:1	8:58; 10:30; 17:1–5; 20:28
In him was life	1:4	5:26; 6:33; 10:10; 11:25–26; 14:6; 17:3
Life is light	1:4	8:12
Conflict between light and darkness	1:5	3:19; 8:12; 12:25, 35, 46
Believing	1:7,12	2:11; 3:16, 18, 36; 5:24; 6:69; 11:25;14:1; 16:27; 17:21; 20:25
Light coming into the world	1:9	3:19; 12:46; 17:14, 15, 16
Rejection of the Logos	1:10–11	4:44; 7:1; 8:59; 10:31; 12:27–40; 15:18; 17:12
Logos/Jesus not received by his own	1:11	4:44; 17:12
Born of God and not of flesh	1:13	3:6; 8:41–42; 17:3
Seeing glory	1:14	12:41; 17:1, 5, 22, 24
One and only son	1:14, 18	3:16; 17:1
Fullness in Logos	1:14, 17	4:24; 8:32; 14:6; 17:17; 18:38
Truth	1:17	14:6; 17:17
Moses/Law and Logos	1:17	1:45; 3:14; 5:46; 6:32; 7:19; 19:29
No one has seen God except the one who comes from God's side	1:18	3:34; 6:46; 8:19, 38; 12:49–50; 14:6–11; 17:3, 8

I first began to suspect that the prologue emerged from the same community as the remainder of the Gospel when I compared parallels between John 1:1–18 and the rest of the book. Some parallels jump out immediately; others are of a more subtle nature. Note particularly the parallels between the prologue and chapter 17 in Table 12.1.

This repetition of common themes should make one hesitant to locate the origins of the prologue outside the Johannine community and should help in answering the question of whether the prologue was written before or after the body of the Fourth Gospel. Yet such has not generally been the case. In general, scholars divide the Gospel of John into a prologue (1:1–18), an epilogue or appendix (ch. 21), and two central sections (1:19–12:50 and 13:1–20:31). Under the continuing influence of Dodd and Brown, these central sections are often called, respectively, the "Book of Signs" and the "Book of Glory" (Dodd 1953, 289; Brown 1966–1970, 1.cxxxviii–cxxxix). Some, following this outline, see John 1:11 ("He came to what was his own, and his own people did not accept him") as a summary of the first division of the book, which tells how Jesus came to his own through a ministry in Galilee and his own received him not. Culpepper sees this verse as pivotal in the chiastic structure of the prologue itself (1980). Verse 12, then, ("but to all who received him . . . he gave power to become children of God") covers the Book of Glory, which contains the words of Jesus to those who do believe in him and narrates his glorification. I personally have never liked nor used this outline, as helpful as it may be. According to 20:30–31, the evangelist seems to think the entire Gospel is a "book of signs," and chapters 13–17 might be seen as the prelude to the "glory," which is clearly the passion.

As already mentioned, many accept the prologue as a literary and theological unity, while others see the prologue as a separate work written after the Gospel and 1 John, all three from the same theological circle and probably composed by the same individual (Miller 1993, 445–46). But do such divisions do justice to the Gospel? Is not the whole Gospel concerned with glory, even the prologue, and is not the whole Gospel concerned with, if not signs, at least the ministry that contains signs, as does the prologue? Can the prologue be so easily separated from the rest of the Gospel, whoever was responsible for it? I suggest that it cannot.[1]

---

[1] "Burney, Black, and Bultmann argue strongly for an Aramaic original for the hymn; the evidence is not conclusive" (Brown 1966–1970, 1.23; see Bultmann 1971, 13–18). Staley detects a massive concentric structure in the Gospel to match a concentric structure in the prologue (1988). Others, e.g. Lund (1931) and Boismard (1957), have also seen a pattern of chiasm in the final form of the prologue, and George Mlakuzhyil, in a thesis for the Pontifical Biblical Institute,

I prefer to see the Fourth Gospel as a narrative with a prologue, similar to other literary works of the time. "The Prologue serves the crucial function of elevating the reader to the implied author's Apollonian vantage point before the spectacle begins. Prologues serving such a purpose were developed by the tragic poets (especially Sophocles) and employed in new comedy as well" (Culpepper 1983, 168). An analysis of Greek drama demonstrates that "the omniscient prologue was almost indispensable in plays that exploited dramàtic irony based on hidden identities" (Harsh 1984, 316). Following this pattern, John's prologue reveals the identity of Jesus at the beginning of the story. As a result, the reader can discover hidden meanings and the recognition of suppressed signals behind or over the characters and events that appear later.

On the topic of the origin of the prologue, I support de Ausejo's suggestion that the poem or hymn underlying the prologue came from the community of the Beloved Disciple (1956). Some find traces of an early hymn within the prologue by comparing it to the second–century Christian Gnostic hymns known as the *Odes of Solomon* (Braun 1959, 224–51). These hymns do have a relationship in style and vocabulary to John's prologue, but the similarities should not be seen as supporting Bultmann's theory that the prologue is based on a Gnostic hymn from the revelation–discourses source written in praise of John the Baptist (Bultmann 1971, 131–38). Both the current version of the prologue and the earlier hymn on which it was based originated in the Johannine community.

The Gospel of John surely is a narrative, a story, and the prologue seems an integral part of the story. But stories involve plot and characters and express the viewpoint of an author. Of course, because this Gospel was composed over several years, as most admit, with at least two or three authors and editors, the narrative that exists now in all probability differs considerably from what might have been originally planned (for example, Brown 1966–1970, 1.xxxiv; Lindars 1972, 51–54). Dodd chose to study the Gospel of John by concentrating on major themes because, in his view, "the structure of the gospel as we have it has been shaped in most of its details by the ideas which seem to dominate the author's thought" (1963, 290). One dominant idea or theme in the Gospel of John is "revelation." The story of revelation, which appears as λόγος in the prologue, becomes Jesus when the word becomes flesh (Ashton 1994, 168–69). In the Gospel of John, Jesus reveals himself. The revelation, the unfolding or unveiling, begins with the prologue and continues through the ministry of Jesus up to his glorification on the cross. In chapter 17,

---

finds chiasms throughout the Gospel (1987). Here again, the image of the whirlwind seems helpful.

the revelation comes to a fitting conclusion in words that will be realized in the crucifixion. The prologue thus sketches the story that is played out in the body of the Gospel. A dominant theme relating to revelation within the prologue is "light," which continues throughout the Gospel as the light confronts darkness. The prologue, however, tells the listener the ending: the darkness does not "master" (κατέλαβεν; 1:5)—or "defeat" or "understand" or "control," depending on which translation one prefers—the light. The same words appear in John 12:35: "Walk while you have the light so that the darkness may not overtake you" (ἵνα μὴ σκοτία ὑμᾶς καταλάβῃ). If revelation forms the fundamental thread that holds the Fourth Gospel together and the prologue begins with the offer of a revelation, then the conclusion at 1:14 ("And the word became flesh") becomes the overriding theme of the rest of the narrative. Chapter 17 is the final explanation of the revelation that relates all believers to God as the "Holy Father" of Jesus.

The Source of John's ΛΟΓΟΣ

Any conclusion concerning the prologue to the Fourth Gospel must of necessity include a study of the origin of the word λόγος ("word"). Within ancient Judaism, some posit a relationship between John's use of λόγος and the *memra* of the Targums. *Memra di YHWH* occurs more than 600 times in different Aramaic Targums of the Pentateuch. Was this *memra* a hypostasis? Can it be equated with the divine "word" of creation or revelation? Is it connected with the λόγος of Philo or the λόγος of John's prologue? Most scholars do not see the *memra* as a hypostasis. The *memra* reveals God in the activity of God in creation. The *Palestinian Targum* attributes to the *memra* different divine reactions, actions, and relations that the Bible attributes to Yahweh. God acts through the *memra*. Under the influence of Greek philosophy, some see the *memra* as a hypostasized being between God and world. But in general the *memra* is not accepted as a hypostasis nor is the *memra* a substitute for the name of God. Rather, the *memra* expresses God's creative and redemptive activity. God communicates through the *memra*. Because these Targums were contemporaneous with the latest writings of the New Testament, the members of the Johannine community could have had access to them through the synagogue (Muñoz Léon 1974, 757ff.).

Certainly, the Gospel of John evidences some Wisdom influences, especially Hellenistic Jewish speculation on the Wisdom traditions. The connection between Wisdom and λόγος becomes explicit in the *Wisdom of Solomon*, and Philo identifies Wisdom with λόγος. In Hellenistic Jewish speculation, the transcendent God needs an intermediary, and

Wisdom λόγος fulfills this role (Tobin 1990, 258–62). For Philo, the goal of the human soul is the knowledge and vision of God. People can become like God through participation in the divine λόγος. The human soul can detach itself from the material world and contemplate the divine λόγος. As Philo speculates on the relationship between his Jewish tradition and his Greek philosophical interests, he portrays Wisdom, Word, creation, light, and life guiding the soul to become like God. Based on parallels between John's prologue and some of Philo's biblical interpretations, the hymn underlying John 1:1–18 may very well be part of the larger world of Jewish speculation on certain biblical texts (Tobin 1990, 268). Of course, John's development of the term λόγος goes beyond the presentation of Wisdom in the Old Testament: there, Wisdom is never displaced by Word, while in John's prologue Word outshines Wisdom. The light and life go far beyond Wisdom because they introduce faith, and then, of course, the λόγος becomes flesh (John 1:14), so unlike any Old Testament interpretation of Wisdom.

In the past, purely Hellenistic Jewish parallels (especially Philo) with the prologue have been emphasized. Recently, however, scholars have looked more into the Old Testament and possible Palestinian origins. Brown studies the Hellenistic background of the prologue and declares, "the basic theme of the prologue is strange to the Hellenistic parallels that have been offered . . . but, in the Old Testament presentation of wisdom there are good parallels for almost every detail of the prologue's description of the word" (1966–1970, 1.520–23). Many exegetes (e.g. Braun, Moeller, and Feuillet) speak of the convergence of Jewish Wisdom speculation and Old Testament Word of God concepts into a single rabbinic motif that influenced the Fourth Gospel. In the Greek world, the term λόγος concerns understanding and is intellectual; in the world of the Old Testament, the "word" is never a human possession but a historical act by which God addresses humanity. The prophetic word and divine wisdom find complementarity and unity in postexilic Judaism. This combination, for many, lies behind the Johannine presentation of the λόγος.

Some historians of the Ancient Near Eastern religions consider the male gods of the pantheon to be the static principles and the goddesses to be the creative and active principles. As the ancient Semitic tribes became Israel and slowly developed a monotheistic outlook, YHWH, clearly a male God, needed some attributes to take over the functions of the god-

---

[2] "The narratives that became the biblical traditions entirely muted any recollection of the female side of divinity, in particular the goddess Asherah whom recent studies have shown to have been a significant figure in Israelite family religion during the monarchy (and perhaps later as well)" (M. Smith 2002b, 648–50).

desses in the ancient pantheon (M. Smith 2002a; 2002b).² The ancient Israelites came to use the concepts Wisdom, Spirit, Word, and Torah to express these creative activities of YHWH. God's creative and redemptive activities became associated with these qualities, which in turn find expression in the understanding of *memra* as the creative activity of God. Philo, influenced by the religious anthropology of the Ancient Near East, his understanding of his Jewish tradition, and his interest in Greek philosophy, recognized that all these concepts contribute to an understanding of λόγος as at least a metaphor for the activity of God in creation and in the redemption of the human soul (Tobin 1990, 257–62).

Much has been written of Wisdom personified or as a poetic figure of speech in Proverbs 8. Certainly, Wisdom is God's attendant and appears as the emanation of God that reflects God's goodness (McKane 1970, 344–58). Jesus is portrayed as the Wisdom of God throughout the Gospel of John (Ashton 1994, 5–35). But λόγος means more than just Jewish Wisdom, and the Johannine Jesus embodies both Wisdom and Word.

As this review indicates, a number of backgrounds for the use of the term λόγος in John 1:1–18 have been suggested. Presuppositions underlie all the theories. Many scholars have accepted one or other of the possibilities, or have combined them. Much, of course, depends upon problems of dating and accessibility: the dating of the *Odes of Solomon* and its relationship to the Johannine community; the dating of the rabbinic literature and the accessibility of Philo's writings to the community of the Beloved Disciple; the existence of a pre–Christian redeemer myth and the interpretation of λόγος by Stoics and other Greek philosophers. One must also note the uncertainty surrounding the meaning of the word *memra*, its dating, and how it might have been understood at the end of the first century. Taken together, all these considerations leave us in unchartered territory with regard to the origin of the term λόγος. Perhaps the most prudent course will be to pay more attention to the simpler Jewish theology of Wisdom, Word, Spirit, and Torah as attributes for God, and to reflect upon how the Johannine Jesus somehow exemplifies all of them.

The Theology of ΛΟΓΟΣ

The Fourth Evangelist uses λόγος as a title for Jesus only in the prologue. Once the Word becomes flesh at John 1:14, the title recedes into the background. But that does not mean that the theology of the Word is absent from the rest of the Gospel. The theology of this title is broader than its use in the first chapter. Jesus is the Word of God, and thus when he speaks, he reveals God. The words of Jesus have been taught to him by the Father (John 8:40; 14:10; 17:8). The content of this Word from the Father concerns the person of the Son and his relationship to the Father and to the disciples. This is particularly true in the farewell discourse. As Word, Jesus reveals the Father and invites individuals to respond to this revelation: "Whoever has seen me has seen the Father" (14:9); "Whoever sees me sees him who sent me" (12:45); "I have made your name known to those whom you gave me from the world. They were yours and you gave them to me, and they have kept your word. Now they know that everything you have given me is from you; for the words that you gave to me I have given to them, and they have received them and know in truth that I came from you; and they have believed that you sent me" (17:6–8). In the body of the Fourth Gospel, the author uses λόγος thirty–nine times and ῥῆμα ("saying"; "something spoken") twelve times. He whom God sends speaks the words (ῥήματα) of God (John 3:34), "and many more believed because of his word (λόγος)" (4:41). Similarly, "anyone who hears my word (λόγος) and believes him who sent me has eternal life" (5:24). These and other examples show how the theology of the Word actually dominates the Gospel, although the titular usage of λόγος appears only in the prologue.

C. H. Dodd contends that "along with the quite ordinary use of the term, the Fourth Gospel uses the term *logos* in a special sense, to denote the Eternal truth (*alaetheia*) revealed to men by God . . . as expressed in words (*raemata*) whether they be the words of Scripture or more especially the words of Christ" (1953, 267). If the term λόγος denotes "eternal truth," as Dodd contends, then chapter 17 makes explicit the meaning of this truth. In Hebrew, דבר is eternal, creative, sustaining, healing, prophetic, and redemptive (Schmidt 1978). By Word, God created all things and the Word of God continues to function throughout the history of Israel. This same Word functions throughout the Gospel of John and should not be limited to the use of the term in the prologue. In chapter 17, the Word speaks and explains the relationship between Jesus and God the Father and the relationship between the disciples and God through Jesus.

THE PROLOGUE AND THE GOSPEL

Both introduce a Gospel, but the prologue of John differs considerably from the prologue of Luke (1:1–4). And although many see some relationship between John 1:1–18 and the beginning of the First Letter of John (chs. 1–4), there are more differences between the two texts than similarities. The close contact between the content of the prologue and the body of the Gospel seems to preclude a loose link to the narrative.

Some even hold that the Fourth Gospel originally began with the reference to John the Baptist at John 1:19ff. and that some of the themes in the prologue are missing from the Gospel (e.g., the preexistence and incarnation of the λόγος), but such a limited relationship between prologue and Gospel proper seems unwarranted. Moreover, the Gospel proper is concerned with the activity and teachings of Jesus (the time of Jesus in the world) and not his heavenly origin. In fact, the prologue is more than a summary of the thought of the Gospel. Usually, a preface that is composed after a work is completed does not go beyond the content of the work, but this certainly is the case with John's prologue.

If one compares the beginnings of the Gospels—Mark, Matthew, Luke, and John, as well as the Acts of the Apostles—it seems that the author of this last Gospel goes beyond all of them in regard to the origin of Jesus. Acts seems to imply that Jesus became God's Son in his resurrection: "God has made him both Lord and Messiah, this Jesus whom you crucified" (2:36). The Gospel of Mark seems to imply that Jesus became Son of God in his baptism: "You are my Son, the Beloved; with you I am well pleased" (1:11). Both Matthew and Luke proclaim Jesus as the Son of God in his conception (Matt 1:20–23; Luke 1:3–35). The author of the Fourth Gospel offers a natural progression by teaching that Jesus was always God's Son because Jesus is eternally the Word of God. The author begins his Gospel with christological reasoning, setting the Word become flesh, Jesus, in the eternity of God. This christological theme finds completion in chapter 17.

Once again, the image of the whirlwind helps. The Gospel of John returns to certain fundamental themes again and again. The most evident theme is the relationship between Jesus and God. An additional theme is the call to faith and rejection—the refusal to believe. The Gospel also includes individuals who offer testimony to Jesus and those who do not. The Gospel proper also frequently calls attention to the "light" and "life" and contains many veiled references to the Old Testament and covenant traditions. The entire movement of the Gospel leads to Jesus' crucifixion and glorification. As the Gospel unfolds, the author brings the reader or listener continually back to these themes and each time brings a deeper understanding of their meaning. The prologue includes all of the same principal themes, and these same ideas are found in the seventeenth chapter. This chapter in the farewell speeches pivots on the relationship between Jesus and God, discusses acceptance in faith and rejection, contains many veiled references to the Old Testament, and directs all to the glorification of Jesus in the crucifixion.

The prologue begins with the Word's relationship to God and concludes with the Word's relationship to God. Faith figures prominently in the prologue. The world knew him not; his own believed in him not, but some believed and they became children of God. John the Baptist offers testimony, first here but also in the first chapter of the Gospel (John 1:6–8, 15; 1:19–34). The references to "grace and truth" and "Moses" (1:17–18) prepare the reader for the further elaboration of Old Testament theology found in the following chapters. The reference to "seeing his glory" at 1:14 is fulfilled as the two perfect disciples, the mother of Jesus and the Beloved Disciple, witness the glory at Calvary. All this suggests that the prologue fits nicely with the general theology of the Gospel and supports the position that it did not exist independent of the Johannine community.

The origin of the title λόγος also should not be found outside this community. The Gospel of John is filled with references to the "Word" of God. Such theology was common in the time of Jesus, because in Jewish tradition God spoke through the prophets and Jesus was more than a prophet. Did other influences affect John's λόγος theology? The Gospel came from an educated community affected by its prevailing culture and philosophy. Some of its members knew Greek philosophy, and incipient Gnosticism existed in the general atmosphere. Surely any or all of these influences could have had some effect on the composition of the prologue and Gospel. Still, the general theology comes from Judaism. George MacRae (1970) has pointed out that the Gospel of John reflects a number of religious currents at the time, and the same is true of the prologue.

For many years, scholars have discussed the possibility of a Johannine school, and most accept the theory that the Fourth Gospel has undergone several revisions. Perhaps there were fewer revisions than some may want, but the Gospel seems not to have been written by one individual in a logical fashion. Or, perhaps we are dealing with a poetic nonstructure that repeats itself. If the Beloved Disciple delivered homilies and if someone compiled these homilies and put them in order as the Beloved Disciple continued to preach about the meaning of Jesus for himself and for his community, naturally he would return to the same themes again and again. Most authors have only so many ideas, and they repeat these ideas over a lifetime. The same would be true for the Beloved Disciple. Certain elements of his understanding of Jesus and his traditions would recur repeatedly. Perhaps the preacher or one of the members of the community had a poetic nature and took some of these ideas and expressed them in rhythmic prose.

Scholarship has proved that the early Christian communities composed hymns (Hengel 1983). Pliny remarks, "What distinguished Christians was the 'singing of hymns to Christ as God'" (*Ep.* 10.96.7; Witherington 1995, 50). Philo relates how the president arises and sings a hymn composed as an address to God, "either a new one of his own composition or an old one by poets of an earlier day" (*Vit. Cont.* 29), and Eusebius interprets Philo's remarks as a reference to early Christian worship (*H.E.* 2.17.21ff; Witherington 1995, 50). The New Testament itself refers to hymn singing (1 Cor 14:26; Col 3:16; Eph 5:19). Frequently in hymns, ideas are repeated and further understanding develops as the hymn unfolds. Perhaps the prologue, coming from a homily, did not originally contain references to John the Baptist (1:6–8, 15), but then because of the importance of individuals giving "testimony" throughout the body of the Gospel, the final editor or someone else included these.

The Gospel of John shows signs of intelligence and poetry throughout, especially the long discourses by Jesus, chapter 17 in particular, and even the parables of the Good Shepherd and the Vine and the Branches. Whether composed by the Beloved Disciple or not, the prologue seems part of the literary heritage of the Johannine community. If chapter 17 can be accepted as coming from a homily preached by the Beloved Disciple, then perhaps the prologue came from a follower of the Beloved Disciple who listened to all of his homilies and in a poetic manner created an overture to the final Gospel.

CONCLUSION

The prologue and chapter 17 originated within the Johannine community. The prologue was not an independent hymn or poem that was then adapted to fit the Gospel. The theology of the λόγος dominates the entire Gospel and should not be limited to the prologue. The source of this term and the theology behind it probably combined several currents of thought at the time. Principally, λόγος theology resulted from reflection upon the activities of God in Jewish history, particularly Wisdom and Word, which are not separated from Spirit and Torah. The Word in the prologue takes on the functions of the Spirit as giving life. The Word fulfills the characteristics of Wisdom in the Old Testament traditions; the λόγος acts like Torah in giving guidance and instruction; and, of course, as Word the λόγος creates. The prologue may have existed as a separate unit, just as many of the parts of the Gospel may have existed as separate homilies, but not outside the Johannine community. The prologue is a literary unity in spite of all efforts to divide it into separate units. The prologue was also part of the original Gospel precisely because of the way its theology begins the whirlwind, which includes the entire composition.

When Jesus acknowledges that he has made himself holy so that his disciples might be holy at John 17:19, he has fulfilled the will of his Father. In the prologue, he gave them the right (ἐξουσία) to be called "children of God"; in chapter 17, they have become holy and so are in fact the children of God. The prologue and chapter 17 have their poetic qualities. Both contain the principal theological themes of the entire Gospel, both come from the same community, and both possibly come from the homilies preached by the Beloved Disciple.

Once within the Gospel of John, the reader or listener goes around and around, growing in an ever–deepening understanding of who Jesus was and what he meant to the Beloved Disciple and to his community, as well as what he means to the Christian community today.

12: RESPONSE

THE PROLOGUE AND JESUS' FINAL PRAYER

Dorothy Lee

What is the literary and theological relationship between the Johannine prologue (1:1–18) and the prayer of Jesus in John 17? As John O'Grady observes in his essay, to ask this question is to raise the wider issue of the relationship between the prologue and the Gospel. O'Grady is not the first to perceive the nexus between the prologue and the prayer, a nexus that, as he demonstrates, is both literary and theological. O'Grady leaves open the issue of whether or not the evangelist originally began with the prologue; he himself locates the origins of the Fourth Gospel in the preaching of the Beloved Disciple, but indicates the importance of reading the Gospel, as we now have it, through the lens of the prologue. His focus is—rightly, in my view—on the final form of the text, setting aside (though not discounting) questions of origin and prehistory.

I would like to explore O'Grady's parallels between the prologue and the final prayer a little further. In theological terms, both passages are concerned with Jesus' identity. That identity is set out at the beginning in majestic terms, disclosing the Word in preexistent union with God (John 1:1–2), in the creation of the world (1:3–5), and in the incarnation of Jesus Christ, who belongs both to the heavenly domain of "glory" and the earthly realm of "flesh" (1:14). That same identity, unfolded for the reader in the intervening chapters through narrative and discourse, sign and symbol, faith and even rejection, is articulated in equally majestic terms in Jesus' great prayer. In other words, the two passages are neither identical nor proximate, but there is an interior correlation between them which, although not perhaps immediately obvious, is nevertheless more than we would expect. The relationship hardly exists in terms of genre, at least not in the narrow sense. The one passage is descriptive of Jesus' provenance and identity—cosmic and earthly—providing a summation of Johannine theology, an overture that sets the mood and tone for the entire Gospel. The other is a prayer, the direct speech of Jesus himself, coming at the conclusion and as the climax of the Last Supper, in which Jesus recapitulates his ministry and prays for his disciples in the context of his impending death. In symbolic terms, however, the two can be seen as fundamentally connected; indeed, once the association is grasped, it is difficult to read the one passage without hearing the reverberances of the other.

The correlation between these two passages can be seen symbolically at a number of levels that I can only touch on here and that O'Grady catalogues more fully. In the first place, what we initially discover of the connection between God and Word (θεός and λόγος), encapsulated in the preposition πρός ("before"; 1:1–2), by the end of the prologue resolves itself, via the incarnation, into the symbolic language of Father and Son (1:14, 18)—symbolism that perdures throughout the Gospel, superseding the more abstract language of the opening sentences. This theological and symbolic move is vibrantly depicted in the prayer, where it is Jesus who now testifies to his own identity and plays out that relationship that is the ground of his being: the eternal Word–Son "turned toward" the Father.

Second, the symbolism of Father–Son, between prologue and prayer, has significantly expanded. This is a point O'Grady rightly stresses. The vague and unspecific "we" of John 1:14 has now become a tangible communion of believers who recognize Jesus' identity as "the one sent from the Father"—those whose birth "from above" the reader has witnessed throughout the symbolic narratives of Jesus' public ministry (1:19–12:50). The relationship between Father and Son is now extended to include overtly the community of God's children, present and future: those who share in the filiation of Jesus himself. The "we" of the prologue, those who are born of God and believe (1:12–13), now take their place within the divine relation. The Son is "turned toward" the Father in both texts, but in the second that stately intimacy has expanded to incorporate "his own"; now it is manifest that to "behold the [my] glory"—a phrase that unites the two passages (1:14; 17:24)—means metaphorically not to observe at a distance but rather to share in the ardor that unites, and has always united, Father and Son. This union is the essence, not only of the

Fourth Gospel's Christology, but also of its ecclesiology: an orbit of faith in which believers are drawn into a preexisting affiliation of love through the abiding Spirit–Paraclete (14:16–26).

The third symbolic aspect of the connection between the two texts concerns the passion narrative, never directly alluded to in the prologue (although hinted at in the references to darkness and rejection) but vividly present to the reader throughout the prayer, as a consequence of both the footwashing and the departure motif in the farewell discourse. In other words, John 17 is as important as a *prolepsis* of the passion as an *analepsis* or recapitulation of the prologue in a different genre. In metaphorical terms, the prayer is an ascent, a dramatization of the significance of the cross: a symbolic "performance" of that glorification that is the inner meaning of the passion in this Gospel. Here, too, there is coherence with the symbolism of the prologue. The cross narrates the identity of the Word made flesh and his ascent, in glory, to the Father; symbolically Jesus enacts that continual ascent to the Father, that eternal "turning toward" that lies at the heart of his identity and mission. Ascent and mutual glorification are imaged, not now in the timelessness of eternity "before the foundation of the world" (17:24), but rather in mortal flesh. The cross attests to the humanity of the Word, and its supreme icon—the flow of blood and water—stands for the incarnation itself and the glory that radiates from it (19:34). And once again, disciples surround the iconography. As with John the Baptist's "intrusions" into the prologue (1:6–8, 15) and the "we" of verse 1:14, and as with the community of disciples who are silent witnesses to—as well as subjects of—the prayer, so now the Beloved Disciple, in company with the mother of Jesus and the holy women, directs the reader's gaze to the life and glory that issue from this crucified, yet ironically birth–giving, body (19:35–36).

These points of contact demonstrate that the question of the interrelationship between the prologue and the prayer goes beyond a diachronic analysis of the Fourth Gospel. Understanding the Johannine symbolic universe is the key to a synchronic analysis, and there is still work to be done. I have argued that not just two but all three passages—prologue, prayer, passion—belong together as "symbolic theology": not touching sides so much as rising like mountains from the foothills of the Gospel, peaks that appear from a distance to be standing side by side. Together, they disclose the core symbolism of Jesus' theological identity, as well as that of the believing community. Within this "whirlwind Gospel" (to use O'Grady's apt metaphor), all three display in image and symbol the revelation of glory in the flesh and its saving significance for the reader, who is invited to enter the divine circle of intimacy with its paradoxical donation of life.

CHAPTER 13

THE SIGNS OF THE MESSIAH AND THE QUEST FOR ETERNAL LIFE

John Painter

Growing up in the country in New South Wales, I inherited a love of wide–open spaces. Paradoxically, my career has placed me in large cities. Much of my early life was spent away from the ocean, but I am never happier than when I find myself where the mountains meet the sea. The opening words of Psalm 121 ("I lift up my eyes to the hills—from where will my help come? My help comes from the Lord, who made heaven and earth") resonate in my being. The mountains and the ocean are living symbols of the wonders of creation and are a source of my experience of wonder in response to God's grace in creation. This sense has deepened with years of reflection. As I look back over my life, I am conscious of the role of reflective memory in enriching life and understanding.

At the age of twenty, I was "called up" to do military service in the days of National Service training. Although I was able to pursue my sporting interests there, as I had at school, the experience was sobering, causing me to reflect upon more serious matters. At the end of my term of service, I decided to attend university and prepare for ministry. After one year of study, I qualified for entry and was accepted for training for ministry in the Anglican Diocese of Sydney, including four years of study at Moore Theological College. There D. W. B. Robinson, a Cambridge graduate who later became Archbishop of Sydney, introduced me to the academic study of the New Testament. I learned from him the importance of giving priority to the primary sources while seeking to discern the appropriate questions in an attempt to read and understand the texts. All that I have subsequently learned has built on the foundation he helped to lay. Looking back, I see that my concern with the importance of grace in creation and the struggle to affirm the reality of human freedom and responsibility arose at Moore College, an institution that is strongly Calvinistic in a way that minimizes grace, freedom, and responsibility outside of Christian faith.

After two years of working in a Sydney city parish, my senior minister encouraged me to pursue further studies in the Northern hemisphere. During the next year, I began to think of where and with whom I would like to work. Having used C. K. Barrett's commentary on John, I decided to apply to Durham (U.K.) and proposed a thesis on "The Idea of Knowledge in the Johannine Literature." With this topic, I hoped I would be assigned to Barrett's supervision. My application was successful, and we arrived in Durham toward the end of January 1965. By this time, I had decided on two limitations for my thesis. First, "the Johannine Literature" would mean, for my purposes, the Gospel and Epistles of John. Second, I decided to explore the work of Rudolf Bultmann and C. H. Dodd as two alternative views of the knowledge issue while also giving priority to Jewish sources, especially the Qumran texts that had been published recently. These seemed to me to support a more Jewish reading of John than either Dodd or Bultmann had offered. By the end of 1967, my thesis was complete.

Working with C. K. Barrett was a life–changing experience in so many ways. I had thought of myself as preparing for ministry, but upon arrival in Durham I found myself in a part–time tutorship at St. John's College, which very soon developed into a full–time position. This allowed what might have been one year of study to extend to the completion of a Ph.D. In the course of this work, the Johannine writings became a part of my life, and since then they have remained a major influence on my understanding of Christianity. Over the years, I have developed a deep bond of fellowship with other Johannine scholars, in the spirit of a veritable Johannine school. Although my thesis has not been published, I continue to live out of the richness that it still has for me.

Because my father was critically ill, we returned to Sydney in 1968, where I was appointed to St. Andrew's Cathedral as Precentor. Though this allowed for occasional teaching at Moore College, it was a demanding and rewarding ministry in the heart of a city full of creative energy. Here, I might have followed a different course. My father died soon after our return to Australia. At the beginning of 1971, I was invited to the

University of Cape Town to teach Early Judaism and Early Christianity, then I moved to Melbourne's La Trobe University in 1977 to do much the same thing. Finally, the move to Charles Sturt University as the foundation Professor of Theology in 1997, where I still teach today. In these university positions, I was the only biblical scholar on the faculty, which led me to maximize opportunities for contact with colleagues by regularly attending and contributing to international conferences. These experiences have sustained me intellectually, and I remain in the debt of those colleagues who have become my friends.

My first book *John: Witness and Theologian* was released in 1975. Looking back on the first edition, I perceive three foundations rooted in my early life and continuing through until today. The first is my recognition of the way John holds together a theology of creation and redemption. The grace of God is revealed in the creative Word and in the incarnate Word. Second, I saw that the grace of God is revealed in the love of God for the world. It is a misreading of John to restrict the love of God to any exclusive group. Third, I realized that God's love is not coercive but seeks to woo all people, indeed the whole of creation, that all may be made whole. This theme has become a focus of some of my later studies.

In 1987, my *Theology as Hermeneutics: Rudolf Bultmann's Interpretation of the History of Jesus* was published. Though Bultmann is scarcely in fashion today, I am aware of the great debt I owe to his hermeneutical work as well as to his work on Jesus, John, and Paul. But that does not mean that I adopt all of Bultmann's conclusions. It does mean, as a bare minimum, that I believe Bultmann identified the big issues confronting scholars in his own day and, although my own approach to John differs from his, I think he provided helpful approaches in responding to those questions. For one thing, like Bultmann, I think that the documents of the New Testament can be most fully understood when read in the context of the diverse nature of early Christianity. This is not to reject a reading of John in the light of the world of our own day, but I do believe the text speaks best to us when read in the context of the assumptions of its own time. A modern reader cannot bypass the past, but rather must at least draw on the work of a translator. The translator needs to be immersed in the world of the language of these texts as well as in the world of the language of translation.

During the 1980s, I prepared a number of papers for meetings of the Studorium Novi Testamenti Societas (SNTS)—in Toronto (1980), Canterbury (1983), Basel (1984), Atlanta (1986), and Cambridge (1988)—and also for an International Society of Biblical Literature meeting in Sheffield (1988). These papers eventually appeared in the journals *NTS*, *JSNT*, and *SJT* and, along with a number of other articles published about the

same time, prepared the way for *The Quest for the Messiah* (Painter 1993b).
Certain streams of thought come together in these contributions, which
began with a paper titled, "The Farewell Discourses and the History
of Johannine Christianity." Here, I argued that the composition of the
farewell discourses (John 13–17) reflects the history of a Jewish group of
believers in Jesus in relation to the broader Jewish community, a relationship that was stormy and full of conflict. The farewell discourses provided
a ground for the ongoing reinterpretation of the Johannine Jesus tradition in the context of new crises in the relationship of this group to the
broader Jewish community. That ground is the inspired remembrance
promised by Jesus in the coming of the Paraclete/Spirit of Truth. Here,
inspired remembrance involves new levels of perception and understanding. Consequently, I came to recognize "watersheds" in the transmission
of the Johannine Jesus tradition. The watersheds are marked by crises in
the life of the believing group, and each crisis created a dam–like interpretive grid through which the tradition passed. The process is clearest in
the farewell discourses but is also evident in other segments of the Gospel
of John (for example, John 6). In some passages, we find evidence of just
one of these crises; in others, multiple levels of reinterpretation.

Toward the end of the 1980s, the relation between creation and
redemption began to come to the forefront of my thinking on John, and
I became aware of the importance of human initiative in the coming of
Jesus' first disciples to him. I also noted that the signs that seem most successful in their overall outcome are initiated by suppliants, not by Jesus—
indeed, signs initiated by Jesus seem to lead to conflict and rejection.
Only later did I come to link this Johannine motif of the "quest for the
Messiah," the quest for eternal life, with important work done by Rudolf
Bultmann, although there is recognition of this in my 1987 book on Bultmann—even though I was not altogether aware of it at the time. The
connection becomes explicit in my essay "Inclined to God—Bultmannian
Hermeneutics and the Quest for Eternal Life" (1996), which was written
for the *Festschrift* for Moody Smith in recognition of the contributions
he has made on Bultmann's interpretation of John. My understanding of
Bultmann draws on his theological and biblical writings in recognizing
the experience of grace in human life and expressed in the search for God,
the quest for eternal life. "God and the Quest for Eternal Life" was the
subject of my inaugural lecture as professor of theology at Charles Sturt
University at the beginning of 1997 (published in 1998). The Johannine
treatment was brought together in *The Quest for the Messiah*.

Since the 1990s, the relationship between creation and redemption
has become the focus of my work on John in a new way, though there
were already intimations of this interest in my "Text and Context in John

5" (1987b) and in my work on the prologue that led to "Theology and Eschatology in the Prologue of John" (1993a). Some directions found in these essays are developed in "Earth Made Whole: John's Rereading of Genesis" (2002a) and "Rereading Genesis in the Prologue of John" (2003a).

During 1996 I was occupied in writing a small commentary on Mark (1997b) and continuing work on *Just James: The Brother of Jesus in History and Tradition* (1997c). The publication of the latter book has resulted in a variety of other contributions on James. Research on both Mark and James has been fruitful and has produced important benefits for the study of John. Then came renewed work on the Johannine Epistles leading to publications in the Eerdmans Commentary on the Bible (2003b) and the Sacra Pagina Commentary (2002b). These projects have led to a number of new insights, and in the remainder of this essay I will focus attention on the elaboration and development of an important theme that has arisen in the course of this work.

Much of my work on John has focused on the rhetorical use of *chreia*, especially in the form of quest stories. Because some of these are miracle quest stories, there is a crucial overlap between the Fourth Gospel's quest stories and "signs" (σημεῖα). In the signs (the Johannine miracle stories), what is significant for everyday life becomes a sign (narrative symbol) of the source of eternal life (John 20:30–31; see Painter 1979; 1986).[1] The remainder of this essay will seek to illuminate this complex Johannine theme. In so doing, it will be necessary to deal summarily with difficult residual problems that have a bearing on the theme before turning directly to the promising perspective of this approach to Johannine interpretation.

Sources, Community, Evangelist

Before proceeding to a discussion of John's "signs," I should state my current thinking on several key points relevant to the background of the Fourth Gospel, including John's possible use of sources, the influence of the Johannine community on the text, and the provenance of the Gospel.

---

[1] The Johannine "signs" are not the miracles per se, but rather the narratives that communicate the signs. This is the point of 20:30–31: the narrative signs in John have been written to lead the reader to believe in Jesus the Messiah, the Son of God, in a way that leads them to eternal life. These signs have been written down to reveal Jesus the Messiah and to communicate eternal life to the believer. Thus, they are featured as the signs of the Messiah in the context of the human quest for eternal life.

My conclusions on these issues (which are dealt with more fully in 1993b, 33–135), will serve as a backdrop for the more focused analysis to follow.

First, fragmentary agreements with one or more of the Synoptics show that the author of John made use of sources. At the same time, the distinctive nature of John's Gospel poses questions that have not been persuasively answered. An apparent growing consensus in one generation breaks down in the next, suggesting that the evidence on this matter is inconclusive and puzzling. I am no more convinced that John used one or more of the Synoptics as his basic source than I am of the existence of a Signs Source/Gospel that, according to some, gives John a significant part of its distinctive character. For the moment, the best we can do is identify tradition where John overlaps one or more of the Synoptics, and perhaps, less confidently, identify tradition in the synoptic–like material in John.

Second, it is common to attribute the shaping of the Fourth Gospel to a community. I am unpersuaded by this view. Distinctive teachers shape communities of this sort. Might not that distinctive teacher be Jesus? Here the distinctive nature of the teaching of Jesus in John matches that of the narrator or evangelist, and Jesus speaks the language of the primary human witness to Jesus. Does the Johannine Gospel speak with the voice of Jesus or does Jesus speak with the voice of John? There may be a degree of truth in each of these propositions, though the Johannization of Jesus in John seems to be significant. It is more likely that the Gospel of John was shaped in and for a community than directly by it, even if the author believed the gospel was a message for the world.

Third and finally, attribution of each of the Gospels to individual "authors" is not the invention of modern individualistic scholars. It is the tradition from the earliest evidence, known to us in the titles of the Gospels and in the accounts concerning their origins collected by Eusebius (320s C.E.). The same evidence makes John the last of the four Gospels chronologically. On the basis of tradition, Irenaeus names John as the fourth of the canonical Gospels (*Against Heresies* 3.1.1; see Eusebius, *HE* 8.2–4). Irenaeus probably assumes the current canonical order, certainly Matthew first and John last. Though he names Mark second and Luke third it is not absolutely clear that he intends to indicate that this represents the order of writing. For our purposes, it is sufficient to note that John is last.

Eusebius also deals with the order of the Gospels. He appeals to Clement of Alexandria and his account in his *Outlines* (*Hypotyposeis*).

> Clement has inserted a tradition of the elders with regard to the order of the Gospels. He says that the Gospels with the genealogies were written first. But the Gospel according to Mark came

into being in this manner. When Peter had publicly preached the word in Rome and by the Spirit had proclaimed the gospel, the many who were present exhorted Mark, as one who had followed him for a long time and remembered what had been said, to write down all that was said. This he did, making his Gospel available to those who asked him. So that when the matter came to Peter's knowledge he neither made objection nor gave special encouragement. Last of all John, aware that the physical facts had been set forth in the Gospels, urged on by his disciples (pupils) and divinely moved by the Spirit, composed a spiritual (πνευματικόν) Gospel. So much for Clement's writings. (*HE* 6.14.4b–7)

According to Eusebius, both Irenaeus and Clement make John the last of the Gospels and, as noted earlier, we can independently confirm the view of Irenaeus. But that may be the extent of the agreement between Irenaeus and Clement, according to Eusebius. The view of Irenaeus presupposes the move of the Johannine tradition from Judea to Ephesus before the composition of that Gospel. Thus, a pre–70 C.E. Judean shaping was followed by further shaping in Asia Minor and composition in Greek. This history of the tradition implies initial shaping in close relationship to Judaism, followed by further shaping through conflict with Judaism and the breakdown of any positive relationship in the period after 70 C.E.

The Puzzle of the Signs and the Resurrection

One notable feature of the Gospel of John is the presentation of Jesus' ministry in a series of distinctive signs (20:30–31). The signs are commonly attributed to a distinctive source. One problem for the signs source family of hypotheses is that distinctive Johannine characteristics are attributed to the source. But if they are characteristically Johannine, they may be a consequence of the distinctive shaping of the Gospel rather than evidence of an underlying source, for which there is no independent evidence. A good example of this problem is the Johannine use of σημεῖον/"sign." There is a concentration of the use of this word in John (17 times, cf. Matt 13 times; Mark 6 times [+2 in the spurious ending]; Luke 11 times; Acts 13 times; Paul 8 times; Hebrews once; Revelation 7 times). The synoptic use is concentrated in the demand for a sign and references to signs in the last days; nowhere are the mighty works of Jesus described as "signs." Characteristically, in John the σημεῖα, some of which are narrated in the Gospel, are Jesus' "works" of healing and benevolence in bountiful provision. Eleven references summarily deal with Jesus' signs, often in the words of the narrator (2:23; 6:2, 14; 12:37; 20:30) but also in the words of various characters (3:2; 4:48; 6:26; 7:31; 9:16; 11:47). The saying at 10:41 implies that Jesus did signs in contrast with John the Baptist, who did no signs. There are also clear references to specific "works" of Jesus as signs (2:11; 4:54; 9:16, which makes the healing of the blind man a representative sign exemplifying Jesus' actions; 12:18).

An important connection between John and the Synoptics is found in the demand for a sign in John 2:18 and 6:30 (cf. 4:48 and Matt 12:38–39; 16:1–4; Mark 8:11–12 [cf. 11:27–33]; Luke 11:16, 29–30). The relationship of John 2:18 to this synoptic tradition is fascinatingly illuminating. The Markan tradition overlaps tradition found in Matthew and Luke (Q), and John resonates with several elements of this tradition. First, there is the challenge for Jesus to perform a sign to establish his authority and thus justify the action he has taken. Second, in both Mark 11:27–33 and John 2:18, what is to be justified is Jesus' action in the temple incident. Third, in John 2:18–22 and the Q version of the tradition, the "sign" that Jesus offers is his resurrection in three days, although this is done in quite different ways. Fourth, although there is a strong tendency to portray Jesus as refusing to provide signs for those who demand them (Mark 8:11–12), this is modified in Q to allow for the exceptional sign of Jonah (Matt 12:38–39; 16:1–4; Luke 11:29–30), which turns out to be a reference to the sign Jesus offers in John 2:19–22, his resurrection. Thus, in Matthew and Luke, as well as John, Jesus offers his resurrection as a sign authenticating his authority. But the sign is not performed on demand. It is a sign for which his critics must wait, and even then they do not see it.

In John, the resurrection is a sign like the other signs performed by Jesus. In Matthew and Luke, it is unclear who performs the sign of Jonah that Jesus announces in advance. In John, Jesus responds to the Jews who demand an authenticating sign by saying, "You destroy this temple and in three days I will raise it up" (John 2:19; translation mine throughout)—the sign that Jesus will perform depends upon the preliminary action of the Jews. The narrator makes clear that the "temple" to which Jesus referred was his body, making the resurrection the sign he offers to establish his authority "to do these things." In John 10:18, Jesus claims the authority, given to him by the Father, to lay down his life and to take it again. Jesus performs the sign of raising himself ("in three days I will raise it up") although the narration of this sign does not occur until John 20. John 2:13–22 is the foretelling of the foundational and climactic sign.[2]

This approach to John 2:13–22 raises questions about John's place-

---

[2] Whether the great catch of fish at John 21:1–14 constitutes the final sign cannot be treated in this paper. I note that it falls outside the boundary of reference indicated by 20:30–31. That does not necessarily make it un–Johannine,

ment of the temple incident. There are reasons to think that the Fourth Gospel underwent modification as well as expansion on the way to completion. Nevertheless, the placement of the temple incident as the first fully public act of Jesus makes very good Johannine sense, and nothing in John's narrative suggests that it was ever the trigger for Jesus' arrest. The first Cana sign is a covert action, explicitly known only to the servants (2:9) but evidently to the disciples as well, because the narrator indicates that they believed in Jesus on the basis of his glory revealed in the sign (2:11). No mention is made of any effect on the servants or the mother of Jesus.

The temple incident is narrated as a fully public event. It is surprising that the response of the Jews (perhaps the temple authorities) is so mild. They demand a sign to establish Jesus' authority for the action he had taken. Although Jesus' offer of a sign is enigmatic, nothing more is said of the Jewish authorities or of any action taken or planned against Jesus at this stage. Instead, the narrator again turns attention to the disciples (John 2:22). But this time, the narrator distinguishes the disciples' lack of comprehension at the time from their subsequent memory of the event after Jesus was risen from the dead. Given that the sign Jesus offered to validate his authority was his resurrection, this foretelling of the sign places Jesus' entire ministry under the sign of the resurrection. The Jesus of John acts and speaks in the light of the resurrection, but within the story the disciples only remember and understand this after Jesus has risen from the dead. The resurrection perspective transformed their memory of Jesus, and this transformation involved a new understanding of the Scripture in relation to the word of Jesus. The paradigm of transformed memory—memory of event, the Scripture, and the word of Jesus—is crucial for John's portrayal of Jesus.

The paradigmatic placement of John 2:13–22 forms an *inclusio* with Jesus' entry into Jerusalem (12:12–19), so that Jesus' public ministry begins in the temple in Jerusalem and ends with his final entry into Jerusalem, the narratives of these two events framing his public ministry. Although the entry is an open public arrival, the narrator again turns the reader's attention to the disciples' failure to understand the event at the time and their transformed memory when Jesus was glorified (cf. 2:22). Again, this transformation involved a new understanding of Scripture and

---

though it seems not to fit the same purpose as the signs of John 1–20. It may be one of "the many other signs" mentioned in 20:30. I am inclined to see John 21 as an addition made at the time of the posthumous publication of the Gospel after the death of the primary author. The addition deals with this author's death, among other things (21:20–25).

what "they (the great crowd) did to Jesus" (12:16). The perspective of the glorification of Jesus was crucial to this transformation of memory. Given the rarity of the use of the language of memory, this *inclusio* seems to place John's account of the ministry of Jesus in the light of the resurrection–glorification of Jesus. This perspective presupposes the role of the Spirit of Truth, who brings about the transformed memory of Jesus' words and deeds (14:25–26; 16:12–15) after Jesus has departed (= is risen/glorified; 16:7).

SIGNS AND WORKS

John's use of σημεῖα ("signs") overlaps with his use of ἔργα ("works"). For the most part, σημεῖα is the term used by the narrator and characters other than Jesus; Jesus prefers rather to speak of his ἔργα. He speaks of his vocation as a whole as his "work" (4:34; 17:4) and also speaks collectively of everything he does, including the words he speaks, as his "works" (5:36). Thus, this description is not restricted to the σημεῖα, but rather it is inclusive of them. Work terminology is rarely used by anyone other than Jesus, a notable exception being 6:30, where the crowd demands a sign by asking Jesus τί οὖν ποιεῖς σὺ σημεῖον . . . τί ἐργάζῃ; ("What sign do you do . . . what do you work?" cf. 6:28). This use of "work(s)" by the crowd is exceptional and picks up Jesus' own idiom in 6:27. Jesus' reference to signs in 6:26 (4:48) is also uncharacteristic. At the same time, the overlapping use of "signs" and "works" in John 6 highlights the overlapping meaning of these terms.

The first occurrence of "work" terminology in the Gospel, in John 3:19–21, is not christological. Jesus, or the narrator, contrasts the evil works of those who choose the darkness rather than the light with the person who does the truth, who comes to the light so that it may be revealed that his works are wrought in God (ἵνα φανερωθῇ αὐτοῦ τὰ ἔργα ὅτι ἐν θεῷ ἐστιν εἰργασμένα). This implies that the believer also (as well as Jesus) does the works of God (cf. 14:12). The characteristic Johannine theme of works is focused on Jesus, who identifies himself as one who lives to do the will of the one (the Father) who sent him and to complete his ἔργον ("work" ; 4:34). Jesus justifies his action on the Sabbath by asserting, "My Father works (ἐργάζεται) until now and I work (ἐργάζομαι)" (5:17; see Painter 1987b, 28–34; 1993b, 213–52). By referring to his works, Jesus identifies his life and actions with the "works" of God (4:34; 5:46; 17:4), among which are the healing and life–giving acts referred to by the narrator as his σημεῖα. Jesus, in the same way as the narrator though with terminological difference, recognizes the important place his signs (works) have in leading people to believe (10:38). There is enough here to show that John does not have a negative view of the signs. Jesus' signs are the works of God that he performs (10:37–38), but not all the works he performs are signs.

THE SIGNS AND A SIGNS SOURCE

Rudolf Bultmann recognized that the Fourth Evangelist uses signs in a positive and constructive way, which he thought was in tension with the view found in the signs source that he proposed. For him, this tension makes it possible to identify the source, which John adopts and develops. In the signs source, the σημεῖα were naive miracle stories, and the evangelist derived the numbered miracle stories of 2:1–11 and 4:46–54, as well as the summaries at 12:37 and 20:30–31, from the source. That

> the evangelist dared to use the ending of the source as the conclusion of his book . . . shows . . . that the σημεῖον is of fundamental importance for him, . . . —if he can subsume Jesus' activity, as he portrays it, under the concept of σημεῖον!—that this concept is more complex than that of the naive miracle story. Rather it is clear . . . the concepts of σημεῖα and ῥήματα (λόγοι) [words] both qualify each other: σημεῖον is not a mere demonstration, but a spoken directive, a symbol; ῥῆμα is not a teaching in the sense of the communication of a set of ideas, but is the occurrence of the Word, the event of the address. (Bultmann 1971, 113–14)

Commenting later on 12:37 ("although he had performed so many signs in their presence, they did not believe in him"), Bultmann observes that

> the astonishing thing is that the ministry of Jesus is described here [12:37] by means of the expression σημεῖα ποιεῖν ["to do signs"] although his σημεῖα were subordinated to his discourses, and his real work was achieved in the revelatory word. [Thus 12:37 and 20:30–31] could be taken over from the σημεῖα–source, in which this way of formulating was regarded as helpful. But the fact that the evangelist was able to adopt it shows how for him the concepts σημεῖα and ῥήματα (λόγοι) flow together: the σημεῖα are deeds that speak, and their meaning is developed in the discourses; moreover the ῥήματα are not human words but words of revelation, full of divine and miraculous power—they are indeed miraculous works. Hence the evangelist also, when

looking back, could characterise the work of Jesus as a σημεῖα
ποιεῖν. (1971, 452)

Commenting on John 20:30–31, Bultmann says:

> As with 12:37, it is at first surprising that the work of Jesus is
> described under the title σημεῖα, but it is comprehensible in view
> of the unity which, in the thought of the evangelist, "signs" and
> words form. As with 12:37, however, the formulation is obvi-
> ously occasioned by the fact that the evangelist is taking over the
> conclusion of the σημεῖα–source. Precisely because in his pre-
> sentation of the Gospel story he has on the one hand made plain
> the meaning of the σημεῖα as deeds that speak, and on the other
> hand represented the words of Jesus as divinely effected event,
> as ῥήματα ζωῆς ["words of life"] (6:63, 68), he is able to use this
> conclusion of the source without fear of misunderstanding, and
> at the same time to conform his book to the form of Gospel lit-
> erature as it had already become traditional. (1971, 698; see also
> 1951–1955, 2.44–45, 59–61)

Although Bultmann rightly characterizes Jesus' signs as deeds that speak
visible words (*verba visibilia*), I do not believe that John identified Jesus'
ministry (as a whole) as a sign or all that he did as signs. This is to treat
σημεῖα as a precise synonym of ἔργα, whereas John's use of the two terms
is overlapping rather than semantically identical. All of Jesus' signs are his
works but not all of Jesus' works are his signs. The error is elementary,
but one that is often made, even by scholars who recognize that John's
use of signs terminology always refers to what we call "miracles."

We may well ask if the theory of an underlying signs source adds
anything to our understanding of the Gospel of John once it is recognized
that the evangelist uses the signs positively and in a way quite essential to
his understanding and portrayal of Jesus. The fact that characters in the
Gospel who do not come to believe in Jesus have a different view of the
signs and demand an authenticating sign is hardly evidence of a source
in which a different view of the signs was present. As noted above, the
demand for a sign is well attested in the synoptic tradition. The evangelist shows incredulity that, in spite of Jesus' many signs, unbelief was the
dominant response to Jesus (John 12:37). The positive use of the word
"signs" in John in reference to the works of Jesus lends no weight to the
signs–source hypothesis, nor does the demand for a sign by those unsym-
pathetic to Jesus.

It is often thought that John 4:48 reveals a seam between the signs tradition and Johannine redaction. There, in response to the nobleman's request that Jesus come down and heal his son, Jesus responds, "Unless you see signs and wonders [ἐὰν μὴ σημεῖα καὶ τέρατα ἴδητε] you will not believe." Certainly there seems to be something incongruous in Jesus' response, because the man's request has the appearance of a request of faith rather than a demand for signs to establish faith. Thus, while the wording of Jesus' response seems to reflect a criticism of signs faith, it does not seem to fit the fact that the man already manifests faith. Further, when the man persists, Jesus complies with his request. The consequence is that, not only did the nobleman believe, so also did his whole household (4:51–53). The report of the expansion of belief on the basis of the known synchronicity of the word of Jesus and the moment of healing is an attestation of the reality of the healing (compare 2:9, 11). How we are to understand Jesus' strange response in 4:48 needs to be examined more closely.

THE CANA SIGNS AS MIRACLE QUEST STORIES

Jesus' criticism of the demand for signs at John 4:48 fits uneasily in the story, but the source–critical solution is unpersuasive. Such clumsy editing is out of character with the evangelist's otherwise skillful literary art. It is more likely that the evangelist shaped this story, including the opening and closing verses (4:46, 54), to link this episode explicitly to the earlier Cana miracle (see 2:1, 11). The Gospel of John presupposes a number of Jerusalem signs between the two Cana signs (2:23; 3:2). The numbering is not of the signs as such, but of the first and second Cana signs (2:1–11; 4:46–54). The evangelist has gone to some lengths to ensure that the reader makes the connection.

Each of the two Cana signs (water to wine and healing the nobleman's son) is initiated by a request to Jesus, the first being an implied request. Of the other signs in John, only the raising of Lazarus is the result of a[n implied] request. In a quest story, the initial request is always tested by an objection or the placing of an obstacle, which the quester must overcome for the quest to be successful.[3] Following this pattern, in each of the Cana

---

[3] On the quest stories in the synoptic tradition, see Tannehill 1981a, 8–10; 1981b, 107–16; Painter 1993b, 163–65, 177–79, 186–91, 208–12. The case for recognizing quest stories in John, including the subcategory of miracle quest stories, is progressively laid out in what follows. The relationship of the signs to quest stories in John is deeply theological. Tannehill identifies inquiry stories, quest stories, and objection stories among a larger group of pronouncement stories in the Synoptics. In working with John, I have built on Tannehill's analysis

stories Jesus' objection is somewhat abrupt. When the mother of Jesus says to him, "They have no wine," he takes this as an implied request for help and replies, "Woman, what concern is that to you and me [τί ἐμοὶ καὶ σοί γύναι]?" (John 2:3–4). This is every bit as strange and abrupt as Jesus' response to the nobleman, especially as the evangelist has introduced this "woman" as "the mother of Jesus." Each of the petitioners had to overcome an apparent rebuff. The mother of Jesus does so by instructing the servants to do whatever Jesus instructs. The nobleman does so by reiterating his request, which is now given in direct speech whereas only the substance of the first request was reported. In each incident, Jesus complies with the persistent request.

The narratives of these two signs can be understood as examples of miracle stories. Francis Moloney's analysis of the two Cana signs follows Bultmann's outline for a miracle story. In its barest form, the miracle story has three components: the problem is described, the means of overcoming the problem are specified, and the successful outcome is attested (Bultmann 1968, 209–43, esp. 221–26). The two Cana signs certainly fit this formal description. Moloney's summary of Bultmann expands this outline, partly on the basis of Bultmann's treatment of the two Cana signs in his commentary on John (Bultmann 1971, 115–18, 204–8). Moloney further modifies Bultmann's classification on the basis of the fact that "the implied reader [of the Cana narratives] encounters a miracle story that is quite untypical." Here I give only the formal description, which underlies Moloney's analysis of the two signs: problem, request, rebuke, reaction, and consequences (Moloney 1993, 89–91, 189–91). This outline is helpful, and Moloney notes that "there are several elements within this structure that make it nontypical of miracle stories"; specifically, "the form of the miracle story is broken as he [Jesus] rebukes the one who raised the problem." I would not say that the form is broken, but rather that what Moloney terms the "rebuke" is not essential to the miracle story form. Rather, the rebuke is the mark of a subcategory of miracle story, the miracle "quest" story. Just as not all quest stories are "miracle" stories, not all miracle stories are "quest" stories. Thus, these two Cana miracle stories have a surplus of meaning, which alerts us to the quest for the Messiah and which turns out to be the other side of the quest for eternal life. Moloney goes on to explain that the "alterations to the traditional form of a miracle story are also the incidents that shape the implied reader in a special way" (Moloney 1993, 90–91). In this, he rightly notes the importance of what he calls the rebuke, yet he does not take account

but have preferred the name "rejection stories" for the Johannine phenomenon classified as "objection stories" by Tannehill.

of the particular *form* of these Johannine stories and their relationship to other formally similar stories. The rhetorical function of a miracle quest story is different from that of a miracle story.

In my view, Moloney mistakenly treats the absence "of the wonder of all who see or hear of the miracle" in John as the omission of an essential mark of a miracle story. The expression of amazement/wonder is but one way in which the actuality of the miracle is attested. Such attestation is provided in both Cana signs. In the water–to–wine narrative, the servants know what has happened (John 2:9), and it is implied that Jesus' disciples beheld his glory revealed in the sign and came to believe in him in a new way (2:11). In the second Cana sign, the father of the boy Jesus healed at a distance verifies that the healing took place at the very time that Jesus said, "Your son lives." It is implied that this knowledge was shared with his household because he "believed along with his whole household" (4:51–53). In each case, the actuality of the "miracle" is attested. When this is recognized, full attention falls on the objection or obstacle to the fulfilment of the quest as that which, with the initial request, distinguishes these stories from other miracle stories and marks them specifically as "miracle quest stories." Miracle stories need not be initiated by a request; indeed, the miracle stories of John 5:1–9a; 6:1–15; 9:1–12 portray Jesus taking the initiative without any suppliant.

As an addendum to these observations on the Cana stories, I might note in passing that a similar dynamic is at work in a third miracle quest story in the Gospel of John—the raising of Lazarus. In the Lazarus quest story, the obstacle to the fulfilment of the quest is established by Jesus' deliberate delay until Lazarus is already dead (John 11:6, 11–14, 17). The willful delay, as with the the rebuke of 2:4 and 4:48, creates an obstacle to the fulfilment of the implied request. That this obstacle was felt is implied by the words of Martha in 11:21, "Lord, if you had been here, my brother would not have died," words that are repeated (with slight variation in order) by Mary in 11:32. Healing a sick man is one thing; raising a dead man quite another, especially after four days in the tomb. Hence, a greater obstacle needed to be overcome, and this is progressively portrayed in Jesus' meeting with Martha (11:21–27). Early in this meeting, she says, "But even now I know that whatever you ask of him, God will give you" (11:22; cf. 11:37). These words show that Martha, even if uncomprehendingly, has surmounted the obstacle constituted by Jesus' delay. In the Lazarus story, Jesus takes more initiative in the latter part of the story, though it is clear that the faith expressed in the initial request is not overwhelmed by Jesus' delay and the death of Lazarus. Nevertheless, the fulfilment of their request was beyond their expectations.

The Theology of Quest Stories and the Signs of the Messiah

In my view, one may better explain John 4:48 in terms of the pattern of a miracle quest story than by suggesting that the evangelist has clumsily redacted a hypothetical signs source. Quest stories were first identified in the study of the Synoptic Gospels, especially Luke, but I have identified a more concentrated, rhetorical, and theological use of quest in John. Rhetorically, this form of story is identified amongst the *chreia* found in the synoptic tradition, Greco–Roman biographies, and rhetorical texts.[4] The literary/rhetorical comparisons reveal something of the social context of the Gospels. The concentration and importance of inquiry, quest, and rejection stories in John opens up something of the distinctive nature of that Gospel.

Theologically, the quest for the Messiah arises from the elusiveness of the Messiah. In Judaism of the time, the Messiah was believed to be "hidden" and, in that sense, elusive (Painter 1993b, 9). In John, this elusiveness is accentuated because Jesus does not fit the common expectations of messiahship. Those who seek him find it difficult to come to terms with the mystery of his person and role. Underlying this mystery is the mystery of God, whom Jesus has come to make known—the God whom no one has seen and who remains mysterious even in being made known (John 1:18). Then, there is the elusiveness of Jesus himself in the face of hostile attempts to arrest or harm him. In John, Jesus' opponents cannot lay hands on him until he is ready to give himself up (John 18:4–11). But there is more to the pervasive and persistent quest for the Messiah in John.

In John, the quest for eternal life is intimately linked with the signs of the Messiah. Indeed, that quest is initially recognized in the quest for the Messiah, which leads into the first of the two Cana signs, which I have identified as miracle quest stories.[5] The intricate relationship between signs and quest is found in the recognition that the quest for the Messiah is the quest for eternal life (John 20:30–31). John builds on the tradition that the Messiah emerges out of obscurity, being hidden. This theme is evident in the questions put to John the Baptist at 1:19–28. Such uncertainty presupposes that the Messiah is unknown. It is even clearer in the controversies in which Jesus' messiahship is rejected because his origin (parents) is known

[4] See Painter 1993b, 163–88. Quest stories are not as common in the Greco–Roman biographies and rhetorical texts as some of the other types of *chreia*.

[5] The first Cana sign is part of a sequence of events linked by a sequence of days (1:29, 35, 43; 2:1) with the marriage taking place on the third day in this sequence.

(6:41–42; 7:26–27). At the same time, it is argued that the signs performed by Jesus weigh in favor of his messianic identity. "Whenever the Christ comes, surely he will not do more signs than this man did?" (7:31). In spite of the absence of clear and independent Jewish evidence concerning the expectation that the Messiah would perform signs, the Fourth Gospel's presentation presupposes this view.[6] The notion that the Messiah would perform signs is strongly implied by the statement of those who believe in Jesus at 10:41–42: "John [the Baptist] did no sign, but whatever John said concerning this man was true." This is a reference back to 1:19–36, where the Baptist, when questioned about the Messiah, identified Jesus as the coming one. The contrast is between the Baptist, who did no sign, and Jesus, who performed the signs of the Messiah.

The synoptic tradition (Matt 11:2–6; Luke 7:18–23; perhaps Q) narrates how John the Baptist sends messengers to Jesus, asking, "Are you the one who is to come, or are we to wait for another?"[7] In both Matthew and Luke, Jesus answers, "Go and tell John what you hear and see." Only Luke reports that, at this time, Jesus healed many people of various life–threatening maladies. Perhaps Matthew's narrative also assumes the performance of healings at this time, but this is not explicit. What these messengers are to tell the Baptist not only summarizes what Jesus has done, but also echoes Isaiah 35:5–6 and 61:1. Clearly, Matthew and Luke understand this message as affirming that Jesus is the coming one, the Messiah. But the specific signs indicated identify him as the healing, helping Messiah. The same is true of the signs in John. The signs of the Messiah are the signs of life—*eternal life*—because the actions dealing with the urgent necessities of daily life have become symbols and communicators of eternal life (20:30–31).

Rhetorically, John carefully introduces the quest for the Messiah by first raising the messianic question in an inquiry story (John 1:19–28) that builds on tradition also known to us from Q (Matt 3:7–12//Luke 3:7–17).[8] In the Synoptics, the introduction of John the Baptist is built on

---

[6] Though Josephus does not speak of certain failed deliverers as "Messiah," they were probably perceived as such by their followers (Painter 1993b, 259–64). They offered Exodus–like signs in the wilderness as evidence of the deliverance they promised to bring.

[7] Matthew has ἕτερον, Luke has ἄλλον. The former perhaps implies "another of a different kind," while the latter makes no assumption of difference.

[8] An inquiry story functions to carry the response to the inquiry. Thus, in John, John the Baptist is not important in himself. He serves as the witness to the inquiry about the Christ. For this reason, neither his activity of baptizing nor the substance of his preaching is described in the Fourth Gospel. Negatively, the Baptist denies that he is the Christ and, positively, points to the one who is.

tradition found in Mark and tradition shared by Matthew and Luke (Q). John is closer to Luke (Q) at certain points. In Luke, the activity of the Baptist provokes some people to question in their hearts whether he is the Christ (Luke 3:15). Evidently, John is a heart reader, because he vehemently denies this impression and contrasts his water baptism with the fiery eschatological baptism of the coming one. But John 1:19–28 is an explicit inquiry story. The priests and Levites who confront the Baptist are sent by the Jews of Jerusalem to ask him, "Who are you?" (1:19, 24). His response, and the discussion that follows, indicate that the inquiry concerned whether or not John was the Messiah. The inquiry story is told to allow the Baptist to distance himself clearly and emphatically from any messianic role, leaving it open for the coming one. The inquiry reveals an expectation of the coming of the Messiah and prepares the way for the development of a quest to find him.

The inquiry is linked to the beginning of the quest by the witness of John the Baptist to the Messiah (John 1:29–34). Because, in the first instance, there is no one to hear the Baptist's witness except Jesus, it seems to be given for the sake of the readers who hear the full witness (1:29; contrast 1:36) with the account of the evidence identifying Jesus as the Messiah, the coming one (1:30–34). Then in 1:35–37, the Baptist has an audience of two disciples who hear only an abbreviated form of his witness without seeing the evidence identifying Jesus as Messiah. Perhaps the reader is to assume that this is a summary of the witness already given, which implies both the full witness and the evidence. As a consequence of John's witness, the disciples *follow* Jesus. The language of following signals the intention of the Baptist's two disciples to detach themselves from him and to attach themselves to Jesus as disciples. In this early story, the first in which Jesus is active, it is notable that, in stark contrast with the synoptic call stories, the initiative is taken by the disciples rather than by Jesus (contrast Mark 1:16–20; 2:13–17). The positive role of their initiative is carefully developed in John.

In this story, Jesus speaks his first words that are, in this Gospel, likely to have been carefully chosen, because the incarnate Word is a teacher who works by his word. Jesus turns, sees two of the Baptist's disciples following him, and asks, "What are you seeking?" (τί ζητεῖτε; John 1:38; translations mine throughout). Not "Who?" but "What?" This first use of "seeking," a term that occurs thirty–four times in the Gospel of John, appears in the first words spoken by Jesus.[9] Many of these occurrences

[9] By contrast, "seek" appears fourteen times in Matthew, ten times in Mark, twenty–five times in Luke, ten times in Acts, nineteen times in the entire Pauline corpus, twice in 1 Peter, and once in Hebrews and Revelation.

express the quest for the Messiah, though there is also concentration on the quest to arrest or kill Jesus. In the first words of the incarnate Word, a marker of the quest for the Messiah is identified. The disciples respond to Jesus' question with another of their own: "Rabbi (which translated means Teacher), where are you living (ποῦ μένεις)?" Jesus answers, "Come and see." The narrator then informs us that "they came and saw where he was staying, and they remained with him that day" (John 1:38–39). This exchange is laden with important Johannine language. First, it is Jesus who identifies the quest in his opening words. His words alert us to the twin themes of seeking and finding, which marks a successful quest (Matt 7:7–8; Luke 11:9–13 = perhaps Q). But, as is characteristic of a quest story, some condition must be met or a difficulty overcome for the quest to be successful. The two disciples, when asked, "What are you seeking?" reply that they wish to know where Jesus dwells. At the surface level, this might mean at which house will Jesus stay the night. But the verb μένω ("remain/abide") has a deeper theological sense in John. It is used forty times in the Gospel of John, twenty–four times in 1 John, three times in 2 John; against these sixty–seven occurrences, μένω appears only three times in Matthew, twice in Mark, seven times in Luke, seventeen times in the entire Pauline corpus, six times in Hebrews, and once in Revelation. The concentration in the Johannine writings is marked. But it is the distinctively theological use of this language by John in reference to the mutual abiding of the Father and the Son, of Jesus and the believer, of the believer and God's/Jesus' word, and of the Spirit that makes clear its importance. Consequently this word, which is featured in Jesus' discourse in John 15, suggests a second level of meaning, because Jesus dwells with the Father (cf. 1:18). Is this the mystery the disciples will learn?

Jesus does not deliver a simple and straightforward answer to their question. If they are to have an answer, they will have to work for it. Jesus responds, "Come [imperative] and you will see [future tense]." The latter constitutes a promise, which the former makes conditional. First they must come. The narrator informs the reader, "Therefore they came and they saw where he abides (present tense) and they abode (aorist tense) with him that day." That something significant has happened is now made clear by this heavy use of μένω.

One of the two disciples who *followed* Jesus was Andrew, the brother of Simon Peter. He first finds his brother and announces to him, "We have found the Messiah (εὑρήκαμεν τον Μεσσίαν) which is translated 'Christ'" (Χριστός; John 1:41). So the seekers announce that they have found the one they were looking for and, having found him, Andrew leads his brother to Jesus. Given that Andrew first (πρῶτον) finds his brother, it is possible, even probable, that he next finds Philip. The process is abbreviated and it is implied that he brings Philip to Jesus, as he brought his brother, and Jesus says to him, "Follow me" (1:43).

This analysis of John 1:19–43, combined with analogies from the use of *chreiai* in Greco–Roman rhetoric and the Synoptic Gospels, allows us to outline the Johannine quest stories as follows (see also Painter 1993b, 177–78; 1996, 357):

(1) The quester makes an implied or explicit request;

(2) The quest dominates the story, and the quester is not simply a foil for Jesus;

(3) The quester seeks something essential for human well–being. In John, something important at a physical level can become important for well–being at a spiritual level;

(4) There is an objection or difficulty to be overcome, and this may redefine the direction of the quest;

(5) The pronouncement of Jesus (a word or an action) holds the key to the resolution of the quest;

(6) The outcome of the quest is of crucial interest and is indicated in the quest story.

Transition from Quest to Conflict and Rejection

Students of the Fourth Gospel have long been puzzled by John 6:1, which suggests that Jesus is in Galilee even though chapter 5 is set in Jerusalem. One solution is to reverse the order of chapters 5 and 6, which makes for a smoother itinerary because John 4 marks Jesus' return to Galilee from Judea via Samaria. But there is no textual evidence to justify this procedure. Thus, if such a transposition has taken place, it must have been very early, perhaps before the initial publication of the Gospel. There is, however, other evidence to support this transposition in the course of composition.

John 6 is an excellent example of the process of composition in the Fourth Gospel, because here it is possible to see in the finished product traces of evidence of the process (Painter 1989, 421–50). This chapter is one of the clearest examples of the Fourth Evangelist's use of tradition shared with the Synoptics. The feeding story, as well as the connected story of the sea crossing, is shared by John and Mark (and the other Synoptists). Those arguing for John's dependence upon the Synoptics have rightly featured this evidence. It is impressive, but John's account also contains an element of tradition not to be found in the Synoptics. It does not express a Johannine point of view, but rather reflects a situation that fits the first–century Jewish context described by Josephus (Painter 1993b, 259–67). Those who saw the feeding sign identify Jesus as the coming prophet (like Moses? see Deut 18:15, 18) and seek to take him and make him king (6:14–15). Jesus' rapid withdrawal makes clear his rejection of this move, which is at odds with a Johannine understanding of his kingship (18:36).

That John 6 builds on tradition is clear, but synoptic dependence is not demonstrably probable. The question is, how does John use this tradition? Though the crowd was following Jesus having seen the signs he performed on the sick (John 6:2), what follows is not a miracle quest story.[10] The feeding miracle story, as with those of John 5 and 9, describes a sign done at the initiative of Jesus (6:5–6). Unlike the two concise and discrete Cana signs, the feeding sign is the initial part of a complex literary development, which remains rooted in the feeding sign. This literary development has all the marks of a complex quest story but ends in failure and rejection. This, and another literary feature to be discussed next, combines to support the view that John 6 was relocated in the process of the composition of the Gospel.

Understood as a complex quest story, John 6 can be analyzed as follows: some of the crowd sees the feeding sign as evidence that Jesus is the Prophet like Moses (John 6:14–15, 30–33). They seek to take Jesus and make him king. We may describe this attempt as an implied request. But Jesus rejects this request because it involves a mistaken understanding of his kingship. This modifies the quest that runs throughout the remainder of the chapter, which concerns what is fundamental to life. Jesus' withdrawal from the crowd constitutes an obstacle to the success of the quest. In this case, his objection not only causes a difficulty for the questers, it demands the reshaping of the quest. Consequently, Jesus does not simply withdraw so that he may continue the discussion at a later time in the same place. The story of the sea crossing, which traditionally followed the feeding, is used to separate Jesus from the crowd and the geographical location of the feeding, which encouraged the thought of gathering for political revolution.

Only in John does the crowd (or some of them) follow across the sea, seeking Jesus (ζητοῦντες τὸν Ἰησοῦν) in Capernaum (John 6:24). This constitutes the renewal of the quest, undaunted by Jesus' withdrawal and departure. But Jesus did not place this obstacle in the path of their quest to test their resolve; his withdrawal was, rather, an objection to their understanding of him. Jesus recognizes their quest and objects to their view of him as one who could be understood wholly in terms of solving the material and economic problems of the people. Their misunderstanding

---

[10] John 6:2 assumes a number of earlier healing signs in Galilee, just as 2:23 and 3:2 assume a number of earlier Jerusalem signs.

is understandable because Jesus had fed the hungry with bread and fish, a feeding that they should have viewed as a Johannine sign. Yet they came seeking Jesus because he had fed them, not because they had seen the sign(s) (6:26). In John 6, we discover the nature of signs as "deeds that speak" or "meaningful actions," "actions full of meaning" where meaning arises symbolically out of the action. This perspective is crucial for a reading of John 6.

Briefly, Jesus' subsequent dialogue with the crowd (6:26ff.) is an effort to clarify and modify what it is that they should seek from him. Jesus moves from the bread of the feeding to the bread from heaven that God gives, the bread of God, who comes down from heaven and gives life to the world (6:26–33). In response they say, "Sir, give us this bread always" (6:34), a request that seems to imply that their quest is about to succeed. First, it is parallel to the response of the Samaritan woman to Jesus' offer of life–giving water, "Sir, give me this water, so that I may never be thirsty or have to keep coming here to draw water" (4:13–15). Second, this water, like the bread Jesus offers in John 6, is the source of eternal life. What follows in John 6:35 is a further clarification by Jesus, which seems to be equally applicable to 4:15: "I am the bread of life. Whoever comes to me will never be hungry, and whoever believes in me will never be thirsty." Just as 6:35 clarifies 6:26–33, there is further dialogue between Jesus and the woman in John 4:16–26 that clarifies the nature of the gift. When the woman leaves, the narrator notes that she leaves behind her water pot and goes into the town where she says to the men, "Come see a man who told me everything I have ever done! He cannot be the Messiah can he?" (4:28–29). The fact that she leaves the water pot empty must be important; otherwise, this detail would not be noted. The woman's priorities have changed. Though often it is rightly noted that the grammatical form of the woman's question to the men of the town can imply a negative answer, the context does not support this reading. It is rather to be seen as a hesitant or tentative suggestion, through which many of the Samaritans came to believe (4:39). When invited, Jesus stayed with them two more days and many more believed, hearing the word of Jesus for themselves (4:40). It may be that 4:41–42 also suggests an advance in their belief, though that is not clear; it may only distinguish hearing the woman speak of Jesus and hearing Jesus himself. The confession provides a suitable concluding Samaritan affirmation of faith for this episode. John 4 portrays the woman as one like Andrew who, having found Jesus, leads others to him (1:35–43). The parallel between 4:15 and 6:34, along with the twin themes of life–giving water and the bread of life, lead the reader to expect a positive outcome for the quest of the crowd in John 6.

Given this expectation, the words of Jesus that follow are shocking (6:36–40). The crowd that has asked, "Give us this bread always" and has heard Jesus' exposition of the bread of life, is given no opportunity for further response. Without any further ado, Jesus rushes on to tell them that they have seen and not believed (6:36). From 6:40–59, Jesus' dialogue partners are identified as "the Jews," and the discussion concludes with the narrator's comment that Jesus "said these things while he was teaching in the synagogue at Capernaum" (6:59). Neither the location in the synagogue nor the identification of Jesus' dialogue partners with "the Jews" fits the dialogue of Jesus with the crowd in 6:25–33, which fits well with 6:34–35. All of this suggests that John 6, as with John 4, originally portrayed a successful quest in which the nature of the quest was transformed in its fulfillment. Eventually, however, John 6 was used to portray a failed quest, and there is a rough transition from the crowd (6:22–35) to the Jews in the synagogue (6:41–59), where a tone of aggression is introduced. This rough transition has an impact on the account of the response of Jesus' disciples, which tells us that many of them ceased to follow him (6:60–71). At issue with the Jews and the disciples is Jesus' claim concerning his heavenly origin and destiny (6:42, 62). The heavenly origin was already asserted in the language of the bread from heaven, from God, with which Jesus identified himself (6:32, 33, 35). The disciples who fell away, like the Jews of 6:41–42, were scandalized by Jesus' claim to be the bread that came down from heaven (6:41–42, 60–61). After all, they knew his father and mother.

This shift in the outcome of the quest story in John 6 seems to be linked with the breakdown of the relationship between the Jews of the synagogue and the Johannine believers. My hypothesis is that John 6 became separated from John 4, with which it shares the theme of Jesus' offer of himself as the source of eternal life, as a result of the breakdown of relationship with the Jews of the synagogue. John 6 also shows some of the impact of this break upon those who had been believers. But it is in Jerusalem that John sets the paradigm for the Jewish rejection of Jesus, based on the twin charges of Sabbath breaking and blasphemy (5:18; Painter 1987b, 28–34). John 6 only partially reveals the grounds of conflict in Galilee, where the problem was less serious. Structurally, John 5 provides the paradigm of rejection, and all that follows falls under its shadow. The surprising rejection of the Galilean crowd now has a precedent in John 5, and the synagogue in Capernaum is named as the place of rejection for Jesus in John 6, foreshadowing the threat of eviction from the synagogue that emerges in John 9:22, 34.

Signs and the Quest for Eternal Life

In John, Jesus' signs are signs of life. Elements of the physical world that sustain physical life become the symbols of the source of eternal life with which Jesus identifies himself as giver and gift. The feeding sign becomes the means by which Jesus offers himself as the source of eternal life (John 6:35). In the same way, the raising of Lazarus becomes the basis for Jesus to offer himself as the resurrection and the life (11:25–26). Between these two signs, Jesus offers himself as the light of the world (8:12; 9:5). The giving of sight to a blind man becomes a third sign that reveals Jesus as the source of life and demonstrates the reality of his saying in 8:12, "I am the light of the world." The summary reiteration of this saying in 9:5 alerts the reader to the connection at the beginning of the sign. Jesus affirms that, because he is the light of the world, those who follow him will not walk in darkness but will have the light of life (cf. 1:4). The light comes from the source of life and is life–giving. To give the blind man his sight was to give him life.

The Johannine creation story provides the basis for understanding the signs as windows into the goodness and bounty of God as the Lord and giver of life. Creation reality underlies the quest for eternal life, so that the prologue affirms harmony and continuity of creation and redemption as foundation and fulfillment (Painter 2002a). Creation finds completion in Jesus' life–giving work. Creation, if flawed, is nonetheless graced, and in the outworking of that grace, creation may be made whole.

Rudolf Bultmann frequently quoted the words of Augustine from the beginning of his *Confessions*: "O God, you have made us for yourself, and our heart is restless until it finds its rest in you." Bultmann repeatedly appealed to these words to support his view that the quest for life and the quest for God are two sides of one quest. This quest is irrepressible in human life and arises spontaneously, whether consciously or unconsciously. For Augustine, this expression of anthropological understanding arose out of his self–understanding, which he extrapolated as an anthropological statement about the human heart. For Bultmann, the quest for life is in reality the quest for God or, in Johannine terms, the quest for eternal life is the quest for the Messiah (John 1:38–39, 41; 20:30–31; Painter 1998, 10–16). It is not inappropriate to term eternal life "authentic life" when it is understood as the life that has its source in God, is revealed in Jesus, and is communicated to those who believe in him.

13: Response

THE JOHANNINE CONCEPTION
OF AUTHENTIC FAITH AS A RESPONSE
TO THE DIVINE INITIATIVE

Paul N. Anderson

It is a high privilege to be invited to respond to John Painter's essay. Among his many contributions to New Testament studies, Professor Painter has alerted us to the ways in which the quest narratives function in John, both traditionally and rhetorically. His article in this volume not only explores the origin and development of key Johannine passages, but it also engages meaningfully their theological and experiential implications. In highlighting the relevance of Painter's earlier work, this essay too is sure to make a difference.

The subject in his paper I would like to focus on and take a bit further involves the divine quest for humanity, a theme that runs alongside the human quests for the divine in the Fourth Gospel. Put another way, if one were to ask *why* the quest narratives in John employ ironic presentations of dead–end aspirations and wrong–headed ventures that are challenged and corrected by Jesus, the answer would lie in the evangelist's conviction that "the One Quest beyond the Many" stands above all human quests. The restlessness of the human heart points us to a more transcendent quest, conveyed—nay, embodied—by the Revealer. This divine quest for humanity, challenging all that is of creaturely origin, calls for authentic faith as a transformative response to the Divine Initiative. This theme is set out in the Fourth Gospel's prologue (John 1:1–18) and climactically calls the reader to encounter at John 20:31. The latter verse stresses that, although other stories attributed to Jesus lie beyond the Johannine witness, these are written so that the hearer/reader might believe.

I appreciate the fact that Painter opens his essay with the story of his own quest: his search for the truth about matters Johannine. John Painter has long been a hero for me, as well as a friend, and his quest and findings also intersect with my own. In addition to reading everything I could find by Professor Painter as I conducted my inquiry into the character and development of Johannine Christology while a student at the University of Glasgow, I too cut my interpretive teeth on Barrett and Bultmann, among others. Their theological interpretations remain solid, but my own testing of the literary evidence for their composition theories yielded critically inadequate results. The Fourth Gospel is not, in my view, an amalgam of unknown sources, nor is it dependent on Mark or another of the Synoptics (P. Anderson 1997a, 48–169). The Fourth Gospel's autonomy is compelling, although its tradition did not develop in isolation; I prefer to think in terms of a "dialogical autonomy" in explaining the relationship between the Fourth Gospel and other Jesus traditions (P. Anderson 2006, 37–41, 101–26).

I was privileged to present a paper, at Professor Painter's invitation, in the Johannine Literature Seminar at the 1993 SNTS meeting in Chicago. Raymond Brown had been scheduled to do a paper on John 6 but had to cancel, and this opened a place for one last paper on the subject before the group moved on. There, I argued that at least four groups were targeted in the evolving Johannine context of John 6, in contrast to Martyn's theory of a single community crisis in the context of John 9 (see P. Anderson 1997b, 24–57). The quests for another feeding (the crowd), religious certainty (the Jewish leaders), easy discipleship (the disciples), and apostolic primacy (Peter) are brought to bear on the life–producing food that Jesus gives and is, in contrast to death–producing alternatives (v. 27). As the Master from Marburg puts it, "The whole paradox of the revelation is contained in this [Jesus'] reply [6:35]. Whoever wants something from him must know that he has to receive Jesus *himself*. Whoever approaches him with the desire for the gift of life must learn that Jesus is *himself* the gift he really wants. Jesus gives the bread of life in that he *is* the bread of life. . . . Whoever wishes to receive life from him must therefore believe in him—or, as it is figuratively expressed must 'come to him'" (Bultmann 1971, 227).

The scandalizing impact of the Divine Initiative upon the world's quests for miraculous signs, religious certainty, costless discipleship, and political power deserves further comment. Indeed, Jesus' challenge to the miraculous evaluation of the feeding ("they ate and were satisfied") was not levied against an inferred, backwater σημεῖα source, but rather, against the prevalent Christian interpretation as conveyed within all five Synoptic feeding narratives. Given John's dialogical autonomy, the anti-thaumaturgic dialectic is more likely to have been conducted between the developing Johannine tradition and its living audiences, rather than a static text, Markan or otherwise. It may even represent a dialogue *within* the Johannine tradition itself, especially if the Fourth Gospel indeed represents an autonomous Jesus tradition developing theologically in its own distinctive ways (P. Anderson 2006, esp. 127–73). Whatever the case, John bridges the apparent contradiction between reports of Jesus' wondrous ministry and the relative dearth of miracles in the later experience of believers by an emphasis on the central theological meaning of the signs (P. Anderson 2004). Blessedness thus extends to those who "have not seen" as a means of including later generations who witness less–than–dramatic results (John 20:29). It is not one's capacity to control human destiny, as the Grand Inquisitor in *The Brothers Karamazov* muses, which motivates Jesus' multiplication of the loaves. Rather, that thaumaturgic interest is the work of the Tempter—a role here played by the crowd—played out otherwise in the Q narratives. As "signs," the works and words of Jesus point to a more basic and sustaining reality than the outward alone can convey. In his being sent to the world from the Father, the world itself is invited to respond to the Father's redemptive love.

A second way in which the Revealer scandalizes the world involves the affront which revelation is to religion. As a human construct, all religious ventures involve human attempts to approach the divine. The problem is an anthropological one, not a theological one: humans do not have the capacity to conceive of divine grace and unmerited love. Grace, in essence, is postconventional, which is why it requires a revelation to be perceived. Because no one has seen God at any time, no one can come (not "may" come) to God except by being drawn by the Father (John 6:44). For this very reason, the Jewish leaders are scandalized in John and equated with the unbelieving world. Tensions between them and Jesus within the narrative are certainly not factors of one form of religious convention against another; they involve the challenge of all religiosity—including Christian forms of it—in the face of revelation. The only hope for humanity is the response of faith to the Divine Initiative, which is why authentic worship can only be in Spirit and in truth (John 4:21–24). Independent of place and form, coming to God authentically moves out of a sense of being drawn by God to a place of openness and faith. The topography of authentic worship is the inward and adoring response of the heart to God, not a cultic place, pattern, or form of creaturely origin. The Spirit convicts persons of sin and of righteousness, and all truth is ultimately liberating. The hope for the world lies not in our love for God, but rather in the fact that God has first loved us. The scandal is that coming to God involves first laying at the foot of the cross not only our sin, but also our creaturely attempts to reach the Divine. God actively seeks such people, working to draw them into an authentic relationship of worship, characterized by receptivity and responsiveness to the movement of the Spirit. The work of the Revealer thus poses a scandal in every generation to every religion—Christian, as well as Judean and Samaritan. The human initiative is of no avail; the only hope for humanity is a believing response to the Divine Initiative: the essence of saving–abiding belief, itself.

A third way in which the Revealer scandalizes the world involves John's juxtaposition of political power and true authority. Whereas Pilate claims to have all power to release Jesus or to put him to death, he is exposed as the "impotent potentate" before the jeering crowd: although he finds "no fault" in Jesus, he is reduced to begging the crowd to let him let Jesus go. The prefect here falls far short of perfect. When Pilate asks whether Jesus is a king, however, Jesus replies with a qualified affirmative: his kingdom is one of truth, and all who abide in the truth are his disciples (John 18:37). Pilate exempts himself from that company, admitting his failure to comprehend the truth. Authority in John is ever a factor of truth, and this is why Jesus' disciples do not fight. The truth cannot be furthered by force or violence, and because it works from the inside out, independent of environment and circumstances, truth alone has the power to liberate (8:32). This principle is also evident in the Johannine presentation of Peter. While Peter retains the role of chief among the disciples, he points centrally to the primacy of Christ, who leads all believers—at least potentially—through the dynamic workings of the Holy Spirit. Peter is presented in John as *Pontus Minimus*, a witness to the conviction that Christ alone is the sole priest and leader of the authentic church because he alone has the words of eternal life (6:68).

More than a century ago, Rufus Jones wrote a book called *The Double Search*. In it, he developed a treatment of humanity's quest for God, but also of God's quest for humanity (Jones 1906). Indeed, our hearts are restless until they rest in God, and to extend the conversation to Blaise Pascal, "thou wouldst not seek Me if thou hadst not found Me" (*Pensees* #552). The inclination to seek is already a reflection of, even a testimonial to, the illuminating work of the Revealer in the world and in our hearts. In Johannine terms, then, authentic faith is essentially the response of beloved humanity to the saving–revealing initiative of God, drawing us at many times and in many ways to a believing response to God's quest for humanity. In the light of "the One Quest beyond the Many," we are invited to seek until we, ourselves, are found.

CHAPTER 14

REMAINING IN HIS WORD
FROM FAITH TO FAITH BY WAY OF THE TEXT

Sandra M. Schneiders, I.H.M.

This is certainly the most unusual project in which I have participated in the thirty plus years I have been engaged in studying and pondering the Fourth Gospel, including teaching it to others and writing about it. The project's initiator and combination shepherd and sheep dog, Tom Thatcher, invited us to reflect upon one of two cluster questions: either upon where we think Johannine Studies has been during our professional lives and where it is headed; or upon our own experience of participating in this scholarly journey. A number of insightful papers, recently read or published, have charted from different perspectives the course of Johannine Studies from the mid–twentieth century to our own day, and I presume that other contributors to this volume will hazard well–founded predictions that will benefit all of us, especially the newer scholars in the field who will have to deal with the emerging challenges. I have therefore decided to reflect upon the second option, "how my mind has, or has not, changed" over the past three decades. Actually, the personal journey of anyone seriously engaged in the academy probably reflects, at least to some extent, what has been going on in the field. So the two sets of questions are more like different ways of dealing with the same question. What has been happening in the field of Johannine Studies over the lifetime of the people involved in this book? How have these developments influenced our personal academic journeys and what might be developing for the future as the result of this history?

Reflecting upon how my own mind has and has not changed since I finished my doctoral studies in 1975 and began teaching in the Graduate Theological Union in Berkeley, California, turned out to be a more interesting mental exercise than I anticipated, because it raised the foundational question of what constitutes "change" when the subject is one's own mind or one's discipline. The intricate interplay of influences that often are not purely intellectual or cleanly rational; the intuitive processes of selection and rejection of ideas, theories, explanations, or approaches; the incorporation of insights, which is often so gradual as to be unnoticed until we hear something coming out of our mouths that we would not have said a few years earlier—all these are signs (revelatory *sēmeia*, perhaps?) that things, or we ourselves, are significantly, even radically, different. But it may not be entirely clear how or in what respect.

I suspect that in both an individual and an academic field, "change" does not happen punctually, with something that is clearly "before" and something clearly "after" (like those photos of successful dieters); change is, rather, something we recognize in hindsight as the product of an organic process of development or evolution. The development, though organic, is often not smooth. Like an adolescent whose nose or feet are suddenly (albeit temporarily) out of proportion to the whole, we go through periods of individual and corporate awkwardness as we experiment with new insights, attitudes, intellectual stances, or sensibilities that, once incorporated, feel so natural that we forget our earlier hesitations or even adamant rejections and refusals. No doubt many established scholars (who today would not think of presenting to a class a bibliography containing only male authors) once considered feminist criticism a passing fad of overheated female brains. When did the profound change that was constituted by the mainstreaming of feminist criticism in the biblical academy happen, to me or to the field?

These reflections led me to realize that, while there might be a useful mental distinction between "what has changed" and "what has not changed" in my approach to the Fourth Gospel, no real separation between them is possible. What has remained substantially the same has been profoundly affected by what has changed, and what has changed has been controlled and shaped by its incorporation into what has remained the same. So, I will begin by trying to say what has remained the same and then devote most of my time and space to detailing the effects of all that has changed on that core datum. The short answer to the question is that what has remained constant for me is my basic concern, my fundamental interest, in studying the Gospel of John, the "what" and "why" of my personal–professional project. And what has changed is virtually everything else.

WHAT HAS REMAINED THE SAME

My love affair with the Gospel of John—and it is that—began sometime before I had any idea of becoming a professional in the biblical academy, and indeed before such was even a realistic goal for a Catholic female. This Gospel spoke to me, even in my youth, at some profound level. It was true and beautiful in a way that captured my mind and my heart. Of course, I did not make the acquaintance of John in isolation. The Fourth Gospel was simply, for me, the most attractive part of the biblical text I encountered in my religious upbringing and studies in the Catholic schools I attended. After entering the religious order to which I have belonged most of my life, my love of theology in general and especially of Scripture led to my being sent, in my thirties, for graduate studies in the field. Over the next seven years of theological study in Paris and in Rome, my circling around the Fourth Gospel eventually led to the choice of a dissertation topic that situated me for good in Johannine Studies, namely, the resurrection narrative in the Gospel of John. And the rest, as they say, is history. But, as I will say shortly, there is a sense in which the rest is precisely *not* history, or at least not about history, and that constitutes the major way in which my mind has changed in relation to what has not changed.

The choice to focus my Johannine Studies on the resurrection narrative was probably at least partly the result of the influence of the tremendous upsurge of interest in the resurrection of Jesus in the late 1960s and 1970s, which reached a fever pitch in the Catholic context of Rome while I was studying there. However, the upsurge of interest in the resurrection was not at all limited to Catholics, as a perusal of the list of monographs, symposia, essays, debates, and books of all sort in the academic and popular press of the period attests. See, for example, the nearly one–hundred–page bibliography compiled by Guiseppe Ghiberti for the Symposium on the Resurrection held in Rome in 1970 (Dhanis, et al. 1974, 651–745). Historians, religious studies scholars, psychologists of religion, linguists, theologians, and biblical scholars buzzed around the topic of the resurrection like bees around a honey jar. Resurrection, that of Jesus and that of the believer, became a virtual cottage industry in the theological academy for a couple of decades, which coincided with the post–conciliar flourishing of Catholic biblical scholarship within which I did my doctoral studies. After a brief recession, intense interest in the resurrection seems to be once again in flood stage, as attested by the recent studies of scholars such as N. T. Wright and John Dominic Crossan (Crossan and Wright 2006),

Luke Timothy Johnson (1999, esp. ch. 3), and also by recent interdisciplinary and ecumenical symposia (e.g., Davis, Kendall, O'Collins 1997)
and studies (e.g., Peters, Russell, and Welker 2002).

I shared the intellectual fascination of my teachers and mentors with
this topic and my interest (although it was not especially fashionable in
the academy to admit it) was not purely academic. It mattered ultimately
to me (and I think to most of the scholars involved in the discussion, even
when they projected the disinterestedness expected of objective scholarship) whether the man Jesus who was crucified under Pontius Pilate actually rose from the dead. Even more, it mattered to me what that statement
could possibly really mean—for Jesus, for his followers, for me, for the
whole of creation. This, I think, is what has not changed in my relationship with the Fourth Gospel, indeed with the whole of the Bible, over the
ensuing decades.

I got into Biblical Studies, I now realize, because I wanted to find out
how the Bible in general, the New Testament in particular, and the Gospel of John specifically, could actually mediate the relationship between
human beings, especially believers, and the God who was incarnate in
Jesus, the Word made flesh, who rose from the dead and is still with us.
My basic interest was and still is in the subject matter of the text in relation to the believing reader, ancient or contemporary. If the biblical text
is a privileged mediation of that relationship, serious study of the Bible
seemed to me the self–evident path to understanding and developing that
relationship. But that is probably the last thing about the project that I
would ever find self–evident! Once I crossed the threshold of the ancient
and mysterious forest that is the Gospel of John, complexity and sim-
plicity, darkness and light, shadows and reality, would be the fascinating
world in which my academic life would unfold.

How a text, especially an ancient one, could mediate a relationship,
especially a relationship with the Transcendent, in the present; whether
this particular text, riddled as it was with problems of a scientific, literary,
historical, and even ethical nature, was trustworthy; how the text was to
be read and understood and how one could know whether one had in fact
understood it correctly; how genuine, "objective" scholarship in relation
to sacred texts was related to ecclesial authority; whether author, text,
or reader had priority in the search for meaning in texts and/or existential significance; whether the results of scholarship determine faith or
vice versa or neither—all of these questions about biblical interpretation,
which are by no means peculiar to the study of the Fourth Gospel, were
rattling around in my head as I worked on John 20, the Johannine narrative of Jesus' resurrection.

My teachers were experts in the use of historical–critical methods for studying the New Testament and were intent upon forming us students in that method. They had little to say on the foregoing questions (which, I would later realize, were primarily hermeneutical and theological rather than exegetical ones), except to warn that pursuing them was a sure–fire way to remain a doctoral student for the rest of one's natural life. It was much better to learn to "do well" what we knew how to do (namely, exegete the text) than to "raise theoretical questions about what we were doing."

But these issues, which were resolutely consigned to the back burner by most of the best biblical scholars of the mid–twentieth century, were bubbling in other disciplinary pots, specifically philosophical, social, literary, and theological ones. I have no regrets now that I was not really allowed to pursue these questions on the nature of texts, the meaning of revelation, the process of interpretation, the meaning of meaning, communication theory, the conflict of interpretations, ideology criticism, the relation of method to truth, the difference between the Bible as human text and the Bible as sacred scripture, the relation of theology and spirituality to Biblical Studies, and so on until after I had learned, by doing, how to use the classical, modern, historical–critical methods of handling texts. Whatever I would later learn about biblical interpretation—whether under the rubric of hermeneutics, methodology, theology, or spirituality—would not invalidate this basic training in historical–critical method and the respect for rigorous and collegially vetted scholarship that it inculcated. But eventually, I would come to realize that historical criticism needed to be incorporated into a larger hermeneutical project rather than being allowed to subsume all other concerns into itself, as it had tended to do in the period between the emergence of higher criticism and the hermeneutical and methodological explosions of the past few decades.

I finished my doctoral studies and began teaching the Gospel of John, but I was caught up in an intellectual and personal dilemma. On the one hand, I was convinced that the interpretive key to the Fourth Gospel was the evangelist's stated purpose, articulated at 20:30–31, that this Gospel was "written that you [i.e., the reader] may come to believe." It was written from a faith lived in the Johannine community to enable and deepen the faith of the reader in the identity and mission of Jesus, in order that the reader might have "life in his name." On the other hand, I had learned that the only way for a serious, academically trained and responsible scholar to fulfill the stated goal of the evangelist was through historical–critical exegesis, a collection of methods that could tell us a great deal (at the time, I thought a good deal more than I now believe to be the case) about what and who produced the text and what it might have meant to some ancient community, but could not tell us very much at all about what the text was meant to produce—namely, salvific faith in the present. That seemed to be a task assigned to, or reserved for, nonacademics like pastors or saints who were not constrained to or by methodological rigor or the demands of consistency, nor accountable to the high standards of the academy. Unfortunately for my peace of mind, I wanted it all: full engagement in the biblical academy and "life in his name" at the same time. I even wanted these two things to be somehow related in my own experience and work. This is when my mind began to change.

How My Mind Has Changed

Bearing in mind the suspicions about the nature of change that I articulated at the beginning of this reflection, I think I can say that except for this central concern about how an academically responsible and methodologically rigorous study of the Fourth Gospel could mediate a transformative engagement with the biblical text, everything else has changed, whether slightly or radically. In hindsight, I would describe this gradual evolution in terms of several overlapping moves resulting from my involvement in developments in New Testament scholarship in general and Johannine Studies in particular. Although they now seem to have succeeded one another chronologically, there is no clear–cut succession and none canceled out completely what it succeeded. It was a development by way of progressive but selective incorporation rather than substitution.

The first period of change modified my understanding of historical–critical methodology and its contribution to biblical interpretation. Early twentieth–century developments in the field of historiography had a delayed impact upon Biblical Studies, but when that wave did hit the biblical shore it undermined the confidence that had reigned well into the 1950s that somehow, done right, historical criticism could tell us "what really happened" in first–century Palestine. In fact, the ongoing efforts of the Jesus Seminar, and especially some of its spinoffs, including the current debates over the resurrection, testify to the fact that the hope of establishing, if not what actually happened, at least what did not happen is still very much alive in our field.

The unsettling (because it sounded irreverent) question that began to nag at me as I followed this discussion was, "So what?" Suppose we could establish that the Johannine Jesus could not possibly have delivered some of the theological monologues attributed to him, such as the discourses in John 14–17. Would these sublime texts be any less authoritative and enriching for Christian faith and life, any less theologically true and enlightening, indeed even less valuable for our knowledge of Jesus himself, than if Jesus had actually spoken them? However, if they do not come from Jesus himself, where do they come from, and what kind of link is there between the real Jesus, the text, and contemporary Christianity?

But discourses are one thing; historical deeds are another. Writers often put words in a character's mouth that express differently what the character did, in fact, substantively say. Indeed, such imputed speech might be more representative of the character's real meaning than a transcript of any actual discourse. Things, however, actually do or do not happen. What if Jesus did not raise Lazarus from the dead? My own historical–critical work on John 11 has gradually led me to the conclusion that it is highly doubtful that the pre–Easter Jesus raised anyone from the dead. And of the three resuscitation stories in the Gospels, the Lazarus event is probably the least likely to be historically factual (Rochais 1981). If the Johannine text presents the resuscitation of Lazarus as the sign that Jesus' resurrection is the source of resurrection for his followers (that is, that he is indeed "the resurrection and the life"), and if Jesus' direct question to Martha, "Do you believe this?" is actually addressed to the reader, what are the implications of a critically based questioning of the facticity of Lazarus' return from the dead?

A further assault on my confidence in the historical–critical method as a comprehensive or even adequate approach to biblical interpretation came from the growing doubt I shared with many other New Testament scholars about the capacity of historical criticism to establish, even in broad strokes, what really happened concerning Jesus except in basic outline. Jesus was born, but was it in Judea, as Matthew and Luke affirm, or in Galilee, as John implies? He was somehow related to John the Baptizer, but was it biologically, or in the Qumran community or Essene movement, or as a prophetic rival, or as one legitimated by John or vice versa? Jesus exercised a brief public ministry of preaching, teaching, and healing, a year or so in length according to the Synoptics or nearly three according to John. He was arrested and executed by crucifixion through some kind of collusion between the temple authorities and the Roman Empire, represented by Pontius Pilate. And somehow he continued to influence his followers after his death, whether by actually rising from the dead (bodily, physically, spiritually, or communally) or through some kind of collective religious or psychological experience on their part. Almost every element even of this basic outline admits of a variety of descriptions and interpretations. And the few elements that are virtually certain historically are not the most critical. If Jesus had died under some Roman official other than Pontius Pilate or by some method of execution other than crucifixion, the story as formative of Christian faith would not be substantially altered. In other words, most of what really matters—e.g., whether Jesus rose from the dead or whether he is really the

Son of God—cannot be established historically, and most of what can be established historically—e.g., that Jesus died by crucifixion rather than flogging—does not matter a great deal. The question this raises for me is, Are we asking the right question when we ask what really happened?

For most New Testament scholars today, the question of "what really happened" gave way some decades ago to the question of what the author intended to say, whether or not that was a statement about historical facts. Writers use historical material in various ways to convey truth, which does not necessarily equate with historical facts. It might be the case that the writers of the Gospels were more concerned with conveying the meaning of Jesus, his identity and project, and God's intention through Jesus, than recounting historical facts about him as a first–century Jew. If that was the case, perhaps they molded historical data or even traditions about historical events in function of theological concerns. But this would not be a falsification of the data if it was not their intention to convey factual data in the first place. Rather, it would be a reworking of historical material for some well–founded purposes, for example, to respond to the needs of an actual early Christian community or so that readers might come to believe in Jesus and through believing have life in his name.

This led to the modification of the exegetical criterion of "historical facticity" by a related but more nuanced criterion, "authorial intention," as the mediator between what really happened and what the text recounts. The notion of authorial intention was intimately related to the emergence of redaction criticism, which focused attention on the community contexts of the various Gospels which, it was hypothesized, controlled the respective authors' intentions. This led, of course, to a realization that the evangelists were real authors responding in original ways to real situations, rather than scribes cutting and pasting traditional material. The circularity of discerning the author's intention by analysis of the community context and the community context by discernment of the author's intention was partially overcome by the possibility of comparing the Synoptic Gospels in light of the two–source theory, based on the assumption of Markan priority. The parallels and their modifications in each Gospel, especially when a pattern in the modifications in a particular Gospel could be established, allowed a mutually reinforcing pair of hypotheses about what issues in the community to whom the Gospel was addressed elicited from the evangelist particular ways of handling common tradition.

John's Gospel, however, offered formidable resistance to this seemingly fruitful approach, because, in the absence of parallels to much of the Johannine text analogous to the synoptic parallels, the community context of the Fourth Gospel seemed permanently inaccessible. The work of R. Alan Culpepper (1975), who found an external analogue for John's community in the ancient schools; D. Moody Smith, who continued to chronicle and evaluate efforts to relate John to the Synoptics (1992); J. Louis Martyn (1979b) and Raymond E. Brown (1979), who discovered internal evidence about the who, when, and why of John's community; and Robert Fortna, who took a linguistic/theological approach to source and redaction in John (1988) contributed to some progress in this area and grounded some redaction–critical hypotheses about the *Sitz im Leben* of John and therefore the intention of the evangelist in recasting the traditional Jesus material in rather radical ways. Despite the recent substantive questioning of these hypotheses about the nature and history of the Johannine community (see, for example, Reinhartz 2001, 37–53), I continue to think that, as long as they are not pushed too far or absolutized, they are enlightening and, in any case, they are still the most coherent and explanatory model we have. This work on the nature and history of the community, and therefore on the intention of the Fourth Evangelist, has been supplemented and furthered by a renewed inquiry into the historical reliability of the Jesus material in John, spearheaded by Tom Thatcher and Robert Fortna (2001) and now carried forward by an SBL group on "Jesus, John, and History."

But, when all is said and done, what we *cannot* establish historically about the pre–Easter Jesus through the Gospel of John, and about the historical Johannine community and its relation to the historical Jesus, is so much more extensive than what we *can* establish that I have become very reserved about how much time and energy I want to spend on the hunt for the historical Jesus, the historical "John," the historical community, or the relationships among them. I am convinced that there was a real Jesus who lived and died in first–century Palestine, that he rose from the dead, and that he is present in his community today. And I am convinced that there was in the first century a Christian community that had a very unique experience of this risen Jesus, i.e., a unique spirituality that led to the production of a highly original and theologically exciting text that we call the Gospel of John. These convictions are derived not from historical facts empirically established, but are based on the text of a Gospel that I believe is reliable witness to real experience.

This brings me to the second cluster of ways in which my mind has changed, a positive development that was the complement to my eroding confidence in the adequacy, to say nothing of the comprehension, of the historical–critical paradigm and program. Gradually, and at first almost unnoticed by me, I began to shift my attention from historical to literary approaches to the Fourth Gospel. This was not simply a methodological shift, from historical criticism to redaction criticism to structural criticism to narrative criticism. It was a hermeneutical/theological shift in regard to where I was locating revelation as event in the present. I found Gail R. O'Day's work on narrative mode and theological claim in John (1986) enlightening, very persuasive, and highly suggestive. I backed up in John 20:30–31 from the purpose of the Gospel, "that you may believe," to the means that the evangelist suggests will lead to this believing, namely, "these are written." The evangelist seems to be saying that while the words and deeds of the pre–Easter Jesus (the many other signs that Jesus did in the presence of his disciples) were the place, the locus, of the revelatory encounter with God for Jesus' contemporaries, the Gospel text, the things that are written, is the place of encounter, the locus of revelation, for subsequent disciples. What history was for the first disciples, the text is for us. The critical question is not how, *through* the text, we can get "back" to the first century in order to find the pre–Easter Jesus and participate imaginatively in the experience of the first disciples; rather, the question is how *in* the text we can encounter the present and active Jesus, thereby having in our own time and place the same experience, in a different mode, that the first disciples had.

Once I became convinced that the text itself, not some past reality to which the text gave us access, was the locus of revelatory encounter, all the new categories and methods of literary criticism took on fresh significance. Work done on symbolism, irony, characterization, narrative, literary structure, communication theory, and so on now appeared to me less as examinations of rhetorical style and more as constituting the very mode of revelatory disclosure. That, of course, raised the question of how the text was related to its subject matter, namely, Jesus in his life, death, and resurrection. If the text was not primarily a historical record of Jesus' life but a literary creation, and if, equally importantly, the historicity of Jesus was not expendable, how was the text as locus of revelatory encounter to be understood?

My own eventual conclusion was twofold: that *witness* was a better category than historiography for understanding the relationship between the Gospel text and its subject matter; and, that *art* was a better way of understanding how the text functions disclosively than was historiography or expository discourse. Paul Ricouer was the most influential thinker in helping me to bring these conclusions together into a coherent theory of the Gospel as revelatory text (Ricouer 1976; 1980; 1981).

There are few developments in literary theory over the past couple of decades that have not, in some way great or small, enriched my understanding of texts. I am aware that I tend, virtually always now, to reframe positivist historical questions about what really happened or what the evangelist intended, or even what was probably going on in the Johannine community, into textual questions. A question such as, "Did Jesus really raise Lazarus from the dead?" (which I consider unanswerable if the question is one of historical facticity), or even, "What did John intend to say about Lazarus?" (which there is also no way to ascertain), makes more sense to me if reframed as, "What does the text say about the raising of Lazarus and what does that *mean*?" The text narrates a resuscitation by Jesus, but there are many clues in the text itself that this is not a historical description or assertion but a theological exposition about the meaning of human death and eternal life. Working on the text itself as part of the literary work we call the Fourth Gospel, while also making use of any available historical data and even relevant extratextual information including subsequent Christian theology and spirituality, seems to me to be a more fruitful approach to "these are written." There really is, I believe, a world behind the text of the Fourth Gospel, which includes the pre–Easter Jesus and his contemporaries in a particular historical time and place as well as the persons and processes involved in the production of the text, even though these are only partially available to us in and through the text. And there is an ever–expanding world in front of the text, the world of Christian discipleship appropriated and expanded by readers past and present in a variety of textual, artistic, pragmatic, liturgical, and mystical ways, both personal and communal. But the world of or in the text—that is, the range of existential possibilities that opens up in the interaction between reader and text—is the real meaning of the text, a meaning that is not imprisoned in the text to be exhumed by exegesis, not fully determined by the intention of the author, not univocal but relatively undetermined and therefore polyvalent, but also not freely created by the reader unconstrained by the features of the text. The text gives rise to a potentially infinite number of valid interpretations in different readers reading in different contexts, but it is not a wax nose or a Rorschach inkblot.

The proliferation of methods in New Testament Studies is, from my perspective, a blessing rather than a curse. But, like rain, there can be too much of a good thing, especially when it all lands in the same place, and I think we have experienced a few disciplinary mudslides that should warn us all not to build very large structures on unstable ground. Yet insofar as new methods arise from authentically new questions, often brought to the text by new cohorts of readers, they are invaluable in providing new perspectives. As you can see, my move from emphasis on history to attention to the text itself was focusing me more and more on the reader and the work, indeed the art, of reading. Once again, just as focus on the text as literary creation did not render historical questions irrelevant, so attention to the reader and the reading strategy and process has not replaced concentration on the text as text. The process of learning to interpret texts, for me, has not been a succession of discrete stages but a progressive "thickening" or deepening of the meaning of interpretation.

This brings me to two recent developments in Biblical Studies generally and Johannine scholarship in particular that have influenced me in recent years and that I am still learning to incorporate into the work of interpretation. The first is ideology criticism generally and feminist criticism in particular. Ideology criticism in relation to John is indirectly descended from Bultmann's realization that there is no such thing as presuppositionless interpretation. The presuppositions Bultmann felt were impeding the access of modern people to the biblical message were the prescientific presuppositions of the biblical writers, in contrast to what he called the scientific cosmology or worldview of moderns. Ideology criticism is a legitimate descendant of demythologization. It differs in that it is less concerned with views of the physical or natural universe and more concerned with cultural, social, and psychological worldviews, especially as these are controlled by and supportive of power arrangements in family, society, and church.

The first major impact of ideology criticism on New Testament Studies came from feminist scholars, and John's Gospel was a kind of positive foil to the negative attention focused on the Pauline writings about women. Johannine scholars such as Raymond Brown (1979, 183–98) and Martin Hengel (1963, 243–56), who certainly would not have called themselves or been called "feminists," had noticed that John's Gospel, in comparison with the Synoptics and Paul, presents a quantitatively and qualitatively striking picture of women in at least one early Christian community. Not only the mother of Jesus, but the remarkably well–drawn figures of the Samaritan Woman, Martha and Mary of Bethany, Mary Magdalene, and even the textually anomalous "Woman Taken in Adultery" stand out in this Gospel of intimate encounters.

John's Gospel became a privileged site in the attempt to exhume the buried story of women in the early Christian community. Elisabeth Schüssler Fiorenza's monumental *In Memory of Her* (1983) was only the rising of a stream of studies that started as a trickle of articles and has developed into a veritable flood of books, including monographs, commentaries, collections, Festschrifts, and theoretical works. Some of the best younger or newer scholars writing on the Fourth Gospel today, such as Rekha Chennattu, Mary Coloe, Colleen Conway, Dorothy Lee, and Amy–Jill Levine, are women whose feminist sensibilities suffuse their work rather than focusing solely on female figures in John or even on roles of women in the Fourth Gospel. And feminist studies of John are not limited to female authors. Even the question of the gender of the evangelist and/or the Beloved Disciple has been raised anew. I am much indebted to the development of feminist ideology criticism in Johannine Studies, which has sensitized me to the importance of other kinds of ideology criticism that need to be applied to the Fourth Gospel: postcolonial, racial, ethnic, and religious, particularly in regard to the ever–neuralgic issue of the Jews and anti–Judaism in the Gospel of John.

The second recent development in Biblical Studies generally and Johannine Studies in particular that has influenced my work is postmodernism, particularly various types of deconstruction (cf. Adam 2000). I am more ambivalent about this development than about ideology criticism. On the one hand, there seems to me to be no question about the need to destabilize and even subvert the hegemonies that have reigned unquestioned in the biblical academy, not only those that privilege certain readers but also those that privilege, even to the exclusion of other possibilities, certain kinds of reading, including but not restricted to historical criticism. My natural—or developed—tendency to focus primarily on the text and the experience of meaning to which the text gives rise in the present, rather than on the history that is presumed to have given rise to the text, predisposes me to sympathy with philosophical antifoundationalism and resistance to logocentrism.

But my primarily existential interest in the biblical text as a place of faith encounter with God in Jesus makes me leery of deconstruction for its own sake. One might say that the ultimate and most radical instrument of deconstruction is mystical experience that subverts all human constructions of meaning in face of the utter Otherness of God encountered. So, whatever subverts our too–facile and too–absolute constructs and makes us attend to what is marginalized, what does not fit, what our vocabulary cannot handle, what we failed to notice, and especially what the interests of power have made invisible or unspeakable is to be welcomed not only as an aid to honesty but even, perhaps, as a propadeutic to divine encounter. We can be grateful that the anonymous or imperial "we" that exonerates the writer from responsibility for her or his interpretive moves or their results has become increasingly rare in contemporary academic writing, and many of us feel a need to claim, almost tediously, our social location before commencing work, lest we appear to universalize our very particular handling of the text. We recognize the need to deconstruct *ourselves* as fully consistent, if not infallible, subjects; to deconstruct our *sacred texts* as inerrant products of divine inspiration; to deconstruct our *ecclesiastical contexts* as all sufficient frameworks of orthodoxy; and to deconstruct the *canons of our academic guild* as the only rules of the game.

All that being said, however, I find that I still take the biblical text utterly seriously as a privileged locus of encounter with the living God.

While I am willing, even eager, to engage the text with a certain creative abandon, to "play" in a certain sense in the garden of the biblical text in hopes of seeing more and better than I have been taught or formed to see, I am still impelled to take off my shoes before the burning bush of the Word of God. Deconstruction that is used to reduce the text to meaningless rubble, to privilege nihilism over meaning, or to showcase virtuosity at the expense of personal engagement or commitment does not, at least at this point in my career, appeal to me. We often enough have to traverse the desert of apparent meaninglessness in our quest for living water within the biblical text—and John's Gospel is a part of the Bible often especially fraught with ambiguity, seeming inconsistency, apparent or real self–contradiction, and symbolic tangles of many kinds—but I remain committed to the quest for meaning, even for that *bête noir* of deconstructionists, coherence, because I think it is more congenial to the human mind and spirit than chaos, not because we are intellectually lazy, terminally addicted to power, or spiritually degenerate, but because we are made in the image of the Logos of God.

So I may have come full circle back to what has not changed despite all that has, namely, my basic interest in the Bible as sacred Scripture, in John's Gospel as a kind of "holy of holies" in the New Testament because of its extraordinary power to mediate the encounter between God and the reader/hearer through the human being Jesus of Nazareth who is the Word made flesh, and of the importance of scholarship that is open to every development—hermeneutical or methodological—that can facilitate that encounter.

Conclusion

By way of conclusion, I will allude to a discussion that was taking place in the March 2006 *SBL Forum* (online) during the time that I was preparing this essay. A number of scholars were debating whether "faith–based biblical study" is compatible with "academic biblical study." Some of the discussants maintained that the two are incompatible, the former having no legitimate place in the academy even if the scholar were a committed believer. One implied that they are simply unrelated, two entirely different enterprises: one private and nonacademic, the other public and properly academic. And another suggested that the task of the Biblical Studies professor is to facilitate the student's transition from a faith–based to an academic approach, which another reader correctly noted suggests that such a move is from an inferior to a more mature approach to the text. None of the discussants seemed to think that faith is a benighted position that should be rooted out of the student, nor that personal faith in the scholar is necessarily an impediment to objective scholarship. It was even admitted that the vast majority of people who go into Biblical Studies do so because the Bible is somehow a privileged text in their experience. But the discussants seemed to agree that, in the interests of scholarship, faith should be checked at the door of the classroom and retrieved on one's way out.

I considered making my contribution to this book a position paper on this subject but decided that, even though I have been working out the relationship between my love for and commitment to the Bible as sacred Scripture and my equally passionate commitment to biblical scholarship throughout my academic career, it would be more interesting to my readers to simply tell the story of that journey rather than enter into an abstract discussion of the meaning of "faith–based" and/or "academic" in relation to New Testament studies, the validity of the category of "objectivity" in relation to scholarship, or the purpose of religious studies in the program of undergraduates.

It is probably obvious by now that I not only see no contradiction or necessary conflict between faith and scholarship, but also that I can see little real point in devoting a lifetime of study to these relatively ordinary texts (literarily and historically speaking) unless one is convinced that they are anything but ordinary (theologically and spiritually speaking). For me, scholarship expended on the biblical texts, especially on the New Testament texts by a Christian, is not motivated by the desire to "prove" anything about or in the text, because the text is not an arsenal of unassailable theological propositions or even unarguable directives for Christian faith and life. Nor, on the other hand, is biblical scholarship a purely secular, to say nothing of methodologically agnostic or actually atheistic, examination of neutral sources of information. Christian faith can and should be nourished by these texts, and I believe that rigorous scholarship is singularly important and helpful in allowing these texts to perform that function. Faith does not distort scholarship nor does scholarship subvert faith, provided that scholarship is honest, responsible, and oriented to genuine understanding, criteria I find more helpful than the slippery criterion of "objectivity." By *honest*, I mean rigorously faithful to the data, denying nothing that presents itself as true no matter how unsettling or challenging it may be, and affirming what the best available methods of investigation can uncover. Scholarship is *responsible* when it is fully "answerable" to all its appropriate dialogue partners, including other scholars, the believing community, the secular academy, and the larger society affected by what religious communities believe. And for me, the ultimate goal of all genuine scholarship in any field, but especially in something such as Biblical Studies, is *understanding*, in both its epistemological and its ontological senses. Epistemologically, understanding is the dialectical partner of explanation, and this dialectic of explanation and understanding, as Ricouer has taught us, is what gives rise to the event of meaning to which all study, in my view, is finally oriented. But the accumulation of events of meaning generates understanding as a progressively expanded and enriched ontological condition, the characteristically human way of being in this world as concerned and committed participant rather than disinterested observer.

It is this final point, the coincidence of understanding as a progressively more adequate *grasp* of what the biblical text means and understanding as an *expansion of being*, as a person, a disciple of Christ, a citizen of the world, that seems to be what I have grasped and what has grasped me in more than thirty years of struggling with, drinking from, falling short of, being healed by, and making available to others the Gospel of John. When all is said and done, biblical scholarship, and especially Johannine scholarship, is, in my view, a lifelong attempt to appropriate the promise of Jesus in John 8:31–32: "If you continue in my word you are truly my disciples; and you will know the truth, and the truth will make you free."

14: Response

IDEOLOGIES PAST AND PRESENT

Colleen Conway

It was with much pleasure and interest that I read Sandra Schneiders's reflections upon her journey as a scholar of the Fourth Gospel. There is much about which we concur, even if I began my own journey in a much different place and now find myself heading in new directions. Whereas Schneiders's path has taken her from strictly historical questions to more literary and ideological interests, I took a literary approach in my dissertation, but since then I have become ever more interested in the historical dimension of texts. However, my interest in history is ideologically flavored. That is, like Schneiders, I also have been influenced by ideological approaches, and like Schneiders, I am interested in contemporary uses of the biblical text. Thus, the question that arises in the intersection between Schneiders's reflections and my thoughts on future directions in Johannine Studies concerns history, ideology, and contemporary interpretations of the text. In what ways do the ideological forces that helped shape the Fourth Gospel in the past have lasting effects on its interpretation and use in the present?

Clearly, the historical element in this question has little to do with a historical–critical method that might tell us "what really happened." It does not concern the historicity of the Gospel accounts, or of John's Gospel versus the Synoptic Gospels. To be sure, I assume that the Gospels are historical documents and I am interested in them as such. But I am not interested in their historical factuality, nor do I think it critically important for the interpretation of these texts. Instead, I consider that insofar as the Gospel of John was generated in a particular time and place, it is a product of a cultural moment. My historical interests are in the cultural forces or ideologies that produced that moment and led to the particularly Johannine way of shaping a story about Jesus.

Moreover, my interest in the historical dimension of a text such as the Fourth Gospel is not only in how it was produced, but also how it contributed to the production of a particular worldview. Rather than assuming that the text simply reflects its context, I assume a degree of reciprocity between the two. By now, those familiar with "the new historicism" will no doubt see it rearing its paradoxical head in this discussion. Admittedly, this perspective has had a major influence on the way I conceive of history and textuality. And while the "new historicism" is not so new anymore in secular literary studies (it is likely quite passé by now), I still believe we have much to learn by considering the Gospel of John in light of the questions raised by this perspective. Such questions concern the production and circulation of texts, the systems of power represented in this textual production, and how the text participates in the symbolic world of a particular culture.

I can provide one example from my own work. Currently, I am focused on the imperial context of the Gospel writers, in particular the gender ideology that was at the heart of the Roman imperial project. In considering the forces that contributed to the shaping of the Johannine Jesus, I examine the masculine ideology of the empire. Because the ideology of masculinity is so prominent in the rhetoric of the Roman Empire, I cannot imagine a presentation of a divine man—in this case, John's presentation of Jesus—that would not engage this ideology in some way. But I do not assume that the Gospel of John merely reflects this ideology. Instead, its presentation of Jesus suggests a complex relationship of accommodation, adaptation, and resistance to imperial masculinity.

In many respects, the Johannine Jesus takes on the characteristics of a truly masculine ideal (self-control, courage, self-sacrifice for a noble cause). But the Johannine Jesus' ultimate stance against the "ruler of this world" (John 12:31) suggests a resistance to imperial authority. Most likely, the author intends this phrase as a reference to the devil, but this does not exclude a reference to the emperor as well—indeed, most people hearing "the ruler of this world" in the first-century Mediterranean context would think first of the emperor. In this way, the Fourth Gospel participates in the broader gender ideology of its culture, but at the same time resists the primary representative of the imperial masculine ideal.

This brings me to the second part of my question. Once we are aware of the ideological forces that contributed to the shaping of the text (and gender ideology is just one example), can we also be attuned to how such ideologies affect our interpretations in the present? Are there places where we can name these ideologies and resist them in our own interpretations? Feminist scholars have intuitively attempted to do this in their emphasis on Jesus as Wisdom—another thread that runs through the Fourth Gospel. But a new historical approach would make a more conscious effort to unmask these ancient ideologies and examine the interpreter's role in perpetuating them.

Schneiders suggests that, for her, the primary reason to study the text is because it is a vehicle of revelation. Whatever one's position is in regard to the revelatory power of the text, I would contend (and I think Schneiders would agree) that we need to be critically aware of the cultural rhetoric that is adopted to communicate that revelation. Such rhetoric has the power to construct a particular cultural reality, especially given the status of the text as sacred Scripture. In other words, to return to the beginning, whether or not the events recorded in the Fourth Gospel ever happened, what does happen is the creation of a worldview in which there are insiders and outsiders, above and below, children of God and children of the devil. For me, how we engage that world, in the midst of our contemporary one, makes all the difference with respect to determining the revelatory significance of the text.

Finally, the point at which I disagree most strongly with Schneiders's reflections is in regard to her discussion of faith, scholarship, and the study of sacred texts such as the Fourth Gospel. She remarks that she "can see little real point in devoting a lifetime of study to these relatively ordinary texts (literarily and historically speaking) unless one is convinced that they are anything but ordinary (theologically and spiritually speaking)." But I personally can readily imagine someone who does not find the text so extraordinary "theologically and spiritually speaking," but still finds it quite extraordinary "historically speaking." One could argue that texts that address a divine presence at work in the lives of human beings, or even the idea of a god taking on human form, are not particularly unusual in the ancient world, even if such texts are not an exact match to the Fourth Gospel. On the other hand, most would agree that what is anything but ordinary is the cultural capital that this text has wielded in the history of its existence. That, in itself, is worth examining, with or without confessing belief in the content of the Fourth Gospel. Many people find this narrative (and the Bible in general) profoundly interesting, even if they do not approach it from a confessional stance. Johannine scholarship, indeed biblical scholarship, would miss the contributions of such scholars should they decide that the study of this text, as an extraordinary cultural and historical phenomenon, was not worth their time.

CHAPTER 15

JOHANNINE STUDIES AND THE GEOPOLITICAL
REFLECTIONS UPON ABSENCE AND IRRUPTION

Fernando F. Segovia

In accounting for the absence of an imperial–colonial focus in early Christian studies, Richard Horsley has repeatedly emphasized a fundamental discursive connection between, on the one hand, the erasure of the geopolitical in the interpretive history of the early Christian writings and historical constructions of the early Christian movement and, on the other hand, a set of basic tenets underlying modern Western ideology in the eighteenth through the twentieth centuries. The most developed and pointed formulation of this linkage is found, to my mind, in Horsley's introduction to the 2001 Rauschenbush Lectures given at Colgate–Rochester Theological School, subsequently published under the title *Jesus and Empire* (Horsley 2003, 1–14). In his proposal, while not altogether unproblematic as formulated, I find a most suitable point of departure for my own reflections upon the role of the geopolitical in Johannine Studies, and toward this end I recall its main postulates.[1]

Horsley's argument begins by foregrounding three key assumptions of Western modernity: the separation between religion and society, the

---

[1] I find it problematic insofar as the postulates are presented as markers of the West in too straightforward a fashion, that is, without critical analysis. To be fair, Horsley does move in the direction of deconstruction, pointing to the gulf between claim and reality. I would argue for a more incisive step in this regard.

primacy of the individual, and the recourse to essentialist categories of classification. First, and indeed foremost, Western thought shifted religion from the public to the private sphere, thereby removing it from political and economic affairs and confining it to the realm of personal faith and piety. Second, Western thinking emphasized the individual over the communal, divorcing human beings from their social and cultural contexts. Third, Western thought relied upon essentialist definitions of ethnicity, nationality, and culture, rendering all such concepts apolitical in the process. Horsley goes on to outline immediate and significant repercussions of the projection of these postulates onto the world of antiquity. In keeping with the received focus on religious concerns, the study of early Christianity bypassed its political and economic dimensions. Similarly, in light of the established wedge between the individual and the communal, such study approached early Christianity in terms of key actors and religious disputes, in isolation from the social–cultural forces and relations in which such debates and figures were embedded and with which they interacted. Lastly, following the dominant influence of essentialism, such study construed early Christianity as a universal and spiritual religion emerging from the local and ethnic religion of Judaism, overriding thereby the gamut of political variations within both "religions."

Not surprisingly, given the sum total of this overarching disciplinary focalization—its religious approach to early Christianity, its concern with individual characters and religious controversies, and its stereotypical evaluation of Jewish–Christian relations—Horsley regards the absence of the geopolitical in early Christian studies as inevitable and determinative in two ways. At the level of the writings and the movement, he notes, critical analysis of early Christian perceptions of, and responses to, the imperial–colonial framework of Rome has been decidedly minimal, as has critical attention to the dynamics of Roman rule over subject territories and peoples and the reactions of such peoples and lands. At the level of academic interpretation, critical reflection upon the use of the biblical writings in the imperial–colonial projects of the West or the relation of the discipline of Biblical Studies vis-à-vis such frameworks has been practically nonexistent. Horsley himself has brought these judgments to bear on Historical Jesus Studies (Horsley 2003) as well as Pauline Studies (Horsley 1997, 1–8). It is a judgment that I find easily transferable to Johannine Studies as well.

MISSING THE GEOPOLITICAL

Indeed, the gap of the geopolitical is just as pronounced in Johannine scholarship, not only in terms of textual production (the exposition of the

Gospel in light of the cultural and social matrix of the text), but also with respect to textual reception (scholarship's vision of and stance toward the Gospel as interpreted in light of its own cultural and social matrices). I find it fair to say, as a rather seasoned observer of Johannine Studies, that the academic interpretation of the Fourth Gospel—whether informed by the more traditional historical approaches or the more recent literary and sociocultural readings—has, by and large, operated out of a critical framework that ultimately draws on the assumptions of modern Western ideology identified by Horsley. Such scholarship has certainly favored religious and theological matters to the detriment of encompassing political and economic affairs, has emphasized the religious tenor of the encounter between the circle of Jesus and his followers and various groups and figures, and has concentrated, whether in support or in challenge, on the process of the separation of the Johannine "community/ies" from its/their parent religious base in the Jewish "synagogue," particularly the origins, dynamics, and ramifications of this split.

The reasons for such a reigning framework are not hard to ascertain. At the level of the "text," two observations are in order. First, the Fourth Gospel is a decidedly religious writing—a text concerned with a world of divine beings, a world of human beings, and the nexus of relations between these worlds. It is also a writing that revolves around conflict, not only between the spiritual and material worlds but also within the material world itself. Inevitably, such conflict takes on a profoundly religious tinge. Second, the Gospel's biographical account of Jesus as Word of God—written at a later time, in a different location, and under different circumstances—is situated and developed in the regions of Galilee and Judea, so that the story and discourse of the narrative, its *what* and *how*, are suffused with elements from the Jewish tradition: its peoples and group formations, its cultural and social surroundings, its beliefs and practices. Consequently, the pivotal conflict also takes on a distinctly Jewish tinge. At the level of "criticism," the interpretive tradition has been determined for decades now by the working hypothesis of a break/expulsion of the Johannine "community" from the Jewish "synagogue." This rupture involves a dialectical relationship along the following lines: on the side of the community, developing and irreconcilable beliefs regarding the figure of Jesus, his identity and role, and problematic practices arising out of such beliefs; on the side of the synagogue, measures taken by the authorities to deal with such developments in their midst. The result of such conflict is the religious separation of Christianity from Judaism.

Within this interpretive model, moreover, the Gospel narrative emerges as a mixture of material coming from two different historical stages and bearing two distinct, though not always easily separable, literary layers: a first phase/level, the once–upon–a–time, represented by the actual ministry of Jesus; a second phase/level, the now–and–here, constituted by the subsequent experience of a Christian community. As such, the Gospel of John becomes a writing in which later Johannine material has been projected onto early Jesus material, yielding a biographical account that constructs an imagined past in light of a living present and that functions as a site of struggle for the Johannine community. In the end, the established critical framework comes about as the result of a symbiotic relationship between a particular construction of the narrative world of the Fourth Gospel and the critical focalization of what might be characterized, given the enduring influence of its founder, as the "Martyn legacy."

The ramifications of this approach for Johannine Studies are easily discernible. In terms of critical attention, the underlying geopolitical matrix involving the imperial–colonial framework of Rome and its impact on the production of the Fourth Gospel has not been addressed in any sort of sustained and systematic fashion. Rome may be said to hover in the background as a massive yet unattended presence. As a result, a number of important concerns lie dormant. How directly or indirectly does the Fourth Gospel deal with and look upon such an imperial presence? How does the text's undeniable, and indeed primary, religious dimension relate to the cultural and social in general and the political and the economic in particular? What transpires when a geopolitical perspective is deployed in the analysis of the Gospel narrative—its settings and conflicts, its characters and formations, its agenda and rhetoric?

In terms of critical discourse, the relationship of Johannine scholarship to a variety of geopolitical matrices, and hence the impact of modern and postmodern imperial–colonial frameworks on the academic reception of the Gospel, has gone singularly unpursued. Here, too, Empire may be said to hover in the background as an imposing but unmasked presence. A number of key questions remain unasked. How does the critical tradition represent and evaluate the presence and role of Rome in the Gospel narrative? What are the subsequent applications and ramifications of such Gospel constructions, most specifically in terms of agenda and rhetoric, in the Christian tradition, across the board? What is the position of the critical tradition regarding its location, character, and interests as a literary product within imperial–colonial frameworks of its own?

Yet, a major change is presently underway. In the course of the 1990s, a further formation of ideological criticism, already well developed in academic circles since the late 1970s, entered the discursive framework of Biblical Studies: postcolonial criticism, with its focus on geopolitics and, more specifically, on the differential relations of power (domination and subordination) at work within imperial–colonial frameworks (Moore and Segovia 2005, 1–22). Its impact on the discipline has been swift and extensive; this is certainly true of its application to the texts and contexts of early Christianity. Interestingly enough, Johannine Studies has played—relatively speaking, given the still incipient character and limited output of such criticism—a leading role in this regard.

Finding the Geopolitical

The move toward a postcolonial outlook in Johannine scholarship is directly linked to the work of Musa W. Dube, whose publications in this area have been numerous and ongoing, including a series of articles in a variety of venues (Dube 1996; 1998; 2000a), all of which are informed and guided by a postcolonial feminist reading of the Bible (Dube 2000b), and a collection of essays, coedited with Jeffrey L. Staley, titled *John and Postcolonialism* (Dube and Staley 2002). Dube's research has set an expansive and foundational framework, methodological as well as theoretical, for any and all further application of the postcolonial optic in Johannine scholarship. All such work reflects, in varying degrees, a multidimensional reading of the text alongside its interpretations and interpreters, modern and postmodern. Such is the case with Dube herself, who focuses both on various passages in the Fourth Gospel and on interpretations within the academy and among African women readers. It is also the case with the contributors to the volume on *John and Postcolonialism*, which includes studies devoted primarily to the text (Staley; Glass; Liew), others concerned with interpretations and interpreters (Huie–Jolly; Guardiola–Sáenz), and a third group that deal with both text and interpretations/interpreters jointly (Lozada; Kim; Reinhartz).

Despite the long–established critical framework, outlined earlier, it should not be surprising that the Gospel of John has attracted such attention. As I have argued in my postcolonial commentary on John (Segovia 2007), the Fourth Gospel is a writing in which the postcolonial problematic is very much in evidence, both prominent and pervasive. It is a writing preeminently religious in nature, but also decidedly political—one that highlights and problematizes, through its primary religious concerns and pursuits, its political context of production. This it does, as I have further argued, through portrayals of conflict at a variety of levels, all of which are interrelated: locally, through regional conflict among various groupings within colonial Palestine; globally, through geopolitical conflict between the colonial and the imperial within the Roman Empire; cosmically, through mythical conflict between suprahuman powers within reality as a whole. Over and beyond the regional or "national" conflict lie both a geopolitical or "international" struggle and a mythical or "transworldly" struggle. Within this overall scenario, moreover, the contending sides on each level, represented in diametrical opposition to one another, line up alongside their counterparts at the other levels in a joint multidimensional encounter. What was needed to bring the global dimension of the Gospel, and its relationship to the local and cosmic dimensions, into proper relief was a different critical lens—the postcolonial angle. Only then would a corresponding shift—or, more accurately, expansion—in interpretive framework, already afoot, take place: a discovery of the shadow of Rome and Empire as englobing and controlling matrices for the Fourth Gospel and for Johannine Studies, respectively.

I should like to reflect upon the beginnings of this emerging critical framework—its positions, its findings, its ramifications—through the collection on *John and Postcolonialism*. I do so for a variety of reasons. First, in laying out a vision for the postcolonial optic in Biblical Studies, I have argued for parallel analysis of the ancient texts, the modern and postmodern readings of such texts, and the modern and postmodern readers behind such readings (Segovia 1998, 56–63). The task envisioned thus qualifies as an exercise in the second dimension of this programmatic vision—a critical give–and–take with, in this case, contemporary interpreters. Second, in my postcolonial commentary on the Fourth Gospel I approached the text directly, without engaging other applications of the postcolonial lens. Here, then, I seek to provide this sort of critical interchange. Lastly, as a collection of studies, *John and Postcolonialism* brings a broad array of voices and interests to bear on the Fourth Gospel within a common interpretive field of vision. Thus, my interaction with these essays will provide a fine opportunity for critical exchange with a wide range of entrées, results, and consequences.

As is the case with any postcolonial exposition of the Gospel of John, such dialogue with other postcolonial readings cannot but have in mind the enormous complexity of postcolonial discourse, with its many variations and profound disagreements on every area of investigation or topic of discussion. To think of the postcolonial approach as essentially incontrovertible—a fairly set method, with a largely established set of procedures; grounded on a fairly secure theoretical foundation, with a mostly undisputed set of postulates; and deployed with a rather distinctive purpose in mind, sporting a largely agreed upon set of aims—would constitute a serious misrepresentation of its discursive apparatus and trajectory. It is much better, therefore, to speak, not of an interpretive "method," but of a postcolonial "optic" or "lens" or "angle" within which the reader, implicitly or explicitly, takes a position on any number of moves and paths, methodological as well as theoretical. Consequently, I should like to structure my reflections upon *John and Postcolonialism* around certain major areas of discussion: the meaning and scope of the "postcolonial," the specific slant and approach adopted, the results derived with regard to Christian community and Roman Empire, and the critical stance taken vis–à–vis such findings.

Representing the Geopolitical

To begin with, a word about the volume as a whole is in order regarding its presentation and its structure. *John and Postcolonialism* opens with an introductory essay whose subtitle, "Travel, Space, and Power in John," readily brings to the fore the major topics of discussion addressed by the contributors (Dube and Staley 2002). The structure of the book is explained in a brief foreword. The leading essay is an early reflection upon the Johannine sense of "place" by Tod Swanson (Swanson 2002), chosen because of its influence on Dube and Staley themselves in their own initial postcolonial explorations of the Gospel; their articles immediately follow. As it turns out, however, this is a somewhat problematic editorial move, as the other contributions establish no connection whatever with this piece and Dube's article is not at all in conversation with Swanson. The placement of the other studies reflects a combination of narrative sequence and overall focus: a series of central essays on particular units of the Gospel of John (chs. 5, 8, 15), followed by two concluding essays of general scope.

At the heart of postcolonialism, the introduction argues, lies the concept of "traveling," involving a crossing of boundaries (the notion of space) and the ensuing contested relationships between colonizers and colonized (the notion of power). All three concepts—movement, boundaries, power relations—are thus interrelated and interdependent. The movement arises among the "visited" or colonized, who seek to claim their humanity and to liberate their geographical spaces, mapped by the "visitors" or colonizers as in darkness, without power, devoid of God. The movement continues as the colonized become "visitors" in turn, venturing into the geographical spaces of the colonizers, now the "visited," though as powerless rather than powerful, travelers. Such struggles for power, unleashed by traveling into other geographical spaces, mark not only the contemporary world but also the narrative of John. Now as in the past, "heavens" are imagined, repositories of "light" and "knowledge," which propel such traveling, both by way of "descent" and "ascent," and engender conflict, in the face of projected "darkness" and "ignorance." Such power struggles lie, the introduction continues, at the core of postcolonial readings: they analyze, across history and culture, the layout and consequences of "heavens"—how domination is constructed and legitimized by the colonizer, how the colonized react to such domination (collaboration; resistance; assertion of rights), and how the colonizer and the colonized engage in travel. Postcolonial readings examine, therefore, how writings contribute to colonization or decolonization, out of concern for justice in the world and with the aim of advancing ways of coexistence without oppression or exploitation.

Such a reading of the Gospel of John, the introduction explains, stands behind the collection. At the level of exposition, the essays in *John and Postcolonialism* examine the traveling that takes place within the narrative and its ramifications—the relations of power established on earthly spaces as a result of such journeying. At the level of criticism, the articles examine the traveling undertaken by readers of the Gospel as they journey into the narrative and interpret the relations of power at work therein in the light of their own geographical spaces and power relations. On the one hand, therefore, the Fourth Gospel emerges as a site of struggle for power, written from one perspective of the conflict (that of "heaven")—emphasizing the power of the Word, speaking for all the "visited," and thus in need of close attention. On the other hand, readers are denied any neutrality in their journeys, either with regard to the Gospel (and its "heaven") or within their own geographical spaces (and their "heavens"). This twofold thrust the different contributors are said to pursue in different ways and from different contexts. At the same time, all are described as engaged in their own geographical struggles for liberating power, in search of a space in which individuals from different worlds can share in the construction of a "world of liberating interdependence."

In light of this envisioned project, the choice of Swanson's article as a leading essay proves at once understandable and curious. Quite curious, in two respects: (1) it is not situated within a postcolonial problematic, not directly anyway, but rather within a discursive juncture involving history of religious studies and Christian studies, and (2) it is not grounded in Johannine Studies but rather touches upon the Gospel of John as a move in a critique of such a juncture. In effect, Swanson argues that the morphological study of religions advocated by Mircea Eliade, involving a disjunction of traditional religious symbols and ethnic sacred places, is itself ultimately based on the Christian claim to universality and transplantation, for which John provides strong support. At the same time, Dube and Staley's choice of Swanson's essay as a frontispiece is readily understandable, given Swanson's reading of "place" in John and his approach toward Western attitudes regarding place.

In the face of a perceived rupture of social harmony as a result of separation from God, signified by multiple attachments of ethnic identities to sacred places, the Gospel of John—in line with broader Hellenistic thinking regarding ethnic diversity and divine unity—advances a Jesus who, as the Word of God, points to a spiritual place in the Father's house, thereby putting an end to all sacred topographies of the world and gathering all peoples together under the one God in a community of the end times. Such a radical project, carried out through reverse reen-actments of foundational events by local heroes establishing ethnic dif-ferentiation and sacred places (John 4 and 6), yields a Christian claim to all territories. Such a claim, in turn, bears enormous consequences, for example, the disenfranchisement of natives who convert (the Samari-tans) and charges of betrayal and murder against those who reject (the "Jews"). The result of abolishing the need for private places, Swanson argues, was clear: "room for unity had actually shrunk, relatedness was asphyxiated, and divisiveness exacerbated" (2002, 28). This legacy from the Fourth Gospel and Christian Origins in general, Swanson adds, was appropriated by the West in its own collapse of ethnic space within the historical project of colonialism: having no sense of its own distinctive ethnic space, it approached all other places as "mission fields"; without a framework for mediating relations of respect, it sought to "over[run] the globe" (2002, 29).

It is precisely such a sense of universality and transplantation, rooted in early Christianity and central to the West, that underlies the proj-ect of morphological comparison of religions and the vision of a new humanism espoused by Mircea Eliade. Here, the true meaning of place may be abstracted from local sacred places, which merely serve to shed light on "place" as a universal category of human imagination. The result of such endeavor is, again, a thorough coopting of indigenous symbols, marked by the impoverishment of unity and a trampling of respect. Con-sequently, Swanson concludes, the presence of place should be viewed as irreplaceable and its meaning as not transferable—"rituals are irreplace-able responses to irreplaceable places" (2002, 30–31). In the end, there-fore, the utopian hope should not be pursued—nor, by implication, the project of colonialism or the comparison of Eliade.

The significance attached to Swanson's essay by the editors of *John and Postcolonialism* can be readily appreciated. First, Swanson's study bears specifically on the Gospel of John and its discursive ideology of spatial construction—a coopting of all sacred spaces and ethnic formations by Christian universality and transplantation. Second, the article further establishes a direct link between John and the West, specifically in terms of the colonialist ideology of spatial construction—the overriding of all spaces and all peoples. Third, Swanson indicts a standing scholarly frame-work of the West involved in the comparison of religions—a devaluation of the local and the ethnic. Finally, it is a study that adopts a critical stance in the face of such discursive and historical projects, demanding attention to spaces and ethnicities and the deployment of an ethos of respect. In other words, Swanson's political reading of the Gospel of John and the West alike represent the beginnings of a move toward a postcolonial problematic. For the editors, Swanson identifies and critiques the "heavens" imagined by John and the West while pointing to a different "heaven" marked by inclusion and coexistence. Such foregrounding and evaluation, in effect, the collection aims to continue in full force within Johannine Studies.

Engaging the Geopolitical

My dialogue with this concerted exercise in the crucible of Johannine Studies and postcolonial studies will begin with a general reflection on whether and how the contributors to *John and Postcolonialism* deal with a central and controverted question in postcolonial discourse: the force and reach of the concept as such. What does it mean when the term "postcolonialism" is invoked? What is the scope envisioned for this term, transhistorically and crossculturally? From these questions, I shall proceed to analyze briefly each essay in the volume in terms of its overall mode and approach, its reading of the Johannine stance on community and world, and the stance it adopts toward such a reading.

Meaning and Scope of the Postcolonial

On the twofold question of the meaning and scope of "postcolonial," I find a broad range of positions. At one end of the spectrum, two studies deal directly with such issues (Dube; Reinhartz); at the other end, four essays largely bypass these issues in favor of other discursive concerns and frameworks, including displacement (Staley), nationhood (Glass), borders (Guardiola–Sáenz), and identity (Liew). All such topics, to be sure, form part of a postcolonial optic, but they are neither introduced nor theorized as such. In the middle, three studies reveal a working definition, but only indirectly so: Lozada (relation of superiority/inferiority), Huie–Jolly (position of domination and universality), and Kim (fragmentation of context). The most explicit positions of Dube and Reinhartz are worth examining in closer detail.

Adele Reinhartz's view of the meaning and scope of the term "postcolonial" is less developed than that of Dube; it is, however, to the point on both scores. Drawing upon one theoretical perspective (Ashcroft et al. 1989), Reinhartz defines meaning and scope directly: the former as what follows the onset of colonization, hence a historical–political category; the latter as involving the study of history and literature from cultures affected by European imperialism. This definition, however, raises another key problem: can "postcolonialism" be applied prior to or outside of European imperial–colonial frameworks? Reinhartz's solution to this quandary is swift and pragmatic: because the texts of the New Testament were composed under the imperial–colonial framework of Rome, the application of a postcolonial approach is justified.

Musa Dube's definition of the meaning and scope of the term "postcolonial" is more substantial than that of Reinhartz, yet not as directly to the point on either score. The issue of scope can be readily ascertained. Pointing to a variety of theoretical perspectives (Maunier 1949; Said 1993; wa Thiong'o 1986), Dube characterizes imperialism as an "ancient institution," with a lineage traced from the ancient near eastern empires through the Greeks and the Romans to the modern European empires and the contemporary imperialism of globalization. What is common to all such formations is an ideology of expansion—a quest to impose control, via the use of diverse forms and methods at different times, over foreign geographical spaces and their populations. The relationship between colonizer and colonized is one of domination and subordination, yielding suppression of diversity and promotion of universal standards. Imperialism, consequently, is transhistorical and crosscultural. The issue of meaning can be readily inferred. Within imperial–colonial frameworks, Dube posits imperializing or expansionist, as well as decolonizing or liberative, strategies. The postcolonial constitutes the decolonizing impulse, thus a social–psychological category: that which problematizes and resists imperialism.

In sum, on the question of the meaning and scope of the term "postcolonialism," the collection is not sufficiently grounded, and its applicability to the early Christian writings is basically presupposed. Only Dube advances a rationale for such an approach to John: imperialism as an "ancient" and enduring phenomenon, with Rome as salient example. The force of the postcolonial, when invoked, is essentially taken for granted. Only Dube suggests a position: resistance. This aspect of the conjunction between academic discourses, understandable as an early exercise therein, stands in need of further development.

Critical Findings

In repeated references to the postcolonial world, Jeffrey Staley's article invokes a set of constitutive material conditions that include globalization processes, diasporic communities, rhizomic fragments, and, above all, displacement. Indeed, the concept of "dis–place"—whose theoretical source is identified but not expounded on—is central to Staley's study. Given his own keen sense of displacement, Staley discloses his interest in the politics of place, which leads him to examine his multidimensional experience of "dis–place" within the United States and the Fourth Gospel's representation of "dis–place" within the Roman Empire. His study thus becomes a comparative analysis of and reflection upon the concept of place in Johannine ideology and scholarship, as well as in his own family history and personal experience.

What Staley finds in emerging studies of place in the Fourth Gospel is agreement on "uprooting": Jesus as spiritualizing the land of Israel (Burge 1994) or laying claim to all lands (Swanson 2002). Behind these studies, Staley finds contemporary political preoccupations at work: in the case of Burge, the consequences of land replacement for American evangelical views of the Palestinian–Israeli conflict; in that of Swanson, the ramifications of land delegitimization for all local religions. Both see John as dis–placing place, although such a move is evaluated quite differently: positively by Burge (place as unimportant); negatively by Swanson (place as irreplaceable). Both readings posit a Gospel ultimately in the service of "colonialist" and "hegemonic" agendas. Instead, Staley suggests, John might be viewed as advancing a "postcolonial geography" that is neither "imperialistic" nor "territorial": a scenario in which all, including Jesus, are victims of Rome, where no place is uniquely privileged as the site of divine presence and power, where all are dis–placed, and where God stands on the side of the oppressed. Staley proposes, in other words, a reading nurtured by the Gospel of John yet resistant to its hard edges.

Such a reading of John, offered by way of intimation, Staley relates to a reading of his own history of "dis–placement"—from the historical westward migrations of his farming ancestors in the nineteenth and twentieth centuries as part of the national story of the United States, through his political upbringing as a child of fundamentalist missionaries in a Navajo reservation in Arizona, to his present personal and familial migrations in search of employment. This history leads him to a twofold sense of place involving attachment to (without irreplaceability) and detachment from place (without spiritualization)—a politics of place that is, always and at once, at home and on the way. From such a vantage point, he ventures, now in the face of a postcolonial world of ever increasing globalization and diasporas, perhaps the Gospel of John can be approached not as a charter for the "dis–placement" of all but as a witness to the "liberation" of all. In the end, a conflicted Gospel, to be sure, but one that can be read, politically, on behalf of the alienated and the dispossessed.

Musa Dube's essay, after positing imperializing as well as decolonizing strategies in all imperial–colonial frameworks and identifying the latter as the postcolonial impulse, calls for analysis of textual production along such lines and for a reading of such production with liberation in mind. Culture figures prominently in the ideology of expansion and in reactions to it. "Imperializing" texts convey the representations and values of imperialism, seeking to promote traveling and to tame the geographical and mental spaces of the colonized. Toward this end, the female gender proves a key feature, not only through the representation of colonized women as such but also in its application to the colonized as a whole. "Decolonizing," which involves reading old texts as well as writing new ones, exposes the relation of domination and exploitation, lays out ways of resistance, and advances alternative visions of relation. Given the centrality of gender throughout her study, Dube's approach is characterized as "feminist postcolonial."

In Dube's view, the postcolonial optic is applicable to biblical criticism in two respects: first, insofar as the texts emerged from an imperial–colonial framework; second, in view of the subsequent use of the Bible as an imperializing text in Western imperial–colonial frameworks. A two-fold decolonizing strategy is thus in order—a criticism attentive to the ideology of the texts themselves (issues of travel, space, and power) and also to the function of the texts in imperial projects (the issue of compatibility). Dube focuses on John 4 as a test case—a "mission" or travel narrative, involving a native (Samaritan) woman, whereby movement across geographical spaces is sanctioned and geopolitical power is deployed. Dube's focus is not on the deployment of the Gospel of John in western expansionism—that is assumed, qua mission text—but rather on the ideological perspective of the text. John 4 is first analyzed as a geopolitical product, and then a critique is advanced from the perspective of the Third World.

Dube's analysis proceeds by way of a close reading of interrelated ideological components in the narrative: imperial setting (occupation yielding a struggle for power among local groups and a turn to Samaria by the Christian group); masked agenda (expansionism concealed by Samaritan invitation); approval of traveling (superiority of Christianity: authority to enter, teach, control); representation of geography and lands (spatial hierarchy: world as negative; Jesus as Savior); characterization (inferior knowledge and invalid faith of Samaria); stance on inclusion and equality (devaluation, replacement, and suppression of the local by the global); gendering (woman and land equated as point of entry); and generic adaptation (inequality of betrothal). The result is a view of John 4 as "imperializing," a text in which a broad array of literary and rhetorical strategies of domination yield a thoroughly intertwined imperial and patriarchal ideology. Dube's critique, correspondingly postcolonial and feminist, is offered by way of a rewriting of the story by a contemporary woman author from Botswana, Mositi Totontle (Totontle 1993). Here, against the context of mine labor immigration and the breakdown of family life in southern Africa, John 4 is reenvisioned as a meeting between two women—one a faith healer and preacher; the other, a despised and outcast local woman. The result is a rereading of John 4 as "decolonizing," a text that creates a space for affirmation, interconnections, and self–realization.

For Dube, mission texts such as John 4 advance geopolitical relations of domination rather than of liberation and thus fit well into imperial–colonial projects. The task of contemporary critics, situated within a global imperial–colonial framework of our own, is to promote decolonization: to offer rereadings of such texts that uncover the ethos of domination and the relations of power at work, and to pen new texts that foster diversity and imagine relations of interdependence. Such is precisely the goal of this essay and of Dube's postcolonial feminist approach in general. Dube's evaluation of John 4 is clear: within a conflicted imperial–colonial world, the text adopts an unrelenting "imperializing" position toward others and is thus to be resisted.

For Francisco Lozada Jr., to read "postcolonially" is to read with liberation in mind, on all fronts and for all peoples, and thus with a vision of a world without the dynamics and legacy of colonialism. Such a reading opts for peace rather than violence and entails ideological analysis of both texts and readings of texts, with the goal of understanding where both stand vis–à–vis the geopolitical problematic. Should either the text or an interpretation thereof (or both) be found wanting in this regard, aligned with the forces of domination rather than of coexistence, an ethical critique is imperative. Such is the intent of Lozada's study of John 5: a postcolonial reading of both the chapter and of a particular interpretation of it from the perspective of Christian missions, with the latter as a point of departure.

Lozada focuses on E. W. Huffard's 1989 essay "Mission and the Servants of God," which finds in the Fourth Gospel in general and in John 5 in particular a solid foundation for the conversion of Muslims. Viewed from this perspective, the Gospel of John is, in effect, an evangelistic tract with emphasis on Jesus' words (close to the Muslim notion of revelation), and chapter 5 provides an ideal theological model of servanthood. Against this reading, Lozada undertakes an extended examination of John 5 as a rhetorical example of *anagnorisis* or "recognition"—a call to true knowledge of Jesus on the part of intratextual as well as extratextual readers. At the heart of this *anagnorisis*, Lozada finds a relation of superiority and inferiority: a hierarchical representation of the Christian community as above all others. He further finds that Huffard has faithfully appropriated this proposed relationship as a charter and pattern for contemporary evangelism, with Christianity portrayed as above all other religions: in effect, a colonialist reading of a colonialist writing, a twofold exercise in cultural imperialism. The consequences of such a position are clear and dangerous: an either/or opposition, in which those who side with Jesus are signified as children of God and those who side against Jesus stand as children of Satan. In the face of such findings, Lozada proceeds to ethical critique: against absolutism, recognizing the relationality of all truth claims; against exclusivism, disavowing the conversion of other religious cultures; against assimilation, espousing pluralism, with respect for different identities. In sum, John 5 is a thoroughly colonialist text and must be thoroughly resisted.

One finds in Marie Huie–Jolly's essay no exposition of a postcolonial approach as such, only a concrete application. Her study brings together two texts: the Gospel of John, through the filter of the debate between Jesus and the "Jews" in 5:10–47, and the Maori in New Zealand from the 1830s through the early 1900s, through a recurring—though by no means universal—self–definition as "Jews" rather than "Christians." This conjunction is based not on explicit intertextuality, for no claim is made of direct Maori invocation of John 5, but on parallel Christological constructions involving similar Christian claims of superiority and dominance. Huie–Jolly's study thus undertakes a twofold ideological analysis of universalizing claims at work in both the Gospel of John and among the Maori, with the aim of examining why Maori Christians would refer to themselves as "Jews," a term signifying unbelief in the Gospel of John and in early Christianity generally.

On the one hand, a critical analysis of John 5 surfaces an absolute claim to the divine sonship of Jesus, with those who reject such a claim, the "Jews," placed outside the fold and under divine judgment. Behind the chapter's forensic framework, Huie–Jolly argues, lies a feud between a marginal Johannine group and the authorities of "synagogue observant Judaism." On the other hand, critical analysis of the Maori situation brings out the imperial–colonial framework of Great Britain and thus exposes a people facing a close imperial connection between government and religion: absolute claim to power in administration, a colonial rule marked by alienation from the land; absolute claim to power in religion, a missionary Christianity grounded in the divine sonship of Jesus as enshrined in the Western creeds. The result is a view of those who refuse such claims as outside the realm and unbelievers. Behind this social framework lie the enormous economic and political apparatus of imperial rule and the role of Christianity as the normative religion. Thus, what had been the absolute claim of marginal Johannine Christology has now become the absolute claim of dominant Western Christendom. Consequently, the self–conferral of the term "Jews" by some Maori becomes for

Huie–Jolly an act of resistance and empowerment in the face of colonialism, a leaving behind of "the way of the Son" through identification with both the Israelites of the Hebrew Bible, a people captive and dominated by a foreign ruler, and the "Jews" of the Fourth Gospel and other early Christian writings, unbelievers who would not bow to absolute power.

While Huie–Jolly's study is primarily devoted to critical exposé, setting forth the power relations at work in early Christian texts and Western creedal statements, a driving sense of purpose may be fleetingly captured when she addresses the present consequences of John 5: its negative characterization of "the Jews" reinforces anti–Judaism; its absolutism threatens indigenous cultures and alternative responses; its forensic dimension lays blame on those who refuse to accept. For her, therefore, the Gospel of John is ultimately a dangerous writing, both in itself and in its Western reception, and calls for a postcolonial, or resistant, reading. Quite interesting in this regard is her assertion that Johannine Christology did not have Rome in mind at all, only Judaism.

Jean K. Kim specifically describes her work as "postcolonial feminist," has recourse to various concepts and strategies of postcolonial theory, and invokes throughout her article imperial/colonial terminology; at the same time, she offers no overall critical account of the optic or the approach. From her concrete analysis of John 7:53–8:11, however, a sense of mode and approach can be discerned, a vision centered on women within the highly fragmented context of postcolonial societies. Kim's point of departure is the story of the "woman caught in adultery," viewed in light of its narrative construction and its interpretive history. Why, Kim asks, is there no attention to the adulterer (who never appears in the story) and no concern for the woman other than as object (forgiven by Jesus or exposing official hypocrisy)? In effect, the woman is granted neither subjective agency in the narrative nor any potential for subjectivity in criticism. In the face of such collusion between "elite" writing and reading and the text's untoward ramifications for women in any number of areas, Kim argues that destabilization is imperative: a resistant reading must foreground women's voicelessness through historical contextualization and social memory, with empowerment in mind.

Such a reading is described as "intercontextual," bringing together a postcolonial text (Gospel of John) and a postcolonial context (woman as cultural symbol). Behind this juxtaposition lies a structural analysis of postcolonial frameworks, which allows Kim to shift and apply from context to context, at once engaging in historical construction and drawing upon social memory. Such a portrait is put together from a number of sources. To begin with, all postcolonial contexts are marked by contestation of legitimate authority between client local authorities, guarantors of the status quo and tradition under the rule of empire, and local voices of protest and change. In addition, within such contexts indigenous women become sites of cultural struggle—assigned upholders of honor for national identity (purity) and potential bearers of pollution under hybridized culture (impurity). Lastly, sexually compromised local women, given foreign military presence and practices, are marginalized (whoring and adultery) and silenced under patriarchal nationalist ideology. Drawing upon such comparative knowledge and social memory, then, a contextualization of John 7:53–8:11 is advanced: a debate regarding legitimate authority in Judea, involving the religio–political authorities and Jesus as challenger, with an indigenous woman, sexually compromised by a Roman soldier, as a site of cultural identity. The result is evident: the adulterer goes unmentioned, while the woman is marginalized as impure and silenced in the narrative and in criticism alike.

Such a reading, Kim claims, rescues the subjectivity of this hybrid woman in John and destabilizes the constraining authority of tradition by focusing on the voicelessness of women in fractured postcolonial contexts. The woman stands no longer imprisoned as a site of im/purity, immoral on account of adultery, but is released as a site of resistance against the "disease" of Roman colonialism as well as of Jewish patriarchal nationalism. In such a reading, which refrains from judgment regarding the positions in question, the Gospel of John emerges as guilty of marginalization and silencing, insofar as it joins the fray over nationalist ideology. Indeed, while his stance toward the woman is not explicitly pursued, Jesus himself does not fare well either, given his role as a disputant within such a gendered contestation of authority. The loser, both in the text and in criticism, is the woman, and ultimately all women within the Christian tradition and beyond. Consequently, Kim concludes, it is imperative to surface the subjectivity of silenced women in texts and against criticism, so that women in ongoing postcolonial contexts can be empowered to puncture their voicelessness and recover their subjectivity.

One finds in Leticia Guardiola–Sáenz's essay much having to do with the postcolonial problematic—the impact of the Third World on Western biblical interpretation; the author's own social and cultural context in the borderlands between Mexico and the United States; a reading of John in terms of border–crossing—but no critical reflection as such on either the postcolonial optic or a postcolonial approach. The emphasis throughout is, rather, on borders, from the combined perspective of border theory and hybridity. The overall approach is grounded in cultural studies: a view of all reading as localized and interested, meaning that analysis of the text requires attention to both the context of its production and to that of its consumption. As a result, all readings create hybrid texts—"crossroads texts" with multiple meanings—and all readers, especially marginalized voices outside the West, constitute hybrid identities. Guardiola–Sáenz's own approach is rooted in her hybrid experience as a bicultural Mexican American, from the borderlands and living in diaspora, and seeks the empowerment of minority readers from the Third World. This study in particular represents a "cultural, regional" reading of John 7:53–8:11, retitled as the story of Jesus and the "Accused."

Guardiola–Sáenz's article emphasizes the delimiting but unstable role of borders (literal and metaphorical) in creating identity and exercising power as sites of control and crossings at once. As such, borders signify the ever–shifting margins of identity and the fringes of power, and hence are highly charged sites for distemper and change. This is certainly true of Mexican Americans, like herself, from the borderlands: border–crossers steeped in a life of ambiguity and tension, marked by constant change and an ethos of survival—a hybrid reality in defiance of all borders (political, religious, moral, cultural) and yielding, for her, a vision of justice and liberation. From the point of view of the text's production, the study advances a reading of John 7:53–8:11 as a meeting between border–crossers in the face of patriarchy—a hybrid reality resisting all boundaries and offering a vision of transformation. Close analysis of contact zones in the story (spatial borders, gender/moral codes, political/religious factions, communication modes) reveals a scenario of liberation: Jesus, the border–crosser par excellence, contesting all power structures in favor of a new reality; the accused woman, a border–crosser from a society that has denied her identity, now freed from oppression and a model for a hybrid and marginalized Johannine community. Context and interpretation go hand in hand. Out of the borderlands, a reading emerges not found in the interpretive tradition of the story from the center—precisely the aim of the project in keeping with a view of the text as a crossroads of interpretation. It is a reading, moreover, that empowers those in the margins and the fringes—precisely the aim of the exercise as well, as a reading against oppression and liberation. In such a reading the Gospel of John clearly emerges on the side of political change and radical alternatives.

In the view of Zipporah G. Glass, any postcolonial project must involve not only critical exposition of empire and its characteristic strategies of homogenization, but also a critical intervention into empire through strategies of heterogeneity from the periphery. Glass has such a project in mind with respect to both the modern nation–state and the ancient biblical text—a dual analysis of the construction of community and identity in light of geopolitical power relations. She describes such a postcolonial approach as an exercise in "positional criticism": a reader engaged in self–conscious and theorized analysis of her own "socio–cultural position" as a point of entry into the Gospel text. In her case, the context involves a twofold racial vision: multiple jeopardy in Germany as an Afro–Deutsch by birth, a *Mischling* of African and German union; precarious status in the United States as an African–American by adoption, an American Negro with a tradition of rights and privileges denied. The text under consideration is the vision of community and identity advanced by the image of the vine in John 15.

Analysis of modern nation–building reveals two homogenizing principles at work in the creation of such "imagined communities" (B. Anderson 1991): citizenship and assimilation. Through these processes, heterogeneous groups are transformed into a unified identity delimited by geographical boundaries, molded by the dominant group, and granted access to power. Although the dynamics of inclusion differ—common blood in Germany or civic ideology in the United States—the process always entails exclusion of the internal other. On both sides of the Atlantic, a phenotypical concept of race has always played a crucial role in nation–building processes to the detriment of all those of African "blood": the German national culture excludes immigrants and mixed–blood children; the U.S. civic culture provides citizenship to liminal groups but without full access to power. Glass's analysis of John 15 shows the same homogenizing principles at work in the creation of the Johannine "imagined community": citizenship in and assimilation to the nation–ness of Jesus the vine. Again, heterogeneous peoples are metamorphosed into a unified identity delimited by religious boundaries, shaped by the dominant group, and yielding access to power. Such inclusion entails exclusion as well: over against Israel, Jesus is the true vine; within the vine itself, the branches must bear fruit or face removal.

As a reader, therefore, Glass, both Afro–Deutsch and African–American, finds herself caught in national relations of power involving a complex and shifting process of ideological negotiation. Within such contexts, situated at the periphery of nation states, individuals of African descent face a situation of internal colonization. As a reader of John 15, Glass finds parallel, national–like relations of power emerging out of a similar process of ideological negotiation in the text. Within its context, situated at the margins of the Roman imperial–colonial framework, the Fourth Gospel constructs its own colonizing center, dynamics of homogenization, and processes of inclusion/exclusion. For a positioned reader, the conclusion is clear: all such strategies of "national" identity and assimilation are to be resisted. In the end, however, Glass's study does not move beyond this first aspect of the postcolonial project, as she remains content with the exposition of relations of power in visions of "imagined communities," historical or discursive, without advancing strategies of heterogeneity from either perspective.

Although Adele Reinhartz swiftly grants the applicability of a postcolonial approach to the Fourth Gospel, the question of procedure proves
more difficult. A standard position is delineated: a focus on the relationship between center and margins, calling for the identification of both
and a reading from the margins. With regard to John, however, such a
position is found wanting in two respects. First, its identification of center
and margin is ambiguous, for while the Johannine community represents
the margin vis-à-vis Rome, Johannine Christology constitutes the center
vis-à-vis all other groups, such as Jews and Samaritans. Second, John's
position on outsiders is controverted. His position on Rome is unclear,
since there is no explicit reflection upon relations between community
and empire, and his position on other groups is mediated, given their
representation only through the narrator's voice. The Fourth Gospel is
thus characterized by silence in the face of Rome alongside John's silencing of neighboring groups. The way out of this quandary is provided by
a foundational analysis of Reinhartz's native country, Canada, as at once
colonized and colonizing. This insight leads to a comparative postcolonial reading of Gospel and nation, for which the Canadian context functions as a point of entry into the Johannine context.

Reinhartz approaches the Gospel of John sequentially, first as a text
of the colonized and then as a colonizing text. In each case, Reinhartz
utilizes examples from Canadian society and culture to explore how the
margins might have responded to the colonization processes at work.
On the relations between Christian community and Roman Empire, she
imagines the Gospel as "the voice of a marginal group" that accepts the
inevitability of Roman rule while espousing a limited and specific mode of
resistance (markers: use of spatial language; adoption of realized–future
eschatology; colonizing language of superior spirituality [especially toward
"the Jews"]). On relations between the Christian community and other
groups, Reinhartz constructs a Gospel with a "colonizing message"—
absolute, universal, and exclusive. Relations with the Baptist's disciples
are depicted as harmonious, but relations with "the Jews" are portrayed
as largely adversarial. Both representations reveal tensions—overt in the
case of the Jews (markers: verbal resistance; violence; betrayal to Rome),
subtle in the case of the Baptist's followers (markers: separate activities;
sense of usurpation; role as informers).

In the end, the appropriateness, value, and mode of a postcolonial
reading is affirmed. Such a reading is appropriate, provided that (1)
groups may be viewed as both colonized and colonizer, leading to analysis of the various perspectives at play, and (2) conflict among marginal
groups is granted, highlighting the control of the narrative. Such a read-

ing is valuable, given the insights gained into ancient text and contemporary context alike; such a reading is resistant insofar as it is conducted from the margins, wherever situated. For Reinhartz, therefore, it may be said that an imperial–colonial framework emerges as highly complex, full of tension and divisions in the margins; that, within their respective imperial–colonial frameworks, the text of John emerges, like the text of Canada, as highly conflicted; and that a postcolonial reading signifies a resistant reading, in any and all imperial–colonial frameworks, although the vision behind such resistance remains unuttered.

The final essay in *John and Postcolonialism*, by Tat–siong Benny Liew, addresses neither the dynamics of a postcolonial optic nor the mechanics of a postcolonial approach, but rather the way in which the Gospel of John, as a cultural symbol, engages in community construction and functions as a site of struggle in the creation of community. For this exercise, Liew draws on a broad theoretical base, with particular emphasis on processes of community formation (Cohen 1985; B. Anderson 1991) and key cultural codes—the dialectic of consent and descent and the ideology of ascent—within the "(multi)cultural dynamics" of the United States (Sollors 1986). In so doing, Liew pursues a joint critical analysis of the symbolic or imagined Johannine and U.S. national communities from his own context and perspective as an Asian–American critic.

On the side of the Fourth Gospel, by far the greater focus of attention in this article, Liew highlights John's pervasive concern for relations and boundaries, with contrastive definition as the main strategy, as well as the Gospel's twofold vision of community based on consent and ascent. On the one hand, belonging is by consent as opposed to descent and dissent, open to all by choice, with confession in Jesus, Savior and Word of God, as the absolute requirement; on the other hand, community membership confers ascent, upward mobility of all sorts as well as expansive growth. John thus envisions a community built on a surface rhetoric of unity and love. At the same time, however, Liew finds profound contradictions throughout the Fourth Gospel: on the side of consent, appeals to descent of various sorts as well as indications of dissent and mingling on various fronts; on the side of ascent, concern for the future and marginalization of outsiders. In this respect, John's envisioned community is belied by an underlying rhetoric of hierarchy and exclusion. In the case of the United States, Liew notes a similar contradiction between projects of consent and ascent, involving a rhetoric of rebirth and love on the part of the dominant culture alongside an apparatus of descent and erasure involving a strategy of hierarchy and exclusion toward racial and ethnic minorities. Within such conflicted cultural politics, Asian–Americans, Liew claims, occupy a highly ambiguous space as "almost–white–but–not–quite," a model minority: not only a part of the "other," included as "white" only when convenient, but also an "obscure other," beyond differentiation as a group.

The result is a deconstructive study of both community constructions (Johannine and American) and a stance of critical ambivalence. John's construction emerges as appealing (radical vision of consent and prominence of community) and yet off–putting (hierarchical boundary and emphasis on consent). As cultural symbol, moreover, John's construction can be and has been read in ambiguous ways: rather than simple consent or dissent, from within the Christian tradition, in terms of indebtedness as well as regret. Yet, Liew concludes, there is no room for ambivalence regarding critical evaluation, interpretation as contextual and ethical, and a commitment to continuous critique.

Surveying the Geopolitical

In summarizing my impression of the postcolonial optic as employed in *John and Postcolonialism*, I will follow the three areas of discussion identified earlier: mode of inquiry and approach to the biblical text, the relationship between Roman Empire and Johannine Christianity, and the interpreter's critical stance.

On the question of mode of inquiry, all contributors to *John and Postcolonialism* address the Fourth Gospel as cultural product rather than the material matrix of the text. As such, the emphasis throughout is on the literary, rhetorical, and ideological dimensions of the Gospel rather than on its social and cultural context. To be sure, references to the latter are to be found, but by way of background rather than as primary object of inquiry. With regard to the text as such, the focus varies: while some essays address the narrative as a whole (Staley; Reinhartz; Liew), most focus on individual units (Dube; Lozada; Huie–Jolly; Kim; Guardiola–Sáenz; Glass). On the question of approach, all contributors look beyond the text of the Fourth Gospel to its history of interpretation and/or their own social and cultural contexts. In the process, a range of options can be readily discerned: the majority address the critical tradition and their own locations (Staley; Lozada; Kim; Glass; Reinhartz; Liew); others emphasize the ecclesial–missionary tradition (Dube; Huie–Jolly); one essay concentrates on personal framework (Guardiola–Sáenz). The specific angle of attention varies widely: the concept of place (Staley); the ideology of traveling, with gender as signifier (Dube); religious construction of self and others (Lozada; Huie–Jolly); voicelessness of women (Kim); drawing and crossing of borders (Guardiola–Sáenz); community construction and identity (Glass; Liew); and construction of outside groups (Reinhartz).

The spectrum of positions regarding the Johannine stance on community and world within the imperial–colonial framework of Rome is broad but lopsided. At one end, the Gospel of John emerges as a decidedly positive intervention, a voice of resistance. Guardiola–Sáenz, however, is the only critic in this quarter, viewing John 7:53–8:11 as a crossroads text pushing beyond boundaries and toward transformation. At the other end, the Fourth Gospel stands as a resolutely negative insertion, a voice of oppression. This sector is the most populated: Dube, who views John 4 as an imperializing mission text of expansion and domination; Lozada, who views John 5 as a colonialist text espousing religious absolutism, exclusivism, and assimilation; Huie–Jolly, who sees John 5 as a dangerous text of religious universalism and accusation; Kim, who contends that John 7:53–8:11 is an oppressive text denying subjectivity to the woman character, a site of struggle for patriarchal nationalism; and, Glass, who views John 15 as a colonizing text of exclusion in its imagined vision of community and identity. In the mid–range, the Gospel of John appears as a conflicted maneuver, at once positive and negative, a controverted voice of resistance and oppression. This space is also well populated: Staley, who sees the Gospel as a political text with a complex ideology of displacement, of all by Jesus alongside of all including Jesus; Reinhartz, who views the Gospel as a text both marginal, over against Rome, and colonizing, over against non–Christian groups; and, Liew, who concludes that the Gospel of John is an ambivalent text in its construction of community, involving consent and descent, ascent and exclusion.

Finally, all the contributors to *John and Postcolonialism* in varying degrees argue for and undertake a critical evaluation of the text. Depending upon the approach in question, such critique may extend to the interpretive tradition and contemporary ramifications. These critiques deploy varying strategies, and then issue from different ethical and political visions. Following the delineation of the Johannine stance on community and empire, a broad range of evaluations may be observed, from solidarity through wrestling to rejection.

In full backing of the Gospel, the sole voice is that of Guardiola–Sáenz, rooted in a personal vision of justice and solidarity for those marginalized by the West (John 7:53–8:11 as advancing a sharp vision of political change from the borderlands). Struggling with the Gospel, three voices come to the fore: Staley, from a personal commitment to a postcolonial geography of attachment to and detachment from place (looking past displacement by Jesus to displacement by Rome in the Gospel); Reinhartz, grounded in theoretical commitment to postcolonial ambiguity involving conflict among marginal groups and clashing stances within groups (Gospel as resisting Rome while marginalizing the Jews and the Baptist's

followers); Liew, proceeding from personal commitment to ongoing critique in light of his controverted status as Asian–American (highlighting
the Gospel's recourse to hierarchy and consensus as well as to consent
and community). In full disaccord with the Fourth Gospel, the voices
are many: toward the liberation of the traveled–to, Dube (a decolonizing reading of John 4, with gender as key signifier, through rewriting
by a woman author from the Third World); in quest of a world without colonialism and with liberation for all, Lozada (a resistant reading of
John 5 with pluralism and respect for others in mind); harking back to a
historical tale of Western political–ecclesial expansionism in the Pacific
and arguing for respect for indigenous and alternate voices, Huie–Jolly
(identification with the unbelieving Jews of the Gospel as resistance to
the absolutism of Christian claims); in solidarity with the role of women
as cultural sites of struggle in postcolonial societies, Kim (rescuing the
subjectivity of the woman in John 7:53–8:11 through historical exposé);
and, finally, grounded in suspicion of all homogenization strategies as
both Afro–Deutsch and African–American, Glass (puncturing the project of inclusion/exclusion advanced by John 15 through heterogeneous
intervention).

A Nonconcluding Comment

The preceding overview reveals basic agreement on various dimensions
of a postcolonial reading of John: extension of critical attention to the
history of reception as well as to the contemporary contexts of criticism;
attention to the narrative construction of relations between community
and empire; and the call for critical reaction regarding such construction.
The overview has also surfaced insufficient interaction with postcolonial
theory, especially in matters of meaning and scope. The overview further
reveals considerable diversity in fundamental foci of inquiry among the
various postcolonial readings of John: point of entry into the text; deter-
mination of the Gospel's representation of relations between community
and empire; and critical evaluation of such representation. As a whole, I
would describe *John and Postcolonialism* as a solid point of reference for all
further attention to the realm of the geopolitical in Johannine Studies.
In joining such a line of inquiry, I would describe my own approach as
sharing in such agreements, committed to such interdisciplinary dialogue
with postcolonial studies, and adding to such diversity.

I would summarize the main lines of my own approach as follows.
On meaning and scope, I view the postcolonial as a social–psychological
category (the problematization of an imperial–colonial relation of domination and subordination within any type of historical–political situation)

and regard it as applicable to imperial–colonial frameworks across history and culture (with due specificity regarding the different social and cultural formations in question). Regarding point of entry, I approach the Gospel of John as a constructive cultural–material intervention within the imperial–colonial framework of Rome as imagined and represented, and I pursue its critical analysis from a combined literary, rhetorical, and ideological perspective. Regarding the representation of community–empire relations, I see the Fourth Gospel as deeply conflicted: espousing, on the one hand, a radical postcolonial vision and program in the face of Rome and all worldly power—a manifesto of exposé, rejection, and resistance; yet deploying, on the other hand, severe imperial–colonial policies of its own vis-à-vis all those deemed outside such a vision and program—a strategy of exclusion, dismissal, and condemnation. On critical stance toward the Gospel, I regard engagement with the text as imperative in the light of our own cultural and material contexts and find the Gospel both diametrically opposed to and readily succumbing to a geopolitical relation of domination and subordination. Finally, I would extend such engagement with the text to its history of interpretation in the modern and postmodern periods as well as to the individuals and communities behind such interpretations.

In the end, therefore, I would argue, incumbent upon all of us is a thorough and pointed conversation with the Gospel of John, with our various readings of the text, and with one another as critics of the text within our respective social and cultural locations. Why? First, because the Gospel itself constitutes, as argued earlier, a religious writing with sharp political overtones and thus calls for a response in kind from all its readers. In effect, its rhetorical thrust and ideological claims reach beyond its original readers to all modern and contemporary readers. Second, such conversation is incumbent because the era of scientific objectivity and neutral detachment in biblical criticism, as all across the social and human sciences, has been theoretically punctured and displaced. In an era of cultural and social constructionism, each and every reading emerges as a construction of the text with political and ethical ramifications of its own. Lastly, because all of us, as readers of the text in the postmodern era, are not just passive scholars of the ancient world of the Mediterranean basin and early Christianity but also active citizens of our own world—a world in which a global economy, neoliberal capitalism, and a geopolitical hyper–power, a United States of America at once immensely powerful and eerily fragile, stand atop the web of international relations. Consciously or not, we read this text from an imperial–colonial framework of domination and subordination within our own geopolitical formation of differential relations of power, and our readings become, as the Gospel itself, cultural–material interventions in our own social and cultural contexts.

I came to such a critical realization, as a product of and agent in my own times, in the aftermath of the social and cultural upheavals of the 1960s and the profound transition in biblical scholarship, as in all academia, from the mid–1970s on. From such a vantage point, I find, in agreement with Richard Horsley, that the sense of the geopolitical has been strangely missing in biblical criticism in general and in Johannine Studies in particular. Such a focus has been an intensely present absence throughout my generation and should come to the fore with the next generation. Fortunately, *John and Postcolonialism* shows that this geopolitical gap is rapidly drawing to a close and that the irruption of the postcolonial has begun in earnest. My own theological and political interaction with the Gospel, its readings and readers, must, however, wait until another time—to cast it in Johannine terms, if I may, a not yet that is already here.

15: RESPONSE

TOWARD AN INTERDISCIPLINARY
APPROACH TO JOHANNINE STUDIES

Francisco Lozada Jr.

In "Johannine Studies and the Geopolitical: Reflections Upon Absence and Irruption," Fernando F. Segovia calls the next generation of scholars to take seriously the geopolitical matrix of the Johannine Literature, particularly the imperial–colonial framework of Rome, in the production and interpretive history of these texts. Segovia opens this call with a brief analysis of Richard Horsley's *Jesus and Empire* (2003), not only to highlight Horsley's critical perspective on why geopolitical considerations are absent from early Christian studies generally, but also to launch his own argument that such discussion is missing from Johannine Studies in particular. Segovia, however, sees an irruption, sparked by postcolonial criticism (postcolonial optic), of new efforts to engage the broad range of geopolitical issues and arenas vis–à–vis Johannine Studies, as reflected in Dube and Staley's *John and Postcolonialism* (2002). The majority of Segovia's reflections take the form of a critical engagement with the essays in this important volume, which serves as a point of departure for critical exchanges regarding their author's understandings, approaches, and interpretations of various Johannine texts from a postcolonial optic that aims to engage the geopolitical.

I certainly agree with Segovia's assertion that the geopolitical question needs much more attention in Johannine Studies, but I would like to ask, "What would it take for the next generation to answer this call?" I would argue that to address this question, Johannine scholars must become much more informed about three interrelated arenas of the geopolitical: (1) the *cultural* arena, with its various competing discourses of power; (2) the *economic* arena and its range of policies and ramifications; and (3) the *political* arena, with its assortment of models of governance and their effects. Essentially, I would argue that Johannine scholars must move toward a more interdisciplinary approach to address these arenas. In other words, I am suggesting that to address the question of the geopolitical in Johannine Studies, the next generation of scholars will need to be just as aware of the world they live in as they are of the world behind the text, for it is this world now that continues to inform our questions and approaches to the Fourth Gospel. The remainder of my remarks will briefly outline key considerations related to these three arenas.

One area that I believe needs closer attention is the study of *culture and society*, particularly with a focus on ways that race/ethnicity, sexuality, ability, citizenship, gender, nationality, class, and language function to define or construct identities. A focus on how these social identity factors are related to one another and how they are related to power within a society is also very important. I see all of these identity factors as part of the geopolitical dimension in Johannine Studies. For example, exploring culture and society through the lens of these contested identity factors in the Johannine text is essential to a better understanding of how notions of identity and difference have (and still do) affirm racial, ethnic, class, and gender distinctions, how they were once applied within European colonial powers, and how they are now elaborated among neo–colonial powers. The question of belonging and exclusion, the increase of politics of identity, especially centered on religious concerns, shows no sign of abating within the period of the next generation of Johannine scholars.

A second area that warrants closer examination is the study of *economics*, with a focus on globalization and its powerful neo–colonial ramifications. I do believe that there are benefits to globalization, but there are also negative effects that call for a closer analysis of how it is applied throughout various international local and global economies. Informed by a contemporary examination of these issues, Johannine scholars will better understand various ancient forms or glimpses of globalization, particularly its effects on the homogenization of culture. In other words, if one studies the global development of capitalism and its effect of converging cultures and lifestyles across the globe (e.g., Starbucks–drinking or McDonald's–eating), one might better understand how the Fourth Gospel converged ancient communities, for example in relationship to universalism and particularism, which eventually produced various outcomes for the Johannine community and within various communities in our world.

The final area that I see as part of the geopolitical question is the study of *politics*, which focuses, for example, on the question of empire. The next generation of Johannine scholars will need to be informed on many issues relating to colonialism and neo-colonialism. For instance, the interplay between neoconservative and neoliberal policies, the transformation of the United Nations and the status of multilateralism, legacies of earlier imperial and colonial formations, migration and diasporic cultures, state power, and even house bills (e.g., S. 2611, the Hagel–Martinez compromise immigration bill) and foreign policies (e.g., preemptive military action) are all topics or texts that could be read alongside the Fourth Gospel to further understand various geopolitical aspects within the world of the Johannine text and how they might be played out within its world and this world. I am thinking, for example, of a comparative analysis of how U.S. imperial power maintains a unilateral world in a post–Cold War era with how the Johannine text maintains a unilateral world centered around its universal belief in Jesus as the Son of God.

In short, Segovia's call to the next generation of Johannine scholars to focus on the geopolitical in Johannine Studies is very important. To address this challenge, an interdisciplinary approach to Johannine Studies is a must, one that takes seriously the cultural, economic, and political arenas that make up the geopolitical dimension. Yet this is not an easy task. It will call many scholars to retool or to be "born anew," and it will call many graduate curricula to either lengthen their reading lists or to scratch and renew their readings lists in order to lead the next generation of scholars in the direction of an interdisciplinary approach to Johannine Studies, as well as to Christian Origins.

CHAPTER 16

THE PROBLEM OF HISTORY IN JOHN

D. Moody Smith

Christian faith's interest in history is, and always has been, fueled by the historical fact claims of the New Testament itself. Modern historical criticism has, of course, raised serious questions about those claims, and these questions are nowhere more acute than in the case of the Fourth Gospel. My own interest in the Gospel of John grew up alongside an equal interest in the quest for the historical Jesus, particularly the presentation and critique of Albert Schweitzer. The Gospel of John plays no role in Schweitzer's great work, being laid aside as "theology" rather than "history" despite its apparent fact claims (John 19:35; 21:24). Bultmann's commentary on John might have seemed to provide an alternative to Schweitzer's dismissal of this Gospel (Bultmann 1971). Bultmann correctly saw that the historicity of Jesus was crucial in John, but only his "thatness," not his "whatness." According to Bultmann, the affirmation that the Word became flesh (1:14) is essential for Johannine, or for any, Christology. Yet the Johannine portrayal of Jesus is, for the most part, a Christian theological construction. One might say that, for Bultmann, John is the final step (and the right step) within the New Testament in the development of a proper Christology. As such, the Fourth Gospel represents an inner–Christian theological development, one not dependent upon Judaism or on the historical figure of Jesus. Yet matters could not come to rest there, as with a new generation of exegetes fresh questions about history and the Gospels were being raised.

As a graduate student, one of the first things I read in Paul Minear's New Testament Theology seminar at Yale in the fall of 1957 was James M. Robinson's noteworthy monograph *The Problem of History in Mark*. I did not grasp the full significance of this book at the time, nor did I think to ask whether there is a comparable problem of history in John. In little more a decade later, however, J. Louis Martyn was to publish his groundbreaking study *History and Theology in the Fourth Gospel* (1968; 3rd ed. 2003). For Martyn, the problem of history in John was the problem of the history and conflicts of the Johannine community. The Jesus of that history was the Jesus present by means of the Spirit–Paraclete to that community. The Fourth Gospel's narrative moves at two levels, that of the Johannine community or church in its struggle against (other) Jews who do not accept Jesus as the messiah and, underneath so to speak, the *einmalig* ("onetime") level of Jesus or the old tradition about Jesus and his ministry. Martyn did not dismiss the *einmalig* level. Indeed, it is essential to his thesis, but he focused on the other, higher level in the two–level drama, whose ultimate unity was vested in the work of the Paraclete.

Nevertheless, John is a narrative of Jesus' ministry. Like the Synoptics, it begins with the appearance of John the Baptist and ends with the passion narrative. Moreover, the narrator says, "We have seen his glory" (John 1:14), and Nathanael is told that he will see "the angels of God ascending and descending upon the Son of Man" (1:52). The piercing of Jesus' side has been seen by the true witness (19:34–35), who is apparently the source of this Gospel (21:24). Does not the Fourth Gospel deserve to be taken seriously for what it claims to be?[1]

Moreover, 1 John emphasizes as strongly as the Gospel the importance of Jesus as a real, historical figure, but the Epistle seldom if ever figures in discussions of this issue. Yet the Epistle's prologue (1:1–3) emphasizes even more than the Gospel's (John 1:1–18) the visibility, audibility, and tangibility of the Word of life. If the Gospel's prologue is here in view—and 1 John 1:1–3 would otherwise make little sense—Jesus himself is in view. Moreover, Jesus keeps reappearing in this letter, even when his name is not explicitly called. There is continual reference to "the beginning" (ἀρχή) throughout the document. True, the Jesus who

---

[1] Ernst Käsemann once addressed this question eloquently: "But if John felt himself under constraint to compose a Gospel rather than letters or a collection of sayings, Bultmann's argument is revealed as very one–sided. For it seems to me that if one has no interest in the historical Jesus, then one does not write a Gospel, but, on the contrary, finds the Gospel form inadequate" (1969, 41).

died and is now the Paraclete/Advocate with the Father (1 John 2:1) presides over the scene. But at the same time, he is inseparable from his historical past. This is evident as soon as his commandments come into view. It is not just a matter of keeping commandments, however, but walking as that one (masculine singular) walked (2:6). The one whose walk is to be emulated is obviously Jesus. If this were not clear enough already, there is a telling play on the "new commandment" that Jesus issues in the Gospel of John (13:34). When an old commandment replaces the new commandment (1 John 2:7), it is described as "the one which you had from the beginning," obviously from Jesus himself ("the word that you have heard").

The importance of Jesus as a real human being is underscored by the condemnation of Christological heresy in 1 John 4:1–3. Who is from God (or "of God") and who is not? Obviously, the crucial criterion is confessing that Jesus has come in the flesh, meaning as a real human being. Denial of the humanity of Jesus is the heresy that has divided the community (cf. also 2:18–25). Interest in the historical figure of Jesus is not academic. The interest is not in history per se, but in doctrine, but the doctrine depends upon the historical reality of a human being.

First John makes clear what the Word's becoming flesh (John 1:14) means. The Epistle is more explicit on this point than the Gospel, although it is a proper interpretation of the Gospel, for which the humanity of Jesus is a basic ingredient. Rarely is Jesus spoken of as the son of Joseph in the Synoptic Gospels, but Philip introduces him to Nathanael as Jesus son of Joseph from Nazareth (John 1:45). After Jesus has referred to himself as the bread from heaven (6:41), the Jews, who are apparently his fellow Galileans, say, "Is not this Jesus, the son of Joseph, whose father and mother we know? How can he now say 'I have come down from heaven'?" (6:42). Jesus is a human being whose natural origins are known. His claims, taken literally, are inconceivable, and therefore presumably false. But they are not to be taken literally. They must be demythologized, as the evangelist has demythologized the myth of the descending and ascending redeemer. For Gospel as for Epistle, the humanity and historical reality of Jesus are basic.

Of course, historical skepticism about John's portrayal of Jesus did not begin yesterday. That the Johannine Jesus is preaching the gospel of the post–resurrection church has been apparent to most exegetes since the rise of historical criticism. Moreover, we are asked to believe that Jesus gave sight to a man blind from birth and raised from the dead a man who had been dead for four days. Really? Jesus' supernatural power is too much in evidence for Bultmann's modern man or woman (Bultmann 1957a). Yet such power is already manifest in the synoptic Jesus; John only enlarges it or goes out of his way to call attention to it. Here, as in other cases, John makes what is latent in the Synoptics patent or explicit. Obviously, in John Jesus' "deeds of power" become signs, which they are not in the Synoptics. Yet even there, they are more than humanitarian acts: they signify Jesus' mission as a commission from God. They betoken the inbreaking rule of God (Matt 12:28; Luke 11:20) as they likely did for Jesus himself and for his followers. They have a latent christological function.

The sayings of Jesus in John are another matter, in that the Johannine Jesus talks Christology quite explicitly and debates his role with his opponents. Although this does not happen in the Synoptics, in Mark for example, the question about Jesus' mission and role lurks constantly in the background and moves the narrative forward. In John, it is answered at the beginning and the narrative lacks the same movement; the question is only who will accept Jesus' claims and who will not. This is an excellent example of what is latent in the Synoptics being patent in John. Although the anachronistic character of the Johannine Jesus' preaching has long been recognized, significant progress has been made in setting the character and content of his speech in the context of a conflict with Judaism, or better, within Judaism, about the validity of the emerging church's claims for Jesus. Moreover, as the Gospel itself makes clear, the continuing revelation of Jesus, through the ever-present Jesus speaking to his church, is the work of the Spirit or Paraclete, which Jesus himself promised (John 14:25–26; 16:12–15).

The problem of John's historical value as a source for Jesus or genuine Jesus tradition is, of course, closely related to the question of John and the Synoptics (see further D. M. Smith 2001). Where does John stand among the Gospels? But the resolution of that issue is not the necessary *a priori* for addressing the question of Jesus tradition in the Gospel of John. There are various positions on the question of John and the Synoptic Gospels that may tilt the answer to the Jesus tradition question one way or the other, but they do not necessarily decide it. Take for example the view that John knew and used one (usually Mark) or more of the Synoptics. One may decide that the historical substance of John is derived from the Synoptics and any departure from them is a product of John's apologetic or theological interests. This is an arguable position and has been set out recently by Maurice Casey (1996). Frans Neirynck, on the other hand, argues that John knew and used all the Synoptics, but as far as I know he has not suggested that because of this the Fourth Gospel can contain no historical data not found in the others. Similarly, de Solages believes John knew the Synoptics, but he argues that where the Fourth

Gospel's differs from them it is likely more accurate historically. The author is, in his view, John the Beloved Disciple, who knew because he was there (de Solages 1979).

On the other hand, the position that John is independent of the Synoptics, as enunciated by P. Gardner–Smith (1938) and developed by his Cambridge colleague C. H. Dodd (1963), is quite congenial with the historical value of John. Dodd certainly thought so, and his masterful *Historical Tradition in the Fourth Gospel* is as impressive an effort to demonstrate that as one can imagine. If John did not use the Synoptic Gospels, what were his sources? Although Bultmann had argued for a signs source and a passion source and Fortna would soon advocate a Gospel of Signs, Dodd favored oral tradition. In any event, as Gardner–Smith saw, John's independence opens the door to its historicity. Yet the earliest gospel evidence from outside the New Testament shows that independence from the Synoptics does not necessarily imply historicity. Do any of the apocryphal Gospels that we know, albeit mostly in fragmentary form, seem to be based upon Mark (or the Synoptics)? Apparently they are not, and they are at least in this sense independent. Moreover, they are for the most part patently fictional, although elements of old tradition may underlie the *Gospel of Peter* at a few points, and *Thomas* may contain independently transmitted sayings. In fact, a three–Gospel canon seems to have formed around Mark and suppressed other Gospels. Its only lasting rivals were the Gospel of John and, in some circles in the fourth century and later, the *Diatessaron*. But the *Diatessaron* was, of course, a compilation of the canonical four. John, like all Gospels outside the Markan canon, largely went its own way, but followed a general Gospel (though not necessarily the Markan) outline or structure.

Recent investigation and discussion of the synoptic problem suggests that, although the two or four source hypothesis is as good as we can do, synoptic relationships may be more complex. If that is the case, and it may be, any relationship among all four Gospels, and perhaps others, would, in the nature of the case, be even more complex. To make any conclusion about history or historical tradition in John dependent upon the resolution of this problem would likely be tantamount to postponing it indefinitely.

In a forthcoming article in the *Handbook of the Study of the Historical Jesus* (Leiden: Brill), I will deal with the question of the historical value of John's Jesus tradition more extensively than is possible in a piece such as this. Here, it will only be possible to look at a few representative instances: first, several in which John contradicts or differs from the Synoptics; and, second, some in which John differs from Matthew and Mark while agreeing with Luke.

Obviously in John, Jesus' ministry is spread over as much as three years, certainly more than two (three Passovers; 2:13; 6:4; 11:55), while in the Synoptics it is limited to one year—really less than one (one Passover; Mark 14:1). Moreover, the Johannine Jesus is frequently found in Jerusalem or Judea, while in the Synoptics he never goes there until the end. While one may scarcely speak of demonstration or proof, in principle the Johannine version is more probable, particularly since the Synoptics' version is based solely on Mark, whose framework owes as much or more to theology than to history. Yet even the Markan account of the growing impact of Jesus and opposition to him suggests a ministry of more than one year rather than less. And even in Mark, there are suggestions that Jesus has spent more time in Jerusalem, probably prior to his final visit. At his arrest, he alludes to a period of time spent teaching in the temple ("day by day"; Mark 14:49). He seems to have made previous preparation for his entry into Jerusalem (11:1–6) and for the room for the Last Supper (14:12–16). Both pericopes can be viewed as Markan compositions intended to portray Jesus' advance knowledge (presumably supernatural) yet we cannot be sure that this is the case—possibly both scenes assume Jesus' longer or previous presence in Jerusalem. (Parenthetically, it is strange if John had been following Mark that he omitted these scenes that so fully correspond to his view of Jesus' foreknowledge and power.) Moreover, it is altogether likely that Jesus went up to Jerusalem regularly, not only for Passover but other feasts, just as John suggests (cf. John 5:1; 7:2).

Both John and the Synoptics portray Jesus' ministry as beginning with John the Baptist, but with striking differences. In the Synoptics, Jesus' encounter with John, during which he is baptized, is separate from the account of the calling of the disciples, the brothers Peter and Andrew and James and John, from their work as fishermen on the Sea of Galilee (Mark 1:16–20). In Mark, Jesus commands they follow—in fact, they seem to follow only because Jesus commands and without any prior knowledge. In John, the similar account of their encounter does not mention baptism, but instead has the Baptist sending his disciples to Jesus. Disciples of John the Baptist thus become disciples of Jesus. That is a more plausible historical scenario than Mark's, if less dramatic. Although in John's version Jesus is shortly thereafter declared to be Messiah (1:41), Mark's call scene is also theologically pregnant. Jesus has only to command and his would–be disciples obey. The Baptist reappears later in all four Gospels, but only in the Fourth Gospel is Jesus portrayed as conducting a ministry alongside the Baptist. Mark has the Baptist's work end before the ministry of Jesus begins (Mark 1:14), in what appears to be a neat, theologically motivated, compartmentalization. The Fourth Evangelist goes out of his way to emphasize Jesus' superiority to John the Baptist (1:15, 30), yet he depicts Jesus and John baptizing in a kind of rivalry (John 3:22, 26; 4:1). Although this portrayal is promptly corrected (4:2), the correction seems to be a sort of afterthought in which it is stated that not Jesus himself, but only his disciples baptized. But that is also something found in no other Gospel. Throughout this Johannine scene, the statements of Jesus and the Baptist bear all the marks of later theological reflection, but the data about their relationship are in all likelihood historical, despite their absence from the Synoptics.

John's differences from the Synoptics, particularly Matthew and Mark, are often accompanied by peculiar contacts or affinities with Luke. This is nowhere more evident than in the trial of Jesus before the Sanhedrin, which is entirely missing from John, although a place has, so to speak, been left for it with the mere mention of Caiaphas the high priest (John 18:24, 28). Instead, John describes a brief and theologically inconsequential hearing before Annas (18:13–14, 19–23). At the same time, Mark's lengthy and theologically weighty account of Jesus' formal trial before the Sanhedrin (14:53–64), in which witnesses are sought and heard, a confession under questioning is made by Jesus, and a verdict rendered, is missing from John. Remarkably, Luke, who is clearly using Mark in his rendition of the Sanhedrin scene, omits just these juridical elements (Luke 22:66–71). In Luke, it is no longer a trial. The historical difficulties of the Markan trial account have long been observed by Jewish and Christian commentators, notably the fact that it violates a number of stipulations governing a capital trial laid out in the Mishnaic tractate *Sanhedrin*. Did it happen? The simpler Johannine account of a hearing before Annas does not present comparable difficulties and is more likely historical.

Ironically, on John's accounting one such difficulty could be removed: the evening of Jesus' arrest and arraignment is not Passover itself, a high holy day on which the trial and other events as recounted in Mark (and Matthew) are scarcely conceivable, but the day previous. John states and reiterates that Jesus' death occurred the afternoon *before* Passover rather than the day *after* (John 18:28; 19:14, 31, 42; cf. 13:1). Has John changed the date so that Jesus dies as the Passover lambs are slain? Despite John 1:29 and 36, as well as 19:36, this is not noted in John. That is, the slaughtering of the lambs while Jesus is dying is not explicitly mentioned. Moreover, in John, Jesus' death is not explained in terms of the sacrificial cult—the temple altar—as it is in the words of institution of the Lord's Supper, which are, of course, found only in the Synoptic Gospels and Paul. The differing Johannine chronology of Jesus' trial and death relieves the historical problems created by the synoptic accounts and does not really support clear and explicit Johannine theological themes.

On this point of divergence, there is not a Lukan parallel to John, but there are others. The trial scene, of course, stands out. But in the death scene also Luke and John agree in omitting the so–called cry of dereliction (Mark 15:34; Matt 27:96; cf. Ps 22:2). Luke, clearly following Mark, has Jesus say instead, but in the same "loud voice," "Father, into thy hands I commit my spirit" (24:46). In John, not obviously following Mark, Jesus says only, "It is finished," but the narrator adds, "and bowing his head he gave over the spirit." Spirit figures in both John and Luke. So, in pericopes that are found in all four Gospels, Luke often diverges from Mark and Matthew at the same points John does. For further examples, John's account of the calling of the disciples differs from Mark (and Matthew) as we observed, and Luke also differs radically (Luke 5:2–11; cf. John 20:1–14), although in a different manner. Matthew and Mark have two feeding narratives, Luke and John have only the feeding of five thousand. Only Luke and John report speculation over whether John the Baptist was the Messiah (Luke 3:15; John 1:20). And while John does not report Jesus' baptism at all, Luke barely mentions it after it has occurred, and does not describe the act (Luke 3:21).

If there is any dependence between John and Luke, which way does it run? Is it likely that John, who is not following Mark, whether or not he knew Mark, would have elected to go with Luke at some points, having both before him (or knowing both)? Or is it more likely that Luke, who used Mark, would have been influenced by an alternative, perhaps Johannine, account that differed at many points? I believe the latter is more probable. The cry of dereliction cited above is a relevant instance. Unquestionably, Luke is following Mark in his story of Jesus' death; John, whether or not he knew Mark, is not. How is it that Luke and John agree both in the deletion of the cry and its replacement with a reference to the spirit, whether Jesus' or God's? Which way does dependence go? The answer is not a given, but the conclusion that Luke is swayed from his dependence upon Mark by his knowledge of John, or a John–like narrative, is both plausible and inviting. Luke would have changed a statement about Jesus' death (John 19:30; "gave up his spirit" or "expired") into an appropriate word of a dying martyr, after which he similarly "expired" (Luke 23:46; using the verbal rather than John's nominal form of *pneuma*). Of course, Johannine priority does not necessarily imply historicity, but again it opens the door for it.

So, is there a problem of history in John? There is little doubt that there is. The problem of the historical setting of John is a problem of history that is as close to resolution as it ever has been. Jesus stands over against "the Jews." Who are these "Jews"? For that matter, who is this Jesus? Most exegetes would now agree that he is not the "historical" Jesus.

Why is he opposed by "the Jews" when he and his disciples are themselves Jewish? Why should Jesus' would–be disciples fear expulsion from synagogues (John 9:22; 16:2)? Or why should they even think of such a thing? The answer to these and similar questions lies in the reconstruction of the setting of the Fourth Gospel in, or at the edge of, a Judaism that rejects the claims of Jesus' (still Jewish) followers, who have been or anticipate being rejected themselves ("put out of the synagogue"). They want to remain Jews, but as it is turning out, they will not. This reconstruction remains hypothetical, but it fits the data of the text remarkably well. This is why it has been gaining ground among Johannine scholars.

What about the historical figure of Jesus in the Gospel of John? That John's Jesus is not the same as the historical figure of early first–century Galilee is clear enough, although sometimes he may be glimpsed through the Johannine lens. But when we ask about Jesus tradition in John, that is a different issue. What is at stake in this case is old tradition and quasi–historical data. In this essay I have aimed to survey the territory; indicate the issues involved (e.g., John and the Synoptics); suggest how they play out with regard to this problem; and point to evidence for Jesus tradition, in the sense of data pertinent to the historical ministry of Jesus, in the Gospel of John.

I began these reflections by setting Martyn's *History and Theology in the Fourth Gospel* alongside James Robinson's *The Problem of History in Mark*, with the intention of discussing the problem of history in the Fourth Gospel. It may be worthwhile now to look again at Robinson's comments on Mark to take stock of any parallel between his work and Martyn's on John. As a side note, I might mention that, in a small seminar on Mark at the University of Zurich in the academic year 1963–1964, Professor Eduard Schweizer, in discussing some feature of Mark, would sometimes ask what it is reminiscent of, and the answer would usually be "*das Johannesevangelium.*"

Robinson's presentation is set against the context of the then–current (mid–1950s) Continental discussion, which pivoted on the exegetical and theological work of Rudolf Bultmann. Although an active partner in that discussion, Robinson set forth a position on Mark that ran counter to Bultmann's theological position and interests. Robinson emphasized that Mark speaks for a community (or church) for which history and historicity were important. Further, historicity meant more to this community than the punctiliar moment in which one encounters and accepts the kerygma. Because of this, Robinson conjectures, Mark (and the Synoptics generally) are relegated to a relatively minor role in Bultmann's classic *Theology of the New Testament* (Robinson 1957, 18, esp. n. 1). For Robinson, however, the history of the Markan community recapitulates the history of Jesus. Mark "sees Jesus and the Church engaged in the same cosmic struggle against the same demonic force of evil" (1957, 63). Moreover, "since the church sees its history founded in Jesus' history, it can witness to and explain its religious experience better by writing the history of Jesus as the Messiah than by describing its own religious life" (Robinson 1957, 13). Could not the same be said of John? If so, there is a significant analogy between the problem of history in John and the same problem in Mark. In both cases, the evangelist tells the story of his community while at the same time telling the story of Jesus' ministry. If this were not the case, neither Gospel would have been written. This is a real and important parallel. Of what does Mark remind us? Obviously, "*das Johannesevangelium.*"

At the same time, quite obvious differences exist between John and Mark. Their eschatological perspectives are different, as Robinson's treatment of Mark makes clear. Up to the Passion narrative, they apparently drew upon different traditions. In John, Jesus preaches a Gospel about himself, which Mark also shares but without putting it on the lips of Jesus. Mark is closer to the historical figure of Jesus than is John, although no less committed to a theological perception of him that affects the way he shapes and structures his Gospel. It is all the more remarkable, then, that at just those points where the Fourth Gospel differs from Mark and the other Synoptic Gospels, John's version is often preferable historically.

There is a "problem of history in John" not unlike that in Mark. Mark presents problems when evaluated historically, but greater problems arise when history is left out of account. The same is true of John. For all their differences, Mark and John are obviously about the same protagonist. Not only is he named Jesus, but he is a Galilean Jew who carries out his mission within the boundaries of biblical Israel. He teaches, he performs healings and other extraordinary miracles, and he goes to Jerusalem to face death. What Mark obviously believes about Jesus John puts on his lips.

Both John and Mark are extraordinary biographies. They are extraordinary in two senses: first, because of claims made for the protagonist; but, second, because the nature of those claims has fundamentally shaped the character and context of the narration. The crowning and most significant event of his life was his death, but it was not the end. He rose from the dead. At least that is what the authors of these rather unique documents believed, and they represent groups of followers who were equally convinced. Their differences seem to fade before these common factors.

16: RESPONSE

GENRE, SOURCES, AND HISTORY

Craig S. Keener

Professor Smith's essay helpfully places the problem of history in the Gospel of John in the context of other ancient Gospels, the most natural setting for understanding John. In view of this approach, what light does the issue of "Gospel genre" shed on historical questions? Moreover, what can we say about history in John without resolving more specifically the controversial question of sources?

On the question of genre, Richard Burridge's work on the Gospels as biographies (developing the earlier work of Talbert, Shuler, Aune, and others) has had a major impact on how we approach these texts. For example, analogies with other ancient biographies have important implications for how the Gospel writers viewed their enterprise. Ancient biographers addressed real characters of history (or, for the distant past, those they believed were real) using existing traditions. Biographers selected and adapted traditions, and some took more liberties than others. But biographers such as Cornelius Nepos, Plutarch, Arrian, Tacitus, Suetonius, and Diogenes Laertius did not invent events; rather, they drew upon prior biographic and historic accounts, collections of sayings, oral traditions, and legends. Of course, no one claims that all their sources are reliable. But in general, sources written closer to the events they depict depend upon more genuinely historical, as opposed to legendary, information, as ancient writers themselves acknowledged. Although scholars often cite works such as Xenophon's *Cyropedia* and Pseudo–Callisthenes' *Alexander Romance*, which were composed far more freely, these works differ so greatly in character from mainstream biographies (falling closer to novels about historical characters) that they belong in a different category. (As with other novels, they remain relevant for literary comparisons, but they differ substantially from the biographies of authors just mentioned.)

Appeal to the biographic genre cannot resolve all historical questions, however, not least because the category (even with the caveat offered above) remains a broad one. Plutarch (and certainly Philo) took more liberties than Suetonius; John clearly took more liberties than, say, Luke. I believe that genre can predispose us to doubt that John simply invented the events that he describes, but genre does not help us evaluate his sources for such events or the degree to which he has adapted details in those sources.

Moreover, although ancient historians sometimes adapted speeches in their sources, many also composed speeches freely where necessary (Josephus, for example, introduces Hellenistic speeches into the biblical narrative). Whereas John's narratives are, as Prof. Smith points out, synopticlike, the Fourth Gospel's speech material (with its explicit Christology) appears more problematic. Synoptic comparison nevertheless helps. Some of Jesus' sayings in John parallel those in the Synoptics but obviously reflect a Johannine idiom. This observation may permit us to suppose that some of Jesus' other sayings in the Fourth Gospel that do not enjoy multiple attestation may also represent earlier tradition that has been recast in Johannine idiom.

John does, after all, claim eyewitness tradition. Andrew Lincoln has recently argued that the eyewitness tradition claim is a fictitious literary device that would be so recognized by ancient readers (2005, 23–25). Were John writing an apocalypse, this would be the case, but biographers who claimed to be present at events or who cited others present there were making historical claims (Keener 2006). (One could counter with Philostratus' Damis in *Life of Apollonius*, but this work is closer to Pseudo–Callisthenes than to the biographies we have noted.) Extrinsic confirmations, such as topographic accuracy long after 70 C.E, also differentiate John from ancient novelists.

More sensitive to narrative cohesion than in the past, scholarship today tends to be more skeptical of source theories, which, despite their frequent brilliance, have so often produced contradictory results. The unity of John's style invites attention to John's story as a whole; at the same time, scholars today are often unconvinced by hypothetical reconstructions of sources no longer extant. Unlike such sources, comparison with the Synoptics can afford an objective basis for comparison. Yet as Prof. Smith has pointed out, though historical questions often return to the relation between John and the Synoptics, they do not stop there. If we assume that John was independent of the Synoptics, his inclusion of Synoptic events and sayings suggests that he has included prior traditional material. If this is the case with material that independently surfaces in the Synoptics, it is probably the case for much of the rest of his material as well.

But let us assume for a moment that John depended upon one or more of the Synoptic Gospels (which, on most views of dating, should have been circulating in the churches by his time). Would not the same caveat obtain? That is, if John depends upon the Synoptics at points, he writes not as a pure novelist but as one who at least sometimes works from tradition. Is it reasonable to suppose that he depends only upon sources that happen to have remained extant (i.e., the Synoptics), yet freely invents everything else? Dare we suppose that the sources now extant were the only stories about Jesus in circulation, when Luke claims that there were "many" (Luke 1:1)? It is true that we cannot verify John's use of sources at such points, but neither can we dismiss them. Given John's use of sources where we can test him (that is, where they remain extant), the burden of proof should generally favor prior tradition in John in particular cases where we lack other deciding factors. On the whole, it seems likely that John, an ancient biographer claiming an independent eyewitness source, does in fact preserve much older information.

To argue that John contains information about events does not explain what he does with that information, a question that can be tested only by examination. For example, in my own work on John (Keener 2003), I found no reason to believe that most of this Gospel specifically "depends upon" the Synoptics (though I do believe that John knew of them and other works). The case appears to me different, however, in the Passion narrative, where John seems to adapt the familiar passion story: instead of Judas dipping in the cup with Jesus, Jesus gives him the bread; instead of a Last Supper evoking the paschal context of Jesus' death, the crucifixion itself falls on Passover; instead of Simon bearing the cross, Jesus carries his own. I believe that John adapted (or at least selected) some details from the traditional passion story in a way that is theologically significant and that he expected his audience to notice.

In the final analysis, most scholars agree that the Gospel of John includes and adapts some historical tradition. Because so much data no longer remains extant, scholars differ on the quantity of tradition and the nature of its adaptation. The Synoptics help provide an objective control for our approaches, inviting a greater appreciation for John's historical value.

CHAPTER 17

TRADITION, EXEGETICAL FORMATION, AND THE LEUVEN HYPOTHESIS

Gilbert Van Belle

No single book in the history of Western civilization has exerted greater influence on the way we live than the Bible. Throughout the centuries, this "Word of God" has served the Christian community as both canon and point of reference. The Bible has been used and abused for countless purposes, so much so that readers are often surprised to find that one and the same text has been explained in a variety of often highly disparate ways.[1] For many, the Bible represents a source of inspiration for selfless engagement and sacrifice on behalf of the community, but it nevertheless remains evident that biblical texts have not infrequently been used to serve personal interests and, in some instances, even to legitimate political regimes. In spite of the 2,000–year gap between our postmodern society and the Semitic and Hellenistic worlds, and in spite of evidence of a degree of disinterest, the Bible continues to inspire many. The last two centuries of the previous millennium witnessed many changes in how biblical texts are explained, especially within the Catholic Church. As Frans van Segbroeck has observed:

[1] One example will serve to illustrate this point. During the Nazi regime, the phrase "salvation comes from the Jews" (John 4:22) was removed from the German Children's Bible because it did not square with anti–Jewish Nazi ideology (Van Belle 2001).

Little of the traditional understanding of inspiration has sur-
vived. Instead of the concept 'infallible,' taken for centuries to
be the Bible's greatest quality, we now speak in terms of 'truth,'
a concept that leaves open considerable room for interpretation.
The Bible as Word of God has also become a human book, a
book in which human persons in all their diversity are far from
strangers. (2001, 128–30, quote 130)

In this article, I will endeavor to explore the future of biblical exegesis
from my particular perspective as a Catholic exegete and a professor at
K.U.Leuven (Belgium). An exegete must be aware of his background and
training. A number of factors play a significant role in one's research:
denominational heritage (Catholic, Protestant, Pentecostal, or secular—
note that Belgium is predominantly Catholic); whether one studies at a
seminary or a university; whether the institution is progressive or conservative in its thinking; whether one's degree focuses on the arts and
sciences or theology. I was trained at a Faculty of Theology in a Catholic
University (K.U.Leuven), which stands in a particular relation to Rome.
Moreover, one's professional role at an institution—for example, whether
one is engaged as a teaching professor or a researcher—inevitably influences the questions that are asked, the methods employed, the themes
treated, and the stances taken. All these factors were important to the
development of my career as an exegete, but my research was especially
influenced by my experiences as an assistant to Prof. Frans Neirynck during the 1970s and 1980s, the period that saw the emergence of the "Leuven School" in Johannine Studies.

Frans Neirynck, a diocesan priest, was born on May 15, 1927, in
Wingene (West Flanders). He studied Greek and Latin at the secondary
school in Tielt (1940–1946), philosophy in Roeselare (1946–1947), classical philology at K.U.Leuven (1947–1949), and theology at the Great
Seminary in Bruges (1949–1953) and at K.U.Leuven (1953–1957). He
served as professor in Sacramentology and Ecclesiology at the Great
Seminary in Bruges (1957–1960) before his appointment as Professor of
New Testament Exegesis at Leuven in 1961. Neirynck retired in 1992
(see Van Segbroeck et al. 1992, 1.1–89; Focant 1993, xiii–xxxix; Van Belle
1997, 95–121).[2] Neirynck's exegetical work must be seen in relation to
that of his colleague at K.U.Leuven, Maurits Sabbe (1924–2003), also a
priest of the diocese of Bruges who had a passion for the Fourth Gospel

---

[2] Neirynck's collected essays appear in Neirynck 1982; Neirynck 1991; Neirynck 2001. On John and the Synoptics, see also Neirynck et al., 1979.

(Van Belle 2004; 1997, 119–21). On completing his doctorate in 1953, Sabbe was appointed a professor at the Great Seminary in Bruges and was responsible for teaching courses in the Old Testament and New Testament. He also served as librarian, reflecting his love for books—appropriately, the library of the faculty of theology at K.U.Leuven is named after him. Sabbe was appointed to the faculty of K.U.Leuven in 1967 and retired in 1989. In the preface to an important collection of his articles, Sabbe characterizes the era of his teaching career as "a time of significant changes within the Church and of growing opportunities for critical biblical scholarship" (Sabbe 1991).

My remarks here will focus on Neirynck's influence on the rich and evolving exegetical tradition at K.U.Leuven, and particularly on the emergence of the so–called "Leuven Hypothesis" on the Gospel of John.[3] First, I will reflect upon the task of the exegete, specifically describing three facets: the exegete as historian and philologist; the exegete as believer and theologian; and, the exegete in dialogue. I will then formulate what I believe to be the major challenges facing exegesis at the present time. My remarks in these first two sections will interact with a number of passages from the document of the Papal Biblical Commission on "The Interpretation of the Bible in the Church" (15 April 1993), which also outlines "the task of the exegete."[4] I believe this document to be determinative for the future of Catholic exegesis and biblical theology, which stands in relation to and dialogue with other denominations and approaches, as well as classical philology, literary theory, science, and philosophy. Note that, in the discussion to follow, citations in [brackets] refer to page numbers in Joseph Fitzmyer's 1995 commentary on this document. Finally, I will conclude with remarks on the Leuven School's approach to the Gospel of John.

---

[3] Portions of the following discussion are a revised version of my 2003 essay "Dialogue with Tradition" (Van Belle 2003). Note that K.U.Leuven is located in Flanders, the Dutch–speaking region of Belgium. In 1968, the university split: the French–speaking Université Catholique de Louvain moved to a new campus in Louvain–la–Neuve, and the Dutch–speaking Katholieke Universiteit Leuven remained in Leuven. Note that all references to the post–1968 situation at K.U.Leuven refer to the Dutch campus in Leuven.

[4] The English text appears in *The Interpretation of the Bible in the Church: Address of His Holiness Pope John Paul II and Document of the Pontifical Biblical Commission* (Rome: Libreria Editrice Vaticana, 1993); see also *Origins* 23 (1994), pp. 498–524. For other commentaries on this document, see Houlden 1995; Williamson 2001, esp. 273–88.

THE EXEGETE'S TASK

As noted, the exegete plays three roles: historian and philologist; believer and theologian; and, participant in an ongoing dialogue. As a *historian*, I have been taught to study and explain the Bible, which is read in the church community as "the Word of God in human language" [26]. The Bible consists of a collection of ancient literary texts written in Hebrew, Aramaic, and Greek. As such, the initial task of the exegete is to acquire a thorough and effective knowledge of these languages. The texts of the Bible, written in the aforementioned ancient languages, ought to be explained in the same scientific fashion as any other literary work stemming from antiquity. This perspective on the exegesis of the Bible was already considered a necessity by J. J. Wettstein in the eighteenth century, who argued that "since we read sacred books, the decrees of a ruler, and all books ancient and new with the same eyes, we are obliged to apply a same set of rules for the interpretation thereof, which we use for their understanding."[5]

At K.U.Leuven, the scientific study of the significance of ancient texts employs the historical–critical method as its primary and most essential tool. This methodological approach allows us to establish a contextualized picture of the significance of what the authors and redactors of the Bible had in mind when they wrote. As a research method, historical–critical analysis includes several different stages: reconstruction of the original text; linguistic (morphological and syntactic) and semantic analysis; study of the structure of the text and its various component textual units; reconstruction of the sources employed; study of the literary genre; and research into the transmission and redaction of the text. In this light, it is essential that any explanation of the text's historical situation be coordinated with reading the text (literary, rhetorical, narrative, structural, and semiotic analyses), measuring one's reading against other methods rooted in tradition (canonical interpretation, Jewish interpretive traditions, and the study of the *Wirkungsgeschichte* of the text), and comparing one's conclusions to approaches based primarily in the human sciences (sociological, cultural–anthropological, psychological and psychoanalytical analyses) as well as the so–called "contextual approaches" (liberation theologies and feminist readings).

As a *believer* and *theologian*, I have been taught that the Bible is the Word of God "in which, as in a mirror, the pilgrim Church contemplates

---

[5] Cf. *Novum Testamentum Graecum* (Amsterdam, ex officina Dommeriana, 1752), 2.875: "Sicut autem iisdem oculis & libros sacros· & edicta Principis, & libros omnes veteres novosque legimus: ita etiam eaedem regulae in interpretatione illorum sunt adhibendae, quibus ad horum intelligentiam utimur."

God, the source of all her riches" (*Catechism* 28/§97). For the church community, the Bible is thus not only a collection of historical documents related to its origins; it is first and foremost the Word of God addressed to the community and to the entire world. The Bible is a book of the church and for the church. "The Bible came into existence within believing communities. In it the faith of Israel found expression, later that of the early Christian communities" [156–57]. In other words, the Bible is the source within which the Christian community seeks its identity. It should be noted at this juncture that the Catholic tradition does not recognize the *sola scriptura* principle maintained in the Protestant tradition. In addition to the Bible, tradition as a source of theological reflection plays an important role for Catholics. It was with this in mind that the *Dogmatic Constitution on Divine Revelation* of the Second Vatican Council declared that the church accepts the biblical writings together with the sacred tradition as its primary rule of faith (*Dei Verbum* §21; compare §24).

As a believer, the exegete is compelled to ensure that the content of the Bible is passed on in an always authentic manner. Thus, the exegete is obliged to pay due attention to hermeneutical approaches that can contribute to the recovery of the actual significance of the Bible's message [108–193]. The work of the exegete is incomplete, therefore, if he or she restricts his or her endeavors to the establishment of the text of a biblical book, reconstructing its sources, describing its literary forms and employed procedures, or determining the period and location of its origins. Exegetes will only achieve their purpose "when they have explained the meaning of the biblical text as God's word for today" [156]. They must therefore pay due attention to the actualization and enculturation of the biblical message [170–78]. In addition, they are obliged to account for the various ways in which the Bible is employed in the church: in liturgy, in *lectio divina*, in pastoral work, in catechism, and in the ecumenical movement [179–88]. Given the fact that the Bible can serve as "the soul of theology" for a believer [163], exegetes are required to explain its Christological, canonical, and ecclesial significance [156–57].

Finally, the task of the exegete is not that of the scholarly recluse. On the contrary, the exegete must enter into *dialogue* with a variety of different groups in a variety of different contexts. Following this principle, professors of biblical exegesis at K.U.Leuven introduce their students to the different methodologies that are used to study biblical texts, making it clear that the Scriptures must be studied with great care and objectivity if their literary, historical, social, and theological values are to be discovered. Rooted in a profound respect for the Word of God, the education of students in the exegetical endeavor needs to attain a high intellectual content, adapted, nevertheless, to the environment in which it is undertaken and to the partners whom it also serves. "More technical in university faculties, this teaching will have a more directly pastoral orientation in seminaries" [159]. Given that exegesis should be understood as an undertaking within the theological sciences (*fides quaerens intellectum*), exegetes need to enter into dialogue with systematic and dogmatic theology, moral theology, liturgy, pastoral theology, missiology, and catechism [161–169, 179–188].

As one aspect of this dialogue, K.U.Leuven places a high priority on the publication of research results. Publishing in high–ranking, internationally acclaimed academic venues brings Catholic exegetes into contact with the broader scientific world. Through more popular publications, the exegete comes into contact with different readers: the general public, educated adults and children in catechetical programs, Bible study groups, apostolic movements, and congregations [160–161]. By making the results of their research accessible to the broader public, exegetes bear in mind the significant questions of their time, questions relevant to both the church and the world at large.

The Bible also has a universal and a missionary aspect. "Moreover, since the Bible tells of God's offer of salvation to all people, the exegetical task necessarily includes a universal dimension. This means taking account of other religions and of the hopes and fears of the world of today" [157]. The exegete will thus be obliged to enter into specific dialogue with other religions that have established their foundations on a "sacred book."

The Exegete's Challenges

The working environment of faculty members at K.U.Leuven is no longer that of our professors, even when we wish to continue in their traditions. As a consequence of secularization, a number of profound changes have taken place in the study of the Bible. Here I will simply note five such changes that seem particularly significant. First, in contemporary Belgian society the study of theology and exegesis has declined for the simple reason that faith itself has declined. Second, the availability of courses in exegesis at many universities and seminaries has been considerably reduced. In many universities, theology now faces strong competition from religious studies. As more time is devoted to the study of other religions, less time is available for theological courses and, as a consequence, for exegesis. Seminaries likewise devote considerable time to the development of pastoral skills at the cost of the other theological courses (Johnson and Kurz 2002, 38–39). Third, one is left with the impression that, despite the efforts of the Second Vatican Council, the study of the Bible in the context of Catholic education and in the church as a whole continues to occupy a secondary position. The fact that many Catholics own their own Bible does not mean that they enjoy the same culture of reading Scripture evident among members of other denominations. Fourth, in our secularized society, the study of exegesis tends to be located more frequently within the study of the humanities in general or in departments of religious studies. As a result, in most cases the academic environment in which biblical exegesis is studied is at best neutral and at worst hostile toward the community of faith in which the Bible is understood as canon (Johnson and Kurz 2002, 38 n. 12). Fifth and finally, interest in ancient languages, so essential for the study of the biblical text, has diminished considerably in recent decades. All these cultural changes present dramatic challenges to the task of exegesis.

If Christianity still hopes to offer a relevant response to questions concerning the meaning and value of life, then the significance of the Christian message expressed in the Bible needs to be translated, rephrased, and explained anew. At the same time, however, the tasks of exegesis now transcend the capacities of a single individual. In the future, the various tasks of interpretation outlined before will doubtless be divided and shared as scholarship continues to move toward specialization [157–58]. What then are the priorities that such a division of labor should establish in today's world? I will focus here on four issues: the importance of philology, the centrality of the historical–critical method, the need for integrated exegetical research, and the unavoidability of dialogue with church and world.

First, exegetes must be challenged to provide quality philological research. A profound and scientific knowledge of the biblical languages (Hebrew, Aramaic, and Greek) and of Latin is of primary importance. Although each group and generation of Christians throughout the world has a right to its own translation of the Bible, the provision of such translations brings with it a complex process of study and dialogue that not only enjoys religious significance but also has social and cultural importance. Every translation, moreover, is a rewording and an interpretation, whereby the enculturation of the Bible is set in motion. "The theological foundation of enculturation is the conviction of faith that the Word of God transcends the cultures in which it has found expressions and has the capability of being spread in other cultures, in such a way as to be able to reach all human beings in the cultural context in which they live" [176].

Second, the historical–critical method developed and used by my predecessors is indispensable for the interpretation of the Bible and, I would contend, is still the most appropriate method for interpretation of the foundational texts of Christianity. "The eternal Word became incar-

nate at a precise period of history, within a clearly defined cultural and
social environment. Anyone who desires to understand the Word of God
should humbly seek it out there where it has made itself visible and accept
to this end the necessary help of human knowledge" [189]. For this reason, the Pontifical Biblical Commission correctly insists that

> the very nature of biblical texts means that interpreting them will
> require continued use of the historical–critical method, at least
> in its principal procedures. The Bible, in effect, does not present
> itself as a direct revelation of timeless truths but as the written
> testimony to a series of interventions in which God reveals him-
> self in human history. In a way that differs from tenets of other
> religions, the message of the Bible is solidly grounded in history.
> It follows that the biblical writings cannot be correctly under-
> stood without an examination of the historical circumstances
> that shaped them. [190]

It should be noted, in addition, that the historical–critical method is a
most effective antidote to fundamentalism and misuse of the Bible.

Third, the flood of publications in the field of exegesis reveals a great
need for integrated approaches in which the results of scientific research
are presented with clarity and depth. Exegesis at K.U.Leuven has also
given a high priority to biblical–theological studies, and monographs and
articles in service of dogmatic theology, ethics, pastoral theology, and
liturgy are encouraged.

Fourth and finally, an exegete who is a member of a church community must accept this reality as his or her greatest challenge. Exegetes
cannot remain indifferent to the changes that have taken place in present–day culture. They are obliged to accept with conviction their task
of proclamation, endeavoring to make the richness and relevance of the
Bible accessible to their contemporaries. In fulfilling this task, they do
not serve in isolation but rather in dialogue with others and the church
community. The Bible came into existence in a community rooted in a
living tradition and serves as canon for the church today; in other words,
the Bible is and always has been community–establishing. Outside the
church the Bible is a lifeless text, but within the church it is of sacred and
formative significance. For Christians, the Bible is not just a book like any
other; it is the Book of books, a mirror for life, the Book of the faithful
and the Book about the faith. The clarification of this principle for people
of the twenty–first century is the primary challenge faced by exegetes
today. This is a point that exegetes need to take into consideration when
conducting their scientific research.

THE GOSPEL OF JOHN AND THE LEUVEN SCHOOL

In 1966, I began studies in the Faculty of Theology at the Catholic University of Leuven. From this vantage point, I was privileged to witness the birth of the Leuven Hypothesis on the Gospel of John. The remainder of my remarks will situate this hypothesis within the tradition of the faculty and then briefly outline my current thinking on the relevant issues.

At the end of the nineteenth century, Albinus Van Hoonacker (1857–1933), professor of Old Testament, and Paulin Ladeuze (1870–1940), Professor of New Testament, in cooperation with church historian Alfred Cauchie (1860–1922), brought renewal to the Leuven theology faculty by introducing the historical–critical method. In the twentieth century, Joseph Coppens (1896–1981) and Lucien Cerfaux (1883–1968) followed the precedent of Van Hoonacker and Ladeuze by initiating a comprehensive scientific oeuvre. As professors of Old and New Testament, they served on the editorial board of the periodical *Ephemerides Theologicae Lovanienses* (established in 1924). They also founded the annual Colloquium Biblicum Lovaniense (1949). Their students, Frans Neirynck and Maurits Sabbe, continued in the tradition of historical–critical biblical research and applied this method to the study of the Gospel of John.[6] As dean of the Faculty of Theology from 1968–1972, Neirynck insisted that "the Louvain tradition demands serious scientific labor, critically analyzing the historical growth of Christian thought. Continuing to practice the critical method and introducing it to young theological students. This remains its most important task" (Neirynck 1969, 225–33, quote 233).

Of course, one of the most significant historical–critical questions regarding the Gospel of John is the problem of the relationship between John and the Synoptics. This relationship became an important field of research for Neirynck and Sabbe during the 1970s. Both scholars argued vehemently that the Fourth Evangelist did not make use of traditions lying behind the Synoptic Gospels, but rather used the Synoptic Gospels themselves as sources. By taking this approach, Neirynck and Sabbe naturally distanced themselves from the diachronic methods employed by those who maintained that they could reconstruct sources or distinguish a sequence of redactional phases in the evolution of the Fourth Gospel. In contrast to these scholars, Neirynck and Sabbe tended to favor the literary unity of the Gospel of John, with emphasis on the creativity of the evangelist. Through their influence and writings, the theory of

---

[6] When I studied theology, Neirynck and Sabbe's colleagues in New Testament were Jan Lambrecht, Raymond F. Collins, and Joël Delobel. In 1969, Frans van Segbroeck became Neirynck's most important assistant (Van Belle 1997, 121–44).

John's dependence upon the Synoptics came to be known as the "Leuven Hypothesis."

Neither Neirynck nor Sabbe has given a full description of the interpretive method behind their conclusions. Two of Neirynck's doctoral students, Gabriel Selong and Johan Konings, offered tentative descriptions of the Leuven method in their dissertations (see esp. Selong 1971, 1.123–37; Konings 1972, 1.285–306). According to them, Neirynck's working hypothesis was governed by two principles. First, under no circumstances can exegetical inquiry be based on dubious preconceptions; rather, it must be organized from the known to the lesser known. Concretely, this means that:

> instead of beginning with some a priori consideration (the affirmation of the authenticity or of the historical value of the Fourth Gospel), one should start with the study of the text; in place of trying to recover a presumed primitive order of the text, one has to make an effort to understand and to explain that order as it lays before us; instead of resorting to unknown conjectural sources or traditions, attention must be given first of all to the Synoptics as the possible sources of the Fourth Gospel. (Selong 1971, 1.124)

Second, no tradition or source can be postulated unless there is sufficient reason (*Entia non sunt multiplicanda sine ratione*). Building on this basic framework, Selong and Konings suggest that Neirynck's approach to the Gospel of John followed six major guidelines, which essentially form the framework of the Leuven Hypothesis.

First, the Fourth Gospel is a theological work and not a history. The evangelist deliberately chose the literary genre "Gospel" as the vehicle of his message, a genre that originated in early Christianity (Neirynck 1993, 258–59). Therefore, corresponding to the Gospel genre, John describes the life and teachings of Jesus in a connected narrative from the teaching of the Baptist to Jesus' death and resurrection. But the Gospel of John is not simply a narrated account of Jesus' career; rather, it is an interpreted account of the significance of his person and teachings. As such, the Johannine narrative is a dramatic presentation of the theological significance and meaning of the incidents narrated, including even the events of the passion. The narrative elements are, furthermore, treated as "signs" or symbols of unseen realities, and this symbolic character goes deeply into the whole of the work (Selong 1971, 1.124). Moreover, and perhaps most importantly, it must be emphasized that the uniqueness of the Fourth Gospel is located in the fact that it finds the eternal reality conclusively revealed and embodied in a historical person who actually lived, worked, taught, suffered and died, with direct historical consequences. This principle is clearly expressed in John 1:14: "And the Word became flesh" (cf. Dodd 1953, 444).

Second, textual criticism forms a crucial part of the Leuven Hypothesis simply because exegesis must focus on the evangelist's text. Therefore, an attempt should be made to establish, provisionally at least, the most probable reading of the passages in question. Consideration must also be given to "variant readings," because these might reflect the earliest interpretations of the text (Selong 1.124).

Third, the so-called aporias in the Gospel of John—abrupt changes in the flow of the narrative, artificial transitions, inconsistencies in grammar or logical sequence—are also important considerations in assessing the relationship between literary unity (and literary criticism) and historical reliability. Aporias could indicate that the evangelist used material "which originally stood in a different context" or combined "material deriving from the source and material coming from the Evangelist"; they could also indicate "the use of material taken from two different places of the source" (Selong 1971, 1.124–25). In stark contrast to the many attempts to uncover hypothetical sources behind the Fourth Gospel, proponents of the Leuven Hypothesis insist that the Gospel of John should first be compared to the Synoptics, not only because they are of the same genre but also because they have similar structures and content—at least, far more similar than any other known (that is to say, "not postulated"), documents. Furthermore, even an "early date" of writing cannot threaten the literary dependency of the Fourth Gospel on the Synoptics, because stylistic, theological, and historical research has indicated with some certainty that the Gospel of John was written after the break with Judaism (Konings 1972, 1.301).

Fourth, John's creativity should not be restricted, for, just as the authors of the Synoptics went about their work freely and creatively, so also did the Fourth Evangelist (Selong 1971, 1.124–25). John reworked the synoptic material in various ways within the boundaries of his creative freedom. Thus, he sometimes distributed elements of particular passages from the Synoptics throughout his Gospel, and in other instances combined different passages from the Synoptics into one scene. The creativity and freedom that characterize the Fourth Evangelist's work can be illustrated by studying his use of the Old Testament. He uses the same freedom when referring to the words of Jesus (Van Belle 1997).

Fifth, the possibility should not be dismissed that material unique to John (and thus not found in the Synoptics) might reflect important theological interests of the evangelist. In fact, this should be expected

in a work that aims to interpret the theological significance of the life
and ministry of Jesus. Thus, when the differences between the Fourth
Gospel and the Synoptics are established, it is necessary to determine
whether or to what degree these reflect John's unique terminology, style,
and motives (Selong 1971, 1.125).

Sixth and finally, to ascertain John's possible employment of sources
and possible transformation of those sources, it is crucial to pay particular
attention to the author's vocabulary, grammar, style characteristics, literary tendencies (use of synonyms, dramatization, parenthetic comments),
themes, motifs (of reminiscence, of misunderstanding, for instance), and
ways of thinking (Selong 1971, 1.125). This being said, it is nevertheless
important to note that uniqueness of vocabulary, which may arise simply
from uniqueness of subject matter, does not necessarily indicate that John
has used a special source. The priority of the Synoptics in the interpretation of the Fourth Gospel leads proponents of the Leuven Hypothesis to
elucidate the proper place, in our view, of the use of other background
material as follows:

> Only after comparisons have been made between John and the
> Synoptics is it feasible to make comparisons with other texts
> (such as the apocrypha, Gnostic literature, texts from Qumran
> and Nag Hammadi, Hellenistic, Jewish and Rabbinic literature)
> and to use such texts in the interpretation of the fourth gospel.
> (Konings 1972, 1.302)

Based on this working hypothesis, the most significant results of
my own research as a Johannine exegete and a member of the "Leuven
School" may be formulated briefly as follows. First, the language and
style of the Gospel of John are so homogenous, and the craftsmanship of
the evangelist is so creative, that it is impossible to distinguish alternative
sources or traditions apart from the Synoptics. Second, the homogenous
Christological and theological language of the evangelist, his symbolism,
and the structure of the text, lead the reader to see, within the framework
of Christology and soteriology, "the Word made flesh"—that is, not the
historical Jesus, but the faith of the Johannine community. According to
this faith, Jesus is the Messiah, the "Son of God," who was sent to the
world for our salvation. Third, as a result of the first two conclusions, the
possibility of authentic historical tradition in the Fourth Gospel can be
neither denied nor proven.[7]

---

[7] Compare my remarks here to the cautious conclusion of C. M. Tuckett on
the historical reliability of the Fourth Gospel: "These differences [i.e., the differences between John and the Synoptics] make it very difficult to see both John

Conclusion

The teaching of Scripture, wherever it takes place, must continue to submit itself to the demands of strict scientific research. For me, this implies the continuation of the tradition of historical–critical research in which I was formed, but in dialogue with other methodological approaches to the Bible. With regard to the Gospel of John particularly, I continue to use the method of the Leuven School. As an exegete in a faculty of theology, however, the postmodern context in which we live obliges me to make it clear that the Bible is more than just another ancient text; it contains the Word of God in the language of human persons. It is for this reason that I am able to give my full support to the document of the Pontifical Biblical Commission, which describes the goal of the exegete as follows: "the aim of the exegete is to shed more and more light on the biblical texts themselves, helping them to be better appreciated for what they are in themselves and understood with ever more historical accuracy and spiritual depth" [161].

---

and the Synoptics as equally accurate reflections of the historical Jesus. . . . [T]he teaching of the historical Jesus is likely to be more accurately reflected in the Synoptic tradition than in John's Gospel. This does not mean that John's Gospel is historically worthless in terms of any quest for the historical Jesus. Some details of John's account appear more historically plausible than the Synoptic accounts and may well be historical" (Tuckett 2001, 126–27).

17: RESPONSE

THE LEUVEN HYPOTHESIS IN
C/cATHOLIC PERSPECTIVE

Peter J. Judge

As Professor Van Belle indicates in his essay, the Catholic University at Leuven is home to a rich tradition of biblical interpretation, one that is fully self–conscious of hearing, reading, and understanding the Scriptures in the midst of a community of faith. As Van Belle points out in his summation of the Pontifical Biblical Commission's document *The Interpretation of the Bible in the Church*, this community is *Catholic* in an obvious and official sense in that it responds to the guidance of the teaching office that speaks for and in the name of the whole church. In a related but perhaps less juridical sense, this is a *catholic* community in that it reads the Bible together and knows that the meaning of the Bible emerges from this dynamic reading as church, as People of God, whose collective wisdom is always more than the sum of the parts. This tradition of reading and interpretation is also *catholic* in that it reaches back and rests upon the wisdom, both scholarly and spiritual, of those whose voices are now silent and whose pens are long still, but who remain eloquent in a new way. Of course, this approach is certainly not unique to Roman Catholic Bible readers, nor are all Catholic readers aware of or in agreement with such an outlook. But this description does, I believe, encapsulate the spirit that generally pervades the Catholic scholarly approach to reading and interpreting sacred Scripture, whether in the historical–critical tradition for which K.U.Leuven is well known or through newer, post-modern methodologies.

When it comes specifically to the interpretation of the Gospel of John, the approach of those who are groomed in the Leuven tradition could also be said to be rather *Catholic*. This emphasis is epitomized in the first "guideline" in the framework of the Leuven Hypothesis that Van Belle elicits from Selong and Konings: "the Fourth Gospel is a theological work and not a history"; it "is not simply a narrated account of Jesus' career; rather it is an interpreted account of the significance of his person and teachings." At first blush, hardly anyone would take issue with such statements, yet they make a simple point that becomes a kind of ethos. One could fairly say that modern Catholic scholarship has not been characterized by a focus on the historical Jesus, nor by efforts to isolate a core of so–called authentic words of Jesus or biographical material. Such concerns are not absent, but in general it seems to me that Catholic exegetes are more oriented to the study of the Gospels as vehicles for discovering the proclaimed Jesus, the Christ. Somewhat paradoxically, the Christian proclamation of good news in a saving encounter with God is without doubt "embodied in a historical person"—"the Word became flesh" (John 1:14)—yet the real value of reading and studying the Gospel of John comes not from mining the text for historical data but rather from engaging the Christology and soteriology—that is to say, the faith—of the Johannine community. Van Belle notes that "authentic historical tradition in the Fourth Gospel can be neither denied nor proven"; in fact, it is not even the point of the scholarly endeavor. What is important is not how much or how well the Gospel of John preserves the historical Jesus, but rather how the Fourth Evangelist has (re–)interpreted the meaning of the "real" Jesus Christ for faith.

Reading John as a Gospel brings us to another sense in which the Leuven approach is catholic in the more general sense. I was first inclined to call this an extended meaning of the term in view of what has been mentioned earlier, but in fact it is listed as the very first definition of the word "catholic" in my Webster's Dictionary: "comprehensive." Leuven scholars have endeavored to read John among the Gospels in a comprehensive way, as a relatively late first–century Christian proclamation in the form of a rather unique literary genre shared with the Synoptics. In points 3 through 6 in his framework of the Leuven Hypothesis, Van Belle stresses the necessity of understanding the Johannine Gospel, its language, style, and presentation of events, first and foremost in comparison and contrast to the Synoptic Gospels, with a full openness to the evangelist's unique creativity precisely vis–à–vis these earlier Gospels. A crucial aspect of this approach, moreover, is the importance of doing such study with careful attention to the redactional history of the Synoptics themselves.

Anyone who knows the so–called "Leuven Hypothesis" knows that its center of energy comes from the encyclopedic and tireless study of Prof. Frans Neirynck. The first paper Neirynck ever delivered at an SNTS meeting (Neirynck 1968) signaled his program, upon which he would insist over and again, "to study carefully the tradition–redaction problem of the Synoptic texts before drawing any conclusion about the origin of the Synoptic-like elements in John" (1977, 94).[1] Following this logic, in his survey of research on "John and the Synoptics" at the 1975 *Colloquium Biblicum Lovaniense*, Neirynck remarked, "It is . . . an inherent difficulty in the commentaries on John that parallel texts from the Synoptics are abundantly quoted but scarcely examined from the viewpoint of redaction criticism" (1977, 77). Twenty years later, in a critique of a published *Akzessarbeit* on the Centurion/Royal Official story (John 4:46–54), Neirynck again noted that examining tradition and redaction in both the synoptic and the Johannine pericopes before discussing their relationship is a good method, but insisted that premature acceptance of a pre–Johannine source "*oriente déjà les options synoptiques*" ("already predisposes the synoptic options"; 1995, 178).

At the same time, Neirynck did not propose that John relied exclusively on the Synoptics. He argued, rather, that one should exhaust every possibility of a thorough redaction–critical approach to the Synoptics and to John before exploring the Fourth Evangelist's possible dependence upon other (hypothetical) written sources.[2] John's creative use of synoptic material, influenced by developments both theological and sociological in the author's own community, can be fully explained without recourse to independent sources.

An important crux of the debate came home to me during an exchange between Professors Neirynck and D. Moody Smith at the evening *Carrefour* at the Louvain Biblical Colloquium on "John and the Synoptics" in 1990. Neirynck and Smith were discussing their respective conceptions of the nature of redaction–criticism as applied to the Fourth Gospel. It

---

[1] In an earlier study, Neirynck had declared that examination of the Fourth Evangelist's redaction "should not be done without a careful analysis and an evaluation of all potentialities implied in the Synoptic narrative" (1975, 129).

[2] See the "Additional Note" to *John 5, 1–18 and the Gospel of Mark: A Response to P. Borgen*, where Neirynck objected to the assertion that his approach was simply to reject any unknown or hypothetical sources for John in favor of sole reliance upon the Synoptics: "I am not aware that I ever gave such exclusiveness to the Synoptic Gospels as to exclude John's use of oral–tradition or source material" (Neirynck 1991, 711–12).

became clear that Smith defined redaction–criticism rather narrowly as the examination of a biblical author's editorial reworking of a specific source text. For Neirynck, on the other hand, the study of the Fourth Evangelist's redaction was much more a matter of analyzing a creative *relecture* of synoptic material (Neirynck 1992, 15; 2001, 15). Some recent publications would suggest that Neirynck's approach is becoming more *catholic*, as it seems to be found now beyond the confines of Leuven.

Neirynck's way of working continues to shape the research and writing of a new generation of Leuven scholars. Van Belle's own work on the linguistic and stylistic unity of the Fourth Gospel and his monograph–sized review and critique of the signs–source hypothesis are now well known and widely used.[3] Others are examining the Fourth Gospel and/or its individual pericopes from both historical– and narrative–critical perspectives, and some are addressing anew the question of John's value for our knowledge of the historical Jesus. These studies do not follow simple source– and redaction–critical models by which an evangelist can be shown to have redacted or edited a clearly distillable source text. I see them, rather, as literary applications of the notion that the Fourth Evangelist provides us with an extremely insightful understanding of Jesus, even though his narrative may not be the most historically factual presentation.[4] If we can exhaustively examine all the potentialities of the Matthew, Mark, and Luke redactions of the Gospel, can we not then examine the Fourth Gospel from the perspective that the evangelist creatively made use of these earlier iterations to provide a deeper, more lasting appreciation of the real meaning of the story, at least from the Johannine perspective?

[3] See, for example, Van Belle 1985, 1997b, 2001, 2003a; also Van Belle 1994 (on the signs–source hypothesis). I should also mention his rather comprehensive Johannine Bibliography (Van Belle 1988).

[4] This notion is borrowed from John Painter's paper, "Interface of History and Theology in John," delivered to the John, Jesus, and History group at the 2004 Society of Biblical Literature Annual Meeting. Note that Painter is inclined to accept John's knowledge of, but not dependence upon, the Synoptics.

CHAPTER 18

THE ROAD AHEAD
THREE ASPECTS OF JOHANNINE SCHOLARSHIP

Urban C. von Wahlde

In 1973, when I began work on my doctoral dissertation, Prof. Noel Lazure, my director, suggested that I adopt some position regarding the literary origin of the Gospel of John and move on in my study of the symbolism of the "crowd" (ὄχλος) in the Gospel. Three years before that, Robert Fortna had published *The Gospel of Signs* (1970). I was impressed with the care with which he did his work and the way he set out criteria for determining what belonged to the signs source and what did not. As I worked on the instances of ὄχλος in John 7, my attention was also called to a dissertation by M. C. White on "the Jews" in the Fourth Gospel (1972). White pointed out that John uses two sets of terms for "authorities" and that these alternate in the text. The one set comprises of "Pharisees," "chief priests," and "rulers," and the other is represented only by the term "the Jews." White referred to Wellhausen's earlier work on chapter 7, which had argued the same position. I was struck by that observation and began to notice other features that were consistent with the material associated with these two sets of terms. As a result of my work on this subject, Professor Lazure suggested I petition for a change of topic—because I had already written three hundred pages on the literary analysis of the Gospel! And so, my dissertation came to set forth the beginning of a theory regarding the origin of the Fourth Gospel.

With the demands of teaching, two institutional moves and a growing family, my research proceeded slowly. In 1982, Raymond Brown published his commentary on the Johannine epistles and I was asked to write
a review of it. The thoroughness of the reading necessary for the review
led me to understand in a whole new way both the First Letter of John
and its relationship to the Fourth Gospel. I began to notice that much of
the material that I could not account for in my study of the composition
of the Gospel had considerable similarities to the views of the author of 1
John. At the same time, much of the material in the second of the literary
strata I had already identified in the Gospel of John seemed similar to
the beliefs of the opponents that were being confronted by the author of
1–2–3 John. The more I studied, the more this seemed to be borne out
in the text.

In 1982, I published a study of all the texts in the Gospel of John
that contain the term οἱ Ἰουδαῖοι ("the Jews") as a way of distinguishing
the various uses of this word (von Wahlde 1982). This eventually led to
my becoming concerned with the very important question of possible
anti–Semitism in the Gospel. In the meantime, I had moved again (to my
current position at Loyola University in Chicago) and in 1987 was asked
to chair the department at a time when we were developing a doctoral
program. Again, research on a large scale slowed down, although two
preliminary explorations of the Fourth Gospel appeared in book form. In
1989, I was asked by Michael Glazier to do a commentary for a series he
envisioned. A sequence of unfortunate incidents resulted in his company
being taken over by Liturgical Press, and as it became clear that the type
of commentary I had proposed would not be a good fit with the vision
of the new editors, I was released from my contract but decided to finish
the commentary before seeking another publisher. When I was almost
finished with the first draft, I approached Professor David Noel Freedman, editor of the Anchor Bible series. Unbeknownst to me, Professor
Freedman had just been appointed editor of the new Eerdmans Critical
Commentary series. An agreement was reached for a multivolume commentary in that series, which is now in the final stages of completion.

Beginning about 1998, yet another aspect of the Gospel of John
began to engage my attention. While doing work on my commentary,
I became impressed with the specificity and detail of the Gospel's references to places where narrated events occurred. About this time, Prof.
James Charlesworth of Princeton invited me to give a paper in Jerusalem
in 2000 at a conference on "Jesus and Archaeology." I suggested that I
explore the topic "The Gospel of John and Archaeology," and he agreed.
This led me into a third area of work that has blossomed into a number
of articles.

Since that time, my interests in alleged anti–Judaism and anti–Semitism in the Fourth Gospel, the literary origins of the text, and connections between John and archaeology have continued to dominate my scholarly work. It is from the perspective of these three areas that I would like to make some observations on the present state of Johannine scholarship.

Methods of Interpreting the Gospel of John

My forthcoming commentary attempts what some will judge a futile task—a detailed description of the processes of composition and editing by which the Gospel of John reached its present form. For more than one hundred years, scholars have attempted to identify and define this process without substantial success. This is not surprising, because there are a number of problems that such commentaries must face and that make them fragile works.

The first problem in reconstructing the composition–history of the Fourth Gospel is a general *a priori* skepticism about the feasibility of the project. Although Raymond Brown, in his Anchor Bible commentary (1966–1970), put forward a view of the composition of the Gospel and, in some cases, was quite specific about attributing individual passages to specific periods in the overall process, toward the end of his life he returned to a discussion of the issue and expressed his conviction that scholars should be skeptical about "any commentator's attempt to tell us down to the half–verse what belongs to what edition" (Brown/Moloney 2003, 61; Brown 1994, 23, 75–93).

A second problem is, of course, that such commentaries are necessarily complex and require a considerable commitment of time and effort to critique. This complexity in and of itself is enough to prevent some scholars from fully testing a theory. Yet at the same time, it has to be said that, if the composition of a Gospel was in fact a complex process, no understanding of it will be complete until that complexity is accounted for. It has often struck me that scholars who are not committed to preaching on a Gospel regularly are, in some ways, better situated to undertake such study, because they are not compelled by an immediate need to "make sense" of a text and to apply it to the spiritual needs of a congregation. Such pressure to make sense of a passage or an entire text can get in the way of facing fully the range of problems that it presents.

The third problem is that, inevitably, human beings interpret the same words or passages differently. "Real" readers interpret "real" texts in *really* different ways! One need only peruse a number of recent commentaries to be reminded of this fact. When one includes the Johannine

Epistles in this overview, the situation becomes even more acute. There
are widely (one is tempted to say "wildly") differing views of the nature of
the crisis that divided the Johannine community. There are widely different views even of the relation of the First Letter to the composition of the
Gospel—was 1 John composed before the Gospel or after it or, as I would
hold, at one stage during the process of composition of the Gospel?

The fourth problem with any attempt at reconstruction is that a commentary tends to be dismissed quickly as a whole if the view of the origin
and development of the Gospel and the Letters that it presents proves to
be unconvincing. Such commentaries are looked upon as subjective and
idiosyncratic and, consequently, as minimally useful.

I am well aware that my own commentary will run this very same risk
and that it will do so at a time when many may doubt the possibility of
success. Yet it is my conviction that this is the type of project that ultimately must be pursued, and that when it is accomplished it will provide
the most important kind of understanding of the Johannine tradition and
a new depth and clarity of insight into the Gospel by recognizing that
there is not a *single* Johannine theology evident in the Fourth Gospel but
rather a development of theology. If we are able to provide a history of
the development of the Johannine tradition (and clearly there was a history to its development), we will get a much more precise understanding
of the Gospel text itself and also of the development of early Christian
reflection upon the identity and meaning of Jesus. And, if we are able to
understand more clearly the literary development of the Gospel, we will
also understand better the various issues that the Johannine community
faced in its relationship to the synagogue and in relationships within the
community itself.

Up to this point, scholars have not been successful in unlocking
the secrets of the Fourth Gospel's developmental history. As a result,
they have sought to locate new approaches that will prove more fruitful
in dealing with the Gospel and the letters. When I entered the field of
Johannine Studies, practically the only approach was historical criticism.
However, in the last twenty–five years, there has been a methodological
explosion resulting in a variety of approaches that now include narrative criticism and its variants—social science criticism, cultural criticism,
and feminist criticism, to name only a few. Hermeneutical issues such as
deconstruction were far over the horizon. Among these various methods,
the methodology that has had the greatest impact on Johannine Studies is narrative criticism and its variants. This method was first applied
to Johannine Studies in a substantial way by R. Alan Culpepper in his
Anatomy of the Fourth Gospel (1983). In the twenty–five years since the
release of that book, narrative criticism has become a major force not
only in Johannine Studies but in Biblical Studies in general.

The values of narrative criticism are obvious. There can be no doubt that the Gospels are put forward in narrative form and contain elements of true narrative. It cannot be denied that there are elements of plot in the Gospel of John. One of the most obvious is the "hour" of Jesus. From the time of his first miracle at Cana, there is the indication that the notion of Jesus' "hour" is important and that his "hour" will be a time of great significance. Throughout the Gospel, there are references to the fact that Jesus' hour has not yet arrived. But in John 12:23, we read finally that "the hour has come for the Son of Man to be glorified." Another example may be seen in the notion of Jesus' two "glorifications." For the reader who is familiar with the traditional account of the passion, Jesus' description of both his public ministry and of what is about to transpire in his passion as a "glorification" create not only a radically new perspective but also a sense of a narrative turning point of major significance. As a third instance, in the introductory elements of both the healing of the blind man in chapter 9 and the raising of Lazarus in chapter 11, the author creates suspense with Jesus' remarks about a "day" that contains twelve hours that will lead into a "night" when he is not able to work. This motif of "the coming night" continues to build throughout chapter 12 (cf. 12:35–36, 46–50) and culminates in the comment of the narrator in 13:30 that, when Judas left the upper room, "it was night." In these and many other instances, narrative approaches offer valuable insights on the text.

Yet there are also dangers in the narrative approach, although they are, at times, more subtle. Just what sort of narrative the Fourth Gospel is, is often not addressed. The primary focus of this narrative is an understanding of the theological meaning of the ministry of Jesus, rather than the drama of Jesus' life. Are all elements of the narrative of equal importance, or has the narrator given signals that some elements are more important than others? In the first Cana miracle (John 2:1–11), is the primary focus on the "unquestioning acceptance of the word of Jesus" by his mother (Moloney 1998a, 69) or on the response of the disciples? In the second Cana miracle (4:46–54), is the focus on the official's acceptance of the word of Jesus that his son will be healed or on the belief that results when the official finds out the son was indeed healed? Both readings would seem legitimate—a fact that suggests there may be ambiguities in the text that cannot be completely resolved on the narrative level.

One might argue that an "alert" reader would notice the so–called "aporias," the various kinds of literary disjunctures and inconsistencies, that pervade the Gospel of John. But narrative critics argue that the first–century reader would be accustomed to such problems and would move beyond them. A prime example of such a problem is the relation of chapter 21 to the remainder of the Gospel. Most narrative critics treat this chapter as integral to the literary and theological purposes of the original author. Yet Francis Moloney, a prominent narrative critic, points out that the elements of this chapter that conflict with the remainder of the Gospel are considerable. So considerable, one might argue, that if the critic chose to take them into account, his or her reading might be quite different. However, by adopting the narrative approach, the critic chooses to be selective, focusing on some elements of the narrative and ignoring other elements that, in many cases, are anything but insignificant.

The notion that the present text of the Fourth Gospel "made sense to someone" is one I would agree with, but perhaps not in quite the same way as its proponents intend. I would ask the question, What *kind* of sense does it intend to make? There is narrative sense, which seeks to present an effective literary work, and there is theological sense, which uses the vehicle of narrative but seeks to focus on the proper expression of the author's theological perspective. The primary focus of the Fourth Gospel is theology, and the narrative is the servant of theology. If chapter 21 makes use of material with another origin, it is possible to recognize this, and at the same time, to recognize that its addition was clearly not for literary reasons but for theological ones. If chapters 5 and 6 are reversed, then it means that at least this aspect of the *narrative* sequence (of course, distinguished from the issue of *historical* sequence) is not of great importance. What can we say about the narrative value of the explanation of the parable of the shepherd in John 10? Applying the standard literary criteria to John 10:1–17, the passage fails to have a genuine sense of unity or coherence; and exactly where the emphasis is intended to fall within the verses is indeed difficult to tell. In John 7:37–39, Jesus promises that rivers of living water will flow from his side; in 19:34, both water *and* blood flow forth. Was the author careless in chapter 7? The text seems much too important for him to be careless. For the author of John 19:34, the fact that the blood of Jesus issued forth in addition to water is very important. Could it be that John 19 is a complement and a development of the thought of 7:37–39? If the Fourth Gospel is more interested in theology than in narrative niceties, then we have an explanation.

As a result of my years of teaching, I am convinced that students (from undergraduate to doctoral) tend to see what they are taught to see. We all need to develop a sensitivity to the text in our attempts to derive meaning from it. If I teach a course using a narrative commentary, I find that students will attend to certain aspects of the text and are easily convinced by the viewpoint of the commentator we are reading. After all, these commentators are intelligent professionals who are able to connect elements of the narrative in a plausible way. At the same time, I have found that students who study the Gospel of John this way are all too able to read the Gospel without noticing the obvious literary problems raised by the text itself. For example, some commentators argue that chapters 1–4 report incidents in which various individuals and groups respond properly to the word of Jesus and come to belief (Moloney 1998a, 156–58). At the same time, other commentators reading the same text come to the conclusion that no one in the Gospel ever comes to complete belief before the resurrection (Witherington 1995, 221). Yet another example of how radically different interpretations can be is found in the various treatments of the "sacramentalism" (or lack thereof) in the Fourth Gospel. Is this diversity of opinion the result of inherent ambiguity or is it the result of differing viewpoints within the text itself? If there are numerous viewpoints within the text, some criteria must be established for determining the reason for those viewpoints and their hierarchy.

In short, I am led to the conclusion that, at the present time, Johannine scholarship needs to be more attentive to historical and literary approaches to the Gospel and to recognize the need to explore both the question of editing as well as the question of narrative focus. Scholarship on the Fourth Gospel has produced more and more nuanced studies of the vocabulary of this text, and this enables us to study the Gospel with more precision. If not all instances of the term οἱ ᾿Ιουδαῖοι ("the Jews") have the same meaning, they should not be uncritically grouped together; if all instances of ἔργον ("work") have the same meaning, they should not be grouped together uncritically, either.

Attention to the possibility of editing is an essential issue in the study of all areas of canonical and noncanonical literature of the Jewish and early Christian tradition. The Gospel of John cannot be an exception, however difficult the matter may be.

The Fourth Gospel's Attitudes toward Jews and Judaism

A second area of Johannine Studies that I have had the opportunity to be personally involved with is the Fourth Gospel's presentation of Jews and Judaism. In the chronology of my own research, my first interest in this topic centered around the fact that, in some passages, "the Jews" are identified as a distinct group from others in the text who were also religiously and ethnically "Jews." In these texts, "the Jews" function as religious authorities alongside other groups that also function as religious authorities, but who are identified as "Pharisees," "chief priests," and/or "rulers." Moreover, as I remarked earlier, I noticed that in the texts where "the

Jews" has this meaning, there are other consistent features. For example, in these texts, the discussion regularly involves high Christology and contains elements that are anachronistic to the ministry of Jesus but proper to the situation of a Jewish Christian community at the end of the first century. Thus, I saw the term as significant for identifying strata in the composition of the Gospel (von Wahlde 1979; 1989, 176–88).

However, John's use of the term "Jews" has much broader implications for an understanding of the Fourth Gospel. Twice, I had the opportunity to survey the literature on the subject (von Wahlde 1982; 2000). In the fifteen years between these two surveys, the approaches taken to the investigation of the topic expanded enormously. Now there were articles that took a social science view, a narrative view, a psychological view, as well as a number of new perspectives within the realm of traditional historical–critical methods. A new perspective in the study of this topic is gained by scholars who are not Christian but whose readings bring a fresh and distinctive perspective to these texts.

Opinion on the referent of the term "Jews" has varied over the decades, but there seems to be emerging agreement that the instances that are most explicitly hostile do not attempt to represent the entire Jewish populace but only the position of official Judaism. Undoubtedly many of the populace held views similar to those of the religious authorities, but the views expressed by "the Jews" in the Gospel of John seem to represent the official religious opposition to Jesus (or to the views regarding Jesus espoused by the Johannine community) within Judaism. At the same time, disagreement continues even with regard to this. Some argue that the term always refers to "Judeans" rather than "Jews," and there remains considerable disagreement about which passages refer to religious authorities and which refer to the Jewish people at large.

In addition to concern regarding the meaning of the term "the Jews," there is also growing concern about the Fourth Gospel's broader attitude toward the Jews as a people and toward Judaism as a religion. Throughout history, people (mainly Christians) have made use of the Gospel of John as a justification for the hatred, condemnation, and killing of Jews. The debate on this issue has intensified in the past ten years with the appearance of numerous proposals that the Gospel is inherently and irretrievably anti–Jewish. The range of opinion on this matter is reflected in the papers of the 2000 Leuven Conference on Anti–Judaism in John's Gospel (see Bieringer et al. 2001). This issue is often complicated by the variety of ways in which the relevant terms are used and understood. What is the meaning of "anti–Jewish"? Does this refer to Jews in the ethnic sense or in the religious sense? What is the relation of this term to "anti–Semitism"? Is the Gospel of John "supercessionist," meaning that it sees Judaism as an obsolete forerunner to Christianity? If so, does this imply that Judaism as a religion has no right to exist after Jesus? What is the relation of supercessionism to belief in Jesus as the "fulfillment" of Judaism?

Of course, the resolution of the question of the Fourth Gospel's alleged anti–Judaism has considerable implications for the understanding of this text as Scripture. If the Gospel of John is indeed intrinsically hateful, it is important to come to grips with this fact. But, it may also be that those who see the Gospel as intrinsically anti–Jewish fail to interpret the text against its historical background in a sufficiently thoroughgoing way. This is certainly one of the most important aspects of the issue and one that requires additional discussion.

Even if the Gospel of John is not intrinsically hateful toward Judaism or Jewish people, there remains the considerable task of dealing with these texts in a pastoral or liturgical setting. Should they simply be excluded from public liturgical reading? If so, does this imply that such texts do not carry the message of God? Does it sidestep the need to come to grips with the text itself and the need to educating the public? Should the term "the Jews" be replaced in readings by such terms as "the Jewish religious authorities"? These issues continue to confront both scholars and preachers and continue to require attention. The issues are so sensitive that sometimes the rhetoric involves unscholarly labeling and impuning motives. Future discussion will also flourish more freely when such language is avoided.

THE GOSPEL OF JOHN AND ARCHAEOLOGY

A much less contentious area of scholarship is the contribution that modern archaeology can make to the understanding of the Gospel of John. Unfortunately, archaeology is often associated with those extreme literalists who would use it to prove the absolute historicity of the Bible. In fact, it has a broader and more scholarly relevance than some might imagine. In the Gospel of John, there are thirteen geographical references not mentioned in the other Gospels. If we include in our list those places about which we learn details not mentioned in the other Gospels, the number increases to twenty. From what we now know from archaeological and literary sources, these references are not symbolic creations, as was once thought, but are accurate and detailed references that reveal aspects of Jesus' ministry not otherwise known. Of course, the accuracy of these references cannot be used to argue for the truthfulness of the gospel message, but it does reveal that at least one of the authors of the Fourth Gospel was quite familiar with Palestine of the first century.

Ongoing archaeological work continues to reveal more and more information pertinent to our understanding of the Gospel of John. For example, we now know that the southern basin of the Pool of Bethesda was a very large and very deep *miqveh* (Gibson 2005), a pool for ritual purification, rather than a reservoir, as has been claimed in earlier literature and as is explained in the tourist information given at the pool. This is significant in itself, but it is even more significant that, in the summer of 2004, Ronny Reich and Eli Shukron uncovered the remains of an even larger *miqveh* adjacent to what was traditionally known as the Pool of Siloam (Reich and Shukron 2005; Shanks 2005). The discovery of this ritual purification pool will require that scholars revise their opinions of just what ancient references to "the Pool of Siloam" actually mean: the smaller northern pool at the exit of Hezekiah's tunnel or the larger stepped pool now discovered slightly to the south. It is significant that the pools at Bethesda and Siloam are mentioned only in the Gospel of John (5:1–9; 9:7–11). It is also significant that these pools are *miqvaot*. Such large, public *miqvaot* were natural meeting places for large numbers of people. In the case of Bethesda, Jesus is explicitly said to be present himself at this large, public *miqveh* at the *northern* edge of the city. In such a place, the healing would have been witnessed by a considerable number of people. Similarly, the healing of the man born blind takes place at the Pool of Siloam. This pool, as we have seen, was a large, public *miqveh* at the *southern* edge of the city. Just how close to the pool Jesus himself was is not clear from the account, but again, the healing would have been witnessed by many.

There are also other examples of archaeological discoveries that significantly affect our understanding of John's Gospel. The discovery of Bethsaida, east of the Jordan River, at the northern edge of the Sea of Galilee, enables us to locate with certainty the town from which Andrew, Peter, and Philip came. And the proximity of the town to Gentile areas helps explain the Hellenistic names of those disciples. Equally perplexing has been the location of "Bethany Beyond the Jordan," mentioned at John 1:28 as the place where John the Baptist and the disciples first meet Jesus. Although the evidence for the identification of this site is not as compelling as it is for the sites just mentioned, archaeological excavations at Wadi Kharrar on the east side of the Jordan, across from the pilgrim site of Bethabara, have provided substantial evidence that this was the Bethany Beyond the Jordan.

The Gospel of John is among the most influential writings of the New Testament. Literature on this Gospel continues to be produced at such a rate that it seems no one single individual could truly master it all. This production means that progress will continue. As the Gospel of John and 1–2–3 John continue to be examined with the array of methods that have developed in the past thirty years, and as these books are examined from new perspectives both from within and from without the Christian world, we will certainly continue to grow in our understanding and appreciation of this remarkable literature.

18: Response

COMBINING KEY METHODOLOGIES IN JOHANNINE STUDIES

Felix Just, S.J.

Professor von Wahlde's reflections highlight three disparate aspects of Johannine scholarship: the relationship between historical and literary criticisms as applied to the Fourth Gospel and the Johannine Epistles; the question of potential anti–Judaism or anti–Semitism in the Gospel; and, the contributions that recent archaeological discoveries can make to our understanding of John. My response will primarily raise two questions. The first is related to von Wahlde's first point: How might historical and narrative methodologies better complement one another in future Johannine scholarship? The second combines his two other topics: How might new archaeological discoveries not only advance our understanding of the historicity of the Fourth Gospel, but also inform the question of its anti–Jewish aspects at various stages of its composition history?

As von Wahlde emphasizes, Johannine Studies must move beyond a dualistic mentality that either applies historical methodology (sometimes to the point of ignoring the canonical form of the texts) or focuses on the literary aspects of the Gospel and Epistles in their final forms (while often neglecting any historical questions). All questions are legitimate, and different questions require different methodologies. Although reality is often very complex, one should resist the temptation to reduce its complexity by focusing only on certain aspects of a question that interest us while ignoring other elements that may be just as important.

All but a small minority of readers today accept the proposal that the Fourth Gospel was not written all at once by only one author. The double endings at John 20:30–31 and 21:25, along with the third–person reference in John 21:24 to the Beloved Disciple as the author of the (main portion) of the Gospel, make it virtually indisputable that the text was edited and expanded at least once, if not numerous times. Yet if there were several stages in the composition of the Fourth Gospel, why should one not attempt multiple narrative–critical readings of John? One objection to this proposal is that it seems too speculative to attempt a narrative analysis of a hypothetically reconstructed earlier version of the text. Following this argument, many scholars propose that one can only deal with the final, received text. Yet what text is that? As is well known, but not always taken into consideration, we possess not just one, but numerous versions of the "final" text of John. The version reproduced in Nestle–Aland 27 is itself a hypothetical reconstruction of what textual critics suggest may have been the original form of the Gospel, whereas the versions contained in the extant manuscripts differ significantly from one another. The most obvious difference is in the inclusion or omission of the *pericopae adulterae* (7:53–8:11), yet other verses are also missing in some of the preserved manuscripts (e.g., 5:4), and there are hundreds of smaller textual variations throughout the twenty–one chapters of the Fourth Gospel.

Thus, each narrative–critical analysis will be different, at least slightly, depending on which version of the text based on which manuscripts one uses. Similarly, although we (unfortunately!) do not possess any ancient manuscript of John that actually ends at 20:31, it is not unreasonable for a narrative reading to omit chapter 21 from consideration. Although the same procedure admittedly becomes more speculative when applied to other hypothetically reconstructed "earlier" versions of the Gospel (e.g., omitting chapters 15–17, or reversing chapters 5 and 6), applying careful narrative–critical analyses to the different reconstructions proposed by various source critics might help determine which of the proposed reconstructions are more plausible than others. Thus, the fundamental insight of narrative criticism—that the text must have "made sense to someone"—might helpfully be applied not only to the final stage, but also to earlier, albeit hypothetical, stages in the composition of the Fourth Gospel.

A related issue that must be investigated further, even though much ink has already been spilled over it throughout the centuries, is the question of the authorship of the Gospel and Epistles attributed to John. If there actually were many stages in the composition and expansion of the Fourth Gospel, then one cannot responsibly avoid asking who and how many different people were involved in the production of the text. Yet here the terminology quickly becomes complex and confused, betraying the competing stances of various scholars. Did the Fourth Gospel have several different "authors"? Or just one "main author" who later revised and expanded his own text? Was there a separate final "redactor"? And if some older texts were incorporated by the "main author," how should one best refer to those who wrote these earlier "sources"? Moreover, which of all these people should be called "the evangelist"? And how do the Johannine Epistles fit into the picture? Despite nearly two millennia of discussion on such issues, there is still no consensus among Johannine scholars, but rather a confusing mix of terminology applied to the sources, author(s), redactor(s), and evangelist. If any consensus could ever be reached regarding the historical identity of the "disciple whom Jesus loved" (John the son of Zebedee, John the Elder, Thomas, Lazarus?)—at least to rule out some of the more speculative suggestions (such as John the Baptist or Paul of Tarsus)—then our understanding of the historical processes of oral transmission and written composition of the Johannine material might advance as well.

Even if we cannot know for certain how often and to what extent the texts were edited and expanded, we should not ignore the question altogether and assume that only the "final" editions matter. The biblical texts were not yet "fixed" at the end of the first century. Rather, the first generations of Christians felt quite free to adapt and expand older writings (just as Matthew and Luke expanded upon Mark and other sources, and even Mark was lengthened at some point in time). Thus, it might be helpful to apply narrative analysis to various proposed reconstructions of earlier versions of the Fourth Gospel, in order to understand better the meaning the text might have held for its readers at earlier stages of its development in the first century.

As to von Wahlde's second point, although much progress has been made in recent decades regarding the question of possible anti–Judaism in the Fourth Gospel, there is still no scholarly consensus on this highly charged and divisive issue. It remains difficult to reconcile the observations that the Fourth Gospel appears to be both more Jewish and more anti-Jewish than the Synoptics. Yet once again, a combination of historical and literary approaches would clearly be more productive than an either/or approach that privileges historical criticism to the neglect of literary analysis, or vice versa.

Recent decades have also provided many new archaeological discoveries in the Holy Land, which have not only given us additional bits of trivia related to certain Johannine pericopae (e.g., the pools of Bethesda and Siloam), but are also in the process of fundamentally shifting our assessment of the historical value of the Fourth Gospel as a whole. As more and more scholars are coming to realize, the provenance of this Gospel is more closely connected with Jerusalem and its environs than was previously considered possible. It should by now be obvious to everyone that Mark's Gospel is not an objectively historical or chronologically accurate account of Jesus' life, but much historical Jesus research still privileges Mark (whether tacitly or explicitly) to the neglect of John. Yet, the more that archaeology increases our awareness of the historical accuracy (or at least plausibility) of many details in the Fourth Gospel, the more this Gospel will be accepted as a potentially reliable historical source for the life of Jesus.

Thus, the relationship between John and the Synoptics needs to be investigated anew, but from a different vantage point. If both the Synoptics and John preserve historically reliable, albeit independent, traditions about the historical Jesus, a fuller explanation must be given as to why Mark did not include some of the most significant Johannine materials, as well as why John did not include many of the key Synoptic materials. Did they not know each other's traditions? If not, how can this be explained? For example, if the stories of the man born blind or the raising of Lazarus have any historical basis, is it conceivable that Mark might not have known about them? Or did he know them and intentionally omit them for some reason?

The more we realize that the Synoptic traditions have a Galilean provenance and reflect an anti–Jerusalem bias while the Johannine accounts are based on Judean sources that may not have been aware of many Galilean traditions about Jesus' ministry, the more scholars could accept the historical value of Mark and John as complementary, rather than contradictory, and thus avoid unduly privileging one to the neglect of the other.

There is not space here to develop these proposals in greater detail, but such questions seem worthy of further investigation in the years ahead, because they might one day advance our understanding not only of the Gospels as narrative texts but also of the historical Jesus and the early Christian communities in their close but increasingly conflictual relationships to other forms of Judaism in the first century.

WORKS CITED

Adam, A. K. M. 1995a. *Making Sense of New Testament Theology: "Modern" Problems and Prospects."* Studies in American Biblical Hermeneutics 11. Macon: Mercer University Press.

———. 1995b. *What Is Postmodern Biblical Criticism?* GBS, New Testament Series. Minneapolis: Fortress.

———, ed. 2000. *Handbook of Postmodern Biblical Interpretation.* St. Louis: Chalice Press.

Alexander, Philip S. 2001. "The Church and the Jewish People: The Past, the Present, and the Future." Lectures to the School of Fellowship in Alderly Edge, Cheshire. Fall Term.

Alter, Robert. 1981. *The Art of Biblical Narrative.* New York: Basic Books.

Anderson, Benedict. 1991. *Imagined Communities: Reflections on the Origins and Spread of Nationalism.* Rev. ed. New York: Verso.

Anderson, Janice Capel. 1991. "Mapping Feminist Biblical Criticism: The American Scene, 1983–1990." Pages 21–44 in *Critical Review of Books in Religion.* Atlanta: Journal of the American Academy of Religion and the Journal of Biblical Literature.

Anderson, Paul N. 1997a. *The Christology of the Fourth Gospel: Its Unity and Disunity in Light of John 6.* WUNT 2.78. Valley Forge: Trinity Press International.

Anderson, Paul N. 1997b. "The *Sitz im Leben* of the Johannine Bread of Life Discourse and Its Evolving Context." Pages 1–59 in *Critical Readings of John 6*. BIS 22. Edited by R. Alan Culpepper. Leiden: Brill.

———. 2004. "The Cognitive Origins of John's Christological Unity and Disunity." Pages 127–48 in *Psychology and the Bible: A New Way to Read the Scriptures*. Edited by J. Harold Ellens and Wayne Rollins. Westport: Praeger.

———. 2006. *The Fourth Gospel and the Quest for Jesus: Modern Foundations Reconsidered*. London: T&T Clark.

Ashcroft, Bill, Gareth Griffiths, and Helen Tiffin, eds. 1989. *The Empire Writes Back: Theory and Practice in Post-Colonial Literatures*. New York: Routledge.

Ashton, John, ed. 1986. *The Interpretation of John*. IRT. Philadelphia: Fortress.

———. 1991. *Understanding the Fourth Gospel*. New York: Oxford University Press.

———. 1994. *Studying John: Approaches to the Fourth Gospel*. New York: Oxford University Press.

Attridge, Harold W. 2006. "Johannine Christianity." Pages 125–43 in *Origins to Constantine*. Edited by Margaret M. Mitchell and Frances M. Young. Cambridge: Cambridge University Press.

Aune, David E., Torey Seland, and Jarl H. Ulrichsen, eds. 2003. *Neotestamentica et Philonica: Studies in Honor of Peder Borgen*. NovTSup 106. Leiden: Brill.

Barrett, Charles K. 1947. "The Old Testament in the Fourth Gospel." *JTS* 48:155–69.

———. 1972. "The Prologue of St. John's Gospel." Pages 27–48 in *New Testament Essays*. London: SPCK.

———. 1978. *The Gospel According to St. John: An Introduction with Commentary and Notes on the Greek Text*. 2nd ed. Philadelphia: Westminster.

Barthes, Roland. 1974. *S/Z*. Translated by Richard Miller. New York: Hill & Wang.

Bartlett, David. 2006. "Interpreting and Preaching the Gospel of John." *Interpretation* 60:48–63.

Bauckham, Richard, ed. 1998a. *The Gospels for All Christians: Rethinking the Gospel Audiences*. Grand Rapids: Eerdmans.

———. 1998b. "For Whom Were Gospels Written?" Pages 9–48 in *The Gospels for All Christians: Rethinking the Gospel Audiences*. Edited by Richard Bauckham. Grand Rapids: Eerdmans.

———. 2001. "The Audience of the Fourth Gospel." Pages 101–11 in *Jesus in Johannine Tradition*. Edited by Robert T. Fortna and Tom Thatcher. Louisville: Westminster John Knox.

Bauer, Walter. 1934. *Orthodoxy and Heresy in Earliest Christianity*. Reprint 1971. Edited by Robert A. Kraft and Gerhard Krobel. Philadelphia: Fortress.

Beutler, Johannes, S.J. 1972. *Martyria: Traditionsgeschichtliche Untersuchungen zum Zeugnisthema bei Johannes*. Frankfurt: Knecht.

———. 1975. "Psalm 42/43 im Johannesevangelium." *NTS* 25:3–57.

———. 1984. *Habt keine Angst: Die erste johanneische Abschiedsrede (Joh 14)*. Stuttgart: Katholisches Bibelwerk.

———. 1991. "Response from a European Perspective." Pages 191–202 in *Semeia 53: The Fourth Gospel from a Literary Perspective*. Edited by R. Alan Culpepper and Fernando F. Segovia. Atlanta: Scholars Press.

———. 1997. "The Structure of John 6." Pages 115–27 in *Critical Readings of John 6*. BIS. Edited by R. Alan Culpepper. New York: Brill.

———. 1998. *Studien zu den johanneischen Schriften*. Stuttgart: Katholisches Bibelwerk.

———. 2000. *Die Johannesbriefe*. Regensburg: Pustet.

Beutler, Johannes, S.J., and Karl P. Donfried, eds., 2000. *The Thessalonian Debate*. Grand Rapids: Eerdmans.

Beutler, Johannes, S.J., and Robert T. Fortna, eds., 1991. *The Shepherd Discourse of John 10 and Its Context: Studies*. New York: Cambridge University Press.

Bieringer, Reimund, Didier Pollefeyt, and Frederique Vandecasteele-Vanneuville, eds. 2001. *Anti-Judaism and the Fourth Gospel: Papers from the Leuven Colloquium, 2000*. Louisville: Westminster John Knox.

Blomberg, Craig L. 2002. *The Historical Reliability of John's Gospel: Issues and Commentary*. Downers Grove, Ill.: InterVarsity Press.

Booth, Wayne. 1961. *The Rhetoric of Fiction*. Chicago: University of Chicago Press.

Borgen, Peder. 1959. "John and the Synoptics in the Passion Narrative." *NTS* 5:246–59.

———. 1965. *Bread from Heaven: An Exegetical Study of the Concept of Manna in the Gospel of John and the Writings of Philo*. NovTSup 10. Leiden: Brill.

———. 1970. "Observations on the Targumic Character of the Prologue of John." *NTS* 16: 288–95.

———. 1972. "Logos Was the True Light." *NovT* 14:115–30.

———. 1983. "Bread from Heaven: Aspects of Debates on Expository Method and Form." Pages 32–46 in *"Logos Was the True Light" and Other Essays on the Gospel of John*. Trondheim: Tapir Academic Publishers.

Borgen, Peder. 1986. "God's Agent in the Fourth Gospel." Pages 67–78 in *The Interpretation of John*. Edited with an introduction by John Ashton. Philadelphia: Fortress.

———. 1987a. *Philo, John, and Paul: New Perspectives on Judaism and Early Christianity*. BJS 131. Atlanta: Scholars Press.

———. 1987b. "The Prologue of John—as Exposition of the Old Testament." Pages 75–101 in *Philo, John, and Paul: New Perspectives on Judaism and Early Christianity*. BJS 131. Edited by Peder Borgen. Atlanta: Scholars Press.

———. 1987c. "Creation, Logos, and the Son: Observations on John 1:1–18 and 5:17–18." *ExAud* 3:88–97.

———. 1990. "John and the Synoptics: A Reply to Frans Neirynck." Pages 408–37 in *The Interrelations of the Gospels*. BETL 95. Edited by David L. Dungan. Leuven: Leuven University Press.

———. 1991. "The Sabbath Controversy in John 5:1–18 and Analogous Controversy Reflected in Philo's Writings." *Studia Philonica Annual* 3:209–21.

———. 1992. "The Independence of the Gospel of John: Some Observations." Pages 1815–33 in *The Four Gospels 1992: Festschrift Frans Neirynck*. 3 vols. BETL 100. Edited by Frans van Segbroeck, et al. Leuven: Leuven University Press.

———. 1993. "John 6: Tradition, Interpretation, and Composition." Pages 268–91 in *From Jesus to John: Essays on Jesus and New Testament Christology in Honour of Marinus de Jonge*. JSNTSup 84. Edited by Martinus de Boer. Sheffield: Sheffield Academic.

———. 1996a. *Early Christianity and Hellenistic Judaism*. Edinburgh: T&T Clark.

———. 1996b. "The Gospel of John and Hellenism: Some Observations." Pages 98–123 in *Exploring the Gospel of John: In Honor of D. Moody Smith*. Edited by R. Alan Culpepper and C. Clifton Black. Louisville: Westminster John Knox.

———. 1997. *Philo of Alexandria: An Exegete for His Time*. NovTSup 86. Leiden: Brill.

———. 2000. Review of Michael Labahn, *Offenbarung in Zeichen und Wort. Untersuchungen zur Vorgeschichte von Joh 6,1–25a und seiner Rezeption in der Brotrede*. *JTS* 53:215–23.

———. 2005. "Some Crime-and-Punishment Reports." Pages 67–80 in *Ancient Israel, Judaism, and Christianity in Contemporary Perspectives: Essays in Memory of Karl-Johan Illman*. Edited by Jacob Neusner, et al. Lanham, Md.: University Press of America.

Boismard, Marie–Émile. 1957. *St. John's Prologue*. Translated by Carisbrooke Dominicans. Westminster, Md.: Newman Press.

Boyarin, Daniel. 2002. "The *Ioudaioi* in John and the Prehistory of 'Judaism.'" Pages 216–39 in *Pauline Conversations in Context: Essays in Honor of Calvin J. Roetzel*. JSNTSup 221. Edited by Janice C. Anderson, et al. Sheffield: Sheffield Academic.

———. 2004. *Border Lines: The Partition of Judeo–Christianity*. Philadelphia: University of Pennsylvania Press.

Braun, François-Marie. 1959. *Jean le Theologien et son évangile dans l'église ancienne*. Vol. 1 of *Jean le Theologien*. 2 vols. Paris: Gabalda.

Brodie, Thomas L. 1992. "Fish, Temple Tithe, and Remission: The God–based Generosity of Deuteronomy 14–15 as One Component of Matt 17:22–18:35." *RB* 99:697–718.

———. 1993a. *The Quest for the Origin of John's Gospel. A Source-Oriented Approach*. New York: Oxford University Press.

———. 1993b. *The Gospel According to St. John: A Literary and Theological Commentary*. New York: Oxford University Press.

———. 2000. *The Crucial Bridge: The Elijah–Elisha Narrative as an Interpretative Synthesis of Genesis-Kings and a Literary Model for the Gospels*. Collegeville, Minn.: Liturgical Press.

———. 2001. *Genesis as Dialogue: A Literary, Historical, and Theological Commentary*. New York: Oxford University Press.

———. 2004. *The Birthing of the New Testament: The Intertextual Development of the New Testament Writings*. Sheffield: Phoenix Press.

Brodie, Thomas L., Dennis R. MacDonald, and Stanley E. Porter, eds. 2006. *The Intertextuality of the Epistles*. Sheffield: Phoenix Press.

Brown, David. 1999. *Tradition and Imagination: Revelation and Change*. New York: Oxford University Press.

———. 2000. *Discipleship and Imagination: Christian Tradition and Truth*. Oxford: Oxford University Press.

Brown, Raymond E. 1961. "Incidents That Are Units in the Synoptic Gospels but Dispersed in St. John." *CBQ* 23:143–60.

———. 1966–1970. *The Gospel According to John: Introduction, Translation, and Notes*. 2 vols. AB 29-29A. Garden City: Doubleday.

———. 1971. "Jesus and Elisha." *Perspectives* 12:86–104.

———. 1979. *The Community of the Beloved Disciple*. New York: Paulist Press.

———. 1982. *The Epistles of John*. AB 30. Garden City: Doubleday.

———. 1994. *The Death of the Messiah: From Gethsemane to the Grave. A Commentary on the Passion Narratives in the Four Gospels*. 2 vols. ABRL. New York: Doubleday.

———. 2003. *An Introduction to the Gospel of John*. ABRL. Edited by Francis J. Moloney. New York: Doubleday.

Bultmann, Rudolf K. 1941. *Das Evangelium des Johannes*. Göttingen: Vandenhoeck & Ruprecht.

———. 1951–1955. *Theology of the New Testament*. 2 vols. Translated by Kendrick Grobel. New York: Scribners.

———. 1957a. "The New Testament and Mythology." Pages 1–44 in *Kerygma and Myth: A Theological Debate*. Edited by and with contributions from Hans Werner Bartsch. Translated by Reginald H. Fuller. London: SPCK.

———. 1957b. "Ist voraussetzungslose Exegese möglich?" *TZ* 13:409–17.

———. 1958. "Modern Biblical Interpretation and Existential Philosophy." Pages 45–59 in *Jesus Christ and Mythology*. Edited by Rudolf Bultmann. New York: Scribner.

———. 1960. "Is Exegesis without Presuppositions Possible?" Pages 289–97 in *Existence and Faith: Shorter Writings of Rudolf Bultmann*. Selected, translated and introduced by Schubert M. Ogden. New York: Meridian Books.

———. 1968. *The History of the Synoptic Tradition*. 2nd ed. Translated by John Marsh. Oxford: Basil Blackwell.

———. 1971. *The Gospel of John: A Commentary*. Translated by G. R. Beasley-Murray, R. W. N. Hoare, and J. K. Riches. Philadelphia: Westminster.

Burge, Gary M. 1994. "Territorial Religion, Johannine Christology, and the Vineyard of John 15." Pages 384–96 in *Jesus of Nazareth, Lord and Christ: Essays on the Historical Jesus and New Testament Christology*. Edited by Joel B. Green and Max Turner. Grand Rapids: Eerdmans.

Burnett, Fred W. 1990. "Postmodern Biblical Exegesis: The Eve of Historical Criticism." Pages 51–80 in *Semeia 51: Post-Structural Criticism and the Bible: Text/History/Discourse*. Edited by Gary A. Phillips. Atlanta: Society of Biblical Literature.

———. 2000. "Historiography." Pages 106–12 in *Handbook of Postmodern Biblical Interpretation*. Edited by A. K. M. Adam. St. Louis: Chalice.

Carson, D. A. 1982. "Understanding Misunderstandings in the Fourth Gospel." *TynBul* 33:59–89.

———. 1991. *The Gospel According to John*. Leicester: InterVarsity Press.

———. 2001. "Mystery and Fulfillment: Toward a More Comprehensive Paradigm of Paul's Understanding of the Old and New." Pages 393–437 in *The Paradoxes of Paul*. Vol. 2 of *Justification and Variegated Nomism: A Fresh Appraisal of Paul and Second Temple Judaism*. WUNT 2.140. Edited by D. A. Carson, Peter T. O'Brien, and Mark A. Seifrid. Tübingen: Mohr Siebeck.

Carter, Warren. 2006. *John: Storyteller, Interpreter, Evangelist*. Peabody, Mass.: Hendrickson.

Casey, Maurice. 1996. *Is John's Gospel True?* New York: Routledge.

Catechism of the Catholic Church. 1994. London: Chapman.

Chatman, Seymour B. 1978. *Story and Discourse: Narrative Structure in Fiction and Film*. Ithaca, N.Y.: Cornell University Press.

Chennattu, Rekha M. 2006. *Johannine Discipleship as a Covenant Relationship*. Peabody, Mass.: Hendrickson.

Chesterton, G. K. 1957. *Orthodoxy*. Garden City, N.Y.: Image Books.

Cohen, Anthony P. 1985. *The Symbolic Construction of Community*. New York: Tavistock and Ellis Horwood.

Collins, Adela Yarbro. 1988. "Narrative, History, and Gospel." Pages 145–53 in *Semeia 43: Genre, Narrativity, and Theology*. Edited by Mary Gerhart and James G. Williams. Atlanta: Scholars Press.

Cope, Lamar. 1987. "The Earliest Gospel Was the 'Signs Gospel.'" Pages 17–24 in *Jesus, the Gospels, and the Church: Essays in Honor of William R. Farmer*. Edited by E. P. Sanders. Macon, Ga.: Mercer University Press.

Crossan, John Dominic. 1995. *Who Killed Jesus? Exposing the Roots of Anti-Semitism in the Gospel Story of the Death of Jesus*. San Francisco: HarperSanFrancisco.

Crossan, John Dominic, and N. T. Wright. 2006. *The Resurrection of Jesus: John Dominic Crossan and N. T. Wright in Dialogue*. Edited by Robert B. Stewart. Minneapolis: Fortress.

Cullmann, Oscar. 1975. *The Johannine Circle*. Translated by John Bowden. Philadelphia: Westminster Press.

Culpepper, R. Alan. 1975. *The Johannine School: An Evaluation of the Johannine–school Hypothesis Based on an Investigation of the Nature of Ancient Schools*. SBLDS 26. Missoula, Mt.: Scholars Press.

———. 1980. "The Pivot of John's Prologue." *NTS* 27:1–31.

———. 1983. *Anatomy of the Fourth Gospel: A Study in Literary Design, Foundation, and Facets*. Philadelphia: Fortress.

———. 1984. "Story and History in the Gospels." *Review and Expositor* 81:467–78.

———. 1985. *1 John, 2 John, 3 John*. Knox Preaching Guides. Atlanta: John Knox.

———. 1987. "The Gospel of John and the Jews." *Review and Expositor* 82:273–88.

———. 1994. *John the Son of Zebedee: The Life of a Legend*. Columbia: University of South Carolina Press.

———. 1995. "The Gospel of Luke." Pages 1–490 in *The New Interpreters Bible*. Vol. 9. Nashville: Abingdon.

Culpepper, R. Alan. 1997a. "The Theology of the Johannine Passion Narrative: John 19:16b–30." *Neotestamentica* 31:21–37.

———, ed. 1997b. *Critical Readings of John 6.* BIS 22. Leiden: Brill.

———. 1998. *The Gospels and Letters of John.* Nashville: Abingdon.

———. 2000. *John the Son of Zebedee: The Life of a Legend.* Minneapolis: Fortress.

———. 2001. "Anti–Judaism in the Fourth Gospel as a Theological Problem for Christian Interpreters." Pages 61–81 in *Anti-Judaism and the Fourth Gospel: Papers from the Leuven Colloquium, 2000.* Edited by Reimund Bieringer, Didier Pollefeyt, and Frederique Vandecasteele-Vanneuville. Louisville: Westminster John Knox.

———. 2002a. *Eternity as Sunrise: The Life of Hugo H. Culpepper.* Macon, Ga.: Mercer University Press.

———. 2002b. "Inclusivism and Exclusivism in the Fourth Gospel." Pages 85–108 in *Word, Theology, and Community in John.* Edited by John Painter, R. Alan Culpepper, and Fernando F. Segovia. St. Louis: Chalice Press.

———. 2005a. "Designs for the Church in the Gospel Accounts of Jesus' Death." *NTS* 51:376–92.

———. 2005b. The Legacy of Raymond Brown and Beyond: A Response to Francis J. Moloney. Pages 40–51 in *Life in Abundance: Studies of John's Gospel in Tribute to Raymond E. Brown, S.S.* Edited by John R. Donahue. Collegeville, Minn.: Liturgical Press.

———. 2005c. "Review of Charles E. Hill, *The Johinnine Corpus in the Early Church.*" *CBQ* 67:346–48.

———. 2007. *The Gospel of Mark.* Smyth & Helwys Bible Commentaries. Macon, Ga.: Smyth & Helwys.

Culpepper, R. Alan, and C. Clifton Black, eds. 1996. *Exploring the Gospel of John: In Honor of D. Moody Smith.* Louisville: Westminster John Knox.

Dahl, Nils A. 1962. "The Johannine Church and History." Pages 124–42 in *Current Issues in New Testament Interpretation: Essays in Honor of Otto A. Piper.* Edited by William Klassen and Graydon F. Synder. New York: Harper.

Daube, David. 1984. *Das Alte Testament im Neuen: Aus jüdischer Sicht.* Konstanz: Universitatsverlag Konstanz.

Davis, Stephen, Daniel Kendall, and Gerald O'Collins, eds. 1997. *The Resurrection: An Interdisciplinary Symposium on the Resurrection of Jesus.* New York: Oxford University Press.

De Ausejo, Serafin. 1956. "Es in un himno a Cristo el prólogo de Juan?" *EstBib* 15:381–427.

De Boer, Martinus C. 1992. "Narrative Criticism, Historical Criticism, and the Gospel of John." *JSNT* 47:35–48.

———. 1993. *From Jesus to John: Essays on Jesus and New Testament Christology in Honour of Marinus de Jonge.* JSNTSup 84. Sheffield: Sheffield Academic.

———. 1996. *Johannine Perspectives on the Death of Jesus.* CBET 17. Kampen: Pharos.

———. (forthcoming). "Johannine History and Johannine Theology: The Death of Jesus as the Exaltation and the Glorification of the Son of Man." In *The Death of Jesus in the Fourth Gospel.* Edited by G. Van Belle. Leuven: Peeters.

De Jonge, H. J. 2001. "'The Jews' in the Gospel of John." Pages 121–40 in *Anti-Judaism and the Fourth Gospel: Papers from the Leuven Colloquium, 2000.* Edited by Reimund Bieringer, Didier Pollefeyt, and Frederique Vandecasteele-Vanneuville. Louisville: Westminster John Knox.

De Jonge, Marinus. 1968. *De Brieven van Johannes.* Nijkerk: Callenbach. With revised editions in 1973, 1978, and 1988.

———. 1977a. *Jesus: Stranger from Heaven and Son of God: Jesus Christ and the Christians in Johannine Perspective.* SBLSBS 11. Edited and translated by John E. Steely. Missoula, Mt.: Scholars Press.

———, et al., eds. 1977b. *L'Évangile de Jean. Sources, rédaction, théologie.* BETL 44. Leuven: Leuven University Press.

———. 1988. "The Christology of the Gospel and the Letters of John." Pages 140–51 in *Christology in Context: The Earliest Christian Response to Jesus.* Edited by Marinus de Jonge. Philadelphia: Westminster.

———. 1990. "John the Baptist and Elijah in the Fourth Gospel." Pages 299–308 in *The Conversation Continues: Studies in Paul and John in Honor of J. Louis Martyn.* Edited by Robert T. Fortna and Beverly R. Gaventa. Nashville: Abingdon.

———. 1992a. "The Radical Eschatology of the Fourth Gospel and the Eschatology of the Synoptics." Pages 481–87 in *John and the Synoptics.* BETL 101. Edited by Adelbert Denaux. Leuven: Leuven University Press.

———. 1992b. "Christology and Theology in the Context of Early Christian Eschatology, Particularly in the Fourth Gospel." Pages 1835–53 in *The Four Gospels 1992: Festschrift Frans Neirynck.* 3 vols. BETL 100. Edited by Frans van Segbroeck, et al. Leuven: Leuven University Press.

———. 1993. "The Conflict between Jesus and the Jews and the Radical Christology of the Fourth Gospel." Pages 15–34 in *Perspectives, Witness, and Translation: Essays in Honor of John E. Steely.* Edited by Clayton N. Jefford. Lewiston: Edwin Mellon.

De Jonge, Marinus. 1995. "Monotheism and Christology." Pages 225–37 in *Early Christian Thought in Its Jewish Context*. Edited by John Barclay and John Sweet. New York: Cambridge University Press.

———. 1996. *Johannes: Een praktische bijbelverklaring*. Kampen: Pharos Press.

———. 2000. "Christology, Controversy, and Community in the Gospel of John." Pages 209–29 in *Christology, Controversy, and Community: New Testament Essays in Honour of David R. Catchpole*. NovTSup 99. Edited by David G. Horrell and Christopher M. Tuckett. Leiden: Brill.

Denaux, Adelbert, ed. 1992. *John and the Synoptics*. BETL 101. Leuven: Leuven University Press.

de Ruyter, B. W. J. 1998. *De gemeente van de evangelist Johannes: haar polemiek en haar geschiedenis*. Delft: Eburon.

de Solages, Bruno. 1979. *Jean et les Synoptiques*. Leiden: Brill.

Dettwiler, Andreas. 1995. *Die Gegenwart des Erhöhten: Eine exegetische Studie zu den johanneischen Abschiedsreden (Joh 13,31–16,33) unter besonderer Berücksichtigung ihres Relecture-Charakters*. Göttingen: Vandenhoeck & Ruprecht.

Dhanis, Édouard, Barnabas Mary Ahern, and Giuseppe Ghiberti, eds. 1974. *Resurrexit: actes du symposium international sur la résurrection de Jésus, Rome 1970*. Vatican City: Libreria editrice vaticana.

Dodd, Charles H. 1953. *The Interpretation of the Fourth Gospel*. Cambridge: Cambridge University Press.

———. 1963. *Historical Tradition in the Fourth Gospel*. Cambridge: Cambridge University Press.

Dube, Musa W. 1996. "Reading for Decolonization (John 4:1–42)." Pages 37–59 in *Semeia 75: Postcolonialism and Scriptural Reading*. Edited by Laura E. Donaldson. Atlanta: Scholars Press.

———. 1998. "Savior of the World but Not of This World: A Postcolonial Reading of Spatial Construction in John." Pages 118–35 in *The Postcolonial Bible*. BP 1. Edited by R. S. Sugirtharajah. Sheffield: Sheffield Academic.

———. 2000a. "Batswakwa: Which Traveler Are You (John 1:1-18)?" Pages 150–62 in *The Bible in Africa: Transactions, Trajectories, and Trends*. Edited by Gerald West and Musa W. Dube. Leiden: Brill.

———. 2000b. *Postcolonial Feminist Interpretation of the Bible*. St. Louis: Chalice.

———. 2002. "Descending from and Ascending into Heaven: A Postcolonial Analysis of Travel, Space, and Power in John." Pages 1–10 in *John and Postcolonialism: Travel, Space, and Power*. BP 7. Edited by Musa W. Dube and Jeffrey L. Staley. New York: Sheffield Academic.

Dube, Musa W., and Jeffrey L. Staley, eds. 2002. *John and Postcolonialism: Travel, Space and Power.* BP 7. New York: Sheffield Academic.

Dunn, James D. G. 2001. "The Embarrassment of History: Reflections on the Problem of 'Anti-Judaism' in the Fourth Gospel." Pages 47–67 in *Anti-Judaism and the Fourth Gospel: Papers from the Leuven Colloquium, 2000.* Edited by Reimund Bieringer, Didier Pollefeyt and Frederique Vandecasteele-Vanneuville. Louisville: Westminster John Knox.

———. 2003. *Jesus Remembered.* Grand Rapids: Eerdmans.

Eckart, Dietrich. 1924. *Der Bolschewismus von Moses bis Lenin: Zwiegespräch zwischen Adolf Hitler und mir.* München: Hoheneichen.

Egger, Wilhelm. 1987. *Methodenlehre zum Neuen Testament: Einführung in linguistische und historisch-kritische Methoden.* Freiburg: Herder.

———. 1996. *How to Read the New Testament: An Introduction to Linguistic and Historico-critical Methodology.* 1st English ed. Peabody, Mass.: Hendrickson.

———. 1999. *Methodenlehre zum Neuen Testament: Einführung in linguistische und historisch-kritische Methoden.* 5th ed. Freiburg: Herder.

Esler, Philip J. 1998. "Community and Gospel in Early Christianity: A Response to Richard Bauckham's *Gospels for All Christians.*" *SJT* 51:235–53.

Evans, Christopher F. 1957. "The Central Section of Luke's Gospel." Pages 37–53 in *Studies in the Gospels: Essays in Memory of R. H. Lightfoot.* Edited Dennis E. Nineham. Oxford: Basil Blackwell.

Fanning, Buist M. 1990. *Verbal Aspects in New Testament Greek.* Oxford: Clarendon.

Felton, Tom, and Tom Thatcher. 2001. "Stylometry and the Signs Gospel." Pages 209–18 in *Jesus in Johannine Tradition.* Edited by Robert T. Fortna and Tom Thatcher. Louisville: Westminster John Knox.

Fitzmyer, Joseph A. 1995. "The Biblical Commission's Document, 'The Interpretation of the Bible in the Church': Text and Commentary." SubBi 18. Rome: Pontifical Biblical Institute.

Focant, Camille, ed. 1993. *The Synoptic Gospels: Source Criticism and the New Literary Criticism.* BETL 110. Leuven: Leuven University Press.

Fortna, Robert T. 1970. *The Gospel of Signs: A Reconstruction of the Narrative Source Underlying the Fourth Gospel.* SNTSMS 11. Cambridge: Cambridge University Press.

———. 1988. *The Fourth Gospel and Its Predecessor: From Narrative Source to Present Gospel.* Philadelphia: Fortress.

Fortna, Robert T., and Tom Thatcher, eds. 2001. *Jesus in Johannine Tradition.* Louisville: Westminster John Knox.

Frey, Jörg. 1997–2000. *Die johanneische Eschatologie.* 3 vols. Tübingen: Mohr.

———. 2004a. "Das Bild 'der Juden' im Johannesevangelium und die Geschichte der johanneischen Gemeinde." Pages 33–53 in *Israel und seine Heilstraditionen im Johannesevangelium.* Edited by Michael Labahn, et al. Paderborn: Schöningh.

———. 2004b. "Auf der Suche nach dem Kontext des vierten Evangeliums." Pages 3–45 in *Kontexte des Johannesevangeliums: Das vierte Evangelium in religions- und traditionsgeschichtlicher Perspektive.* Edited by Jörg Frey and Udo Schnelle. WUNT 175. Tübingen: Mohr Siebeck.

Frey, Jörg, and Udo Schnelle, eds. 2004. *Kontexte des Johannesevangeliums: Das vierte Evangelium in religions- und traditionsgeschichtlicher Perspektive.* WUNT 175. Tübingen: Mohr–Siebeck.

Gardner-Smith, Percival. 1938. *Saint John and the Synoptic Gospels.* Cambridge: Cambridge University Press.

Genette, Gérard. 1980. *Narrative Discourse: An Essay in Method.* Translated by Jonathan Culler. Ithaca, N.Y.: Cornell University Press.

Gibson, S. 2005. "The Pool of Bethesda in Jerusalem and Jewish Purification Practices of the Second Temple Period." *Proche-Orient Chrétien* 55:270–93.

Guardiola-Sáenz, Leticia. 2002. "Border-Crossing and Its Redemptive Power in John 7.53–8.11: A Cultural Reading of Jesus and the Accused." Pages 129–52 in *John and Postcolonialism: Travel, Space, and Power.* BP 7. Edited by Musa W. Dube and Jeffrey L. Staley. New York: Sheffield Academic.

Gunkel, Hermann. 1901. *Genesis, übersetzt und erklärt von Hermann Gunkel.* Göttingen: Vandenhoeck & Ruprecht.

Guthrie, George. 1999. "Boats in the Bay: Reflections on the Use of Linguistics and Literary Analysis in Biblical Studies." Pages 23–35 in *Linguistics and the New Testament: Critical Junctures.* JSNTSup 168. Studies in New Testament Greek 5. Edited by Stanley E. Porter and D. A. Carson. Sheffield: Sheffield Academic.

Haenchen, Ernst. 1980. *Das Johannesevangelium: Ein Kommentar.* Tübingen: Mohr.

———. 1984. *John: A Commentary on the Gospel of John.* 2 vols. Translated and edited by Robert W. Funk. Philadelphia: Fortress.

Harrisville, Roy A., and Walter Sundberg. 2002. *The Bible in Modern Culture: Baruch Spinoza to Brevard Childs.* 2nd ed. Grand Rapids: Eerdmans.

Harsh, Philip. 1984. *A Handbook of Classical Drama.* Palo Alto, Calif.: Stanford University Press.

Hawkins, David. 2005–2006. "The Bible and the Modern World: Taking It Personally." *The Bulletin.* Canadian Society of Biblical Studies 65:1–17.

Heidegger, Martin. 1992. *Being and Time.* Translated by John Macquarrie and Edward Robinson. New York and Evanston: Harper & Row.

Hengel, Martin. 1963. "Maria Magdalena und die Frauen als Zeugen." Pages 243–56 in *Abraham unser Vater: Juden und Christen im Gespräch über die Bibel: Festschrift für Otto Michel.* Edited by Otto Betz, Martin Hengel, and Peter Schmidt. Leiden: Brill.

———. 1974. *Judaism and Hellenism: Studies in Their Encounter in Palestine during the Early Hellenistic Period.* 1st English ed. 2 vols. London: SCM Press.

———. 1983. "Hymns and Christology." Pages 78–86 in *Between Jesus and Paul: Studies in the Earliest History of Christianity.* Edited by Martin Hengel. Translated by John Bowden. Philadelphia: Fortress.

———. 1993. *Die johanneische Frage: Ein Lösungsversuch.* WUNT 67. Tübingen: Mohr Siebeck.

———. 1999. "Das Johannesevangelium als Quelle für die Geschichte des antiken Judentums." Pages 293–334 in *Judaica, Hellenistica et Christiana.* Kleine Schriften II. WUNT 109. Tübingen: Mohr Siebeck.

———. 2000. *The Four Gospels and the One Gospel of Jesus Christ: An Investigation of the Collection and Origin of the Canonical Gospels.* Harrisburg: Trinity Press International.

———. 2004. "The Four Gospels and the One Gospel of Jesus Christ." Pages 13–26 in *The Earliest Gospels: The Origins and Transmission of the Earliest Christian Gospels—The Contribution of the Chester Beatty Codex P^{45}.* Edited by Charles Horton. New York: T&T Clark.

———. 2005. "Eye-Witness Memory and the Writing of the Gospels." Pages 77–96 in *The Written Gospel.* Edited by Markus Bockmuehl and Donald A. Hagner. Cambridge: Cambridge University Press.

Hens–Piazza, Gina. 2000a. "Lyotard." Pages 160–66 in *Handbook of Postmodern Interpretation.* Edited by A. K. M. Adam. St. Louis: Chalice.

———. 2000b. *The New Historicism.* GBS. Edited by Dan O. Via Jr. Minneapolis: Fortress.

Hill, Charles E. 2004. *The Johannine Corpus in the Early Church.* New York: Oxford University Press.

Hirsch, Eric D. 1967. *Validity in Interpretation.* New Haven: Yale University Press.

———. 1976. *The Aims of Interpretation.* Chicago: University of Chicago Press.

Hoegen–Rohls, Christina. 1996. *Der nachösterliche Johannes: Die Abschieds-reden als hermeneutischer Schlüssel zum vierten Evangelium*. WUNT 2.84. Tübingen: J. C. B. Mohr.

Holt, J. 1943. *Études d'aspect*. Copenhagen: Universitetsforlaget Aarhus.

Hooker, Morna D. 1975. "In His Own Image?" Pages 28–44 in *What about the New Testament? Essays in Honour of Christopher Evans*. Edited by Morna D. Hooker and Colin Hickling. London: SCM Press.

Horbury, William. 1982. "The Benediction of the *Minim* and Early Jewish-Christian Controversy." *JTS* 32:19–61.

———. 2005. "'Gospel' in Herodian Judea." Pages 7–30 in *The Written Gospel*. Edited by Markus Bockmuehl and Donald A. Hagner. Cambridge: Cambridge University Press.

Horsley, Richard A., ed. 1997. *Paul and Empire: Religion and Power in Roman Imperial Society*. Harrisburg: Trinity International Press.

———. 2003. *Jesus and Empire: The Kingdom of God and the New World Disorder*. Minneapolis: Fortress.

Houlden, J. L., ed. 1995. *The Interpretation of the Bible in the Church*. London: SCM Press.

Huffard, E. W. 1989. "Mission and the Servants of God (John 5)." Pages 84–96 in *Johannine Studies: Essays in Honour of Frank Peck*. Edited by James Priest. Malibu: Pepperdine University Press.

Huie–Jolly, Marie. 2002. "Maori 'Jews' and a Resistant Reading of John 5:10–47." Pages 94–110 in *John and Postcolonialism: Travel, Space, and Power*. BP 7. Edited by Musa W. Dube and Jeffrey L. Staley. New York: Sheffield Academic.

The Interpretation of the Bible in the Church: Address of His Holiness Pope John Paul II and Document of the Pontifical Biblical Commission. 1993. Translated by John Kilgallen and Brendan Byrne. Rome: Libreria Editrice Vaticana.

Isaacs, Marie E. 1991. "Exegesis and Homiletics, Spirituality and Scripture." *The Way Supplements* 72:32–47.

Iser, Wolfgang. 1974. *The Implied Reader: Patterns of Communication in Prose Fiction from Bunyan to Beckett*. Baltimore: Johns Hopkins University Press.

Johnson, Luke Timothy. 1999. *Living Jesus: Learning the Heart of the Gospel*. San Francisco: HarperSanFrancisco.

Johnson, Luke Timothy, and William S. Kurz. 2002. *The Future of Catholic Biblical Scholarship: A Constructive Conversation*. Grand Rapids: Eerdmans.

Jones, Rufus. 1906. *The Double Search: Studies in Atonement and Prayer*. Philadelphia: John C. Winston.

Käsemann, Ernst. 1968. *The Testament of Jesus: A Study of the Gospel of John in Light of Chapter 17.* 1st English ed. Philadelphia: Fortress.

———. 1969. *New Testament Questions of Today.* Translated by W. J. Montague. Philadelphia: Fortress.

Katz, Steven T. 1984. "Issues in the Separation of Judaism and Christianity after 70 C.E.: A Reconsideration." *JBL* 103:43–76.

Keener, Craig S. 2003. *The Gospel of John: A Commentary.* 2 vols. Peabody, Mass.: Hendrickson.

———. 2006. "Review of Andrew T. Lincoln, *The Gospel According to St. John.*" *Review of Biblical Literature.* Online: http://www.bookreviews.org/pdf/5024_5292.pdf.

Kelber, Werner. 1983. *The Oral and the Written Gospel: The Hermeneutics of Speaking and Writing in the Synoptic Tradition, Mark, Paul, and Q.* Bloomington: Indiana University Press.

Kim, Jean K. 2002. "Adultery or Hybridity? Reading John 7.53–8.11 from a Postcolonial Context." Pages 111–28 in *John and Postcolonialism: Travel, Space, and Power.* BP 7. Edited by Musa W. Dube and Jeffrey L. Staley. New York: Sheffield Academic.

Kimelman, Reuven. 1981. "*Birkat Haminim* and the Lack of Evidence for an Anti-Christian Jewish Prayer in Late Antiquity." Pages 2.226–44, 391–403 in *Jewish and Christian Self-Definition.* 2 vols. Edited by E. P. Sanders with A. I. Baumgarten and Alan Mendelson. Philadelphia: Fortress.

Kitzberger, Ingrid R. 1998. "'How Can This Be?' (John 3.9): A Feminist-Theological Rereading of the Gospel of John." Pages 19–42 in *What is John?* Vol. 2: *Literary and Social Readings of the Fourth Gospel.* SBL Symposium Series 7. Edited by Fernando F. Segovia. Atlanta: Scholars Press.

Klauck, Hans-Joseph. 1989. "Gespaltene Gemeinde: Der Umgang mit den Sezessionisten im ersten Johannesbrief." Pages 59–68 in *Gemeinde–Amt–Sakrament.* Neutestamentliche Perspektiven. Würzburg: Echter.

———. 2005. "Community, History, and Text(s)." Pages 82–90 in *Life in Abundance: Studies of John's Gospel in Tribute to Raymond Brown, S.S.* Edited by John R. Donahue. Collegeville, Minn: Liturgical Press.

Koester, Craig R. 1995. *Symbolism in the Fourth Gospel: Meaning, Mystery, Community.* Minneapolis: Fortress.

Konings, Johan. 1972. "Het johanneïsche verhaal in de literaire kritiek. Historiek—Dossier van Joh. I–X—Redactiestudie van Joh. VI,1–2." 3 vols. Unpublished doctoral dissertation. K.U.Leuven.

Köstenberger, Andreas J. 1998. *The Missions of Jesus and the Disciples According to the Fourth Gospel.* Grand Rapids: Eerdmans.

Köstenberger, Andreas J. 2001. "Early Doubts of the Apostolic Authorship of the Fourth Gospel in the History of Modern Biblical Criticism." Pages 17–47 in *Studies in John and Gender: A Decade of Scholarship.* Edited by Andreas J. Köstenberger. New York: Peter Lang.

———. 2002. "John." Pages 2–216 in *Zondervan Illustrated Bible Backgrounds Commentary.* Vol. 2. Edited by Clint A. Arnold. Grand Rapids: Zondervan.

———. 2004. *John.* Baker Exegetical Commentary of the New Testament. Grand Rapids: Baker Academic.

———. 2005. "The Destruction of the Second Temple and the Composition of the Fourth Gospel." *Trinity Journal* 26:205–42.

Kysar, Robert. 1975. *The Fourth Evangelist and His Gospel: An Examination of Contemporary Scholarship.* Minneapolis: Augsburg.

———. 2005a. " 'He Gave up the Spirit': A Reader's Reflection on John 19:30b." Pages 161–72 in *Transcending Boundaries: Contemporary Readings of the New Testament. Essays in Honor of Francis J. Moloney.* Edited by Rekha M. Chennattu and Mary L. Coloe. Rome: LAS.

———. 2005b. "The Whence and Whither of the Johannine Community." Pages 65–81 in *Life in Abundance: Studies of John's Gospel in Tribute to Raymond E. Brown, S.S.* Edited by John R. Donahue. Collegeville, Minn.: Liturgical Press.

———. 2005c. *Voyages with John: Charting the Fourth Gospel.* Waco, Tex.: Baylor University Press.

Kysar, Robert, and Joseph Webb. 2006. *Preaching to Postmoderns: New Perspectives for Proclaiming the Message.* Peabody, Mass.: Hendrickson.

Labahn, Michael. 1999. *Jesus als Lebensspender: Untersuchungen zu einer Geschichte der johanneischen Tradition anhand ihrer Wundergeschichten.* BZNW 98. New York: de Gruyter.

———. 2000a. *Offenbarung in Zeichen und Wort: Untersuchungen zur Vorgeschichte von Joh 6, 1–25a und seine Rezeption in der Brotrede.* WUNT. Tübingen: Mohr Siebeck.

———. 2000b. "Controversial Revelation in Deed and Word: The Feeding of the Five Thousand and Jesus' Crossing of the Sea as a Prelude to the Johannine Bread of Life Discourse." *IBS* 80:146–81.

———. 2004. "Die παρρησία des Gottessohnes im Johannesevangelium: Theologische Hermeneutik und philosophisches Selbstverständnis." Pages 321–63 in *Kontexte des Johannesevangelium: Das vierte Evangelium in religions- und traditionsgeschichtlicher Perspektive.* WUNT 175. Edited by Jörg Frey and Udo Schnelle. Tübingen: Mohr Siebeck.

Labahn, Michael, and Manfred Lang. 2004. "Johannes und die Synoptiker: Positionen und Impulse seit 1990." Pages 443–515 in *Kontexte des Johannesevangeliums: Das vierte Evangelium in religions- und traditionsgeschichtlicher Perspektive.* WUNT 175. Edited by Jörg Frey and Udo Schnelle. Tübingen: Mohr Siebeck.

Labahn, Michael, Klaus Scholtissek, and Angelika Strotmann, eds. 2004. *Israel und seine Heilstraditionen im Johannesevangelium: Festgabe für Johannes Beutler SJ zum 70. Geburtstag.* Paderborn: Schöningh.

Lee, Dorothy A. 2002. *Flesh and Glory: Symbolism, Gender, and Theology in the Gospel of John.* New York: Crossroad.

Lee, John A. L. 2003. *A History of New Testament Lexicography: Studies in Biblical Greek.* New York: Peter Lang.

Levie, Jean. 1961. *The Bible: Word of God in Words of Men.* Translated by S. H. Treman. London: Geoffrey Chapman.

Lewis, C. S. 1975. "Modern Theology and Biblical Criticism." In *Fern-Seed and Elephants, and Other Essays on Christianity.* Edited by Walter Hooper. London: Fontana.

Liddell, Henry G., and Robert Scott. 1958. *A Greek-English Lexicon.* Rev. ed. Oxford: Clarendon.

Liew, Tat-siong Benny. 2002. "Ambiguous Admittance: Consent and Descent in John's Community of 'Upward' Mobility." Pages 193–224 in *John and Postcolonialism: Travel, Space, and Power.* BP 7. Edited by Musa W. Dube and Jeffrey L. Staley. New York: Sheffield Academic.

Lincoln, Andrew T. 2005. *The Gospel According to Saint John.* BNTC. Peabody, Mass.: Hendrickson.

Lindars, Barnabas. 1972. *The Gospel of John.* London: Oliphants.

Lozada, Francisco. 2002. "Contesting an Interpretation of John 5: Moving beyond Colonial Evangelism." Pages 76–93 in *John and Postcolonialism: Travel, Space, and Power.* BP 7. Edited by Musa W. Dube and Jeffrey L. Staley. New York: Sheffield Academic.

Lund, Nils W. 1931. "The Influence of Chiasms on the Structure of the Gospels." *AThR* 13:41–46.

MacRae, George. 1970. "The Jewish Background of the Gnostic Sophia Myth." *NovT* 12:86–101.

Malatesta, Edward. 1978. *Interiority and Covenant: A Study in* εἶναι ἐν *and* μένειν ἐν *in the First Letter of Saint John.* AnBib 96. Rome: Biblical Institute Press.

Martyn, J. Louis. 1968. *History and Theology in the Fourth Gospel.* 1st ed. New York: Harper & Row.

———. 1977. "Glimpses into the History of the Johannine Community from Its Origin through the Period of Its Life in which the Fourth Gospel was Composed." Pages 149–75 in *L'Évangile de Jean. Sources, rédaction, théologie.* BETL 44. Edited by Marinus de Jonge, et al. Leuven: Leuven University Press.

Martyn, J. Louis. 1979a. *The Gospel of John in Christian History: Essays for Interpreters.* New York: Paulist Press.

———. 1979b. *History and Theology in the Fourth Gospel.* 2nd ed. Nashville: Abingdon.

———. 1997. *Theological Issues in the Letters of Paul.* Nashville: Abingdon.

———. 2003. *History and Theology in the Fourth Gospel.* NTL. 3rd ed. Louisville: Westminster John Knox.

Mateos, Juan. 1977. *El aspecto verbal en el NT.* Madrid: Ediciones Cristiandad.

Maunier, René. 1949. *The Sociology of Colonies: An Introduction to the Study of Colonies.* Vol. 1. Edited and translated by E. O. Lorimer. London: Routledge.

McKane, William. 1970. *Proverbs: A New Approach.* Philadelphia: Westminster.

McKay, Kenneth L. 1994. *A New Syntax of the Verb in New Testament Greek: An Aspectual Approach.* Studies in Biblical Greek 5. New York: Peter Lang.

Meeks, Wayne A. 1972a. "The Man from Heaven in Johannine Sectarianism." *JBL* 91:44–72.

———, ed. 1972b. *The Writings of St. Paul.* New York: Norton.

———. 2002. "The Man from Heaven in Johannine Sectarianism." Pages 55–90 in *In Search of the Early Christians: Selected Essays.* Edited by Allen R. Hilton and H. Gregory Snyder. New Haven: Yale University Press.

Menken, Maarten J. J. 1997. "John 6:51c–58: Eucharist or Christology." Pages 183–204 in *Critical Readings of John 6.* BIS. Edited by R. Alan Culpepper. Leiden: Brill.

Miller, E. L. 1993. "The Johannine Origins of the Johannine Logos." *JBL* 112:445–57.

Mitchell, Margaret M. 2005. "Patristic Counter-Evidence to the Claim That the Gospels Were Written for All Christians." *NTS* 51:36–79.

Mlakuzhyil, George. 1987. *The Christocentric Literary Structure of the Fourth Gospel.* Rome: Pontifical Biblical Institute.

Moloney, Francis J. 1977. *The Word Became Flesh.* Theology Today 14. Dublin: Mercier Press.

———. 1978. *The Johannine Son of Man.* 2nd ed. BSR 14. Rome: LAS.

———. 1986. *The Living Voice of the Gospel.* The Gospels Today. New York: Paulist Press.

———. 1993. *Belief in the Word: Reading John 1–4.* Minneapolis: Fortress.

———. 1996. *Signs and Shadows: Reading John 5–12.* Minneapolis: Fortress.

———. 1997. "Who is 'the Reader' in/of the Fourth Gospel?" Pages 219–33 in *The Interpretation of John*. 2nd ed. Edited by John Ashton. Edinburgh: T&T Clark.

———. 1998a. *The Gospel of John*. Sacra Pagina 4. Edited by Daniel J. Harrington. Collegeville, Minn.: Liturgical Press.

———. 1998b. *Glory Not Dishonour: Reading John 13–21*. Minneapolis: Fortress.

———. 2003. "Can Everyone Be Wrong? A Reading of John 11.1–12.8." *NTS* 49:505–27.

———. 2005a. "The Gospel of John as Scripture." *CBQ* 67:454–68.

———. 2005b. "The Gospel of John: The Legacy of Raymond E. Brown and Beyond." Pages 19–39 in *Life in Abundance: Studies of John's Gospel in Tribute to Raymond E. Brown, S.S.* Edited by John R. Donahue. Collegeville, Minn.: Liturgical Press.

———. 2005c. *The Gospel of John*. Sacra Pagina. 2nd ed. Collegeville, Minn.: Liturgical Press.

———. 2006. "What Came First—Scripture or Canon? The Gospel of John as a Test Case." *Salesianum* 68:7–20.

Moore, Stephen D. 1989. *Literary Criticism and the Gospels: The Theoretical Challenge*. New Haven: Yale University Press.

———. 1993. "Are There Impurities in the Living Water that the Johannine Jesus Dispenses? Deconstruction, Feminism, and the Samaritan Woman." *Biblical Interpretation* 1.208–27.

———. 1994. *Poststructuralism and the New Testament: Derrida and Foucault at the Foot of the Cross*. Minneapolis: Fortress.

Moore, Stephen D., and Fernando F. Segovia. 2005. "Postcolonial Biblical Criticism: Origins, Trajectories, Intersections." Pages 1–22 in *Postcolonial Biblical Criticism: Interdisciplinary Intersections*. Edited by Stephen D. Moore and Fernando F. Segovia. New York: T&T Clark.

Muñoz Léon, Domingo. 1974. *Dios Palabra: Memra en los Targumin del Pentateuco*. Granada: Editorial Santa Rita.

Murray, Paul. 1991. *T. S. Eliot and Mysticism: The Secret History of Four Quartets*. London: Macmillan.

Mussner, Franz. 1967. *The Historical Jesus in the Gospel of John*. QD 19. Translated by W. J. O'Hara. New York: Herder.

Neirynck, Frans. 1968. "Les femmes au tombeau. Étude de la rédaction Matthéenne." *NTS* 15:168–90.

———. 1969. "De Nederlandstolige Faculteit der Godgeleerdheid." *Onze Alma Mater* 23:225–33.

———. 1975. "The 'Other Disciple' in Jn 18, 15–16." *ETL* 51:113–41.

Neirynck, Frans. 1977. "John and the Synoptics." Pages 73–106 in *L'Évangile de Jean: Sources, rédaction, théologie*. BETL 44. Edited by Marinus de Jonge, et al. Leuven: Leuven University Press.

———. 1982. *Evangelica [I]. Gospel Studies—Études d'évangiles*. BETL 60. Edited by Frans van Segbroeck. Leuven: Leuven University Press.

———. 1990. "John and the Synoptics: Response to P. Borgen." Pages 438–50 in *The Interrelations of the Gospels*. BETL 95. Edited by David L. Dungan. Leuven: Leuven University Press.

———. 1991. *Evangelica [II]. 1982–1990. Collected Essays*. BETL 99. Edited by Frans van Segbroeck. Leuven: Leuven University Press.

———. 1992. "John and the Synoptics: 1975–1990." Pages 3–62 in *John and the Synoptics*. Edited by Adelbert Denaux. Leuven: Leuven University Press.

———. 1993. "Gospel, Genre of." Pages 258–59 in *The Oxford Companion to the Bible*. Edited by Bruce M. Metzger and Michael D. Coogan. New York: Oxford University Press.

———. 1995. "Jean 4,46–54. Une leçon de méthode." *ETL* 71:176–84.

———. 2001. *Evangelica [III]. 1992–2000. Collected Essays*. BETL 150. Edited by Frans van Segbroeck. Leuven: Leuven University Press.

Neirynck, Frans, in collaboration with Joël Delobel, et al. 1979. *Jean et les Synoptiques: Examen critique de l'exégèse de M.-É. Boismard*. BETL 49. Leuven: Leuven University Press.

Neusner, Jacob, ed. 1968. *Religions in Antiquity: In Memory of E. R. Goodenough*. SHR 14. Leiden: Brill.

———, et al., eds. 2005. *Ancient Israel, Judaism, and Christianity in Contemporary Perspectives: Essays in Memory of Karl-Johan Illman*. Lanham, Md.: University Press of America.

Nicholson, Godfrey C. 1983. *Death as Departure*. Chico: Scholars Press.

North, Wendy E. S. 2003. "John for Readers of Mark? A Response to Richard Bauckham's Proposal." *JSNT* 25:449–68.

Obermann, Andreas. 1996. *Die christologische Erfüllung der Schrift im Johannesevangelium*. WUNT 2.83. Tübingen: Mohr.

O'Day, Gail R. 1986. *Revelation in the Fourth Gospel: Narrative Mode and Theological Claim*. Philadelphia: Fortress.

———. 1997. "John 6:15–21: Jesus Walking on Water as Narrative Embodiment of Johannine Christology." Pages 149–59 in *Critical Readings of John 6*. BIS 22. Edited by R. Alan Culpepper. Leiden: Brill.

O'Donnell, Matthew Brook. 2005. *Corpus Linguistics and the Greek New Testament*. Sheffield: Phoenix Press.

O'Neill, John C. 1972. *The Recovery of Paul's Letter to the Galatians*. London: SPCK.

Pagels, Elaine. 2003. *Beyond Belief: The Secret Gospel of Thomas*. New York: Random House.

———. 2006. "The Gospel of Truth." Op-ed page in *The New York Times*. April 8.

Painter, John. 1975. *John: Witness and Theologian*. London: SPCK.

———. 1979. "Johannine Symbols: A Case Study in Epistemology." *JTSA* 27:26–41.

———. 1986. "John 9 and the Interpretation of the Fourth Gospel." *JSNT* 28:31–61.

———. 1987a. *Theology as Hermeneutics: Rudolf Bultmann's Interpretation of Jesus*. Sheffield: Sheffield Almond Press.

———. 1987b. "Text and Context in John 5." *ABR* 35:28–34.

———. 1989. "Tradition and Interpretation in John 6." *NTS* 35/3:421–50.

———. 1993a. "Theology, Eschatology, and the Prologue of John." *SJT* 46.1:27–42.

———. 1993b. *The Quest for the Messiah: The History, Literature, and Theology of the Johannine Community*. 2nd ed. Nashville: Abingdon.

———. 1996. "Inclined to God: The Quest for Eternal Life: Bultmannian Hermeneutics and the Theology of the Fourth Gospel." Pages 346–68 in *Exploring the Gospel of John: In Honor of D. Moody Smith*. Edited by R. Alan Culpepper and C. Clifton Black. Louisville: Westminster John Knox.

———. 1997a. "Jesus and the Quest for Eternal Life." Pages 61–94 in *Critical Readings of John 6*. BIS 22. Edited by R. Alan Culpepper. Leiden: Brill.

———. 1997b. *Mark's Gospel: Worlds in Conflict*. New York: Routledge.

———. 1997c. *Just James: The Brother of Jesus in History and Tradition*. Columbia: University of South Carolina Press.

———. 1998. "God and the Quest for Eternal Life." *St. Mark's Review* 173:10–16.

———. 2002a. "Earth Made Whole: John's Rereading of Genesis." Pages 65–84 in *Word, Theology, and Community in John*. Edited by John Painter, R. Alan Culpepper, and Fernando F. Segovia. St. Louis: Chalice Press.

———. 2002b. *1, 2 and 3 John*. Sacra Pagina 18. Edited by Daniel J. Harrington. Collegeville, Minn.: Liturgical Press.

———. 2003a. "Rereading Genesis in the Prologue of John." Pages 179–201 in *Neotestamentica et Philonica: Studies in Honor of Peder Borgen*. NovTSup 106. Edited by David E. Aune, Torrey Seland, and Jarl Henning Ulrichsen. Leiden: Brill.

Painter, John. 2003b. "1, 2, and 3 John." Pages 1512–28 in *Eerdmans Commentary on the Bible.* Edited by James D. G. Dunn. Grand Rapids: Eerdmans.

———. (forthcoming). "Does John Have a Coherent and Unified View of the Death of Jesus? A Discussion of the Tradition, History, and Theology of John." In *The Death of Jesus in the Fourth Gospel.* Edited by Gilbert Van Belle. Leuven: Peeters Press.

Palmer, Richard E. 1969. *Hermeneutics: Interpretation Theology in Schleiermacher, Dilthey, Heidegger, and Gadamer.* Northwestern University Studies in Phenomenology and Existential Philosophy. Edited by John Wild. Evanston, Ill.: Northwestern University Press.

Pancaro, Severino. 1975. *The Law in the Fourth Gospel: The Torah and the Gospel: Moses and Jesus, Judaism and Christianity According to John.* NovTSup 42. Leiden: Brill.

Parsenios, George L. 2005. *Departure and Consolation: The Johannine Farewell Discourses in Light of Greco-Roman Literature.* NovTSup 117. Leiden: Brill.

Patte, Daniel, ed. 2004. *Global Bible Commentary.* Edited by J. Severino Croatto, Nicole Wilkinson Duran, Teresa Okure, and Archie Chi Chung Lee. Nashville: Abingdon.

Penner, Myron B., ed. 2005. *Christianity and the Postmodern Turn: Six Views.* Grand Rapids: Brazos Press.

Peters, Ted, Robert John Russell, and Michael Welker, eds. 2002. *Resurrection: Theological and Scientific Assessments.* Grand Rapids: Eerdmans.

Phillips, Gary A. 1990. "Exegesis' Critical Praxis: Reclaiming History and Text from a Postmodernist Perspective." Pages 7–49 in *Semeia 51: Post-Structural Criticism and the Bible: Text/History/Discourse.* Edited by Gary A. Phillips. Atlanta: Society of Biblical Literature.

Piper, Ronald A. 2005. "The One, the Four, and the Many." Pages 254–73 in *The Written Gospel.* Edited by Markus Bockmuehl and Donald A. Hagner. Cambridge: Cambridge University Press.

Plantinga, Alvin. 2003. "Two (or more) Kinds of Scripture Scholarship." Pages 19–57 in *"Behind" the Text: History and Biblical Interpretation.* Scripture and Hermeneutics. Edited by Craig Bartholomew, et al. Grand Rapids: Zondervan.

Popp, Thomas. 2001. *Grammatik des Geistes: Literarische Kunst und theologische Konzeption in Johannes 3 und 6.* Leipzig: Evangelische Verlagsanstalt.

Porter, Stanley E. 1989. *Verbal Aspects in the Greek of the New Testament with Reference to Tense and Mood.* Studies in Biblical Greek 1. New York: Peter Lang.

Powell, Mark Allen. 1990. *What Is Narrative Criticism?* GBS. Minneapolis: Fortress.

Preiss, Theo. 1954. *Life in Christ.* SBT 13. Translated by Harold Knight. Chicago: A. R. Allenson.

Pryor, John. 1992. *John: Evangelist of the Covenant People.* London: Darton, Longman & Todd.

Rabinowitz, Peter J. 1989. "Whirl Without End." Pages 81–100 in *Contemporary Literary Theory.* Edited by C. Douglas Atkins and Laura Morrow. London: Macmillan.

Radcliffe, Timothy, O.P. 1999. *Sing A New Song: The Christian Vocation.* Springfield: Templegate Publishers.

Reich, Ronald, and Eli Shukron. 2005. "Siloam." *Qadmoniot* 38:91–96.

Reinhartz, Adele. 1998a. "The Johannine Community and its Jewish Neighbors: A Reappraisal." Pages 111–38 in *What is John? Vol. II: Literary and Social Readings of the Fourth Gospel.* SBL Symposium Series 7. Edited by Fernando F. Segovia. Atlanta: Scholars Press.

———. 1998b. "On Travel, Translation, and Ethnography: The Gospel of John at the Turn of the Century." Pages 249–56 in *What is John? Vol. II: Literary and Social Readings of the Fourth Gospel.* SBL Symposium Series 7. Edited by Fernando F. Segovia. Atlanta: Scholars Press.

———. 2001. *Befriending the Beloved Disciple: A Jewish Reading of the Gospel of John.* New York: Continuum.

———. 2002. "The Colonizer as Colonized: Intertextual Dialogue between the Gospel of John and Canadian Identity." Pages 170–92 in *John and Postcolonialism: Travel, Space, and Power.* BP 7. Edited by Musa W. Dube and Jeffrey L. Staley. New York: Sheffield Academic.

———. 2003. "Women in the Johannine Community: An Exercise in Historical Imagination." Pages 14–33 in *A Feminist Companion to John.* Vol. 2. Edited by Amy-Jill Levine. Sheffield: Sheffield Academic.

Richter, Georg. 1969. "Zur Formgeschichte und literarischen Einheit von Joh 6:31-58." *ZNW* 60:21–55.

Ricoeur, Paul. 1976. *Interpretation Theory: Discourse and the Surplus of Meaning.* Fort Worth: Texas Christian University Press.

———. 1980. *Essays on Biblical Interpretation.* Edited and introduced by Lewis S. Mudge. Philadelphia: Fortress.

———. 1981. *Hermeneutics and the Human Sciences: Essays on Language, Action, and Interpretation.* Edited, translated, and introduced by John B. Thompson. New York: Cambridge University Press.

Robinson, James M. 1957. *The Problem of History in Mark.* SBT 21. Naperville: Allenson.

Robinson, John A. T. 1985. *The Priority of John.* London: SCM.

Rochais, Gérard. 1981. *Les récits de résurrection des morts dans le Nouveau Testament*. Cambridge: Cambridge University Press.

Ruckstuhl, Eugen. 1977. "Johannine Language and Style: The Question of Their Unity." Pages 125–47 in *L'Évangile de Jean: Sources, rédaction, théologie*. BETL 44. Edited by Marinus de Jonge, et al. Leuven: Leuven University Press.

———. 1988. *Die literarische Einheit des Johannesevangeliums: Der gegenwärtige Stand der einschlägigen Forschungen*. NTOA 5. Göttingen: Vandenhoeck & Ruprecht.

Ruckstuhl, Eugen, and Peter Dschulnigg. 1991. *Stilkritik und Verfasserfrage im Johannesevangelium*. Göttingen: Vandenhoeck & Ruprecht.

Runia, David T. 1984. "The Structure of Philo's Allegorical Treatises: A Review of Two Recent Studies and Some Additional Comments." *VC* 38:209–56.

———. 1987. "Further Observations on the Structure of Philo's Allegorical Treatises." *VC* 41:105–38.

———. 1991. "Secondary Texts in Philo's *Quaestiones*." Pages 47–79 in *Both Literal and Allegorical: Studies in Philo of Alexandria's Questions and Answers on Genesis and Exodus*. BJS 232. Edited by David M. Hay. Atlanta: Scholars Press.

Russell, Letty M., ed. 1985. *Feminist Interpretation of the Bible*. Philadelphia: Westminster.

Sabbe, Maurits. 1977. "The Arrest of Jesus in Jn. 18,1–11 and Its Relation to the Synoptic Gospels: A Critical Evaluation of A. Dauer's Hypothesis." Pages 202–34 in *L'Évangile de Jean: Sources, rédaction, théologie*. BETL 44. Edited by Marinus de Jonge, et al. Leuven: Leuven University Press.

———. 1991. *Studia Neotestamentica: Collected Essays*. BETL 98. Leuven: Leuven University Press.

———. 1992. "The Trial of Jesus by Pilate in John and Its Relation to the Synoptic Gospels." Pages 341–85 in *John and the Synoptics*. Edited by Adelbert Denaux. Leuven: Leuven University Press.

Said, Edward. 1993. *Christianity and Colonialism*. New York: Alfred A. Knopf.

Schmidt, W. H. 1978. "Dabhar." Pages 101–25 in *TDOT*. Vol. 3. Edited by G. Johannes Botterweck and Helmer Ringgren. Translated by John T. Willis, Geoffrey W. Bromiley, and David E. Green. Grand Rapids: Eerdmans.

Schnackenburg, Rudolf. 1965–1971. *Das Johannesevangelium*. 3 vols. HTKNT 4/1–3. Freiburg: Herder.

———. 1973. *Die Johannesbriefe*. HTKNT 13/3. Freiburg: Herder.

———. 1977. "Entwicklung und Stand der johanneischen Forschung seit 1955." Pages 19–44 in *L'Évangile de Jean: Sources, rédaction, théologie*. BETL 44. Edited by Marinus de Jonge, et al. Leuven: Leuven University Press.

———. 1982. *The Gospel According to St. John*. 3 vols. Translated by Kevin Smyth. New York: Crossroad.

Schneiders, Sandra M. 1977a. "History and Symbolism in the Fourth Gospel." Pages 371–76 in *L'Évangile de Jean: Sources, rédaction, théologie*. BETL 44. Edited by Marinus de Jonge. Leuven: Leuven University Press.

———. 1977b. "Symbolism and the Sacramental Principle in the Fourth Gospel." Pages 221–35 in *Segni e Sacramenti nel Vangelo di Giovanni*. SA 67. Edited by Pius-Ramon Tragan. Rome: Editrice Anselmiana.

Schneiders, Sandra M. 1991. *The Revelatory Text: Interpreting the New Testament as Sacred Scripture*. San Francisco: HarperCollins.

Schnelle, Udo. 1992. *Antidocetic Christology in the Gospel of John: An Investigation of the Place of the Fourth Gospel in the Johannine School*. Translated by Linda M. Maloney. Minneapolis: Fortress.

———. 1998. *Das Evangelium nach Johannes*. HTKNT. Leipzig: Evangelische Verlagsanstalt.

———. 2002. *Einleitung in das Neue Testament*. 4th ed. Göttingen: Vandenhoeck & Ruprecht.

———. 2005. *Einleitung in das Neue Testament*. 5th ed. Göttingen: Vandenhoeck & Ruprecht.

Scholtissek, Klaus. 1999–2004. "Johannes auslegen." *SNTSU* 24–25, 27, 29. Part I:34–84 (1999); Part II:98–140 (2000a); Part III:117–53 (2002); Part IV:67–118 (2004a).

———. 2000b. *In Ihm sein und bleiben: Die Sprache der Immanenz in den Johanneischen Schriften*. HBS 21. Freiburg: Herder.

———. 2000c. "Relecture und réécriture: Neue Paradigmen zu Methode und Inhalt der Johannesauslegung aufgewiesen am Prolog 1,1–18 und der ersten Abschiedsrede 13,31–14,31." *Theologie und Philosophie* 75:1–29

———. 2004b. "The Johannine Gospel in Recent Research." Pages 444–72 in *The Face of New Testament Studies: A Survey of Recent Research*. Edited by Scot McKnight and Grant R. Osborne. Grand Rapids: Baker Academic.

Schottroff, Luise. 1970. *Der Glaubende und die feindliche Welt: Beobachtungen zum gnostischen Dualismus und seiner Bedeutung für Paulus und das Johannesevangelium*. WMANT 37. Neukirchen-Vluyn: Neukirchener Verlag.

Schüssler Fiorenza, Elisabeth. 1983. *In Memory of Her: A Feminist Theological Reconstruction of Christian Origins.* New York: Crossroad.

Schweitzer, Albert. 2001. *The Quest of the Historical Jesus: The First Complete Edition.* Edited by John Bowden. Minneapolis: Fortress.

Scott, Bernard B. 1985. *The Word of God in Words: Reading and Preaching.* Fortress Resources for Preaching. Philadelphia: Fortress.

Segovia, Fernando F. 1991. *The Farewell of the Word: The Johannine Call to Abide.* Minneapolis: Fortress.

———. 1996. "The Tradition History of the Fourth Gospel." Pages 179–89 in *Exploring the Gospel of John: In Honor of D. Moody Smith.* Edited by R. Alan Culpepper and C. Clifton Black. Louisville: Westminster John Knox.

———. 1998. "Biblical Criticism and Postcolonial Studies: Toward a Postcolonial Optic." Pages 49–65 in *The Postcolonial Bible.* BP 1. Edited by R. S. Sugirtharajah. Sheffield: Sheffield Academic.

———. 2000. *Decolonizing Biblical Studies: A View from the Margins.* Maryknoll, N.Y.: Orbis.

———. 2005. "Mapping the Postcolonial Optic in Biblical Criticism: Meaning and Scope." Pages 23–78 in *Postcolonial Biblical Criticism: Interdisciplinary Intersections.* Edited by Stephen D. Moore and Fernando F. Segovia. New York: T&T Clark.

———. 2007. "The Gospel of John." In *A Postcolonial Commentary on the New Testament Writings.* Edited by Fernando F. Segovia and R. S. Sugirtharajah. New York: T&T Clark.

Seland, Torrey. 1995. *Establishment Violence in Philo and Luke: A Study of Non-Conformity to the Torah and Jewish Vigilante Reactions.* BIS 15. Leiden: Brill.

Selong, Gabriel. 1971. "The Cleansing of the Temple in Jn 2,13–22: With a Reconsideration of the Dependence of the Fourth Gospel upon the Synoptics." 3 vols. Unpublished doctoral dissertation. K.U.Leuven.

Shanks, Herschel. 2005. "The Siloam Pool in Jesus' Time." *BAR* 31.5:16–23.

Siegert, Folker. 2004. *Der Erstentwurf des Johannes: Das ursprüngliche, judenchristliche Johannesevangelium in deutscher Übersetzung vorgestellt, nebst Nachrichten über den Verfasser und zwei Briefen von ihm (2.3 Joh.).* MJS 16. Münster: Lit.

Sim, David C. 2001. "The Gospel for All Christians? A Response to Richard Bauckham." *JSNT* 84:3–27.

Smith, Dennis E. 1991. "Narrative Beginnings in Ancient Literature and Theory." Pages 1–9 in *Semeia 52: How Gospels Began.* Edited by Dennis E. Smith. Atlanta: Society of Biblical Literature.

Smith, D. Moody. 1984. *Johannine Christianity*. Columbia: University of South Carolina Press.

———. 1990. "The Contribution of J. Louis Martyn to the Understanding of the Gospel of John." Pages 275–94 in *The Conversation Continues: Studies in Paul and John in Honor of J. Louis Martyn*. Edited by Robert T. Fortna and Beverly R. Gaventa. Nashville: Abingdon.

———. 1992. *John among the Gospels: The Relationship in Twentieth-Century Research*. Minneapolis: Fortress.

———. 1995. *The Theology of the Gospel of John*. New Testament Theology. Cambridge: Cambridge University Press.

———. 1999. *John*. Nashville: Abingdon.

———. 2001. *John among the Gospels*. 2nd ed. Columbia: University of South Carolina Press.

———. 2003. "The Contribution of J. Louis Martyn to the Understanding of the Gospel of John." Pages 1–23 in *History and Theology in the Fourth Gospel*. New Testament Library. 3rd ed. Louisville: Westminster John Knox.

———. 2005. "Future Directions in Johannine Studies." Pages 52–62 in *Life in Abundance: Studies of John's Gospel in Tribute to Raymond E. Brown, S.S.* Edited by John R. Donahue. Collegeville, Minn.: Liturgical Press.

Smith, Jonathan Z. 1978. "Good News Is No News: Aretalogy and Gospel." Pages 190–207 in *Map Is not Territory: Studies in the History of Religions*. Edited by Jonathan Z. Smith. Leiden: Brill.

Smith, Mark S. 2002a. *The Early History of God: Yahweh and the Other Deities in Ancient Israel*. Grand Rapids: Eerdmans.

———. 2002b. "Remembering God." *CBQ* 64:631–51.

Soares–Prabhu, George M. 1984. *Wir werden bei ihm wohnen: Das Johannesevangelium in indischer Deutung*. Freiburg: Herder.

Sollors, Werner. 1986. *Beyond Ethnicity: Consent and Descent in American Culture*. New York: Oxford University Press.

Staley, Jeffrey L. 1988. *The Print's First Kiss: A Rhetorical Investigation of the Implied Reader in the Fourth Gospel*. SBLDS 82. Atlanta: Scholars Press.

———. 1995. *Reading with a Passion: Rhetoric, Autobiography, and the American West in the Gospel of John*. New York: Continuum.

———. 2002. " 'Dis Place, Man': A Postcolonial Critique of the Vine (the Mountain and the Temple) in the Gospel of John." Pages 32–50 in *John and Postcolonialism: Travel, Space and Power*. BP 7. Edited by Musa W. Dube and Jeffrey L. Staley. New York: Sheffield Academic.

Steinmetz, David. 1980. "The Superiority of Pre-Critical Exegesis." *Theology Today* 37:27–38.

Stibbe, Mark W. G. 1992. *John as Storyteller: Narrative Criticism and the Fourth Gospel.* New York: Cambridge University Press.

———. 1993. *The Gospel of John as Literature: An Anthology of Twentieth-Century Perspectives.* Leiden: Brill.

———. 1994. *John's Gospel.* New York: Routledge.

Strauss, David F. 1972. *The Life of Jesus, Critically Examined.* Edited with an introduction by Peter C. Hodgson. Translated from the 4th German edition by George Elliot. Philadelphia: Fortress.

Sugirtharajah, R. S. 2002. *Postcolonial Criticism and Biblical Interpretation.* New York: Oxford University Press.

Swanson, Tod D. 2002. "To Prepare a Place: Johannine Christianity and the Collapse of Ethnic Territory." Pages 11–31 in *John and Postcolonialism: Travel, Space, and Power.* BP 7. Edited by Musa W. Dube and Jeffery L. Staley. New York: Sheffield Academic.

Swift, Jonathan. 1975. *Gulliver's Travels.* Introduction by Clive T. Probyn. London: Dent.

Tannehill, Robert C. 1981a. "Introduction: The Pronouncement Story and Its Types." Pages 1–13 in *Semeia 20: Pronouncement Stories.* Edited by Robert C. Tannehill. Atlanta: Society of Biblical Literature.

———. 1981b. "Varieties of Synoptic Pronouncement Stories." Pages 101–19 in *Semeia 20: Pronouncement Stories.* Edited by Robert C. Tannehill. Atlanta: Society of Biblical Literature.

Templeton, Douglas A. 1999. *The New Testament as True Fiction: Literature, Literary Criticism, Aesthetics.* Sheffield: Sheffield Academic.

Thatcher, Tom. 2001. *The Legend of the Beloved Disciple.* Pages 91–99 in *Jesus in Johannine Tradition.* Edited by Robert T. Fortna and Tom Thatcher. Louisville: Westminster John Knox.

Theobald, Michael. 2006. "Das Johannesevangelium—Zeugnis eines synagogalen 'Judenchristentums'?" Pages 107–58 in *Paulus und Johannes: Exegetische Studien zur paulinischen und johanneischen Theologie und Literatur.* WUNT 198. Edited by Dieter Sänger and Ulrich Mell. Tübingen: Mohr Siebeck.

Thompson, Marianne Meye. 1996. "The Historical Jesus and the Johannine Christ." Pages 21–42 in *Exploring the Gospel of John: In Honor of D. Moody Smith.* Edited by R. Alan Culpepper and C. Clifton Black. Louisville: Westminster John Knox.

Thüsing, Wilhelm. 1970. *Die Erhöhung und Verherrlichung Jesu im Johannesevangelium.* 2nd ed. Neutestamentliche Abhandlungen 21/1. Münster: Aschendorff.

Thyen, Hartwig. 1977. "Entwicklungen innerhalb der Johanneischen Theologie und Kirche im Spiegel von Joh. 21 und der Lieblingsjüngertexte des Evangeliums." Pages 259–99 in *L'Évangile de Jean. Sources, rédaction, théologie*. BETL 44. Edited by Marinus de Jonge, et al. Leuven: Leuven University Press.

———. 2005. *Das Johannesevangelium*. HNT 6. Tübingen: Mohr Siebeck.

Tobin, Thomas. 1990. "The Prologue of John and Hellenistic Speculation." *CBQ* 52:258–62.

Tolmie, D. François. 1995. *Jesus' Farewell to the Disciples: John 13:1–17:26 in Narratological Perspective*. BIS 12. Leiden: Brill.

Totontle, Mositi. 1993. *The Victims*. Gaborone: Botsalo.

Tovey, Derek. 1997. *Narrative Art and Act in the Fourth Gospel*. Sheffield: Sheffield Academic.

Toynbee, Arnold J. 1954. *A Study of History*. 12 vols. New York: Oxford University Press.

Trebilco, Paul. 2006. "Christian Communities in Western Asia Minor in the Early Second Century: Ignatius and Others as Witnesses Against Bauer." *JETS* 49:17–44.

Trueman, Carl. 2005. "Sherlock Holmes and the Curious Case of the Missing Book." *Themelios* 30/3:1–5.

Tuckett, Christopher M. 2001. "Source and Methods." Pages 121–37 in *The Cambridge Companion to Jesus*. Edited by Markus Bockmuehl. Cambridge: Cambridge University Press.

Underhill, Evelyn. 1911. *Mysticism: A Study in the Nature and Development of Man's Spiritual Consciousness*. London: Methuen.

Vana, Liliane. 2003. "La *Birkat Haminim* est-elle une prière contre les Judéo–chrétiens?" Pages 201–41 in *Les communautés religieuses dans le monde Gréco-Romain: Essai de définition*. Edited by Nicole Belayche and Simon C. Mimoune. Turnhout: Brespols.

Van Belle, Gilbert. 1985. *Les parenthèses dans l'Évangile de Jean: Aperçu historique et classification, texte grec de Jean*. Leuven: Leuven University Press.

———. 1988. *Johannine Bibliography 1966–1985. A Cumulative Bibliography on the Fourth Gospel*. BETL 82. Leuven: Leuven University Press.

———. 1994. *The Signs Source in the Fourth Gospel. Historical Survey and Critical Evaluation of the Semeia Hypothesis*. BETL 116. Leuven: Leuven University Press.

———. 1997a. "Het onderzoek: Bijbelwetenschap." Pages 63–154 in *De Faculteit Godgeleerdheid in de K.U. Leuven, 1969–1995*. ANL 39. Edited by L. Gevers and L. Kenis. Leuven: Peeters.

———. 1997b. "L'accomplissement de la parole de Jésus: La parenthèse de Jn 18,9." Pages 515–21 in *The Scriptures in the Gospels*. BETL

131. Edited by Christopher M. Tuckett. Leuven: Leuven University Press.

Van Belle, Gilbert. 2001. "Salvation Is from the Jews: The Parenthesis in Jn 4,22." Pages 368–98 in *Anti-Judaism and the Fourth Gospel: Papers from the Leuven Colloquium, January 2000*. Jewish and Christian Heritage Series. Assen: Royal van Gorcum.

———. 2003a. "Repetition, Variation, and Amplification: Thomas Popp's Recent Contribution on Johannine Style." *ETL* 79:166–78.

———. 2003b. "Dialogue with Tradition: Confronting Exegesis and Biblical Theology in the 21st Century." *Louvain Studies* 28:3–11.

———. 2004. *In Memoriam Maurits Sabbe*. ANL 50. Leuven: Leuven University Press.

———. 2005. "The Death of Jesus in the Fourth Gospel." *Colloquium Biblicum Lovaniense* LIV (2005). *ETL* 81:567–79.

———. (forthcoming). *The Death of Jesus in the Fourth Gospel*. Leuven: Peeters.

van der Horst, Pieter W. 1993–1994. "The *Birkat ha–minim* in Recent Research." *ExpT* 105:363–68.

van der Watt, Jan G. 2000. *Family of the King: Dynamics of Metaphor in the Gospel According to John*. BIS 47. Leiden: Brill.

———, ed. 2005. *Theology and Christology in the Fourth Gospel: Essays by the Members of the SNTS Johannine Writings Seminar*. Leuven: Leuven University Press.

Van Segbroeck, Frans. 2001. "Katholieke Bijbelexegese in de laatste twee eeuwen." Pages 128–30 in *Internationaal Commentaar op de Bijbel*. Edited by E. Eynikel, E. Noort, T. Baarda, and Adelbert Denaux. Kampen: Kok.

Van Segbroeck, Frans, Christopher M. Tuckett, Gilbert Van Belle, and Joseph Verheyden, eds. 1992. *The Four Gospels 1992: Festschrift Frans Neirynck*. 3 vols. BETL 100. Leuven: Leuven University Press.

Visotzky, Burton L. 2005. "Methodological Considerations in the Study of John's Interaction with First Century Judaism." Pages 91–107 in *Life in Abundance: Studies of John's Gospel in Tribute to Raymond E. Brown, S.S.* Edited by John R. Donahue. Collegeville, Minn.: Liturgical Press.

von Balthasar, Hans Urs. 1986. *Prayer*. Translated by Graham Harrison. San Francisco: Ignatius.

von Wahlde, Urban C. 1979. "The Terms for Religious Authorities in the Fourth Gospel: A Key to Literary Strata?" *JBL* 98:231–53.

———. 1982. "The Johannine 'Jews': A Critical Survey." *NTS* 28:33–60.

———. 1989. *The Earliest Version of John's Gospel: Recovering the Gospel of Signs*. Wilmington, Del.: Glazier.

————. 1990. *The Johannine Commandments: 1 John and the Struggle for the Johannine Tradition*. Mahwah, N.J.: Paulist Press.

————. 1993. "The Gospel of John and the Presentation of Jews and Judaism." Pages 67–84 in *Within Context: Essays on Jews and Judaism in the New Testament*. Edited by David P. Efroymson, Eugene J. Fisher, and Leon Klenicki. Collegeville, Minn.: Liturgical Press.

von Wahlde, Urban C. 2000. " 'The Jews' in John's Gospel: Fifteen Years of Research (1983–1998)." *ETL* 76:30–55.

————. 2006. "The Gospel of John and Archaeology." Pages 523–86 in *Jesus and Archaeology*. Edited by James Charlesworth. Grand Rapids: Eerdmans.

wa Thiong'o, Ngugi. 1986. *Decolonising the Mind: The Politics of Language in African Literature*. London: James Currey.

Ward, Keith. 2005. "True Protestants Allow Diversity." *Church Times*. December 2.

Warnock, Mary. 1994. *Imagination and Time*. Cambridge: Blackwell.

Webb, Joseph M. 1998. *Pluralism and Preaching: Communication, the Bible, and the Postmodern Pulpit*. St. Louis: Chalice.

Weems, Renita J. 1988. *Just a Sister Away: A Womanist Vision of Women's Relationships in the Bible*. San Diego: Luramedia.

Westcott, B. F. 1971. *The Gospel According to St. John: The Authorized Version*. Grand Rapids: Eerdmans.

White, Martin C. 1972. "The Identity and Function of Jews and Related Terms in the Fourth Gospel." Ph.D. Dissertation. Ann Arbor: University Microfilms.

Williamson, Peter S. 2001. *Catholic Principles for Interpreting Scripture: A Study of the Pontifical Commission's "The Interpretation of the Bible in the Church."* Subsidia Biblica 22. Rome: Pontifical Biblical Institute.

Wink, Walter. 1973. *The Bible in Human Transformation: Toward a New Paradigm for Biblical Study*. Philadelphia: Fortress.

Witherington, Ben. 1995. *John's Wisdom: A Commentary on the Fourth Gospel*. Louisville: Westminster John Knox.

Zimmermann, Ruben. 2004. *Christologie der Bilder im Johannesevangelium: Die Christopoetik des vierten Evangeliums unter besonderer Berücksichtigung von Joh 10*. Tübingen: Mohr Siebeck.

Zumstein, Jean. 2004. "Zur Geschichte des johanneischen Christentums." Pages 1–14 in *Kreative Erinnerung: Relecture und Auslegung im Johannesevangelium*. 2nd rev. & exp. ed. ATANT 84. Zürich: Theologischer Verlag Zürich.

CONTRIBUTORS

Note: Senior contributors are listed alphabetically by last name; respondents are listed following their respective senior colleagues.

JOHN ASHTON lectured on New Testament studies at the University of Oxford until his retirement in 1996. He has edited a collection of articles on John, entitled *The Interpretation of John* (1997) and is the author of *Studying John: Approaches to the Fourth Gospel* (1998) and *Understanding the Fourth Gospel* (1993; rev. ed. 2007).

WENDY E. S. NORTH lectured in New Testament at the University of Hull (England) from 1980 to 1999. Her publications include *The Lazarus Story within the Johannine Tradition* (2001); "Monotheism and the Gospel of John: Jesus, Moses and the Law" in *Early Jewish and Christian Monotheism* (2004); and "'The Jews' in John's Gospel: Observations and Inferences," which will appear in a forthcoming Festschrift for Professor Maurice Casey. Her current interest is exploring the relationship between John and the Synoptics.

JOHANNES BEUTLER, S.J. is professor emeritus of New Testament exegesis at the Pontifical Biblical Institute in Rome. His publications on John include *Martyria* (1972), *Habt keine Angst* (1984), and *Die Johannesbriefe* (2000). A number of his articles were collected and published in 1998. His research focuses on John's roots in the Old Testament and Judaism, and he is currently preparing a book on this topic in English.

CARSTEN CLAUSSEN is lecturer in New Testament theology at the Protestant Theological Faculty, University of Munich (Germany). His publications include "Das Gebet in Joh 17 im Kontext von Gebeten aus zeitgenössischen Pseudepigraphen" in *Kontexte des Johannesevangeliums* (2004) and "The Eucharist in the Gospel of John and in the Didache" in *Trajectories through the New Testament and the Apostolic Fathers* (2005). His research focuses on ancient Jewish and early Christian prayer literature, ancient synagogues, Jesus research, the Qumran literature, and Johannine Studies.

PEDER BORGEN is professor emeritus at the University of Trondheim, NTNU (Norway). He currently lives in Lilleström, near Oslo. His book *Bread from Heaven* (1965; 1981) set the stage for his subsequent studies in the Gospel of John. Collections of his essays appear in his *Philo, John, and Paul* (1987) and *Early Christianity and Hellenistic Judaism* (1996); the latter volume includes his exchanges with Frans Neirynck on John and the Synoptics. His research interests also include Philo and Pauline studies.

MICHAEL LABAHN is postdoctoral researcher in New Testament at Katholieke Universiteit Leuven (Belgium). He is the author or editor of numerous books and articles in German and English, including *Jesus als Lebensspender* (1999), *Offenbarung in Zeichen und Wort* (2000), and *Heilstraditionen im Johannesevangelium. Festgabe für Johannes Beutler S.J.* (with Klaus Scholtissek and Angelika Strotmann, 2004). He currently serves as editor of the ESCO series and is a member of the LNTS series editorial board. His research focuses on the Fourth Gospel and the Sayings Gospel, and he is currently preparing a commentary on the Apocalypse of John.

THOMAS L. BRODIE. O.P. is director of the newly founded Dominican Biblical Institute in Limerick, Ireland. His publications include *The Gospel According to John: A Literary and Theological Commentary* (1993), *The Quest for the Origin of John's Gospel: A Source–Oriented Approach* (1993), and *The Birthing of the New Testament: The Intertextual Development of the New Testament Writings* (2004). His research traces literary continuity from the Old Testament into some Matthean logia, the epistles, and thereby into

Proto–Luke (modeled on the Elijah–Elisha narrative), Mark, Matthew, John, and Luke–Acts.

CATRIN H. WILLIAMS is senior lecturer in New Testament studies at the University of Wales, Bangor (U.K.). She is the author of *I Am He: The Interpretation of 'Anî Hû' in Jewish and Early Christian Literature* (Mohr Siebeck, 2000) and is currently working on the reception of the book of Isaiah in late Second Temple Judaism and in the Fourth Gospel.

D. A. CARSON is a Canadian serving as research professor of New Testament at Trinity Evangelical Divinity School, Deerfield, Illinois. He is the author or editor of fifty articles and books, including *The Gospel of John* in the Pillar series.

ANDREAS J. KÖSTENBERGER is director of Ph.D. studies and professor of New Testament at Southeastern Baptist Theological Seminary in Wake Forest, North Carolina. He serves as the editor of the *Journal of the Evangelical Theological Society* and is the author or editor of numerous books, including *John* (BECNT), *God, Marriage, and Family*, and *Women in the Church*. A native of Austria, Köstenberger holds doctoral degrees in Biblical Studies and economics/social sciences. His research interests include hermeneutics, biblical theology, gender issues, and John's Gospel.

R. ALAN CULPEPPER is dean of the McAfee School of Theology at Mercer University in Atlanta, Georgia. Among his many publications are *The Johannine School* (1975; 2007), *Anatomy of the Fourth Gospel* (1983), *John the Son of Zebedee* (1994), and *The Gospel and Letters of John* (1998). His commentary on the Gospel of Mark (Smyth and Helwys Bible Commentaries) was published in 2007, and his current research focuses on the death and resurrection of Jesus in the Gospel of John.

STAN HARSTINE is associate professor of Bible at Friends University in Wichita, Kansas. He is the author of *Moses as a Character in the Fourth Gospel* (2002) and "Un–Doubting Thomas: Recognition Scenes in the Ancient World" (*PRS* 4, 2006). His research focuses on identifying ancient audience conventions for improved understanding of audience responses to ancient texts.

ROBERT T. FORTNA is Weyerhaeuser Professor of Biblical Studies, emeritus, at Vassar College in Poughkeepsie, New York, where he taught for thirty–two years. His publications include *The Gospel of Signs* (1970), The

Fourth Gospel and Its Predecessor (1987), and *Jesus in Johannine Tradition* (with Tom Thatcher, 2001). He has been a member of the Jesus Seminar almost from its inception and has published a number of related articles and, most recently, a commentary on Matthew in the Scholars Bible series (2005).

Tom Thatcher is professor of Biblical Studies at Cincinnati Christian University (Ohio). He is the author or editor of numerous books and articles, including *The Riddles of Jesus in John* (2000), *Jesus in Johannine Tradition* (with Robert Fortna, 2001), and *Why John Wrote a Gospel: Jesus, Memory, History* (2006). He is also the founder and current co–chair of the John, Jesus, and History Group in the Society of Biblical Literature. His research focuses on the ancient media context of the New Testament, the Johannine Literature, and the historical Jesus.

Marinus de Jonge was professor of New Testament and early Christian literature in the Faculty of Theology of Leiden University (The Netherlands) from 1966 until 1990. He has written commentaries in Dutch on the Johannine Epistles (four editions, 1968–1988) and the Fourth Gospel (1996). A number of his articles on John appeared together in *Jesus: Stranger from Heaven and Son of God* (1977). In 1975, he served as president of the Colloquium Biblicum Lovaniense devoted to the Gospel of John and edited the resulting conference volume *L'Évangile de Jean. Sources, rédaction, théologie* (1977). His other research interests include the *Testaments of the Twelve Patriarch*s and the earliest Christian responses to Jesus.

Peter G. Kirchschlaeger is a member of the steering committee of the research project "Exclusivity of the Claim of Truth of the Johannine Christ and Interreligious Dialogue" at the University of Zurich (Switzerland), where he is preparing his doctoral thesis. He is the author of several articles, including "Der jüdisch–christliche Dialog: Idealvorstellungen und Wirklichkeiten" (2005) and "Karl Thieme und der christlich–jüdische Dialog: Beiträge im Freiburger Rundbrief" (2002), and has edited books on the methodology of transferring scientific results to society and on human rights issues. His research focuses on the Gospel of John, Early Christianity, and Judaism.

Robert Kysar taught at Candler School of Theology and Emory University in Atlanta, Georgia, before retiring in 1999. He is the author of numerous books and articles, including, most recently, *Voyages with John: Charting the Fourth Gospel* (2005), *Preaching to Postmoderns* (with Joseph

Webb, 2006), and the third edition of *John: The Maverick Gospel* (2007). He is currently a Heilbrun Fellow at Emory University and is working on a new book titled *Postmodernism and the Gospel of John.*

DAVID RENSBERGER is professor of New Testament at the Interdenominational Theological Center in Atlanta, Georgia. His book *Johannine Faith and Liberating Community* has been in print since 1988, and he is the author of two commentaries on the Johannine Epistles. He is interested in the intersection of communal and social history and experience, theology, and spirituality in the Johannine writings.

J. LOUIS MARTYN is Edward Robinson Professor Emeritus of Biblical Theology at Union Theological Seminary in New York City. His books and articles have two major foci: the Gospel of John (*History and Theology in the Fourth Gospel*, 3rd ed., 2003; *The Gospel of John in Christian History*, 1979) and the letters of Paul (*Galatians* in the Anchor Bible series, 1997; *Theological Issues in the Letters of Paul*, 1997). A upcoming volume addresses issues of divine and human agency.

ADELE REINHARTZ is the associate vice–president for research at the University of Ottawa, where she holds the position of professor in the Department of Classics and Religious Studies. She is the author of numerous articles and books, including *The Word in the World: A Cosmological Reading of the Fourth Gospel* (1992) and *Befriending the Beloved Disciple: A Jewish Reading of the Gospel of John* (2001). Her Johannine research has focused on the interplay between literary and historical–critical methodologies, with particular attention to the history of the Johannine community and the representation of "the Jews" in the Fourth Gospel. She is currently working on a book on Caiaphas with support from the Social Sciences and Humanities Research Council. Adele was elected to the Royal Society of Canada in 2005.

FRANCIS J. MOLONEY, S.D.B. is professor emeritus of New Testament at the Catholic University of America in Washington, D.C.. He is also professor emeritus of theology at the Australian Catholic University. He is the author or editor of numerous books and articles, including *The Gospel of Mark: A Commentary* (2002), *An Introduction to the Gospel of John* (with Raymond Brown, 2003), *Mark: Storyteller, Interpreter, Evangelist* (2004), *The Gospel of John: Text and Context* (2005), and *The Living Voice of the Gospel: The Gospels Today* (2006). His research focuses on the Jesus of history and the setting and message of the four Gospels.

MARY COLOE holds a joint position as senior lecturer in Scripture at the Australian Catholic University and St. Paul's Theological College in Brisbane, Australia. She is the author or editor of numerous books and articles, including *God Dwells with Us: Temple Symbolism in the Fourth Gospel* (2001) and *Dwelling in the Household of God: Johannine Ecclesiology and Spirituality* (2007). Her research interests focus on the theology and spirituality of first–century Christianity, especially the Gospel of John and the relationship between Jews and Christians during those formative years.

JOHN F. O'GRADY is professor emeritus at Barry University in Miami Shores, Florida. He has written numerous books and articles, including *According to John* (1999), and he is working on a new book titled *Preaching the Gospel of John*. He is currently teaching on the Gospel of John at the Pontifical Biblical Institute in Rome.

DOROTHY LEE is a Scottish–born Australian whose research interests focus on the Fourth Gospel's symbolism and theology. She is professor of New Testament within the United Faculty of Theology in Melbourne, Australia, and is the author of various articles and monographs, including *The Symbolic Narratives of the Fourth Gospel* (1994), *Flesh and Glory: Symbol, Gender, and Theology in the Gospel of John* (2002), and *Transfiguration* (2004). She is currently writing a symbolic commentary on the Gospel of John, exploring the links between symbol and text in art, music, and poetry.

JOHN PAINTER is professor of theology at St. Mark's Canberra Campus, School of Theology, Charles Sturt University in ACT, Australia. He is the author or editor of numerous books and articles, including *John: Witness and Theologian* (1975); *Theology as Hermeneutics: Rudolf Bultmann's Interpretation of the History of Jesus* (1987); *The Quest for the Messiah: The History, Literature, and Theology of the Johannine Community* (2nd ed., 1993); and *1, 2, and 3 John* (2002). His research focuses on Jewish and Christian relationships in the first two centuries C.E. and the theological implications of an understanding of this relationship. He is a keen sportsman and a fanatic about cricket and tennis, who runs daily and kayaks whenever possible.

PAUL ANDERSON is professor of biblical and Quaker studies at George Fox University in Newberg, Oregon. He is the author of more than 140 essays and two books on John, *The Christology of the Fourth Gospel* (1996) and *The Fourth Gospel and the Quest for Jesus* (2006). As well as introducing

"Cognitive Critical Analysis" to the study of Gospel traditions, Anderson is a co–chair and co–editor of the John, Jesus, and History project.

SANDRA M. SCHNEIDERS, I.H.M. is professor of New Testament studies and Christian spirituality at the Jesuit School of Theology and Graduate Theological Union in Berkeley, California. She is author of numerous articles, chapters, and books, including *The Revelatory Text: Interpreting the New Testament as Sacred Scripture* (1999) and *Written That You May Believe: Encountering Jesus in the Fourth Gospel* (2003). Her research focuses on Johannine Studies, biblical hermeneutics, and biblical spirituality.

COLLEEN CONWAY is associate professor of religious studies at Seton Hall University in South Orange, New Jersey. She is the author of *Men and Women in the Fourth Gospel: Gender and Johannine Characterization* (1999) and several articles on Johannine Studies, including "The Production of the Johannine Community: A New Historicist Approach" (2002) and "Gender Matters in John" in *A Feminist Companion to John* (2003). She is currently working on a book titled *Jesus the Man: Greco–Roman Masculinity and New Testament Christology*.

FERNANDO F. SEGOVIA is Oberlin Graduate Professor of New Testament and early Christianity in the Divinity School at Vanderbilt University in Nashville, Tennessee. He is the author of numerous essays and volumes on the Johannine Literature, including *The Farewell of the Word* (1991), *What Is John?* (editor, 1996), and "The Gospel of John" in the upcoming *A Postcolonial Commentary of the New Testament Writings*. His areas of interest also include method and theory, as well as ideological criticism.

FRANCISCO LOZADA JR. is associate professor of New Testament studies and Latina/o church studies at Brite Divinity School in Fort Worth, Texas. He is the author or editor of *A Literary Reading of John 5: Text as Construction* (2000) and *New Currents through John: A Global Perspective* (with Tom Thatcher, 2006). His research focuses on the construction of early Christianity and contemporary approaches to biblical interpretation.

D. MOODY SMITH is George Washington Ivey Professor Emeritus of New Testament at Duke University in Durham, North Carolina, where he taught in the Divinity School and Graduate School. His work on the Johannine Literature began with *The Composition and Order of the Fourth Gospel* (1965) and has continued up to the present. The second edition of *John Among the Gospels*, which reflects his ongoing interest in historical issues, appeared in 2001. The sixth edition of *Anatomy of the New Testament* (with Robert Spivey and C. Clifton Black) was published in 2006.

CRAIG S. KEENER is professor of New Testament at Palmer Theological Seminary in Wynnewood, Pennsylvania. He is the author of numerous books and articles, including commentaries on John (2003), Matthew (1999), and 1–2 Corinthians (2005), several of which have won awards. His research interests focus on the early Jewish and Greco–Roman setting of the New Testament.

GILBERT VAN BELLE is Professor Ordinarius of New Testament at the Faculty of Theology of the Katholieke Universiteit Leuven (Leuven, Belgium). He is general editor of the journal *Ephemerides Theologicae Lovanienses*, the series Bibliotheca Ephemeridum Theologicarum Lovaniensium, and the series Biblical Tools and Studies. He is the author or editor of numerous books and articles, including *Les parenthèses dans l'évangile de Jean* (1985); *Johannine Bibliography 1966–1985* (1988); *The Signs Source in the Fourth Gospel* (1994); *Luke and His Readers: Festschrift A. Denaux* (2004); *Theology and Christology in the Fourth Gospel: Essays by the Members of the SNTS Johannine Writings Seminar* (2005); *The Death of Jesus in the Fourth Gospel* (2007); and *Repetitions and Variations in the Fourth Gospel: Style, Text, Interpretation* (2007). His research focuses on the style of the Gospel of John, Christology, theology, and history of interpretation.

PETER J. JUDGE is associate professor of religious studies and chair of the Philosophy and Religious Studies Department at Winthrop University in Rock Hill, South Carolina. His published work on the Gospel of John includes "A Note on Jn 20, 29" (1992, in the FS F. Neirynck), an English translation of Gilbert Van Belle's *The Signs Source in the Fourth Gospel* (1994), and *John 20,24–29: More Than Doubt, Beyond Rebuke* (2007). His research continues on the redaction of the Johannine Gospel.

URBAN C. VON WAHLDE is professor of New Testament and former chair of the Department of Theology at Loyola University in Chicago. He is the author of *The Earliest Version of John's Gospel* (1989), *The Johannine Commandments* (1990), and nearly forty articles on the Gospel and letters of John. He has recently completed a three–volume commentary on the Gospel and Letters of John for the *Eerdmans Critical Commentary* series.

FELIX JUST, S.J. teaches in the Department of Religious Studies at Santa Clara University (California). Since receiving his Ph.D. in New Testament studies from Yale University, he has also taught at Loyola Marymount University in Los Angeles and at the University of San Francisco. He is the founder and primary author of "Catholic Resources," an internationally recognized website of biblical, liturgical, and related materials (http://catholic–resources.org), including "The Johannine Literature Web." He teaches regularly in the Catholic Bible Institute of Los Angeles, leads annual Gospel–based retreats, and gives frequent public lectures on a wide range of academic and pastoral topics.

AUTHOR/SUBJECT INDEX

Note: The vast majority of biblical citations in this volume relate to the Gospel of John. Biblical books other than the Gospel of John are indexed here alphabetically by the title of the book. Greek terms are listed before the English entries.

confessionalism, *see* "faith, of readers"; "faith and scholarship"
conflict (Johannine theme), 40, 57, 59–60, 78, 112, 118, 143–44, 147, 236, 255, 284, 285–86, 288, 314
construction of meaning, 169–73, 179, 181–82, 210, 273, 279, 281, 284, 302, 311
contextual aporias, 4, 7; *see also* "aporias"
Conway, Colleen, 272
Cope, Lamar, 149
Coppens, Joseph, 333
Cornelius Nepos, 321
Corpus Hellenisticum Novi Testamenti Seminar, 146
Cosby, Bill, 180
Council of Chalcedon, 79
Court, John, 31
Cousar, Charles, 118
covenant, 29, 30, 92, 213, 225
creationism, 10
crimes report, 55–56, 57–58, 62
cross, 91, 95, 96, 120, 133, 137, 207–208, 220, 231, 260; *see also* "crucifixion"
Crossan, John Dominic, 157, 263
crossings, *see* "borders"
crossroads texts, 297–98
crowd(s) (as character), 41, 42, 44, 47–48, 132, 198, 205, 242, 253–55, 258, 259 260, 343
crucifixion, 56, 58, 62, 77, 118–19, 142, 156–57, 206, 207, 221, 225 226, 267–68, 323; *see also* "cross"
Cry of Dereliction, 318
Culley, Robert, 71, 73
Cullmann, Oscar, 137
Culpepper, R. Alan, xv, 7, 8, 36, 37, 45–46, 70, 76, 87, 90, 111, 112, 113 n. 1, 114, 117, 118, 119, 120,

121 n. 2, 123–24, 125, 134–35, 165, 167, 192, 197–98, 212, 219, 220, 269, 346–47
cultural arena (within the geopolitical), 308
Cultural Studies, 17, 297
cultural symbols, 170, 173, 278, 289, 296, 301, 302
Cyril of Alexandria, 25

Dahl, Nils, 40
Daniel (Book of), 195
Darwin, Charles, 173
Daube, David, 27
Davies, W. D., 110
The DaVinci Code, 94
Davis, Stephen, 264
De Ausejo, Serafin, 220
Dead Sea Scrolls, 27, 29, 36, 75, 110, 190, 234, 267, 336
death of Jesus, *see* "crucifixion"
De Boer, Martinus, 121 n. 2, 127 n. 1, 134–37, 139, 142, 143, 144
decision dualism, 184
Deconstruct(ion), 3, 115–16, 172, 174–75, 272–74, 281 n. 1, 302, 346
Dedication (festival), 204
De Jonge, H. J., 136 n. 5
De Jonge, Marinus, 127–28, 130, 131, 132, 132 n. 3, 134, 135 n. 4, 136, 145–46, 148
Delobel, Jöel, 333 n. 6
demythologizing, 31, 272, 313
Denaux, Adelbert, 128
de Ruyter, B. W. J., 136 n. 5
descent (ideology of), 287, 301, 303
de Solages, Bruno, 314–15
Dettwiler, Andreas, 25, 138 n. 8, 212
Deutsche Christen, 189